SOFT-POWER INTERNATIONALISM

Soft-Power Internationalism

COMPETING FOR CULTURAL INFLUENCE IN THE 21ST-CENTURY GLOBAL ORDER

EDITED BY

Burcu Baykurt and Victoria de Grazia

Columbia University Press
New York

Columbia University Press
Publishers Since 1893
New York   Chichester, West Sussex
cup.columbia.edu
Copyright © 2021 Columbia University Press
All rights reserved

Library of Congress Cataloging-in-Publication Data
Names: Baykurt, Burcu, editor. | de Grazia, Victoria, editor.
Title: Soft-power internationalism : competing for cultural influence in the 21st-century
global order / edited by Burcu Baykurt and Victoria de Grazia
Description: New York : Columbia University Press, 2021. | Includes bibliographical
references and index.
Identifiers: LCCN 2020042519 (print) | LCCN 2020042520 (ebook) | ISBN 9780231195447
(hardback) | ISBN 9780231195454 (trade paperback) | ISBN 9780231551335 (ebook)
Subjects: LCSH: Hegemony—Cross-cultural studies. | Cultural diplomacy—
Cross-cultural studies.
Classification: LCC JZ1312 .S66 2021 (print) | LCC JZ1312 (ebook) | DDC 327.1/14—dc23
LC record available at https://lccn.loc.gov/2020042519
LC ebook record available at https://lccn.loc.gov/2020042520

Columbia University Press books are printed on permanent and durable acid-free paper.
Printed in the United States of America

Cover image: FUKT, Sydney, Australia
Cover design: Milenda Nan Ok Lee

Contents

Acknowledgments

This volume represents a truly international and interdisciplinary collaboration over the last five years, one that moved among several countries and has incurred many debts. Our research network was established in 2015 at the initiative of Victoria de Grazia under the auspices of Columbia's European Institute with funding from the President's Global Innovation Fund at Columbia University and the European Institute's Initiative on Cultural Power in International Relations. With Burcu Baykurt's coordination, this group came together at a series of workshops titled "De-Provincializing Soft Power: A Global-Historical Approach." We met at Columbia University in January 2015, in Istanbul in June 2015, in Beijing in June 2016, in São Paolo in March 2017, and again at Columbia University in November 2018. Additional funding for the workshops in Beijing and São Paolo came from a grant from Alliance's Trilateral Initiatives in Emerging Regions. A final meeting at Columbia, "Two Hegemonic Restructuring Projects in Diachronic Perspective: America's Marshall Plan (1948–1951) and China's Belt and Road Initiative (2013–)," had support from the European Institute, the Weatherhead East Asian Institute, the Institute for Social and Economic Research and Policy (ISERP), and the Department of History.

We especially want to thank Safwan M. Masri, executive vice president for Global Centers at Columbia University, together with Ipek Cem Taha in Istanbul, Joan Kaufman and Bin Pei in Beijing, and Thomas Trebat in

Rio de Janeiro, the directors of the local centers, along with their staff, for their assistance in hosting these meetings. At the European Institute, Adam Tooze, the current director, gave his enthusiastic support, as did the institute's peerless staff: François Carrel-Billiard in the lead, Sharon Kim, and their predecessors, Christopher Hill and Lily Glenn.

The ideas shaping this book evolved through conversations with Richard Balme, Peter Katzenstein, Edward Keene, Monroe Price, Robert Vitalis, Vasilis Trigkas, and Yiwei Wang, and at Columbia University with Hisham Aidi, Charles Armstrong, Karen Barkey, Richard John, Andrew Nathan, Victoria Phillips, Pablo Piccato, and Anya Schiffrin. Victoria de Grazia gives special thanks to students in her courses and workshops on Soft Power in Historical Perspective for their lively critique of the mindset that has made "soft power" such a popular term and so easily misconstrued.

As the chapters for the collection began to cohere, Martha Schulman offered her editorial assistance and deftly shepherded the project to completion. Emilie Yu Marine Xie provided sharp translation skills. Our editor, Caelyn Cobb, was thoughtful and responsive in every step of the process. Our warm thanks to the staff at Columbia University Press, and the Press's outside readers, whose astute comments made the manuscript much stronger.

SOFT-POWER INTERNATIONALISM

Introduction

Soft-Power Internationalism

BURCU BAYKURT AND VICTORIA DE GRAZIA

The last decade of the twentieth century started with anticipation—and foreboding—about the opening of a new world. The dismantling of the Berlin Wall, the collapse of the Soviet Union, and the resulting reforms in communist regimes all indicated that the threat of a cataclysmic confrontation between the two superpower alliances was over. Yet there was no settled agreement on what that meant. As journalist William Schmidt, after interviewing everyday Americans across the country, concluded in 1990, "While there was a strong sense that the Soviet Union had probably lost the cold war, few were willing to say the United States had won."[1]

One reason surely was that U.S. foreign policy has a long history of interweaving hard-nosed interests and dulcet values, but this diplomatic deftness always depended on a clearly marked antagonist. "The problem for the United States will be less the rising challenge of another major power than a general diffusion of power," Joseph S. Nye Jr. proclaimed in 1990, while calling for a reevaluation of foreign policy strategy.[2] At the same time, the dissipation of that enemy figure presented the country's policy makers with an opportunity to establish a more expansive, if looser, global hegemony. The unraveling of the Soviet Union without a military conflict and the growing attraction of democratic ideals around the world offered the glimpse of a more stable, less militarized, peace—but also of multiple countries attempting to stake out a role in shaping international politics.

Nye coined the term "soft power" to characterize the policy the United States should employ to give order to the emerging new world. His simple definition of the concept—"getting others to want what you want"—aimed to provide a liberal blueprint for keeping a U.S.-led international system in place. Rather than military might or economic sanctions, Nye suggested, it was cultural attraction, ideology, and international institutions that could align a multipolar, multicivilizational world with the American imperium.

Soft power was an attempt to define a new capacity for foreign policy analogous to military and economic power, one that would make the highly visible American leadership more palatable to the rest of the world. Very much bound up with rebuilding the U.S.-led liberal international order, the concept was offered as a supplement to, not a replacement for, military force and economic control. Soft power would aim to reinvigorate the United States' ability to engage, assist, and communicate with a variety of states and nonstate actors. The effectiveness of this new power would derive from promoting democracy and human rights, collaborating with civil society actors and international institutions, and using information technologies to support cultural programs. In that sense, far from a radical revision of U.S. diplomacy, the United States aimed to mobilize its seemingly irresistible accumulations of symbolic capital and connect them to the surge of democratic feelings and institutions around the world, in tandem with American foreign policy and in the interest of legitimating American global primacy.

Possibly beyond what Nye originally intended, the concept soon took on a life of its own, evolving into a plausible foreign policy agenda outside the United States. Countries engaged in what they called "soft strategies" to enhance their cultural influence and make it commensurate with—or even superior to—their economic, political, and military weight. Inside the European Union (EU), the agenda called for promoting "normative power." As new economic powers began to emerge in the early 2000s, they invested significantly in cultural diplomacy and expanded their toolkits of cultural programs, humanitarian and development aid, public diplomacy, and information technologies to project their ambitions into the world. Academic and business consultancies began to draw up soft-power indices to establish new global hierarchies among nation-states. Civil society organizations and corporations also adopted the idea of soft power in their quest to assert influence worldwide and establish horizontal counterpower against governments. In the process, the term became a marker of a new kind of global interstate political competition, and, potentially, a new model for multilateral global governance in the early twenty-first century—even as the United States has continued to dominate militarily.

This book explores this rapid spread of the concept of soft power across the globe over the last thirty years, but also how it crashed. It traces how the communication networks, normative concepts, and diplomatic practices associated with it imagined—and to an extent made possible—a multilateral, liberal politics that mainly worked to build on the expansion of global markets and tried to mitigate the extremist political reactions, bumptious claims of rising economic powers, and cultural fractures generated by a new world. We start from the paradox that as the concept of soft power was disseminated globally, it became a key word that concealed more than it revealed. Through a comparative lens turned toward the United States, the EU, China, Brazil, and Turkey, we analyze what facilitated the adoption of the American notion of soft power and in what ways this notion evolved as a reaction to global and regional changes. The result is a study both of how a concept has taken hold worldwide and of a global moment in which many countries sensed a shift in international affairs and saw promise in this new phenomenon. It is also a study of the fateful trends undermining that promise. These include the battered economic growth ensuing from the financial crisis of 2008, frustrated regional hegemonic ambitions, and rising nationalism. They also include unabating militarization arising from the U.S.-led global war on terror and the weaponization of the global internet.

Methodologically, we combine a transnational critical theory with a historical-sociological approach to examine soft power as a distinct historical period, from roughly 1990 to 2015. Our goal is to deprovincialize the concept from the Euro-Atlantic locus in which it was initially formulated and debated. These five cases display the range of soft powers that have appeared over the last thirty years at the global and regional level. While the United States tried to claim the original model of soft power, even as it has attempted to modify it several times, the EU sought to develop a coherent alternative to U.S. leadership through norms-making—that is, normative power. China and Brazil became formidable international actors over the last few decades, while Turkey tried to use its momentous economic growth in the 2000s to play an assertive role in the Middle East. All used the soft power turn as a way to rebalance the power of the United States and Europe, framing their values in postcolonial terms. Their appropriations of the idea of soft power revealed dimensions that its American originator had perhaps not conceived of, while also shedding light on the increasingly globalized intrastate competition around the politics of persuasion.

Our genealogy of soft power starts in 1990, following the fall of the Berlin Wall and the bold proclamations about the end of the Cold War; Nye first introduced the term at a time when many countries were trying to understand their place in the world. We end our analysis circa 2015, when a cluster of events challenged the foundations of each hegemon's quest for normative leadership, thereby calling into question the premises of soft power as it originated in the 1990s and after it was taken up by several countries—namely, a multilateral liberal order in international affairs, multivocality in global organizations, and the democratizing capacity of information technologies.

Rather than pinpointing a particular date that marks the concept's demise, we note the resurgent nationalism in domestic and foreign affairs, heightened regional conflicts, and a far more conflictual use of digital technologies as indicators of the recent radical diversion. Turkey's ambitions for regional influence were thwarted by domestic crises and the ongoing Syrian conflict; corruption scandals in Brazil exposed the vulnerability of the country's claim to international leadership; the limits of the EU's power were revealed especially sharply through the conflict with the Russian Confederation in Ukraine; and the weakening of U.S. dominion in global affairs became much more pronounced during the presidency of Donald Trump. Among our case studies, it is only China that continues its commitment to soft power, much reframed but also much more ambitious in scale.

The period between 1990 and 2015 is defined by what we call "soft-power internationalism," wherein aspiring regional or global hegemons not only relied on cultural resources to wield influence, but also actively countered established powers through nonmilitaristic means. Similar to the liberal internationalist project of U.S. foreign policy that aimed for ascendance through the promotion of liberal principles, soft-power internationalism enabled emerging powers to mobilize their own cultural resources in order to project influence.[3] More acutely aware of the history and changing character of American dominance, many countries recognized that conventional military means could not address complex policy conflicts demanding global leadership and interstate collaboration, even as they continued to recognize the military superiority of the United States. These rising leaders turned to issues of human rights, public health, climate change, or cooperative development to pursue national and multilateral interests in international affairs. From the elegantly choreographed ceremonies during the Beijing Olympics to Turkey's plans to reestablish the one-time unity of the eastern Mediterranean, Middle East, and the Horn of Africa to Brazil's attempt at diplomatic leadership in South-South relations, soft-power internationalism became the way to claim a benevolent form of hegemony.

Soft-power internationalism did not necessarily offer an alternative to either the so-called liberal international order or militarism, but it at least raised the prospect of a collective check to the unilateralist vision of American dominion after the Cold War.[4] It offered a new framework and politics of persuasion, whose apparatus now expanded to cultural institutes, development aid, communication technologies, multinational companies, public diplomacy, nation branding, and trade policies. It promised to reinforce global governance and international civil society organizations. As each actor brought distinctive civilizational resources to their endeavors (coming out of metanarratives about their pasts, whether as empires or anticolonialists), staked out different modalities of influence, and developed paradigmatic institutional practices, soft-power internationalism became a terrain on which emerging powers could challenge the hegemony of the U.S.-led liberal international order.

Four features distinguish soft-power internationalism as a mode of governance, the first and most fundamental being that it was unabashedly bound up with the neoliberal project coming out of the 1980s. We see the effort to mobilize normative values and institutions of norms-making as another dimension to the more or less coordinated political project to encase free markets within an interdependent world and to insulate the global economy from the whimsical decisions of nation-states.[5] From that perspective, the development of soft resources went hand in hand with the notion of "sweet commerce," meaning that accelerating global trade would generate a wealth of transnational and international connections. Though reflecting their own national interests, many countries would have to present themselves in the same normative language and thus be ancillary to the dominant nexus of global institutions, including the World Bank, the IMF, and the European Central Bank, and trade agreements like NAFTA and the WTO, to effectively protect international capital from infringement by domestic policies or the unpredictability of democratic politics. The institutional nexus of neoliberalism flourished with the booms and busts of the 1990s and early twenty-first century until the financial crisis in 2008, thereby accounting for the astounding economic growth of the BRICS, Turkey, and the EU. This cycle gave fresh legitimacy not only to these international organizations, but also to the promise that these new global actors—and their soft-power projects burgeoning from the commodity booms that made their states exceptionally well off in those years—could have a voice in them.

Whether China's legitimation of its international image through the WTO, the integration of Europe toward a single market, or Turkey's use of its Ottoman imperial past to develop new markets in the Middle East, soft-power internationalism reshaped diplomacy into market-confirming practices. The relationship between neoliberalism and soft-power internationalism was mutually beneficial. In the 2000s, as more countries accessed international-capital flows, grew their exports, and benefited from rising commodity prices, they ramped up soft-power practices to advance their political and diplomatic standing around the world.

The second feature is that soft-power internationalism created a new kind of interdependence that did not fit traditional definitions of actors, ideologies, and alliances. Not only have many governmental institutions become significantly globalized since the Cold War's end; a new crop of actors shaping political demands and opportunities has emerged in international politics. Multinational firms, civic groups, trade consultants, and transnational NGOs contested and engaged more visibly with conventional diplomats and political leaders as they all grappled with the risks and benefits of globalization. This new "policy interdependence" led not just to forging new kinds of alliances in different jurisdictions, but also highlighted the significance of norms-making and consensus-building in international affairs.[6] While soft-power internationalism generated a new kind of cooperation among state and nonstate actors, its modus operandi presented itself as a pragmatic approach of mutual benefits and shared values, as opposed to pure ideologies. Subalternity, South–South solidarity, or shared histories of poverty, for example, were taken up by countries like Brazil or China to build solidarity, in contrast to the way Western aid had been traditionally framed as unreciprocated gifts and used to reaffirm global leadership.[7]

The evolution of various information technologies into the global internet marks the third feature of soft-power internationalism. The hyperconnectivity enabled by computer networks since the 1990s has led to an intensified circulation of ideas, money, and people. The communicative promises of the global internet to foster social change and cultivate liberal democratic values were deeply embedded within the U.S. narratives of expanding the liberal international order post–Cold War.[8] Simultaneously a global broadcast medium, a gateway to competing in international markets, and a network that ties the critical infrastructures of nation-states to one another, the global internet has significantly changed the pillars of statecraft in the twenty-first century. It created new industries, recast older ones that traditionally relied on global supply chains, and centered strategic communication at the heart of diplomatic initiatives. The global internet was not just a conduit to circulate soft narratives and mold public opinion; it has also become a competitive terrain on which countries, companies, and civil society actors mobilize their values and norms to reshape governmental control over cyberspace as well as techniques of state-to-state and people-to-people communication.[9]

The fourth and perhaps most complicated feature of soft-power internationalism has to do with what it is not, or, better, what it claims not to be: war-making. While a soft approach to power was allegedly an antipode to warfare ("hard power," as Nye called it), it never eliminated war, nor did it necessarily distance itself from the military. Of course, there is nothing new about the fact that soft forms of displaying foreign policy leadership often go hand in hand with making war—even when the link is not at the forefront. From state propaganda to private publicity, governments—and peoples—always mobilize values and belief systems to distinguish between friends and foe in the name of drawing up either alliances or antagonists. But the dialectical relationship between war-making and diplomatic publicity became blatantly obvious in the period of soft-power internationalism. If Nye's concept began to be bruited in the early 1990s, the moment it took hold was in the wake of 2003, when the U.S. military saw soft power as a complement to the global war on terror. Fighting against an unspecified enemy with an always-shifting geographic scope, the military incorporated the techniques and discourse of soft-power internationalism into its never-ending occupations and renamed them "peace-building." As anthropologist Madiha Tahir astutely recognizes, the adversaries in this new war were rarely defined by their ideological or even legal status; they were merely against U.S. culture, or, as George W. Bush once put it, "they hate our way of life."[10] Technological infrastructures that facilitate this war-making from a distance, along with their promise of "precision," were used to keep an illusory distinction between what the robots (making offensive attacks) and people (offering humanitarian support) did.[11] But, in the end, military action always complemented, if not eclipsed, soft-power initiatives.

Nye eventually labeled this co-constitution of soft power and war-making "smart power," which he described as "neither hard nor soft, but the skillful combination of both."[12] (The concept's original inventor was Suzanne Nossel, a long-time actor in U.S. foreign policy, media and human rights advocacy).[13] When Hillary Clinton became secretary of state, she immediately adopted this new term to emphasize the role of "technology, public-private partnerships, energy, economics" that prop up traditional diplomacy, even as she stayed committed to guns, bombs, and tanks.[14] As soft-power internationalism extended beyond the Euro-Atlantic sphere, a similar conflation of humanitarianism with military interventions reverberated through Russia's invasion of Ukraine in 2014 and Turkey's 2019 attack on northern Syria.

Some soft-power critics point to the blurred lines between the soft, hard, and smart versions as indicators of the concept's intellectual weakness, adding that it has always been challenging to measure soft power's effectiveness. Yet we suggest that the vague premises and ambiguous boundaries of soft power are exactly what made the concept generative and appealing enough to cross borders. Even Russia, a country that has emerged as a significant critic of a West-centric liberal international order, has invested in soft-power internationalism to raise its profile in world politics. Stanislav Budnitsky and Melissa Aronczyk catalog Russia's foray into soft power in three phases: "The humble and clumsy attempts to be liked in the West in the early and mid-2000s, the assertive promotion of Russia's standpoint in the global media space after the 2008 Georgia War, and most recently the aggressive push to disrupt and divide the Western narrative following Putin's 2012 return to presidency and especially with the beginning of the 2014 Ukrainian crisis."[15] Russia's most recent soft-power initiatives aim not just to upset what it calls "Western narratives," but also to use tools of the internet and cultural programs to sow suspicion and disarray, thereby challenging the legitimacy of dominant global communication channels.[16] This emerging version of soft power—what some pundits call "sharp power"—appears more state-driven, more centralized, and significantly less liberal, but it nonetheless showcases the deep appeal of managing political narratives, beliefs, and images in international politics.

After a prolific reign around the world for twenty-five years, soft-power internationalism has given way to bellicosity as more countries have started gravitating toward more nationalist, if not authoritarian, styles of domestic governing and adopting inward-looking foreign policies. The new key terms are "trade war," "cyber war," "hybrid war," and "sharp power." This shift clarifies that the illusion of soft-power internationalism as a distinct order of multilateral diplomacy, networked communications, and international civil society was perhaps just that: an illusion. Globally, it seemed to license the belief that countries could substitute cooperation for hostility, generosity for retaliation, and trade partnerships for military force, but it also obscured the fact that the pursuit of geopolitical interests by nation-states would always predominate in international affairs. The paradoxes and contradictions of this international order were bared by the 2008–2009 financial crisis that made it harder to sustain public diplomacy budgets, fractured trade-led global integration, and intensified regional competition. While many countries scrambled to cope with the consequences of austerity, the United States and the EU—so-called protagonists of soft-power internationalism—failed to burnish themselves as models of international liberal order.

But this sharp shift also underlines the fact that soft-power internationalism demonstrated, albeit briefly, that nations outside of the Euro-Atlantic context have the capacity not just to participate in, but to shape international politics. The new hegemons benefited from a thriving global capitalism, broke out of the traditional hierarchies of global governance, created new alliances among countries and peoples, and imagined global public goods collectively. This populist foreign policy environment—certainly not what Nye intended back in the 1990s—aimed to generate new solidarities and sociality outside of the old Western colonial legacies. Trying to bind the world horizontally through connectivity among different state and non-state actors, soft-power internationalism attempted to even out the balance, despite the overwhelming military power exercised by the United States. Most important, this soft diplomatic vitality attempted to respond to the fierce challenges of the twenty-first century.

Rather than deciding whether soft-power internationalism was a momentary illusion or a valid promise, this volume reveals the interlinked histories of how this hierarchy-breaking period of foreign affairs took shape as an intellectual project as well as a diplomatic practice. The chapters in the first section probe the origins of culture, reputation, and global communication in post–Cold War international relations. Victoria de Grazia traces the genealogy of two key terms that appeared at the outset of the 1990s: "soft power" in the United States, and "normative power" in Europe. Through the distinct, yet intertwined, histories of these concepts and their intellectual architects, she reveals the divergent trajectories of Euro-Atlantic hegemony at the turn of the twenty-first century. While normative power fails to gain traction outside of Europe, its mere existence as a coherent program speaks to the rise of the EU as a new leader in international politics. Soft power, in contrast, elicits worldwide attention and cooperation, yet is ultimately a testament to the crisis of the U.S.-led post–Cold War global order.

Burcu Baykurt then examines one of the structural elements of soft-power internationalism: the making of the global internet as it was shoehorned into the larger ideal of creating horizontal, pluralistic, and democratic networks dominated by civilian power. The history of the global internet as a liberal myth parallels the history of soft-power internationalism: both projects began in the 1990s with the marriage of the technological and economic interests of the U.S. dominion; enjoyed a truly international, multilateral phase in the 2000s when various state and nonstate actors circulated across cyberspace even as U.S.-origin companies (and, to an extent, the U.S. government) orchestrated both the material network of internet infrastructures and the soft messaging of global connectivity as a civilizing virtue; and faced challenges from counterhegemons from 2010 onward, as the U.S. origins of both projects were unmasked and nation-states took issue with the mythology of a global internet and sought governmental control over digital information flows.

Chapters on Turkey focus on how the country has asserted itself as a regional power since the mid-1980s (the "Turkish model"), and how it significantly revised its foreign policy ("neo-Ottomanism") after a new government came into power in the early 2000s. After recounting Turkey's long history of reputation-building in global politics, Dilek Barlas and Lerna Yanik suggest that a more pronounced adoption of soft power during the AKP government paralleled Turkey's shift from trying to integrate itself into an international order led by the United States and Europe to claiming a more autonomous role. Its historical and cultural heritage was an important soft-power asset in public diplomacy, and Turkey also exploited the opportunity of trade-driven foreign policy instruments as it tried to build ties with the Balkans, the Middle East, and Turkic-language areas of the former USSR. Mustafa Kutlay recognizes the influence trade-led powers like Japan and Germany exercised coming out of the 1980s to explore Turkey's endeavors from the first decade of the twenty-first century. His chapter on the use of "economy as a problem-solving mechanism" in foreign policy discusses the limits of trade given the economic turbulence, as well as the identity concerns and geopolitical conflicts in the region.

Priding itself on being the "republic of diplomats," Brazil emerged as another ambitious regional influence in the mid-1980s, immediately after the country moved from dictatorship to liberal government. Despite Brazil's uncertainty and suspicion about a new post–Cold War global order, it quickly, as Oliver Stuenkel observes, became a natural leader in South America. From leading the charge in global trade and diplomatic negotiations to opposing the U.S.-led Iraq War, to making winning bids to host the World Cup and the Olympics, Brazil exploited its soft-power capacity to project its regional and global ambitions. Particularly during the presidency of leftist populist Luiz Inácio Lula da Silva, the country expanded its humanitarian aid strategy and presented its domestic success in reducing poverty as a form of expertise in the Global South.

Brazilian soft power mobilized a new kind of South-South diplomacy, in which commitment to democracy and liberalism went along with horizontal solidarity, as opposed to the more traditional North-South developmental aid marked by verticality. Yet, as Fernando Santomauro and Jean Tible point out, this radical reimagining of humanitarian aid and cooperation suffered from the structural demands of global capitalism, geopolitical tensions, and the historical legacy of the country's peripheral status in international politics. What the authors call the country's "hovering illiberal clouds," its dependency on international finance, widespread corruption, selective scrutiny from international organizations, and clashing factions within the political establishment, brought first Lulismo and then the new model of diplomacy under attack. While Brazil's assertive foreign policy in the 2000s had the potential to challenge the hegemony of the Global North, its experience with soft-power internationalism also demonstrates the deep-rooted effects of peripheral dependency.

Among the countries we survey in the volume, China is the only one that has consistently and significantly invested in soft power even as similar initiatives in the United States, EU, Brazil, or Turkey were slowing down. Sustained development assistance in the African continent has been central to Chinese foreign policy. Martina Bassan reviews this relationship, which began in the mid-1950s as a shared struggle against Western hegemony and neocolonialism. Her analysis of China's recent investments and cultural diplomacy efforts in various African countries demonstrates not only the extent of its economic heft and cultural sway, but also the persuasiveness of its alternative views on global issues. China's rapid economic growth in recent decades and ambitions toward global leadership culminated in the 2013 announcement of the Belt and Road Initiative (BRI), intended to link the economies of Europe, Asia, and Africa with roads, rails, ports, and telecom networks. The economic promises and perils of the BRI are a work in progress, but its political message is obvious: China is attempting to build a new model of global leadership in its image.

Zhongying Pang speaks to the paradoxical history of "soft power with Chinese characteristics." When Nye's original conception was first introduced into the People's Republic of China, policy makers seized on it as useful in signaling that China would ease its way into the world order without disrupting it. In the 2000s, as China slowly developed its own understanding of soft power, it took up leadership positions in several regional and international organizations. As the country's influence expanded into global trade, development, higher education, and the internet, however, Chinese soft power appeared to begin embarking on an ambitious project of global leadership (one that mixes the country's soft and hard capabilities). Pang thus suggests that China's path to its current status as an emerging imperium has been neither linear nor neat. He also questions the fluid boundaries between terms such as "soft," "hard," and "sharp" power, especially as they are applied to countries whose practices do not conform to Western traditions.

Anastas Vangeli examines how countries in Central, East, and Southeast Europe (CESEE) have engaged with the BRI and how that reflects on China's symbolic power. The BRI's planetary vision for infrastructure growth prompts policy discussions that legitimate China's centrality in global governance. It also introduces a new frame for partnerships between postsocialist Europe and China, one that, while awkward at times, nonetheless aims to upend established identities of the former socialist countries.

The last two chapters of the volume turn to the so-called main protagonists of soft-power internationalism, the EU and the United States, and account for their failure in burnishing their leadership in international politics. If normative power in Europe had a radical vision, Thomas Diez asks what caused the crisis of EU foreign policy. Rather than placing blame on the waning influence of the United States or interference by domestic groups in EU policy, Diez's answer is both a defense of the moral underpinnings of normative power and a realistic review of institutional capacity in global politics. There was, Diez suggests, a growing gap between the solidaristic vision of normative power, in which states look out not just for their own interests but those of others, and the structure of the EU as well as international society overall, which prioritizes preserving national sovereignty and nonintervention. The radical vision of normative power could only go so far when the structure of international politics remained stubbornly reformist.

Jack Snyder grapples with the worldwide rise of illiberal populist nationalism, and what that means for soft power and international relations. Many countries, advanced democracies as well as rising semidemocratic or even illiberal states, enjoyed the growth and strong partnerships facilitated by soft-power internationalism since the 1990s. Nonetheless, the collective pull toward populist nationalism over the last few years is unmistakable. Drawing on Karl Polanyi, Snyder recognizes this divergence as a response to the tension between unregulated markets and demands for mass participation—a tension that is pervasive in all these countries, albeit in different forms. This contradiction between markets and politics is nothing new; neither is illiberal populist nationalism. But is there potential for building solidarity among these illiberal countries and transitioning to an illiberal form of soft power? Without the structural backbone of economic heft or military might, Snyder suggests, soft interventions alone do not carry much weight. More important, he argues that, without shared principles among illiberal actors other than their commitment to putting self-interest above all else, it is impossible to conjure up an illiberal, nationalist international peace.

Is soft power, then, only conceivable within a liberal international order? The evidence we have from the last thirty years points that way, but there is also emerging empirical work that examines illiberal countries' soft interventions in the era of a waning worldwide commitment to liberal internationalism. Media scholar Bilge Yeşil, for example, investigates how Turkey's soft-power interventions under an undeniably authoritarian regime exploit subalterity and deploy ressentiment to create regional solidarities.[17] Soft power seems to be of use to harsh regimes, but we have yet to see how durable these new solidarities will be in an increasingly antagonistic global politics.

Instead of being seduced by the soft interpretations of soft power, such as the effectiveness of messages or appeal of cultural frameworks, we focus on the political and economic conditions that made this particular epoch possible and how the practice of cultural power in international relations transformed global governance. By making the intellectual baggage and contradictory roots of soft power more visible and showcasing the varieties of soft powers in non-Western contexts, each chapter illuminates the underlying assumptions and expectations of a concept born of the post–Cold War period. At a time when there is a pervasive sense that the liberal international order is unraveling, we hope this book provides insights into what has happened over the last thirty years and what it meant to sustain peace in a multipolar world, in the immediate aftermath of the Cold War.

Notes

1. William E. Schmidt, "American Voices: Doubts as the Cold War Ends—A Special Report: In U.S., Unease as World Changes," *New York Times*, March 11, 1990, https://www.nytimes.com/1990/03/11/us/american-voices-doubts-cold-war-ends-special-report-us-unease-world-changes.html.

2. Joseph S. Nye Jr., "Soft Power," *Foreign Policy* 80 (1990): 153–71.

3. Daniel Deudney and G. John Ikenberry, "The Nature and Sources of Liberal International Order," *Review of International Studies* 25, no. 2 (1999): 179–96.

4. Perry Anderson, "Imperium," *New Left Review* 83 (2013): 5–111.

5. Quinn Slobodian, *Globalists: The End of Empire and the Birth of Neoliberalism* (Cambridge, MA: Harvard University Press, 2018).

6. Henry Farrell and Abraham Newman, "Weaponized Interdependence," *International Security* 44, no. 1 (2019): 17.

7. Gabrielle Hecht, ed., *Entangled Geographies: Empire and Technopolitics in the Global Cold War* (Cambridge, MA: MIT Press, 2011); Emma Mawdsley, *From Recipients to Donors: Emerging Powers and the Changing Development Landscape*, (London: Zed, 2012).

8. Miriyam Aouragh and Paula Chakravartty, "Infrastructures of Empire: Towards a Critical Geopolitics of Media and Information Studies," *Media, Culture & Society* 38, no. 4 (2016): 559–75.

9. Stanislav Budnitsky and Lianrui Jia, "Branding Internet Sovereignty: Digital Media and the Chinese-Russian Cyberalliance," *European Journal of Cultural Studies* 21, no. 5 (October 2018): 594–613.

10. Madiha Tahir, "The Containment Zone," in *Life in the Age of Drone Warfare*, ed. Lisa Parks and Caren Kaplan (Durham, NC: Duke University Press, 2017), 220–40.

11. Samuel Moyn, "A War Without Civilian Deaths?," *New Republic*, October 23, 2018, https://newrepublic.com/article/151560/damage-control-book-review -nick-mcdonell-bodies-person.

12. Joseph S. Nye Jr., "In Mideast, the Goal Is 'Smart Power,'" *Boston Globe*, August 19 2006, http://www.boston.com/news/globe/editorial_opinion/oped /articles/2006/08/19/in_mideast_the_goal_is_smart_power/; Eric Etheridge, "How 'Soft Power' Got 'Smart,'" *New York Times*, January 14, 2009, https:// opinionator.blogs.nytimes.com/2009/01/14/how-soft-power-got-smart/.

13. Hendrik Hertzberg, "Smart Power," *New Yorker*, January 26, 2009, https:// www.newyorker.com/magazine/2009/01/26/smart-power.

14. Zach Silberman, "Hillary Clinton and the Story of Smart Power," *U.S. Global Leadership Coalition*, June 12, 2014, https://www.usglc.org/blog/hillary-clinton -and-the-story-of-smart-power/.

15. Stanislav Budnitsky and Melissa Aronczyk, "The Logics and Limits of (Russia's) Soft Power" (presentation, 65th Annual International Communication Association Conference, San Juan, Puerto Rico, 2015, May 21–25, 2015).

16. Sheera Frenke, Kate Conger, and Kevin Roose, "Russia's Playbook for Social Media Disinformation Has Gone Global," *New York Times*, January 31, 2019, https://www.nytimes.com/2019/01/31/technology/twitter-disinformation -united-states-russia.html.

17. Bilge Yeşil, "Voice of the Voiceless: Role of Religion and Identity in Turkey's Soft Power and Global Media Expansion," presentation, 69th Annual International Communication Association Conference, Washington, DC, 2019, May 24–28, 2019.

PART ONE

Historical and Conceptual Foundations of Soft-Power Internationalism

CHAPTER I

Soft-Power United States Versus Normative Power Europe

Competing Ideals of Hegemony in the Post–Cold War West, 1990–2015

VICTORIA DE GRAZIA

Most of the contributors to this volume explore how rising hegemons outside the transatlantic area calculated the cultural and political baggage that came with the concept of soft power as they unpacked it and put it to work locally. This chapter unpacks that baggage at its place of origin. It takes two related concepts—soft power in its original 1990 made-in-America formulation, and normative power, Europe's home-crafted counterpart, a term that acquired currency circa 2005—and explores their genesis, their evolution, and the competition between them. Reputation, prestige, and legitimacy have always been a concern of statecraft. This chapter asks what historical forces made these two concepts so popular as new kinds of power in foreign policy making, each subject to particular practices and discourses, with specialized agencies, trained personnel, and freshly devised measures of success and failure. It asks what advantages their promoters believed their home countries and the world could gain from them, and who, ideally, they targeted domestically and abroad. What resources were regarded as necessary to turn them into effective instruments of foreign affairs and diplomatic practice? And, finally, how was their success or failure judged?

At the risk of essentializing the differences between these two terms, turning them into yet another of the binaries which since the early nineteenth century have been used to explain the differences between Europe and the United States, it is important to underscore that, from the outset, the terms had a different valence. However differently they were conceptualized by the norm-entrepreneur promoters who are the main focus of this chapter, those differences have to take into account the contrasting cultures of war and peace coming out of the Cold War, the dissimilar traditions and methodologies in thinking about international relations, and the diverging political projects of the United States and the EU from the outset of the twenty-first century.[1]

Soft power starts from the realist premise that if you want power, defined as the ability to get the outcomes you want from others, you can achieve it either by coercion or by attraction and persuasion.[2] While hard power—the ability to coerce—comes from a country's military or economic might, soft power is the ability to attract and persuade. Soft power is the added inducement, the tactical advantage arising from the appeal of the country's culture, values, and political ideals. It is used not to transform the core beliefs of others, but to encourage them to buy into a common logic, partake of a shared agenda, and, ideally, to build on the trust created by this transactional relationship. Soft power puts communication front and central, insofar as it assumes that differences of viewpoint are often caused by miscommunication and are thus surmountable once the proponent has grasped the target audience, honed the message, calculated how information travels (via the state, markets, civil society) and any possible obstacles (censorship, competing messages, or misinformation), and weighed how to calculate failure or success to account to the various stakeholders.

Normative power also claims to work on the basis of shared beliefs, standards, and values, rather than on material incentives or physical force, to bring change in the international order and among or between the nations within it.[3] However, it claims that its power of attraction arises from convincing others of the legitimacy of the principles underlying its agenda, and it adds that the only enduring way to achieve this convergence of interests is to promote these principles coherently and systematically. Normative power is thus best served by identifying itself with historically validated principles underlying international law and institutions—principles like multilateralism, national autonomy, human rights, and social justice. To work, it requires an element of shared ownership, and the measure of success is whether the shared values reproduce themselves institutionally, through, say, democratic regimes, or by establishing constitutional principles to end human rights abuses. Normative power often uses the language of solidarity rather than of transaction, and, to be effective, it calls for a long time frame, like the decades it took for the European Community to evolve into the European Union, or the half-century it took the Western Alliance arising out of Bretton Woods, the Marshall Plan, and NATO to become the spearhead of the anti-Soviet liberal world order. Its success is verified over time and is time-consuming and tolerant of putative missteps.

That said, the origins of the two concepts—and the articulation of their differences—have much in common. Both were born of a desire to establish a new kind of global liberal hegemony and of the realization that, while the interests of different states might diverge, they were still compatible with a shared interest in reinforcing the transatlantic alliance. From the outset, then, both concepts underscored the desirability of foregrounding norms and values in foreign affairs, as if this was something new. Both were grounded on the belief that history had destined the relevant entities—the United States and the EU—to assume the leadership mantle for the new liberal order coming out of the Cold War (the United States, of course, has believed in its special destiny practically since its foundation; the EU's conviction dates from the 1970s). Both presumed that market reforms were the major motor of global change, and both were shaped by rethinking their own and each other's very different capabilities for war-making in this new order, as opposed to whatever other economic, political, and cultural resources they could use to exercise their influence. Both saw their power as based on the new needs they could address—for instance, agenda-setting around complex global problems like the climate, human rights, humanitarian disasters, aging populations, or women's inequality, and by providing public goods toward their solution. Additionally, both recognized that they could capitalize on new institutional and technological means to promote themselves. On the one hand was the unsurpassed growth of international agencies, nongovernmental organizations, and people-to people civil society institutions. On the other hand was the new, more-or-less-direct access to innumerable people as consumers through deregulated markets, the World Wide Web, and the rapid advances in entertainment and cybercommunication industries spurred by both.[4]

For all these similarities, the two concepts evolved very differently. And, when "soft power" emerged as the generic term, the debate over what peaceable, just, and effective international governance might entail lost a great deal of nuance. As "soft power" was succeeded by trivial notions like "smart power" and "sharp power," etc., substantive debate over foreign policy in the United States collapsed. That trajectory, however, signals some of the paradoxes of soft-power internationalism. One is self-evident from the subject of this volume—namely, that soft power (which, in its original formulation, was regarded as a way for the United States to reaffirm its global leadership) was picked up elsewhere by rising hegemons to reinforce their prestige and voice and to rebalance against American military power. The other, which we examine here, sees the United States in the same period as giving a harder and harder edge to its so-called soft resources.

This hardening has occurred on three levels: first, by the expanding of pseudoprivate media platforms that, left to their own devices on the pretense that they are unregulated, have intensified cultural and ideological conflicts transnationally via international civil society channels; second, as an effect of the militarization of cyber- and other public-diplomacy programs, thanks to the reaffirmation of the leadership of the Department of Defense in this domain of public affairs; and, third, through the armed battles sustained in pursuing the global war on terror. These battles, of course, have time and again called on civilian forces to develop a cultural rationale to fight and then to legitimate American power once the fighting ends. All of this has politicized Western norms and values and made them appear deeply imperiled by a complex of civilizational values variously called fundamentalist, tribal, totalitarian, illiberal, and antisecular.

From the perspective of the North Atlantic World, then, the background for promoting the power of values, beliefs, culture, and communication as a foreign policy arm ought not be viewed as a product of the hopeful moment when the Cold War ended—when commerce, multilateralism, and the renewal of the U.S.-led Western alliance seemed almost inevitable— but, rather, as the opening of an interregnum that has seen huge uncertainty about the basis on which Western hegemony would be reinstated once the certainties of the bipolar Cold War world had to be abandoned.

The Great Divergence

March 20, 2003, marks a key moment in this history. On that date, after a globally televised all-night countdown, the president of the United States, with bipartisan backing from Congress, flouted international law and domestic and international protests to invade the Republic of Iraq and over-throw its president. For our purposes, the invasion can be seen as the cap-stone of the social engineering project that emerged from the Washington Consensus of 1989: Operation Enduring Freedom, a latter-day crusader coalition, would end Muslim resistance that saw the United States as the pinnacle of unholy modernity and made it the object of attacks by militar-ily insignificant states and nonstate actors that culminated in the Al Qaeda attacks on September 11, 2001. After the brief, successful military opera-tion, the coalition would rebuild the country as a Western-aligned free market economy under liberal constitutional rule, and Iraq would pay for it, by selling its oil on the global markets that had been closed to it by Western economic sanctions. Crazy that it all seemed so simple.

Robert Kagan, the well-known American foreign policy analyst, who was living in Brussels on the cusp of the invasion, vividly captured the way European political elites writhed over how to respond to their most impor-tant and long-standing ally. Despite the dozen European states (including Italy and Great Britain) that eventually joined the American-led coalition, Kagan announced that, "on the all-important question of power, the effi-cacy of power, the morality of power, the desirability of power, American and European perspectives are diverging."[5]

Kagan's 2003 book, *Of Paradise and Power: Europe and America in the New World Order,* is perhaps best remembered for its captivatingly sexist image of Europe as Venus and the United States as Mars. There was Europe loll-ing like some Rubenesque goddess of love in Kant's utopia of perpetual peace, happy to exercise her seductive wiles and promote her "civilizing mission" as she undermined world order by denouncing American aggression—and here was the ever-vigilant United States, standing guard to prevent a Hobbesian world from descending into global chaos. Kagan also provided what realists on both sides of the Atlantic regarded as a sat-isfying account of the origins of this divergence: real differences in mili-tary capacity coming out of World War II and the early Cold War were then reinforced culturally as successive European generations became dependent on American might and repudiated their militaristic past so thoroughly that the United States had to act unilaterally to shake Europe back to reality. Though Kagan did not use the terms "soft" and "hard," his images of an effeminate, seductively veiled Europe and a virile, trans-parent United States popularized the contrast between the two, while also fanning American nationalism.[6]

Reacting to both the Gulf War and American intellectual war-mongering, historians sought to explain the divergence as related to loosely defined cultures of war: the United States, they said, seemed to want to reprise the ideological and cultural dynamics of the global Cold War in the global war on terror. John Dower, a U.S. historian of World War II, wondered if the cultural legacy of the United States' annihilatory war against the Japanese explained the violent American reaction to 9/11. American political and military historian Andrew Bacevich asked why, in the wake of the collapse of the Soviet bloc, did American partisans of a new peace culture not prevail? And U.S. historian of Germany James Sheehan wondered how the belligerent Europe of the early twentieth century had been transformed into the peace-minded region of the early twentieth century, even writing a book called *Where Have All the Soldiers Gone?*[7]

Here I want to further the exploration of the evolving cultures of war across the North Atlantic by juxtaposing the intellectual moves of the people most responsible for the elaboration of our two concepts. They make an unlikely pair: Joseph S. Nye Jr., the Harvard University political scientist who coined the term "soft power" in 1990 and then in 2004 made it a byword not just of U.S. foreign policy debates, but international diplomacy; and Ian James Manners, an itinerant British professor of international relations. If Manners was not the first to conceptualize Normative Power Europe (NPE) as a way to identify and promote the EU's capacities as a foreign policy actor, his assiduous promotion of the term led the EU's political class, circa 2008, to adopt it to characterize the EU's ambitions for global leadership.

Bringing them together lets us consider not only differences of continent, disciplinary formation, political leanings, and cultural capital, but also the different class and generational cohorts leading the reconceptualization of international relations on both sides of the Atlantic in the wake of the Cold War. The patrician Nye was born in 1937, son of what we might call New Jersey gentry (his father was a stockbroker), and when he first proposed the term in 1990, he was a senior professor. He entered Harvard University in 1964 to study political science after graduating from Princeton summa cum laude and holding a Rhodes scholarship at Oxford, and it remained his academic base until he retired in 2010 as Distinguished Service Professor and Sultan of Oman Professor of International Relations. From the late 1970s on, he moved seamlessly between Harvard and Washington, DC, serving four years in Democratic administrations and speaking at and to inside-the-Beltway think tanks and international forums like the Aspen Institute and Davos. His ideas were published in *Foreign Policy* and *Foreign Affairs,* in op-ed pieces in the East Coast press; he appeared on television and YouTube, and his charmingly written general audience books were well timed, well promoted, and globally disseminated by major commercial presses.[8]

Born in the mid-1960s, Manners, who had just defended his doctoral thesis when he started clarifying his project in the mid-1990s, was more a cobbler of ideas with ideals. His father was a civil engineer; he grew up with stints abroad in the port town/backwater of Portishead near Bristol. After graduating in 1988 from West Virginia University on a track-and-field athletic scholarship, he trained and conducted research in the public sector–led educational landscape of EU Europe. After a stint as a BBC correspondent covering European affairs and attending University College London and Bristol, where he received his PhD degree in international relations in 1994, he started his academic career in red brick universities and between 1995 and 2004 moved from Bristol to the University of Wales at Swansea to the University of Kent at Canterbury. From there he moved to Scandinavia, where, after a period at Malmo (2004–2006); the Danish Institute for International Studies, Copenhagen (2006–2009); and the Institute of Society and Globalization at Roskilde University (2009–2013), he settled into a professorship in the Political Science Department at the University of Copenhagen (punctuated by visitorships at Lund and Sydney). Manners always treated his workmanlike essays as a collaborative undertaking with like-minded scholars; many were elaborated in conferences and networks designed to forge the new field of European studies and disseminated through leading European academic journals, notably *Millennium: Journal of European Public Policy, Journal of Common Market Studies*, and *Cooperation and Conflict.*[9]

Manners's passion was for a united Europe. He grew up in the peace culture of post-Vietnam Europe, which saw Soviet and American nuclear brinkmanship as a horror and had little or no contact with the British military. His training in critical security studies at the University of Bristol reinforced his skepticism about the utility of war, and, once he spelled out his concept of a "normative Europe," he was always attentive to preventing it from being exploited to reinforce the hegemonic inclinations of Brussels Eurocrats. Nye was an American patriot comfortable with defense and national security issues and elites, both at home and abroad. He was always troubled by the specter of Vietnam, and how to resolve the question of what, in terms of American interests, constituted a good or bad war. Even when soft power acquired global currency, he continued trying to make its success and failure elsewhere a tool for and measure of American global influence.

For all of their differences—for the purposes of this analysis—both are "norm entrepreneurs," the term coined by IR scholars Martha Finnemore and Katherine Sikkink. Like promoters of human rights, sustainability, transparency, and environment, over time their ideas can be treated as having evolved "from hobby horses to common sense categories, the basis for reasonable political action at both the domestic and international level."[10] Both Nye's "soft power" and Manners's "normative power" originated as corrections of the IR discipline and critiques of foreign policy, and both men endeavored to define the terms coherently yet broadly enough so that not only individuals, think tanks, and NGOs, but also states and international agencies, could assimilate them more or less seamlessly into their rhetoric.

That said, Manners's goal was to conceptualize how the EU could exploit the processes to which it owed its existence—namely, treaty-making, negotiations, cooperation with international institutions, and the values like transparency that were inherent in them—to make itself more internally cohesive and more globally effective. Nye's project was to convince a skeptical domestic elite that if the United States was to reestablish its leadership in a more interconnected and multilateral international order, it would have to supplement its immense military-political power with its cultural resources. As Nye eventually realized, this required the United States to undertake the kind of domestic reforms that had legitimated its claim to be the preeminent global model in the Progressive Era, under the New Deal, with the Marshall Plan, and as the founding force of the post–World War liberal order with civil society institutions that could be mobilized to operate in tandem with U.S. governmental forces and liberal international institutions globally.

America's Way

The origins of Nye's conception of soft power take us back to 1970s Cambridge, Massachusetts, Nye's academic and intellectual home base. Under the mentorship of the French-Jewish humanist–social scientist Stanley

Hoffman, Nye shook off the hard-edged realism of the Hans J. Morgenthau–Henry Kissinger school of thought. Steeped in the technocratic optimism of the Cambridge area of those years, he confessed that the Austrian political economist and Harvard professor Joseph Schumpeter of "creative destruction" fame was his first great intellectual passion. It was practically impossible in 1960s Cambridge not to embrace the cybernetic utopias of Norbert Weiner that held out the dream of feedback loops of perfect knowledge, nor the flowering of U.S. regional and development studies that brought Nye to study Kenya, Central America, and Japan. As much as any American social scientist of that time, as Nye embraced the master narrative of American progressivism he grasped its corollary that "the ability to persuade other people that you have a picture of the future which is plausible and that this is a way in which they can move, is an important source of power."[11] If concepts were patentable, Nye would have earned millions from branding "soft power." As it was, his books on the subject were global bestsellers.

In the debates about the discipline of international relations that followed the U.S. defeat in the Vietnam War, Nye sided with his cohort—colleagues of great rectitude and intellectual accomplishment like his long-standing collaborator Robert Keohane—against the swaggering realism of a field shaped by the Cold War's brutal military confrontationalism, as if the fight for global order was still being waged against Nazi totalitarianism and the Axis. This older stance had led to the neglect of the problem of reputation and status and the way states regarded one another's interests, prestige, and moral outlooks, thus offering an incomplete framework for analyzing international relations, especially considering the growing role of international institutions. While Nye's first book, *Power and Interdependence*, written with Keohane, was still grounded in key realist tenets that emphasized the centrality of national self-interest and the use of power to satisfy it, it downplayed old winner-take all assumptions in the name of a more liberal give-and-take.[12] In other words, if states regarded institutions like the International Atomic Energy Commission or World Bank as tools of their power and invested in their procedures, they might hesitate to contravene them, sacrificing some benefits for collaboration on issues deemed more important.

Nye had experienced that kind of cooperative undertaking as national security advisor in the Carter administration. Based in the State Department, he liaised with the National Security Council Committee to deal with the nonproliferation of nuclear weapons. In the face of the energy crisis, there was huge interest in building plutonium-powered reactors, which the United States feared could be converted to weapons manufacture. The problem, then, was how the world's leading nuclear power—the United States—could sell the world on what was then a "wildly unpopular" idea—namely, restricting plutonium sales.[13] Nye worked with the Ford Foundation, developed interagency state capacity to draw up guidelines, and coordinated a transnational study group called the International Nuclear Fuel Cycle Evaluation "to buy time to get people to support the problem." The eventual outcome was the launch of an International Atomic Energy Agency and a Nuclear Suppliers Group, meant to turn the "bad idea" of restricting plutonium sales into an international norm that the United Nations (UN) would eventually police.[14]

It was not until 1990, after several years of arguing against American "declinists" who compared Japanese and German prosperity with the United States' slow economic growth, rusted Fordist industry, giant military expenditures, and mounting budget deficits and national debt, that Nye published his initial formulation of "soft power." He was especially keen to respond to Paul Kennedy, the Yale historian, who, in his 1987 book *The Rise and Fall of Great Powers,* had argued masterfully that all empires eventually declined under the weight of their military obligations.[15] In *Bound to Lead,* published just after the Berlin Wall came down, Nye responded that this would not—could not—be the United States' fate. The problem, as his subtitle indicated, was *The Changing Nature of American Power.* The United States, in addition to its unsurpassable military power and economic resilience, possessed another kind of clout: the "soft" cultural resources of its democratic heritage. By virtue of this legacy, the United States was "bound" to renew its leadership as the "agenda-setting" power of the world, especially as the bipolar global order disintegrated. Given their lack of military power, Japan and Germany could never be more than "civilian powers" supportive of U.S. global leadership.[16]

In a 1990 article for *Foreign Policy,* Nye developed the soft-power theme of *Bound to Lead* in a winningly formulaic style that harried congressional staffers could quote to their bosses as they rushed through early morning policy briefings. It was true, he said, that, from the 1970s on, the United States had faced significant challenges to its superpower status, including declining economic competitiveness, overextended military budgets, and the rise of new cross-national organizations like the OPEC Cartel and new regional powers like Japan and the EU. True, some colleagues thought that American foreign policy should rely more on a multilateral world system, respect Soviet Bloc arrangements, and demilitarize. But neorealist Nye wanted the United States to work with institutions of international governance and preserve its authority as the world's "unique agenda setting power." If the United States valorized not only its "hard command," but also the soft power derived from liberal democracy and the American way of life, the nation could achieve its ends in a cost-effective, prudent, and nonideological way, with none of the redemptive crusader rhetoric employed by Woodrow Wilson (or Ronald Reagan).[17]

As a historian, I would tax Nye for being too vague about what he meant by soft-power resources. Let's use Pierre Bourdieu's notion of cultural capital and agree that the United States had accumulated a huge amount of symbolic wealth, in a way that allowed it to establish the master narrative for what the good society meant in terms of standard of living, technological innovation, consumer freedoms, and so on. If this symbolic capital was exhausted, could it be revived? Or did it have to be reproduced from new sources? Arguably, in the wake of great military victories or civic mobilizations of comparable importance, the United States had time and again reinforced its role as the world's leading model, thus the original Wilsonian moment coming out of World War I, Roosevelt's New Deal, and the Four Freedoms mobilizing against the Nazi-Fascist New Order—so, too, the launch of the Marshall Plan at the onset of the Cold War. Without the civil rights movement and the domestic mobilization against American apartheid, the American story of progress could never have responded to the aspirations of anticolonial movements worldwide. In sum, at every moment down to the 1990s, U.S. appeal abroad had been reshaped by social mobilization and reform at home. What old or new forces might be unleashed to mount an equivalent reform for the 1990s and beyond?

Nye's concept of soft power, insofar as it implied a wholesale overhaul of U.S. domestic policy to reposition the United States as a leading model, went nowhere for almost a decade. He ran up against the belief, promoted by pro- and anti-American pundits and political theorists, that, with the triumph of American consumer capitalism over Soviet socialism, the United States could basically rest on its laurels. Now that the barriers were down, market forces would do the rest, or so liberal regime theory in the hands of American liberal pundits—notably Thomas Friedman—contended. The more states converged around the model of liberal capitalist modernity, the less likely they would come into conflict. "No two countries that both have a McDonald's have ever fought a war against each other," according to Friedman's jokey "franchise theory of global conflict prevention."[18] The world had become flat, to recall another of Friedman's conceits, and the 360-degree CNN eye took in everything twenty-four seven. The *Economist* developed "Burgernomics," which used the local cost of the Big Mac to measure global purchasing power parity (PPP) in the face of volatile currencies. UBS developed its "Big Mac Index" to calculate local labor costs by pricing the time it took the worker to purchase one juicy hamburger with all of the trimmings. Walmart heading into China had no need of Uncle Sam as its political effigy when it had the avuncular "Papa" Sam Walton.

On the other hand, Nye had to contend with American cultural pessimists. American materialism, its technological culture, and secular values were generating a huge backlash globally, generating conflicts among peoples that were more and more defined along civilizational and tribal lines. The progressive version came from Benjamin Barber. In his "Jihad vs. McWorld" (the article in 1992, the book in 1995), he argued that the only way to counter the mounting reaction was to forge a global democratic civic culture, drawing on American democratic solidaristic European cultures. The conservative version came in Samuel P. Huntington's "Clash of Civilizations" (the article in 1993, the book in 1996), arguing that the West's diffusion of valueless technology had debased its own humanistic culture and created an intractable antagonism in others, especially in the Muslim world. To defend the West involved a more farsighted, powerful military strategy and a more muscular, Christianized Americanism.

In Washington, the path to foreign policy reform passes through the national security community. Having served in the Clinton administration (1994–1995) as assistant secretary of defense for international security affairs, Nye understood that the Pentagon was a better lobby for new strategies than the State Department. Both departments needed to overhaul operating systems conceived in the early Cold War, when Eastern Europe was the main confrontation site and anticommunist radio information cum propaganda broadcasts were the main weapons. It was true that the military had more resources. It was also under strong pressure from neoconservatives to eliminate its "socialistic" giant bureaucratic apparatus, pursue cybernetic weapons systems, and outsource operations to private contractors. Historically, U.S. public diplomacy had always revved up in view of new military missions, starting from its first iteration during World War I in the Creel Commission. Conceivably, then, the Pentagon would be more receptive than the State Department.[19]

So it happened in the 1990s. As American troops were moved from western Europe into Russian-border states, they were tasked with the work of the diplomatic corps, whose arrival awaited the cessation of civil conflicts. Embracing the notion of the Revolution in Military Affairs (RMA), the military pushed ahead in cybertechnology, and, as it reorganized its bases abroad—moving from Europe to monitor the ex-Soviet space, the Horn of Africa, and the Indian Ocean—it developed its lily pad (as opposed to large footprint) style of small, numerous, flexibly organized, and closely networked bases.[20] Arguably, the military establishment was in closer touch than the State Department with both foreign civil societies and U.S. domestic politics and could thus make a stronger claim than any other government bureaucracy for connecting the real United States (of democracy, upward mobility, and curiosity about the world) with foreign worlds. At home, it recruited, educated, and promoted a more socially and culturally diverse America, including people of color, and, unlike the State Department, it permitted them at their often early retirement to work in think tanks, teach in war colleges, and hold corporate consultancies, offering conduits for connection that were lacking in civilian administration.

Perhaps also calculating that Congress would be more inclined to appropriate funds if soft power was shown to be efficient in military-security terms, in 1995–1996 Nye teamed up with Admiral William A. Owens, vice-chairman of the Joint Chiefs of Staff, to endorse the soft-power turn on military-technocratic grounds. Their *Foreign Affairs* article "America's Information Edge" argued for piggybacking on the American-led cybernetic revolution to put U.S. global hegemony on a new footing militarily, culturally, and diplomatically.[21] The so-called information edge was the perfect neoliberal invention. Militarily, it promised to transform the state-bureaucratic, materièl-heavy mass army into a pared-down, flexible fighting force operating with precision, speed, and range. In terms of communications, the cyber revolution promised to establish an "information umbrella" as effective as the "nuclear umbrella;" it would enable the United States to share its "dominant situational knowledge" with "a wide range of friends, allies, and neutral nations."[22] Able to distinguish friend from foe in the face of the ever-more complicated alignments of the post–Cold War era, this umbrella would isolate and sanction rogue states like Iraq. At the same time, it would prepare the way for "people to build market societies when the opportunities arise."[23] In this technocratic formulation, there was no mention of the revival of the United States' legacy of good values, democratic beliefs, or civic culture, nor of the Marshall plans being discussed at the time in Western Europe to salvage and restructure post-Soviet bloc economies. In effect, the Nye-Owens article conceived the United States as having such a huge "information edge" at that moment that, as long as its incipient regulation favored American interests, it was suffused with democratic, open society values. If Congress and foreign policy–makers gave it its due place in the overhaul of foreign policy, as Nye and Owens concluded, "the 21st century (would) be the period of America's greatest preeminence, not the 20th."[24]

However, the desire to reap the peace dividend resulted not in the reform of the apparatus of public diplomacy so much as the bipartisan decision to downsize it. In 1998, a new Under Secretariat of Diplomacy and Public Affairs (sometimes called Press and Public Diplomacy) was established within the State Department and charged with bringing it up to date with new information technologies and using them to support cultural programs. But, between 1993 and 2001, government funding for information programs and educational and cultural exchanges declined by approximately one-third, and in 1999 the entity most responsible for public diplomacy, the United States Information Agency, was dismantled and absorbed into the very different bureaucratic culture of the State Department. By 2001, academic and cultural exchanges had shrunk from 45,000 to 29,000 annually. The State Department was pensioning off its aging Soviet experts, but had yet to hire Arabic speakers.[25]

Having returned to Cambridge in 1995 to take up the deanship of Harvard's John F. Kennedy School of Government, Nye thrust himself into national domestic affairs to explain the terrible loss of trust in government that had led Gulf War veteran Timothy McVeigh to bomb the federal office building in Oklahoma City that year. Dismayed at seeing President Clinton capitulate to domestic critics by withholding U.S. support for the World Trade Organization accords at the G8's bumptious Seattle meeting, Nye came back to soft power in late 1999, writing an impassioned op-ed for the *New York Times* to enjoin Republican candidates—who were outdoing each another urging isolation and increased military spending—to remember that their idol Ronald Reagan had championed soft power. Soft power, Nye reminded them, "is our ability to get what we want through attraction rather than coercion." He pointed out once more that, "when other countries want the same outcome we want, then we can get what we want without having to spend as much on coercion." He insisted again on the importance of both dimensions of power, hard and soft, and explained that "they work best when they reinforce each other." Rather timidly, as if not to inject too partisan a note into national security questions, he aligned himself with the Democratic party agenda to argue that "the quality of our domestic life—prosperity, social safety nets, equal access to justice, democratic elections—has a strong impact on our international position."[26]

As a foreign policy realist, Nye was not arguing that U.S. global leadership depended first and foremost on its capacity to be a model both materially and ideally; that idea was left to constructivist IR theorists or Gramscian critics of U.S. hegemonic pretentions. But he was surely speaking to Harvard colleagues like Robert Putnam, whose book *Bowling Alone: America's Declining Social Capital* (1995) registered the dwindling of Middle American civil society in the face of the crisis of great corporate employers like IBM and General Motors and the consequent social and cultural fragmentation of middle-class life. As much as restoring social justice at home, Nye wanted to restore America's social honor abroad. Transparency was an age-old American liberal virtue. If the United States didn't want to be seen as hypocritical, he said, the United States had to practice at home what it preached abroad—democracy, human rights, and social justice.

Europe's Turn

Whereas the conceptualization of soft power was bound up with the evolution in the discipline of international relations at its highest academic level at the most elite American universities at the acme of postwar U.S. power, the conceptualization of normative power was built on a critique of the American version of the discipline mounted by a new trans-European middle class, almost all with positions in public universities, trying to reclaim a European voice in the EU and world affairs. While this endeavor dates to the 1970s, if not earlier, the momentum to define the EU as a repository of deeply held European beliefs and values grew over the 1990s. This momentum reflected the effort to compensate for what was called the democratic deficit in representative institutions, to make the EU less technocratic and more the sum of the concerns and interests of its citizenry. It was also part of the effort to confront the civil war and NATO intervention in Yugoslavia and give the EU more capabilities as an international actor. This trend accelerated with the Maastricht Treaty (1992), and gathered more momentum with the adoption of the single currency (2002).

Ian Manners was teaching European studies at the University of Kent in 2002 when he published his first article on normative power. The milieu surely favored it: founded in 1965, the university had come back from the Thatcher-era cuts to higher education and repositioned itself in the 1990s as the most globally engaged institution of higher education in the British public system. Moreover, Manners was in the School of International Relations, a hotbed of critical security studies, Gramscian cultural critiques, and debates about the only real alternative to America's hard-nosed and increasingly scientized realist international relations, the "English school," identified with Australian-born Oxonian, Hedley Bull, heir to the historian of international relations, E. H. Carr.[27] Manners's decision to publish this first piece in the *Journal of Common Market Studies* was strategic—founded in May 1962, it was the oldest of the academic periodicals dedicated to studying European integration, born out of British academics' deep curiosity about the European Community when Britain's entry, though much debated, seemed near, until Charles de Gaulle vetoed it. The editors expected contributions to be nonpartisan in the British sense, meaning that their authors either announced their biases or cut out the parts that showed them too blatantly.[28]

Manners was straightforward about his. He wanted to repudiate Hedley Bull's realism. The idea that an integrated Europe could present itself as a "civilian power" on the world stage was a "contradiction in terms," Bull had insisted in 1982 in the *Journal of Common Market History*.[29] The European Community might have defied both the well-known anarchy of the international system and historical good sense, but, short of having real military capabilities, it could not be a leading power.

Bull's primary target was Franco-British Europhile Francois Duchêne and his idealization of Europe as a "civilian power."[30] A former aide to Jean Monnet, Duchêne had advanced this idea on the fifteenth anniversary of the Treaty of Rome. 1972 was a good year for Europhiles: under German leadership, Western Europe was coping with Nixon's devaluation of the dollar, and any plans to cut off oil to Europe if it joined the United States in supporting Israel in the event of war was still only a glimmer in OPEC's eyes. Britain was entering the EU, and Charles De Gaulle's "grand design" and the German Federal Republic's Ostpolitik or "opening to the East" still held the promise of opening a third way between the superpowers.

None of this convinced Bull, however. If the new Europe wanted to be an independent power, then it should develop a military force. Lacking one, the European Community could not pursue an independent course of action while the Reagan administration was reigniting the Cold War with the Soviet Union. If it remained Atlanticist, it was subordinated to the United States; if it turned neutralist, it risked subordination to the USSR.

In the next half-decade, Bull's—and British liberal skepticism—would be challenged from the Continent from the perspective of European capitalism and commerce. The first writer to speak of Europe as a normative power was American political scientist Richard Rosecrance, whose 1986 *The Rise of the Trading State* had spoken of the open trading system spearheaded by the German Federal Republic and Japan as a civilizing force, a contrast to the atavistic Hobbesian vision of the world ingrained in the U.S.-Soviet rivalry and revived under the presidency of Ronald Reagan.[31] The notion that Europe, with its mixed capitalist economy and relatively good growth rates, could replace the United States as global economic leader dated back to British economist Andrew Shonfield's impressive 1966 book, *Modern Capitalism: The Changing Balance of Public and Private Power*. This aspiration was given new currency in the wake of the dissolution of the Soviet bloc, as Europeans saw Europe, not the United States, as having held out the hope of human rights to the Soviet bloc nations. The victorious capitalist model was not the Washington Consensus with its primitive view of markets, short-term profit-taking, and indifference to societal cohesion, but, rather, as French economist Michel Albert argued, the crossnationally coordinated social market economies of "Rhineland Europe."[32] With their focus on societal consensus, an active state, and a long-term orientation, these economies had outperformed the United States on most socioeconomic indicators. It was the European standard of living—the combination of European style craft and mass goods, welfare state rights, and decent wages, not the American model of ever-cheaper mass goods, made in Asia and financed for the poor by cheap credit and huge trade deficits with China—that was the new Europe-wide standard. Europe's big brands like Carrefour, Ikea, Parmalat, and Benetton saw themselves as post–Fordist and more competitive and innovative than equivalent U.S. firms.

The breakup of the Soviet bloc forced Europeans to rethink foreign and security policy. First, there was the old German problem. It had been fine to theorize the German Federal Republic as the foremost European "civilian" power, to recall Rosecrance's idealization of the German trading state, or to think of it as the pillar of NATO and Atlantic Alliance, as the Americans wanted. But, once the Federal German Republic had annexed the German Democratic Republic and united Germany acquired complete sovereignty in foreign and military affairs, the pressure was on to find new ways to reanchor it within the EU. Nobody wanted this rich, centrally positioned, and once-again-giant state to grow its power with respect to the post-Soviet states or favor the United States' unipolar worldview. Another issue was what to do with the new Europe of the post-Soviet space: the nations of the Warsaw Treaty and Yugoslavia and former Soviet imperial dependencies like Estonia, Lithuania, and Latvia and the Russian Confederation. Should Europeans embrace the Europe that not just Mikhail Gorbachev but many European socialists longed for, one that stretched from the Atlantic to the Urals? Should they create the European unity that the Cold War had forestalled in 1947? Before this could be answered, the urgent crisis in the Socialist Federal Republic of Yugoslavia had to be addressed. Arguably, no issue was more important to testing—and reinforcing—Europe's desire for a foreign policy of its own. (And none, I will argue, would prove more important to reinforcing Europe's development as a normative power).

Suffice it to say that the EU stumbled in the face of its first post–Cold War foreign policy crisis. As the Yugoslavian conflict unfolded, Germany distanced itself from France and Britain's hope of preserving the status quo, by encouraging the Croatian and Slovenian claims to independence that pitched the federation into a decade of civil conflict. Germany's normative thinking on the matter could be characterized as rich and tragically overdetermined: there was the old imperialist Germany, acting out of sympathy for Croatia, its one-time protectorate; and there was so-called good nationalism of united Germany, wanting to demonstrate that its annexation of East Germany was an act of self-determination, not occupation, by supporting another European people's human right; and there was the deep well of anticommunism that said that self-determination was especially important in the face of communist masters, meaning the Belgrade Serbs.

However German rationales were understood, the FRG's horrific bungle upped the pressure to generate a shared understanding of united Europe as a foreign policy actor.

In the face of these challenges, the EU needed a foreign policy narrative. International relations as practiced by American social sciences had focused mainly on the nation-state, and the best and brightest of Keohane's and Nye's students, notably Andrew Moravscik, was painfully ahistorical even when proposing a historical account. If the EU was going to reject soulless American political science's view that the "EU is best seen as an international regime for policy coordination," it needed a narrative that was both historical and comparative, with a keen eye for member states' peculiarities and affinities even as it created a plausible history of their convergence.[33]

Manners's circle addressed the Europeanists' need for a European account of the evolution of the EU on two levels. It built on the English School of International Relations' interest in solidarist international norms, international law, and human rights by integrating into European studies the study of norms that, across the Atlantic, along with the work of Martha Finnemore and Kathryn Sikkink, had led sociologist Ann Florini to publish "The Evolution of International Norms" in 1996.[34] And it collaborated on group projects like the volume Manners coedited with his University of Manchester colleague Richard Whitman to study the differences between, as well as the eventual convergences among, European member states' foreign policies as they evolved in the wake of the Cold War.[35]

This work became an important political as well as scientific project. The more political elites spoke of their commitment to a Federal Europe and the importance of the European social model in resisting global market forces, the more they recognized that the EU needed a stronger cultural integration. Cultural heft would compensate for its institutional democratic deficit. A stronger cultural identity would offset the ever-more-present Americanization in media and the cyberworld. It would help express the European liberal secularist beliefs and humanistic values that would counter Islamic fundamentalism. The second half of the 1990s was thus a godsend for academics and public intellectuals, as universities mobilized, with the EU supporting projects on Euro-identity and Erasmus student exchanges sending tens of thousands of students abroad for a year of schooling.

When Manners responded to Bull's position in 2002, two decades after Bull had formulated it, he was thus in a solid position. In five decades of peaceful negotiations over rules, regulations, and norms, the EU had become a sovereign entity. More than that, it had become the de facto leader of the post-Westphalian world order. Insisting on the EU as "post-Westphalian" let Manners make two points. The first was that all conventional IR theory started from the premise that the modern international order rested on the peace agreement signed by the belligerents at Westphalia ending the thirty-year religious wars of the first half of the seventeenth century. The pact stipulated that the sovereigns would cease interfering with each other's religious practices and henceforth respect one another's autonomy, equality before international covenants, and freedom from intervention.

The second point was that the European Community, in becoming the EU, had turned its back on the balance-of-power and great-power politics that had devastated the continent and the world. For its negotiators to succeed in constituting a post-state entity, they had to operate according to shared values, practices, and rules within the framework of the post–World War II institutions, treaties, and conventions that stipulated them, including the UN Universal Declaration of Human Rights, the Helsinki Final Act, and the Charter of Paris. Having managed to constitute itself without force of arms, the EU was uniquely positioned to persuade other states and international entities to do the same.[36]

How distant, then, was Manners from Nye. Nye had never questioned the basic realist premises that the world was anarchic, that sovereign states were the basic unit of action, and that there was a hierarchy among them based on measures like gross national product and military power. From that perspective, soft power was another weapon. Constructivist Manners, by contrast, saw human interactions as shaping the world. The European Community had negotiated itself into existence via the ideals of the rule of law, human rights, social solidarity, and gender equality, as well as safeguarding the environment, cultural diversity, and privacy, to name a few. These norms, in turn, interacted with the same complex interdependency (as Keohane and Nye called it) being evolved by the UN and other international institutions and positioned New Europe to sustain a new global culture of norms. From this vantage point, Manners could fend off two groups of critics: the Marxists, who argued that normative power was just a jargony way to sanitize Europe's inveterate imperialism; and the realists, who said that Europe boasted of its normative capabilities to compensate for, and excuse, its lack of military might.

Meanwhile, Romano Prodi's term as the EU's first "prime minister" (i.e., the first president of the European Commission), from 1999 to 2004, brought legitimacy to this normative vision. Elected in 1999 with the support of both conservatives and socialists, the one-time Christian Democrat turned Euro-communist was a Catholic in the spirit of the founding fathers (Alcide De Gaspari, Konrad Adenauer, et alia) and a social democrat in the tradition of Jacques Delors. Along with brokering the adoption of the euro in 2002, joining his voice to the many who hailed monetary unification as an act of idealism, Prodi oversaw the "big bang" eastward enlargement in 2004. From late April of that year, on a political tour of the region that started at Trieste and ended at Strasbourg, he told audiences how the EU's quick response to the Soviet collapse had unified Europe, transforming the Europe divided by the Iron Curtain from Stettin on the Baltic to Trieste on the Adriatic into one unified from Tallinn to Valletta. Prodi also paid tribute to the citizens of the union for "developing market economies and open and democratic societies that meet the high standards we laid down in 1993," meaning the Copenhagen meetings where the EU partners established strict EU entrance requirements. He implicitly compared Europe to the United States: "Our vision of integration has exerted an extraordinary power of attraction on neighboring countries. . . . We enjoy the peaceful rule of law. That means peace and dialogue, something the world today badly needs. It means the protection and defense of social rights and the rights of the individual. In the new world order dominated by a single superpower and the dynamics of globalization, our future depends on our ability to remain united."[37] On May 5, in the last speech of his tenure, he told the European Commission that the EU would seek "to extend to the whole of Europe the model of peace, democracy and prosperity that are the hallmarks of the Union" and "to promote across the world its model for managing relations between countries," which he called a "practical response to the deteriorating international situation."[38] He also announced the material resources the EU intended to devote to this cause through the European Neighbourhood Policy, which, as it evolved over the next decade, would entail a hugely funded effort to strengthen individual and regional relationships between the EU and the countries in its eastern and southern "neighborhoods."[39]

Norms-Making Under the Shadow
of NATO Humanism

Prodi's allusions to "right versus might," "peace," and the "deteriorating international situation"—to his audiences, all clear references to the U.S. intervention in Iraq—return us to our starting point: the relationship between hard and soft power, and the contrast between the United States' bellicose coalition building and European pacifism in the face of military necessity Kagan had popularized only a year earlier in the run up to the U.S. War in Iraq.

To a surprising degree, Manners never considered aggression as perhaps the most powerful means of norms-making. "Aggression" here is intended to mean both the practice of "othering" and all-out war-making. The use of binaries, of using a putative "them" as distinct from a putative "us"—a rhetorically powerful device with real consequences in reinforcing bias, exclusion, and annihilation of those deemed to be "other"—had always been present in European discourse, and it could even be heard in Prodi's speeches. While some might regard counterpoising "right and might," the new Europe against the old United States, as generally salubrious, they could also hear in Prodi the old othering, the imperial habit of setting up European norms as superior—for instance, to Turkey, Europe's historical great other, and the European Community's, as well, because its human rights record did not live up to Copenhagen criteria; or toward the United States as less civilized for having the death penalty and opposing the Kyoto Protocol; or Serbia for its violation of human rights.

Assuming that Manners was sensitive to the permanence of these invidious cultural habits, how did he treat war-making? Quite tidily, I believe, though in a conventional way. The EU needed to acquire military capabilities, which it would do within the framework of the European Security and Defense Policy (ESDP). Assuming military means were not prioritized over nonmilitary ones; their deployment was collectively decided upon, solely for defensive purposes. In any case, the EU was devoid of the bellicosity inherent in the origins of normal nation-states, and it would remain first and foremost a normative power.[40]

That argument made sense when one compared developments within the United States and Europe from the 1990s. Consider, for instance, how closely the development of new cybertechnologies in the United States

were bound up with military-strategic considerations and lines of investment that rebuilt on new bases the military-industrial-academic complex
that Nye was so close to. In Europe, in contrast, except through NATO—
which is not to be dismissed as a pivot of the Euro-based knowledge-
military complex—the connections were far more tenuous, and mainly at
the level of single nation-states.

In reality, war-making was pivotal to the formation of the EU, though
not in the current textbook and EU-bureaucracy sense. It is pure hagio-
graphy, argued foremost historian of European integration Alan Milward,
that the founding fathers' overriding concern in the 1950s was not to prevent war altogether or ever again on the continent; their foremost concern
was to address the threat that the Soviet Union and the eventual resurgence of Germany posed to the European order, and they achieved that
end by accepting the United States as guarantor of European security
through the NATO alliance and by hooking western and southern Germany into the Marshall Plan and the European Coal and Steel Commission. Subsequently, as U.S. historian James Sheehan underscores, the long
European economic boom supplanted welfare with warfare as the main
source of national prestige. In time, political elites who derived their legitimacy from protecting their subjects by force of arms gave way to political
elites who legitimated their social contract in terms of European social
democracy by providing for their citizens' well-being through collective
goods like social security, health services, and public education.

In my reading, normative Europe, by which I mean a more or less integrated Europe, legitimating itself with respect to its citizens and constitu-
ents by appealing to its values, is a later development, and major conflicts—
including the failure of European colonialism, the anti-Vietnam
movement, the breakup of the Soviet empire, and the 1990s Balkan wars,
together with protests against the U.S.-led global war on terror—play a
more significant role than has been conceived, together with the resurgence
of the German Federal Republic as an international actor in the 1980s.

At the same time, the EU has cultivated the myth of itself as somehow
alien to warring behavior, not just as if Western Europe had learned its lesson and reformed, but that its bellicosity has somehow disappeared down a
rabbit hole. Accordingly, Sheehan, like many scholars of postimperial
continental Europe, underestimates the belligerence of European states well
after the Suez debacle of 1956; colonial wars continued for another decade,
and the Cold War confrontation between the United States and the USSR

fought proxy wars outside of the European region into the 1980s, by mobilizing personnel and military matériel from their allies on either side of the Wall. Suffice it to say that, from 1982, as chancellor Helmut Kohl aggressively pursued his project of turning Germany into what he called a "normal nation," he found an accomplice in president Ronald Reagan's foreign policy, Hollywood war films' narrative creativity, and European anticommunist revisionism.

In 1984, Reagan relaunched NATO by celebrating the fortieth anniversary of the Allied landing in Normandy in a way that made the USSR, which was uninvited, the main enemy in the war and turned the Federal Republic of Germany into the United States' loyal ally, a stalwart of the West's ongoing antitotalitarian alliance. This rewriting meant the antifascist resistance practically disappeared, the Soviets fell out of the Allied coalition, the Federal Republic of Germany was established as the pillar of peace in Western Europe, and the dead of the Shoah became the only victims worthy of being mourned. It was only a matter of time before post–Cold War historiography removed the site of war from Western Europe to the bloodied marches of Eastern Europe and laid its causes and catastrophic violence to the pathological feud between the two despotic totalitarians, Hitler and Stalin.[41]

Ultimately, it was the return of war to the European continent in the form of the terrible, almost decade-long Balkans conflict that made European intellectuals hold Europe to being a normative power, but not in the way most people—including, perhaps, Manners—recognized. Aside from revealing major differences of interest among Germany, France, and Britain, deep disagreements over whether the key EU principle was the inviolability of sovereignty or the necessity of protecting human rights, intervention on the part of NATO and the UN highlighted the incorrigible Orientalism that made the violence of the Balkan "others" the perfect foil for reinforcing the high-minded humanistic principles forged in western Europe.[42]

It is sobering to recognize that Europe's first major foreign policy move based on European norms, values, and interests was basically an endorsement of what would soon become the "right to intervene": a war-making concept formulated by liberal theorists of post–Cold War U.S. foreign policy. It was also the first time the Revolution in/of Military Affairs was adopted for humanitarian intervention. European supporters, notably the

Green foreign minister of Germany, Joschka Fischer, called it "NATO humanitarianism."[43] Over seventy-eight days, from March 24 to June 9, 1999, the NATO alliance, led by the world's only superpower, ran 38,000 combat missions over Serbia (a country the size of South Carolina). The strikes combined precision bombing that targeted infrastructure and limited civilian casualties (which eventually amounted to about five hundred) with a massive propaganda bombardment that explained the necessity of removing the president of the Federal Republic of Yugoslavia, Slobodan Milosevic, and preventing the genocide of the Kosovar Albanians. Later, when Joseph Nye was asked for an example of the successful deployment of soft power, he spoke of the 1999 campaign.[44]

This intervention advanced the cause of normative power in Europe, much as the U.S. intervention in Iraq advanced the cause of soft power in the United States and globally. Leaving aside the fact that it barely succeeded in its ostensibly limited political aim of overthrowing Milosevic, the intervention prompted a large swathe of one-time leftists, the so-called '68ers, to become passionate norm entrepreneurs, willing to go to war for the sake of European values. It reestablished NATO as an American-led global force, extending its principles and military bases far into Eastern Europe, in violation of pacts with the Russian Confederation, which it excluded. It forced Serbia to submit its war criminals to The Hague for prosecution, thereby demonstrating the negative effects of flouting the rules of the new Europe. Its bombing raids completed the deindustrialization of Yugoslavia, thereby demonstrating the utter failure of socialist economies. It established the beleaguered Kosovar Albanians as subjects for the first costly sustained experiments that the European Neighborhood Policy would undertake to rebuild European communities infused with European normative values.

The Balkan intervention also introduced NATO allies that intended to fight their humanitarian wars to the new "American way of war."[45] Short of obtaining UN approval, Operation Allied Force used the cloak of the multinational coalition to spread responsibility for intervention and thereby lend it legitimacy. It exploited different notions of prestige to recruit individual members, undercutting the solidarity they might have had with one another. It demonstrated that cybernetic war could provide full-spectrum coverage with few or no ground troops. It legitimated massive bombing to destroy infrastructure, as if destroying homes and workplaces had no psychic and physical costs as long as civilian casualties were limited. It showed the usefulness of cyberinformation technology as a tactical device to mobilize public opinion on behalf of the belligerents.

Soft Power Mobilized

By the same token, soft power took life in conjunction with the American war in Iraq. When Joseph Nye returned to advocating for soft power in the summer of 2003, the United States had been at war with Iraq for six months. His purpose, he wrote in *Foreign Affairs,* was not to castigate Bush, even if "some traditional realists" regarded the administration's "Neo-Wilsonian promises to promote democracy and freedom as dangerously unbounded."[46] Nye could agree that the Bush Doctrine was reasonable when it was argued that globalization had worn away the buffers of distance and that democratization of information and war technologies meant that weak states and terrorists were so lethal and agile that they were bigger threats than rival hegemons like China and Russia. However, the United States had to realize that the world was a three-dimensional chess game that had to be played vertically *and* horizontally, and that this could only be done by mobilizing coalitions of forces that it made "feel consulted and involved."[47] Otherwise, it risked undercutting useful institutions like the UN and raising the costs to the United States of waging war. George W. Bush understood this well enough to order the military to embed journalists with the occupying troops. His president father had not had to do that during the First Gulf War: given CNN's total domination of the news cycle, there were no alternative news sources. Now there were Al Jazeera and other Arab broadcasting outfits. If the public were not to believe Saddam Hussein's lies about U.S. soldiers slaughtering civilians, journalists had to be on hand to provide impartial news, including accurate information about civilian casualties.[48]

It was 2004 when Nye delivered his first full book on the subject, *Soft Power: The Means to Success in World Politics.* The United States was mired in Iraq, and the Bush administration had taken hurried stock of the obsolescence of its soft-power apparatus. The moment the Bush administration launched the war on terror, it started talking about the problem. At the first hearings of the House Committee on International Relations on the Role of Public Diplomacy in Support of the Anti-Terrorism Campaign in

2001, the passion was audible. Tom Lantos, Democrat of California and committed cold warrior, denounced the "appalling failure of public diplomacy," claiming that the United States was "literally being outgunned, outmanned, and outmaneuvered on the public information battlefield."[49] Congress voted all of the appropriations asked for. But what would this battle campaign involve? Would it be a recap of the Vietnam-era strategy of "winning hearts and minds"? Or hard-nosed, politically targeted "strategic communication," as the Pentagon called it? Or publicity in the form of "nation-branding," as urged by advertising industry? Would it use the "airwaves," as old-timer Lantos called the radio? It seemed unlikely that big business and dollar-a-year men would collaborate with the government as they had during World War II and the early Cold War: this war was contested, and it would not be simple to motivate American civilians to mobilize on behalf of people-to-people undertakings, as, say, the United States had when Hollywood idols like Frank Sinatra joined forces with Catholic Church groups, the CIA, and Italian Americans to turn out a giant anti-Communist vote in the 1948 Italian elections. The internet blurred the line between what were called "kinetic" and "cold" fronts and permitted a more or less free flow of information between domestic and foreign audiences, letting Americans and everyone else see Osama Bin Laden's taunts on YouTube, read or listen to English editions of the Qatar-based pro-Islamic *Al Jazeera,* or read the unremittingly negative opinions about the U.S. polls of the Muslim world.

The Bush administration would go through four under secretaries of state for Public Diplomacy and Public Affairs, (which meant 37.2 percent of the time there was no confirmed person in the office). First was the ex-CEO of J. Walter Thompson Charlotte Beers, also known as the "Queen of Branding"; next came genteel Margaret Tuttweiler, an old-line Republican diplomat inherited from the administration of Bush I; then Karen Hughes, a yacky Texas political operative and presidential crony who was soon out on the Middle East stump glad-handing veiled Saudi students and telling them about American freedoms like driving their own car. It finally found its bearings in 2008, in the figure of James K. Glassman, a former press executive, a modern-day Cold War Republican dollar-a-year businessman, who finally enlisted the internet.

Nye would not have disapproved of any of these personalities or undertakings themselves: power is "the ability to get the outcomes one wants," and soft power "rests on the ability to shape the preferences of others," as his new book reiterated. He was certain that in the past "government programs combined with private sector actions, had tipped the military balance with the Soviet Union in favor of the United States." And, of course, the United States still had its "special capabilities." But there were caveats now: as attractive as U.S. culture was, it could also be "repulsive." As peerless as its political values were, it did not always live up to them at home and abroad. If its foreign policies were to prevail, they had to be regarded as legitimate; in sum, in order for the United States to exercise its moral authority, it would have to address the need he had alluded to, but never underscored: "The preservation of the kind of nation that is at the heart of America's soft power appeal."[50]

Lord Carnes's 2006 book, *Losing Hearts and Minds? Public Diplomacy and Strategic Influence in the Age of Terror*, may not have been responding to Nye's book, but in tried-and-true conservative style, this eccentric figure saw Nye's notion of soft power as namby-pamby liberalism. A distinguished Aristotle scholar in his own right, professor at the Naval War College, and a national security advisor during the George H. W. Bush administration, Carnes insisted on a "holistic" and "unblinking" policy to "tie public diplomacy to U.S. grand strategy." America's conservative cultural wars against the Left at home had to be reinvigorate foreign cultural diplomacy, and the Oval Office had to coordinate with the Pentagon and intelligence services, "who have a history" of these undertakings.[51]

Surely this more and more integrally conservative turn in U.S. foreign policy encouraged Nye to find new allies to make a political pitch toward the center, in the hope of influencing the candidates in the upcoming 2008 election. That course of action was inherent in the ninety-page policy paper that came out in 2007 under the aegis of the Center for Strategic and International Studies (CSIS), the immensely rich Washington, DC, think tank founded in 1962 to "find ways for the United States to sustain its prominence and prosperity as a force for good in the world." That Nye had Richard L. Armitage as his coauthor might surprise a Washington outsider. Nobody was more experienced in what Max Boot called the "Savage Wars of Peace" of the Reagan and George H. W. Bush administrations.[52] A Navy man, Vietnam veteran, long-time Pentagon consultant, former Defense Department undersecretary, and member of the neoconservative Project for a New American Century, he was one of the "Vulcans," recruited by George W. Bush's mentors to advise him on foreign policy. True, by the time he and Nye joined forces, he had left the Bush administration to manage his consulting firm, Armitage International, whose main clients were arms and oil companies. And, as a globalist, he agreed with Nye that the next president, whether Republican or Democrat, had to overhaul U.S. foreign policy on the basis of three propositions.[53] The first and most basic was that previous administrations had conceived the global war on terror too narrowly. To win it, American strategists had to embark on a generation-long struggle against extremist terrorists; address the problem of the weak states that fed terrorism; and resolve, like British imperial strategists at the apogee of British power, to produce new international public goods. Second, the United States had to put its own "house in order" to make it a "more viable model for the world."[54] Third, government had to recognize that much of the United States' soft power was produced not by government but by civil society. For that reason, Congress should find the means, perhaps with government funding, but behind a "firewall of independent directors . . . to support but not control American private actors in their face-to-face relations with peoples in other countries."[55]

Point three bears particular comment, as it signaled that Nye and Armitage did not trust U.S. civil society alone to regenerate America's attractiveness. What then could? In the past, Nye had placed considerable confidence in America's information edge, but that had no specific content. In the early Cold War, the president could summon a national effort, and advocates of government and private programs were unabashed about their out-and-out propaganda to foreign audiences, especially after the 1948 Smith-Mundt Act prevented any of the information sent abroad from being viewed at home. With the cyberrevolution, however, that separation had become impossible—and, in 2012, the act was revoked. Well before that, domestic cultural battles had polarized Americans about what was acceptable messaging abroad and what the roles of the government, the new cybergiants, and huge foundations like Gates's or Clinton's should be. In that light, Nye and Armitage's recommendation that Congress "find the means" sounded lame. Strong on some specific recommendations like closing the Guantanamo prison, short on a critique of U.S. foreign policy to substantially change it, the report fell back on recommending "sharp power," Nye's term, which essentially meant a carefully calibrated balance between hard and soft power.

In January 2009, when the newly elected president Barack Obama named Hillary Clinton secretary of state, "smart power" became the byword of

U.S. foreign policy. That Clinton's tenure differed in rhetoric from her predecessors—that she sought to rebuild the State Department's authority in the face of the Defense Department, and that she used her position to promote not only women in the State Department but important multilateral and NGO-based global initiatives in support of the rights of women and children—there is no doubt. But the ongoing U.S.-led global war on terror framed the entire effort, not least Clinton's endeavor, strongly backed by the military and advised by the emerging giant power of Silicon Valley, "to place social media at the center of 21st century statecraft."[56] Whether Clinton was trying to carve out a place for State Department with respect to the military is hard to know. Suffice it to say that the military had several years' experience occupying hostile lands by then, and it had relearned the lesson of every past major war—namely, that the fighting forces could not operate without what the military termed "strategic communication." And that was a civilian task. By 2008, the Defense Science Board was making the Eeyore-like prediction that "the United States will fail in meeting 21st century national security challenges if it does not take existing government collaboration with civil society to a new level."[57] Moving beyond the independent government agency it had recommended in its 2004 report to synchronize private with governmental strategic communication activities, the Defense Science Board now called for an independent "Center for Global Engagement" to develop "the deep understanding of cultures, influence networks, or information technologies that can be achieved through close collaboration with global civil society."[58]

The new "networked world" the State Department envisaged as making government policy for the Obama administration "exists above the state, below the state, and through the state," wrote Anne Marie-Slaughter, Clinton's director of policy planning, in 2009. She echoed Nye and Owen's 1996 article by affirming that the "state with the most connections will be the central player," but her claim that the United States had "a clear and sustainable edge" had lost any foundation.[59] Clinton's reinforcement of U.S. governmental connections with the chief executives of Google, Twitter, YouTube, Facebook, and so on, the facts that State Department personnel made Silicon Valley a mecca for training and information technologies, were used to facilitate communications among dissidents in the Muslim world, taking courage from the "Twitter rebellion" in Iran, were a palpable demonstration of the United States' willingness to instrumentalize the new technology for state purposes. 2010 was a key turning point. In the wake of the Republic of China's raid on dissidents' Gmail accounts and Google's short-lived decision to suspend provision, Clinton embraced "tech evangelism" in a major policy speech on January 21, 2010, in which she called the "freedom to connect" a pillar of the United States' foreign policy agenda.[60] 2010 also saw China, Russia, and the EU take stock of the United States' position, its legal precedents, how to obstruct it, and how to promote their own cyberdiplomacy—purposes and content as yet undetermined.

We Are All Normative Powers Now

At the very moment Nye was abandoning soft power as a critical term of U.S. foreign policy, the term was going global. The Google Citation Index of 2008 captures the movement:

According to Google's Ngram Viewer, in 2008, German-language books on Google mentioned "soft power" 7030 times—in English—while French-language books mentioned it 5800 times.[61] At the Seventeenth Communist Party of China's Seventeenth Congress in 2007, general secretary Hu Jintao spoke of China's need to increase its soft power, setting off a rush of interest.[62] In 2008, the term achieved its maturity: the *Annals* of the American Academy of Political and Social Science devoted an issue to "public

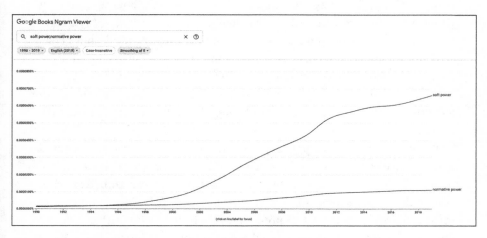

Figure 1.1 Google Ngram Viewer results for "soft power" and "normative power" between 1990 and 2019

diplomacy," with "soft power" as its central theme, joining previous single-term issues including "high-level consumption" (1935), "marketing" (1940), and "Cold War" (1959). At the same time, it is clear that "normative power" never moved outside of academic and regional European circles as a keyword, and its sense was subsumed under the notion of soft power. As practices and policies associated with soft power spread, global rankers stepped in. In 2009, the London-based Institute for Government, in cooperation with the journal *Monocle*, established the first Soft Power Index, which used a composite of statistical metrics and subjective scores to measure national reputations. In the last five years, Chinese scholars have developed more and more sophisticated analytical tools to wrench assessments from the hands of Western analysts.[63]

With the presidency back in Democratic Party hands in 2009, norm-entrepreneurs reached out to would-be converts. Muammar al-Gaddafi was the first great prize, having drawn the right lesson from the overthrow and execution of Saddam Hussein, that closed autocracies were unviable—a lesson that he also received from his son Salif El-Islam, who in 2008 had been awarded his doctoral degree in political science at the London School of Economics on "the role of civil society in the democratization of global governance institutions: from soft power to collective decision making."[64] He was open to conversation with eminent Western experts on the subject. But where to get advice about opening up his regime and improving its public image abroad? In 2010, Gaddafi retained the Monitor Group of Boston, paying them $250,000 a month over a two-year contract, some of which went to hire Harvard faculty. It was on that basis that Nye, after conversing with Gaddafi for three hours on his estate outside Tripoli, concluded that he was a changed man. The one-time visionary of pan-Arabism had abandoned his nuclear plants and collaboration with terrorists and wanted to open up to global trends. He had become "interested in soft power—the art of projecting influence through attraction rather than coercion."[65]

In 2008, the year soft power gave way to smart power in the United States, marked the acme of normative power's success, at least on the regional level. That year, after Manners's 2002 essay was acclaimed as being among the decade's most influential writings on the EU, Jose Manuel Barroso, Prodi's successor as EU president, was heard to boast that "we are one of the most important, if not the most important, normative powers in the world."[66] The European Neighborhood Policy (ENP) was launched in response to the 2004 EU Enlargement, which moved the Union's borders east and south.[67] From 2009, the project had giant budgets to work eastward and around the Eastern and Southern Mediterranean. Part of its remit was to impart the ideal of transparency, along with two new norms—personal responsibility and parsimony—that the EU had advanced to legitimate austerity programs in the wake of the 2008 debt crisis.

That crisis left Europe deeply divided between what in normative terms sounded more and more like a Protestant ethic of capitalism in the northeast, with its capital at Brussels, and the wastrel Catholics—the "Piigs," or Portugal, Ireland, Italy, Greece, and Spain—on the southwestern periphery. It looked more and more like the New Europe had become a "regulatory" or "normative empire": that it was operating at the behest of Brussels Eurocrats and German finance capitalism. That worry would motivate the editorial board of the journal *Cooperation and Conflict* to dedicate its tenth-anniversary issue, in 2013, to historicizing the concept of normative power. In another project, this one funded by the venerable CEPS, founded at Brussels in 1983 and sponsored by Banca di San Paolo and George Soros's Open Society Foundation, Ian Manners and a score of others of varying nationalities, political outlooks, and methodologies tried to answer the question "What does it mean to be a foreign policy actor?" It was important to know that "the 20th century era when the U.S. came to rule virtually alone is over."[68] For our purposes, the most significant result was to end the division between "Soft Power United States" and "Normative Power Europe." American political scientist Daniel Hamilton of Johns Hopkins University spoke of the United States as a normative power, and Manners opened up the notion that both Europe and the United States were using normative power to establish a new hegemony.[69]

Zaki Laïdi offered perhaps the clearest statement on this point in his *Norms over Force: The Enigma of European Power*. Professor of international relations at Science Politique and former aide to Pascal Lamy, the European commissioner for trade in 1999, Laïdi wrote the book when he was foreign policy advisor to Francois Holland. For Laïdi, the EU could never see itself acting in the realist terms of power politics because it was an ongoing political institutional project rather than a state. This was an advantage in institutional bargaining: it always had to combine in some measure national politics, intergovernmental policies, and shared agendas, to maintain an "identity and strategy grounded on a preference for overarching rules of behavior that have been negotiated and not imposed . . . legitimated equally by representative international bodies; and to be enforceable on all actors of the international system notwithstanding their rank within it."[70] That was both its weakness as a power, and its strength. That said, Europe had to develop its own strategic culture and, on that basis, its own military capacities. By 2015, Manners would come to a similar view in the volume he edited with Richard Whitman. They concluded that the more the EU became an operative political entity, the more it would face critical foreign and domestic policy choices, the more its norms would be contested, and the more the project of NPE—Normative Power Europe—would need a strategic culture of its own.[71]

That proposition has only been reinforced since 2016 in the face of the Trump administration's attack on the conventions and institutions of complex interdependency. Perhaps it will not be foreign policy security issues, but rather the overwhelming crises of 2020—of global warming, a pandemic, and economic depression— that will reinstate the trajectory toward a more solidaristic, transparent, and universal complex interdependency.

Notes

1. My approach here sets the contrast between soft power and normative power as a culminating moment in the United States' ongoing challenge to European hegemony over the twentieth century. In that light, soft power would be treated as the latest of a succession of social inventions growing out of U.S. market empire. See Victoria de Grazia, *Irresistible Empire: America's Advance through Twentieth Century Europe* (Cambridge, MA: Harvard Belknap, 2005).
2. For a standard definition, see https://en.wikipedia.org/wiki/Soft_power (accessed September 18, 2020); and, for the only definition that brings the two terms into play with one another, but emphasizing other differences, see Ian Manners and Thomas Diez, "Reflecting on Normative Power Europe," in *Power in World Politics*, ed. F. Berenskoetter and M. J. Williams (New York: Routledge, 2007), 173–88.
3. Ian Manners, "The Concept of Normative Power in World Politics," *DIIS Brief*, May 2009, http://pure.diis.dk/ws/files/68745/B09_maj_ Concept_Normative_Power_World_Politics.pdf (accessed September 18, 2020).
4. This dimension of international society has been a main focus of historical research since the seminal work of Akira Iriye, "Culture and Power: International Relations as Intercultural Relations," *Diplomatic History* 3, no. 2 (April

1979): 115–28, and subsequent books including *Cultural Internationalism and World Order* (Baltimore: Johns Hopkins University Press, 1997) and *The Global Community: The Role of International Organizations in the Making of the Contemporary World* (Chicago: University of Chicago Press, 2002). Iriye's work overlaps with the theorizing of intermediate organizations in international relations, notably that of Robert O. Keohane and Joseph S. Nye Jr., *Power and Interdependence: World Politics in Transition* (New York: Little, Brown, 1977), and Robert O. Keohane, *After Hegemony: Cooperation and Discord in the World Political Economy* (Princeton, NJ: Princeton University Press, 1984).

5. Robert Kagan, *Of Power and Paradise: America and Europe in the New World Order* (New York: Knopf, 2003).

6. See Robert Kagan's earlier formulation in "Power and Weakness," *Policy Review* 113 (June–July 2002): 1–18.

7. The divergence of strategic cultures is examined for Europe by the historian James Sheehan, *Where Have All the Soldiers Gone: The Transformation of Modern Europe* (Boston: Houghton Mifflin, Harcourt, 2008) and journalist T. R. Reid, *The United States of Europe: The New Superpower and the End of American Supremacy* (London: Penguin, 2005). For the United States, see Andrew Bacevich, *The Limits of Intervention: The End of American Exceptionalism* (New York: Metropolitan, 2008); Max Boot, *The Savage Wars of Peace: Small Wars and the Rise of American Power* (New York: Basic Books, 2003); John Dower, *Cultures of War: Pearl Harbor/Hiroshima/9-11/Iraq* (New York: Norton, 2010) and *The Violent American Century: War and Terror Since World War II* (Chicago: Haymarket, 2017); and Alfred W. McCoy, *In the Shadows of the American Century: The Rise and Decline of U.S. Global Power* (Chicago: Haymarket, 2017).

8. For biographical information on Nye, who surely merits the kind of full-scale biography dedicated to idea entrepreneurs of other times, start with his graceful "Essay on Career Choice," in *Power in the Global Information Age* (London: Routledge, 2004), 217–33; also Harry Kreisler, "Theory and Practice in International Relations: Conversation with Joseph S. Nye, Jr.," Conversations with History, Institute of International Studies, University of California, Berkeley, 1998, http://globetrotter.berkeley.edu/conversations/Nye/ (accessed September 18, 2020).

9. Biographical information on Manners is sparse. Start with his home page: https://politicalscience.ku.dk/staff/academic_staff/?pure=en/persons/323164 (accessed September 18, 2020). We augmented this resource with the author's email exchanges with him, January 17, 2020. See, too, Manners's self-effacing reflections on the intellectual evolution of the Copenhagen School, "A Critical Copenhagen Reflection on the European Union as a Global Actor," in *The EU as a Global Actor: A Force for Good in the World?*, ed, Anja Franck and Fredrik Söderbaum (Gothenburg: Centre for European Research [CERGU], 2016),

https://static-curis.ku.dk/portal/files/242794262/Ian_Manners_A_Critical
_Copenhagen_Reflection_on_the_EU_as_a_Global_Actor_2013_2016.pdf
(accessed October 20, 2020).

10. Martha Finnemore and Kathryn Sikkink, "International Norm Dynamics and
Political Change," *International Organization* 52, no. 4 (Autumn 1998): 887–91.

11. Kreisler, "Theory and Practice in International Relations," 4. It is a paradox
of European realist thinking that, although it was hugely interested in prestige, reputation, and so on, its hard-nosed efforts to elevate international relations above history, historical sociology, and the like voided curiosity about
cultural questions, psychological motivation, and, especially, the impact of
domestic politics. See Nicolas Guilhot, "The Realist Gambit: Postwar American Political Science and the Birth of IR Theory," *International Political Sociology* 2, no. 4 (December 2008): 281–304; and Christian Hacke, "Power and
Morality: On the Legacy of Hans J. Morgenthau," *American Foreign Policy Interests* 27, no. 3 (2005): 171–74.

12. Keohane and Nye, *Power and Interdependence.*

13. Kreisler, "Theory and Practice in International Relations," 4.

14. Kreisler, 4.

15. Paul Kennedy, *The Rise and Fall of Great Powers* (New York: Random House,
1987). See also John Agnew, *The United States in the World-Economy: A Regional
Geography* (Cambridge: Cambridge University Press, 1987).

16. Joseph S. Nye Jr., *Bound to Lead: The Changing Nature of American Power* (New
York: Basic Books, 1990).

17. Joseph S. Nye Jr., "Soft Power," *Foreign Policy* 20 (Autumn 1990): 153–71.

18. Thomas L. Friedman, "Foreign Affairs Big Mac I," *New York Times*, December 8, 1998, https://www.nytimes.com/1996/12/08/opinion/foreign-affairs-big
-mac-i.html.

19. Eliot A. Cohen, "A Revolution in Warfare," *Foreign Affairs* 75, no. 2 (1996):
37–54.

20. Alexander Cooley, "Base Politics," *Foreign Affairs* 84, no. 6 (November–
December): 79–92; also his "U.S. Bases and Democratization in Central
Asia," *Orbis* 52, no. 1 (2008): 65–90.

21. Joseph S. Nye Jr. and William A. Owens, "America's Information Edge: The
Nature of Power," *Foreign Affairs* 75, no. 2 (March–April 1996): 20–36. Pub-
lished by the Council on Foreign Relations, this was a bit more influential than
Foreign Policy.

22. Nye and Owens, "America's Information Edge," 27.

23. Nye and Owens, 27.

24. Nye and Owens, 35.

25. All of this is clearly spelled out by "History of the Department of State during
the Clinton Presidency (1993–2001)," Office of the Historian, Bureau of Public

Affairs, U.S. Department of State Archive, June 21, 2001, https://2001-2009
.state.gov/r/pa/ho/pubs/8552.htm, especially parts dealing with the International Information, Educational Exchange, and Cultural Affairs Programs.
Most of the score of white papers issued by think tanks, private foundations,
congressional panels, and other government offices document the basic thrust—
namely, to cut spending and modernize. Historians see a declensionist narrative
here. See Nicholas J. Cull, *The Cold War and the United States Information Agency*
(Cambridge: Cambridge University Press, 2008).

26. Joseph S. Nye Jr., "The Power We Must Not Squander," *New York Times*, January 3, 2000, http://www.nytimes.com/2000/01/03/opinion/the-power-we
-must-not-squander.html. References to the phrase "soft power" multiplied
thereafter.

27. Tim Dunne, *Inventing International Society: A History of the English School* (London: Palgrave, 1998). For the loosening up of European international relations,
see Mark Laffey and Jutta Weldes, "Beyond Belief: Ideas and Symbolic Technologies in the Study of International Relations," *European Journal of International
Relations* 3, no. 2 (1997): 193–237; J. Ann Tickner, "Hans Morgenthau's Principles of Political Realism: A Feminist Reformulation," *Millennium* 17, no. 3
(1988): 429–40; and Ole Wæver, "The Sociology of a Not So International
Discipline: American and European Developments in International Relations," *International Organization* 52, no. 4 (1998): 687–727.

28. Editorial introduction, *Journal of Common Market Studies* 1, no. 1 (March 1962): v.

29. Hedley Bull, "Civilian Power Europe: A Contradiction in Terms?," *Journal of
Common Market Studies* 21, no. 2 (December 1982): 149–70.

30. François Duchêne, "Europe's Role in World Peace," in *Europe Tomorrow: Sixteen Europeans Look Ahead*, ed. Richard Mayne (New York: Fontana/Collins,
1972), 32–47.

31. Richard Rosecrance, *The Rise of the Trading State: Commerce and Conquest in the
Modern World* (New York: Basic Books, 1986).

32. Michel Albert, *Capitalism vs Capitalism: How America's Obsession with Individual
Achievement and Short-Term Profit Has Led It to the Brink of Collapse* (New York:
Basic Books, [1991] 1993).

33. See also Andrew Moravcsik, "Preferences in Power in the European Community: A Liberal Intergovernmentalist Approach," *Journal of Common Market
Studies* 31, no. 4 (December 1993): 473–524.

34. Ian Manners, "Assessing the Decennial, Reassessing the Global: Understanding European Union Normative Power in Global Politics," *Cooperation and Conflict* 48, no. 2 (June 2013): 304–29; Ian Manners, "An Anatomy of
Cooperation: Achieving Common Policy in the New Europe," PhD diss.,
University of Bristol, 1996; Ian Manners, *Normative Power Europe: A Contradiction in Terms* (Copenhagen: Copenhagen Peace Research Institute, 2000);

Ian Manners, *Substance and Symbolism: An Anatomy of Cooperation in the New Europe* (Aldershot: Ashgate, 2000); Ian Manners and Ann Florini, "The Evolution of International Norms," *International Studies Quarterly* 40, no. 3 (September 1996): 363–89.

35. Ian Manners and Richard Whitman, eds., *The Foreign Policies of European Union Member States* (Manchester: University of Manchester Press, 2001).

36. See Manners's three pivotal pieces: "Normative Power Europe Reconsidered: Beyond the Crossroads," *Journal of European Public Policy* 13, no. 2 (2006): 182–99; "European Union 'Normative Power' and the Security Challenge," *European Security* 15, no. 4 (2007): 405–21; and, especially, "The European Union's Normative Strategy for Sustainable Peace," in *Strategies for Peace: Contributions of International Organizations, States and Non-State Actors*, ed. Martina Fischer and Volker Rittberger (New York: Barbara Budrich, 2008), 130–51.

37. Romano Prodi, "Might and Right" (speech, European Commission, Gorizia, Piazzale della Transalpina, Trieste, April 30, 2004), https://ec.europa.eu /commission/presscorner/detail/en/SPEECH_04_217.

38. Romano Prodi, "Might and Right"; "The First Commission of the new Europe European Parliament" (speech, European Parliament, Strasbourg, May 5, 2004), https://ec.europa.eu/commission/presscorner/detail/en/SPEECH_04_225.

39. Prodi, "First Commission."

40. Manners, "European Union 'Normative Power'"; Manners, "European Union's Normative Strategy."

41. Alan Milward, *The Reconstruction of Western Europe, 1945–51* (Berkeley: University of California Press, 1984) and *The European Rescue of the Nation-State* (Abingdon: Routledge, 1992). See also even the most compelling of European Union histories, from which the theme is practically absent—for example, Andrew Moravcsik, *The Choice for Europe: Social Purpose and State Power from Messina to Maastricht* (Ithaca, NY: Cornell University Press, 1998).

42. Thomas Diez, "Europe's Others and Changing Others: Problematizing the Concept of Normative Power Europe," *Millennium* 33, no. 3 (2005): 613–36. This process of othering by western Europe, especially as regards eastern Europe and the Balkans, as well as Turkey, builds on long-standing cultural traditions. To start: Norwegian social scientist Iver B. Neuman, *Uses of the Other: The "East" in European Identity Formation* (Minneapolis: University of Minnesota Press, 1999). A tidy case study is Emma de Angelis, "The European Parliament's Identity Discourse and Eastern Europe, 1974–2004," *Journal of European Integration History* 17, no. 1 (2011): 103–15.

43. U.S. critics immediately got the gist: Noam Chomsky, *The New Military Humanism: Lessons from Kosovo* (Monroe, ME: Common Courage, 1999). For the role of Fischer and other one-time student radicals, notably Bernard Kouchner and André Glucksmann, see Paul Berman, *Power and the Idealists, or The*

Passion of Joschka Fischer and Its Aftermath (New York: Norton, 2005). Younger German historians are just coming to the issue; see, for example, Bettina Gruber, ed., *The Yugoslav Example: Violence, War, and Difficult Ways Toward Peace* (Munster: Waxman, 2014). See, especially, the article by Kurt Gritsch: "War Over Kosovo 24 March 1999–10 June 1999—Beyond and Behind the Scenes: Why NATO Attacked Yugoslavia," 45–62.

44. Joseph S. Nye Jr., "Public Diplomacy and Soft Power," *Annals of the American Academy of Political and Social Science* 616 (March 2008): 100.

45. Bacevich, *Limits of Intervention*; Eliot A. Cohen, *War over Kosovo: Politics and Strategy in a Global Age* (New York: Columbia University Press, 2001); David Hastings Dunn, "Innovation and Precedent in the Kosovo War: The Impact of Operation Allied Force on U.S. Foreign Policy," *International Affairs* 85, no. 3 (2009): 531–46. For the impact on Europe, see Alan W. Cafruny and J. Magnus Ryner, eds., *Europe at Bay in the Shadow of U.S. Hegemony* (Boulder, CO: Lynne Reiner, 2007).

46. Joseph S. Nye Jr., "U.S. Power and Strategy after Iraq," *Foreign Affairs* 82, no. 4 (July–August 2003): 60–67.

47. Mohmmed el-Nawawy, "U.S. Public Diplomacy in the Arab World: The News Credibility of Radio Sawa and Television Alhurra in Five Countries," *Global Media and Communication* 2, no. 2 (2006): 183–203; Giacomo Chiozza, "Disaggregating Anti-Americanism," in *Anti-Americanism in World Politics*, ed. Peter Katzenstein and Robert O. Keohane (Ithaca, NY: Cornell University Press, 2006), 93–126.

48. *The Role of Public Diplomacy in Support of the Anti-terrorism Campaign: Hearing Before the Committee on International Relations, House of Representatives, One Hundred Seventh Congress, First Session, October 10, 2001* (Washington, DC: U.S. Government Printing Office, 2001), 4.

49. Joseph S. Nye Jr., *Soft Power: The Means to Success in Global Politics* (New York: Public Affairs, 2004); the latter quote is from his 1996 "America's Information Edge," with William A. Owens, during the Clinton administration, when he, like other liberals, assumed that liberal centrism would undertake such reforms.

50. Lord Carnes, *Losing Hearts and Minds? Public Diplomacy and Strategic Influence in the Age of Terror* (Santa Barbara, CA: Praeger Security International, 2006).

51. Boot, *Savage Wars of Peace*.

52. Richard L. Armitage and Joseph S. Nye Jr., *CSIS Commission on Smart Power: A Smarter, More Secure America*, February 2007, Washington, DC, https://csis -website-prod.s3.amazonaws.com/s3fs-public/legacy_files/files/media/csis /pubs/071106_csissmartpowerreport.pdf (accessed October 20, 2020). The report was presented at a hearing to the House of Representative's Subcommittee on National Security and Foreign Affairs of the Committee on Oversight and Government Reform on November 6, 2007.

53. Armitage and Nye, *CSIS Commission on Smart Power*.

54. U.S. House of Representatives, *Six Years Later (Part II): Smart Power and the U.S. Strategy for Security in a Post 9/11 World: Hearing Before the Subcommittee on National Security and Foreign Affairs of the Committee on Oversight and Government Reform*, 110th Cong., 1st sess., November 6, 2007 (Washington, DC: U.S. Government Printing Office, January 1, 2009), 4:97–99.

55. *Six Years Later*, 4:99.

56. "21st Century Statecraft," in "Diplomacy in Action," U.S. Department of State, https://2009-2017.state.gov/statecraft/overview/index.htm (accessed September 18, 2020) gives an overview of State Department undertakings since 2009.

57. *Task Force on Strategic Communication* (Washington, DC: Defense Science Board, 2008), xiii. https://www.academia.edu/2898660/STRATEGIC_COMMU NICATION_MANAGEMENT_IS_AMERICAN_POLITIC_AXIS.

58. *Task Force on Strategic Communication*, xiv–xv.

59. Anne-Marie Slaughter, "America's Edge: Power in the Networked World," *Foreign Affairs* 88, no. 1 (January–February 2009): 95.

60. Hillary Rodham Clinton, "Internet Freedom," speech, Newseum, Washington, DC, January 21, 2010, https://foreignpolicy.com/2010/01/21/internet -freedom/.

61. Google Ngram Viewer, https://books.google.com/ngrams/graph?content =Soft+Power&year_start=1800&year_end=2019&corpus=26&smoothing=3& direct_url=t1%3B%2CSoft%20Power%3B%2Cco#t1%3B%2CSoft%20Power% (accessed October 19, 2020).

62. Todd Hall, "An Unclear Attraction: A Critical Examination of Soft Power as an Analytical Category," *Chinese Journal of International Politics* 3, no. 2 (2010): 189–211.

63. Chang Zhang and Ruiqin Wu, "Battlefield of Global Ranking: How Do Power Rivalries Shape Soft Power Index Building?," *Global Media and China*, June 18, 2019, https://journals.sagepub.com/doi/10.1177/2059436419855876.

64. Henry Kenneth Woolf, "The Woolf Report: An inquiry into the LSE's Links with Libya and Lessons to Be Learned," October 2011, http://www.lse.ac.uk /News/News-Assets/PDFs/The-Woolf-Inquiry-Report-An-inquiry-into -LSEs-links-with-Libya-and-lessons-to-be-learned-London-School-of -Economics-and-Political-Sciences.pdf (accessed September 18, 2020), 15.

65. Joseph Nye Jr., "Tripoli Diarist," *New Republic*, December 10, 2007, https:// newrepublic.com/article/65686/tripoli-diarist.

66. John Peterson, "Jose Manuel Barroso: Political Scientist, ECPR Member," *European Political Science* 7, no.1 (2008): 69.

67. The range and richness of people speaking to one another requires a fuller assessment. To start, see Nathalie Tocci, ed., *Who Is a Normative Foreign Policy Actor? The European Union and its Global Partners* (Brussels: CEPS, 2008); Zaki

Laïdi, *Norms Over Force: The Enigma of European Power*, trans. Cynthia Schoh (New York: Palgrave Macmillan, 2008); Pascal Lamy and Zaki Laïdi, "A European Approach to Global Governance," *Progressive Politics* 1, no. 1 (September 2002): 56–63; Sibylle Scheipers and Daniela Sicurelli, "Empowering Africa: Normative Power in EU-Africa Relations," *Journal of European Public Policy* 15, no. 4 (2008): 607–23. See also their previous collaboration, "Normative Power Europe: A Credible Utopia?," *Journal of Common Market Studies* 45, no. 2 (June 2007): 435–57.

68. Tocci, *Who Is a Normative Foreign Policy Actor?*, i.
69. Tocci.
70. Laïdi, *Norms over Force*, 43.
71. Amelia Hadfield, Ian Manners, and Richard G. Whitman, eds., *Foreign Policies of EU Member States: Continuity and Europeanisation* (Abingdon: Routledge, 2017).

CHAPTER II

Circulating Liberalism

The Global Internet and Soft-Power Internationalism

BURCU BAYKURT

I n the introductory chapter of this volume, we suggest that the global
internet is one of the defining features of soft-power internationalism.
As emerging hegemons have turned to cultural resources to exert influence in foreign affairs, the internet, at the same time as it has become the
terrain of huge private and public investment, has been an essential conduit for communicating their messages. While the interdependency
between soft-power internationalism and the global internet may now seem
obvious, I suggest that this was neither inevitable nor always visible. In what
ways did the global internet help circulate the concept and practice of a
new kind of multilateral liberal internationalism undergirded by *soft* forms
of power, while assuming that the United States would stay at helm? How
did soft-power internationalism enable the expansion of an internet in the
service of ubiquitous surveillance and data extraction? Making their debut
around the same time, each project in its own way aimed to create a connected, interdependent, and multilateral world. This chapter explores
how the evolution of the global internet became intertwined with the
development of soft-power internationalism in the years between 1990
and 2015 and aims to underscore the explicit efforts toward that purpose,
as well as the concealed—if not intended—processes that bound them
together.

By "global internet," I do not only mean the network itself, the physical infrastructure that entangles many parts of the world, but also the

companies and protocols that enable the flows of people, products, and ideas across borders. In this chapter, the global internet also includes the collection of entrepreneurs, policy makers, and citizens whose discourses and practices have enabled or constrained cyberspace, albeit not in equal measure. Most important, I use the global internet as an idea—an ideal, even— that has promised to establish a new, decentralized, and unprecedentedly speedy communication infrastructure animated by the seductive potential of innovation. If soft-power internationalism was an interregnum in search of a new kind of global liberal hegemony, the global internet provided the technical and symbolic capabilities undergirding the aspiration of building (or maintaining) empires. Such a broad definition of the global internet is not a lazy dismissal of precision, but instead a way to showcase the extensive entanglement between its materiality and its powerful imaginaries.

This chapter offers two interventions. First, it provides a historical corrective to the recent discussions about a fragmented global internet— wherein the proliferation of 5G networks is framed as an arms race between the United States and China; national governments pursue their own policies around data rights, free speech, privacy, and even financial transfer protocols, ostensibly to splinter the web; and tech companies increasingly act as political agents of their home countries (technonationalism). Despite the hyperconnectivity it has provided, the global internet has always been geopolitical. There was a brief moment when a civilian cyberspace appeared—one that allowed people to easily share information and perspectives from different parts of the world—but it was never a postnational playing field immune to control from governments or tech companies. Rather than seeing nationalist approaches to internet governance as drastic departures, I suggest we focus on how the U.S. government and Silicon Valley companies manufactured a narrative of a borderless world in the era of soft-power internationalism, and how this narrative was unmade as emerging hegemons started challenging U.S.-dominated networks.

Second, I challenge the predominantly *soft* approach to studying soft power and the internet that narrowly examines the circulation of messages or threats by tweets as a means to changing hearts and minds. The global internet's imprint on soft-power internationalism is not limited to broadcasting narratives; it extends to the materiality of telecom and internet infrastructures and to governing issues around ownership, taxation, and control. Cold War anxieties about identifying countries that supposedly presented a danger and threatened the U.S.-led international order were already baked into the internet's design. After the Cold War, both soft power and the global internet originated to reestablish U.S. hegemony under the guise of circulating liberal internationalism and were then taken up by emerging hegemons to counter the United States. It is critical to analyze the communicative infrastructure of soft-power internationalism to better see the sources of power asymmetries among these old and new hegemons. By revealing the political interventions, economic calculations, and conflicted values that underline the messiness and violence of the global internet and soft-power internationalism, this chapter joins the recent calls for centering empire and its infrastructures in media and communications.[1]

As ambassadors of nascent yet seductive ideas at the nexus of various U.S. institutions (from Silicon Valley to academia and Washington, DC) in the early 1990s, soft-power proponents and the early architects of the internet crossed paths regularly, but not always purposefully. First, the Clinton administration mythologized the global internet as part of its larger project of economic globalization. U.S. policy makers actively glorified the information highways as a novel avenue for free speech while attempting to firm up sole control over their governance. The Bush administration's championship of the global internet did not have the same utopian undertones as its predecessor's, but U.S. funding of the global internet continued aggressively in Silicon Valley and around the world post-9/11. In the early-to-mid-2000s, U.S. tech companies started dominating cyberspace even as they inspired the possibility of global civics in defiance of national borders. The ideal of a new internationalism bolstered by global communication reached its acme of novelty at the end of the 2000s, when internet-assisted movements such as WikiLeaks and the Arab Spring seemed to seize on the utopian promise of free and transparent communications to challenge powerful governments. Ironically, however, the epoch that ostensibly accomplished the soft-power enthusiasts' liberal dreams of rampant free speech and democratic organizing around the world has not only revealed the United States' exploitation of the internet, but also undermined the original conception of a new U.S.-led liberal order.

I document three phases of this short history of the global internet and soft-power internationalism. In the first period, roughly between 1990 and the early 2000s, the projects are coeval—that is, they do not refer to one another explicitly (except for a rare foray by Joseph S. Nye Jr. in

1996). The U.S. government and Silicon Valley entrepreneurs were both committed to the global internet and liberal internationalism, but neither theorized cyberspace as the milieu of cultural diplomacy. The second period, between the early 2000s and 2010, is marked by the rise of the global internet as not just a networked public sphere essentially run by Silicon Valley companies, but as a more direct U.S. investment in infrastructure and a liberal mission for global good. It was in the third period, 2010 onward, that U.S. foreign policy explicitly embraced the global internet utopia for cultural diplomacy—yet, ironically, it was also then that the American project of a U.S.-led liberal internationalism and global internet was irreparably damaged when counterhegemons effectively challenged U.S. imperium in both cyberspace and international affairs.

The Beginnings of Soft-Power Internationalism and the Internet, 1990–2000

One of the earliest discussions explicitly connecting soft power and the internet is found in a 1996 essay by Joseph S. Nye Jr. and Admiral William A. Owens, then vice-chairman of the Armed Forces Joint Chiefs of Staff. Titled "America's Information Edge," the piece suggested that not only did the internet provide the U.S. with a clear advantage in collecting and circulating intelligence in the post–Cold War era, but also that information technologies "can strengthen the intellectual link between U.S. foreign policy and military power."[2] Nye and Owens, conscious of the growing unpredictability of a post-1989 international order, recognized digital technologies' potential for building a system of omnipotent surveillance. "The systems of the systems that the United States was building" could provide information that could be used to prevent regional conflicts, or, in a multipolar world, deter countries from becoming hostile—and the rest of the world depended on the U.S. leadership to use such knowledge.[3]

America's information edge was not limited to untangling the new adversaries; the authors also identified the possibility that global cyberspace could propagate liberal values. Riding the wave of a techno-utopianism dominant in the 1990s, they suggested that while information technologies "can enhance the effectiveness of raw military power, [they] ineluctably democratize societies."[4] This new world of computers and digital networks was "a force multiplier of American diplomacy" and constituted the connective tissue between U.S. foreign policy and the military.[5] Nye's later writing displays various iterations of this argument, manifesting as excitement about the speed and declining costs of circulating messages, and raptures about "the irreverent, egalitarian, and libertarian character of the cyber-culture."[6] He certainly was not alone in spelling out a civilizing mission for information highways. "Cyberspace is the land of knowledge," industry consultant Esther Dyson and collaborators proclaimed in 1994, "and the exploration of that land can be a civilization's truest, highest calling."[7] Similarly, policy makers were fascinated by the versatility of a system built by the Department of Defense, but now used "to chat with friends and swap recipes with strangers."[8]

The narrative of a global internet with untrammeled access to abundant information, ideas, and people, all unleashed by the screeching wail of a dial-up model, caught on worldwide. In the countries surveyed in this volume, the internet became publicly available in Turkey in 1993 and in Brazil in 1995. The Chinese government connected to the global network in 1994. With the 1994 launch of Netscape, the world's first commercial browser, liberal discourses of individual freedom, free speech, entrepreneurship, and transparency came to the fore while the internet's military origins and its securitized uses took a backseat.[9] First for the United States, then for the emerging hegemons, the global internet became a vehicle to build and participate in transnational markets, while also giving voice to a myriad of new actors. Despite the dot-com crash of the late 1990s and the global war on terror, optimistic narratives of the internet rarely wavered before the mid-2010s.

The internet's early promises were incorporated into the larger project of economic globalization. Coming out of the 1991 recession, U.S. policy makers saw information superhighways as the number-one priority for improving the country's infrastructure and generating growth.[10] Rather than cultural diplomacy or even military capabilities, the Clinton administration routinely emphasized the importance of building a global infrastructure and supporting a U.S.-based tech industry.[11] In 1994, for example, then–vice president Al Gore announced the Global Information Infrastructure Initiative (GII) at the International Telecommunication Union's (ITU) first World Telecommunication Development Conference. The plan was to wire the world by encouraging deregulation in telecommunications, removing trade protections, and increasing direct foreign investment in global networks.[12] "These highways or, more accurately, networks of distributed intelligence—will allow us to share information, to connect, and to communicate as a global community," Gore proclaimed.[13] He occasionally referenced the prospect of stronger democracies and a peaceful global order that would be spurred by an "increasingly interconnected human family," but the priority was expanding the reach of the global internet.

Many networks and products of the early internet lay within the control of the United States. The early computer networks, for example, required signing up for a connection with a U.S.-based infrastructure (Japan and France were exceptions). Internet traffic initially flowed via the free Netscape browser.[14] To make sure that the governance of this growing network stayed aligned with American interests, U.S. policy makers formed the Internet Corporation for Assigned Names and Numbers (ICANN) in 1998. ICANN was a not-for-profit enterprise tasked with protecting intellectual property rights by managing the domain name system.[15] Even though the organization's scope was international, it had a contract with the U.S. National Telecommunications and Information Administration (NTIA), along with the goal of becoming independent in 2000. However, the United States did not give up leadership until 2016. The seemingly independent, not-for-profit, and multistakeholder-based governance framework of ICANN legitimized the free-flow narrative of the global internet, while allowing the United States to keep its dominance in cyberspace.[16]

The end of the first decade of the global internet had none of the charm of its beginning. Many dot-coms imploded in the early 2000s, and Silicon Valley woke up from its dream of magically making money on the Web. A new investor came to the rescue: the Central Intelligence Agency (CIA). In 1999 the U.S. government founded In-Q-Tel, a not-for-profit corporation to "foster the development of new and emerging information technologies and pursue research and development that produce solutions to some of the most difficult IT problems facing the CIA."[17] Recognizing the innovation potential in Silicon Valley, In-Q-Tel embarked on direct investment, strategic ventures, and sponsorships of open competitions— all without requiring prior CIA authorization or approval for the business deals that the company negotiated. In its first years, In-Q-Tel provided $100 million to twenty companies, including Google and IBM, building an extensive portfolio in computer infrastructure.[18] Its early funding decisions reflected a concern with keeping the internet open and free, but, after 9/11, attention turned to terrorism prevention and detection technologies. In-Q-Tel's overall investments funded many of the commercial internet and data products popular today, from touchscreen technologies to Google Earth.[19]

The Making of a "Global Village," 2000–2010

In the early 2000s, U.S. government priorities shifted from promoting trade to boosting security measures as well as mass surveillance of domestic and foreign actors.[20] Working closely with public agencies, tech companies began receiving more government contracts. As Oracle's David Carey put it bluntly, "September 11 made business a bit easier," adding, "Previous[ly], you pretty much had to hype the threat and the problem."[21] While cyber-security was top priority, the United States continued expanding the reach of the global internet. The Bush administration announced a Digital Free-dom Initiative (DFI) in 2003, intended to overcome barriers to internet access in the developing world. Established within the USAID Africa Global Information Infrastructure, the DFI supported projects in Indonesia (cybersecurity), Jordan (education), Pakistan (telemedicine), Peru (rural internet services), Rwanda (broadband development), Senegal (entrepre-neurship), and elsewhere.[22] In addition to supporting these countries, the initiative aimed to "establish a business-friendly regulatory framework conducive to US investment and partnerships."[23]

What truly marked this decade, however, was the massive international growth of Silicon Valley companies. Founded in 1998, Google was already a global giant by the mid-2000s. Facebook emerged in 2004 and became internationally available in 2007, the same year Apple introduced the iPhone. Twitter, originally dubbed "the free speech engine," was founded in 2006. With the rise of social media platforms and a much larger user base, the global internet soon solidified as a playing field that enabled blog-gers, foreign journalists, and dissidents to reach a mass audience without needing the approval of governments or big media companies. A "networked public sphere" began to take shape, spurred by the prolifera-tion of civic engagement worldwide.[24] A cosmopolitan community of so-called netizens formed to participate in debates over internet governance, seeking their rights to explore uncensored information and contribute to global conversations.[25] These netizens—online activists and developers of technology—conjured, albeit briefly, a new, self-organized world operating transparently and with bottom-up processes. The idea of a global civics driven by netizens seemed to achieve soft-power internationalism's goals, too, with the U.S. values (or professed values) of political freedom, democratic communication, and civil society dominating cyberspace.

While this new networked sphere was predominantly run by U.S.-based companies such as Google, Facebook, and Twitter, it was these corporations' cosmopolitan values and promises, not their American roots, that were on display throughout the decade. As sociologist Zeynep Tufekci once observed, "America's tech entrepreneurs won the world's admiration," becoming the stars of a growing digital culture.[26] At one point, "Google [was] much more popular in China than the USA," according to Chinese blogger Michael Anti (Jing Zhao).[27] In contrast to the contested politics of the 1980s against U.S. cultural imperialism, Silicon Valley had the global capacity to attract politically (taking part in internet governance discussions), financially (making transnational investment decisions), and ideologically (inspiring a global community of wannabe entrepreneurs, digital activists, students, and policy makers).[28]

Toward the end of 2000s, the great paradox of the global internet and soft-power internationalism began to surface: regional hegemons, empowered by soft-power internationalism, started to assert their weight in international development, economic growth, and cultural diplomacy. They turned increasingly to digital infrastructures and internet-enabled global communication, interacting with Silicon Valley companies on their own terms. Despite the techno-utopians' belief that nation-states would succumb to the democratizing potential of technology, many governments began taking control of cyberspace to consolidate domestic power and project influence internationally. At the same time, many internet-powered grassroots movements managed to reorganize national politics, thereby seemingly validating the global internet's capacity for liberalism.[29] The peak of this narrative was, of course, the Arab Spring in late 2010 and early 2011, when digital activists helped to bring down the autocratic governments of Tunisia and Egypt. Tunisian and Egyptian activists' heavy reliance on the internet became so well known around the world that the names of U.S. social media platforms were attached to these political revolutions as if they were the sole enablers of global waves of activism.

It was against this paradoxical background—on one hand, the political as well as economic challenge of rising hegemons against the U.S.-dominated internet, and an activated global civics that testified to the liberalizing potential of the Web, on the other—that the Obama administration and then–secretary of state Hillary Clinton finally acknowledged an intentional connection between soft-power internationalism and the global internet. The deliberate merger of these two projects came with certain modifications. Secretary Clinton adopted the concept of "smart power": a combination of hard and soft power that, arguably, bolstered each other. Next, instead of only abstractly endorsing internet freedom as a liberal value,[30] the State Department began to fund dissident cyberactivists, invested in tools to circumvent censorship, and contacted Silicon Valley giants to postpone routine maintenance that would hinder the work of digital activists in other countries.[31] The Obama administration spent at least $105 million on these programs, which included investment in encryption and filter-circumvention products and support for fighting network censorship abroad.[32]

Internet freedom as U.S. foreign policy agenda harkened back to the Cold War investments (and interventions) in free speech/free press in other countries as an expression of U.S. leadership.[33] At the same time, the widespread use of the global internet, from political organizing to entertainment, also meant that the U.S. internet freedom agenda found large and sympathetic audiences in other countries. Yet the same North American technology businesses that provided the infrastructure for international liberalism were also enabling both repressive regimes abroad and U.S. government agencies to launch digital surveillance and automated combat techniques against other countries. These contradictions were eventually laid bare when first the WikiLeaks and then the Edward Snowden revelations challenged the Obama administration's internet freedom project.[34]

The Acme and Decline of U.S.-Dominated Tech,
2010–2015

On January 21, 2010, Secretary Clinton appeared at the now-defunct Newseum in Washington, DC (a glass-walled museum of news and journalism), and declared internet freedom a new pillar of American foreign policy. "A new information curtain is descending across much of the world," she proclaimed, "and beyond this partition, viral videos and blog posts are becoming the samizdat of our day."[35] With the official launch of the internet freedom agenda, the U.S. government's sheepish approach to intertwining foreign policy and economic interests over the global internet was finally over. Policy makers and tech entrepreneurs began to explicitly cooperate to assert U.S. dominance in cyberspace.

The timing was not coincidental. By the end of the 2000s, many emerging hegemons were explicitly challenging Silicon Valley's dominance of the global internet—either by censorship and regulation or by investing in global software and hardware markets with their own companies. Facebook, for example, was blocked in China in 2009, though Mark Zuckerberg never hides his eagerness to return. Twitter has not been accessible in mainland China since 2009. Even regional hegemons like Turkey occasionally blocked internet platforms and demanded that tech companies comply with national laws.[36] Silicon Valley companies first tried to exert pressure by putting together international coalitions, then expected the U.S. government to get involved. Google's then–legal chief David Drummond, for example, suggested that internet censorship was not just a violation of human rights, but a barrier to U.S. trade.[37]

Less than three months after Secretary Clinton's speech, WikiLeaks, a whistleblower website that posted classified and sensitive documents, released a graphic video of a 2007 U.S. Army assault in Baghdad that left twelve dead, including two Reuters reporters. Called "Collateral Murder," the video was part of the largest leak of classified records in U.S. history. In July 2010, WikiLeaks released a new cache of documents, this time war logs from the field in Afghanistan. And, in November 2010, the site, collaborating with professional news organizations including the *Guardian*, *Der Spiegel*, *Le Monde*, and *El Pais* published confidential State Department cables that U.S. embassies had sent to Washington. The source, Chelsea (then Bradley) Manning, was later sentenced to thirty-five years in prison; she was released early when then–President Obama commuted her sentence.[38]

Secretary Clinton immediately framed the leaks "as an attack on the international community—the alliances and partnerships, the conversations and negotiations, that safeguard global security and advance economic prosperity."[39] U.S. companies including Amazon, PayPal, and MasterCard dropped WikiLeaks as a client, prompting its founder, Julian Assange, to call them "instruments of U.S. foreign policy."[40] The WikiLeaks saga delivered a diplomatic blow to the United States and over the course of 2010 exposed the inconsistencies in the country's soft- (or smart-) power strategies and internet freedom agenda. Some activists in the Middle East, who had become the poster children of the networked public, began to express concerns. Tunisian blogger and activist Sami Ben Gharbia, for example, pointed out the contradiction between the U.S. funding for and support of digital activism in the Middle East and the country's backing of autocratic governments in the region.[41] Nevertheless, Secretary Clinton continued the commitment to internet freedom as a foreign policy priority and gave a second speech in February 2011, announcing an additional investment of $25 million to help online dissidents and digital activists fight state repression.[42]

A bigger challenge to the internet freedom narrative appeared in 2013. In June, the United States and the UK press used documents leaked by Edward Snowden, a former defense contractor, to report on the surveillance activities of the U.S. National Security Agency (NSA). The leaked documents detailed the NSA's global mass surveillance, including political leaders, UN officials, and international businesses such as Google and Petrobras. In addition to revealing hypocrisy in U.S. foreign policy and damaging relations with a number of its closest allies, the leaks severely damaged public trust in U.S. tech and telecom companies, as it became clear that these companies had given the NSA access to their networks.[43] Most important, the Snowden revelations empowered many rising hegemons to attack U.S. leadership in internet governance more boldly. As one policy expert pointed out, it took the leaks about massive NSA surveillance to lay bare the fact that "most of the software and the innovative business models in the internet come from the U.S."[44]

Just two weeks after the first leaks, German chancellor Angela Merkel, who was also the target of NSA surveillance, appeared in a joint press conference with U.S. president Barack Obama and called the internet "uncharted territory for all."[45] She said, "It makes it possible for enemies and opponents of our democratic order to endanger our way of life, with entirely new means and entirely new approaches."[46] In response, many nation-states, including Germany, India, and Brazil, expressed discontent with the existing open internet and signaled interest in forming national or regional intranets outside the domain name system. After canceling a state visit to Washington, DC, Dilma Rousseff, then-president of Brazil, spoke at the UN and called for a new internet governance framework to prevent "cyberspace from being used as a weapon of war, through espionage, sabotage, and attacks against systems and infrastructure of other countries."[47] Together with Merkel, she proposed a nonbinding UN resolution protecting the privacy rights of internet users; it was adopted on December 18, 2013.[48] Next the California-based Internet Corporation for Assigned Names and Numbers (ICANN), which was subject to U.S. law, came under scrutiny. The European Commission criticized U.S. dominance over the organization governing the internet,[49] and Brazil convened the NETmundial meeting in April 2014 to encourage a new model of internet governance that would be less susceptible to U.S. influence.[50] In 2016, after two years of negotiations, the U.S. government agreed to transfer its oversight of the ICANN to a multistakeholder group, though details have not yet been made available.[51]

Riding the global wave of discontent with U.S. tech companies, Turkey's then–prime minister Recep Tayyip Erdoğan attacked social media at a rally in 2014, shutting down Twitter a few hours later in an effort to assert "the power of the Turkish Republic" against international companies that did not comply with national laws.[52] In addition, European regulators have amped up legal pressure on U.S. tech firms to counter the economic and social influence of Silicon Valley companies. In addition to hitting Google with a record $2.7 billion fine for antitrust[53] and fining Apple $15.4 billion for unpaid taxes,[54] the European Union recently introduced the General Data Protection Regulation (GDPR), which strengthens European rules governing data and privacy.[55] Setting new privacy and regulatory standards to manage U.S. tech companies and lobbying Brazil and Japan to pass similar laws, the European Union has emerged as "the world's tech watchdog."[56]

Meanwhile, China has been massively shaping the global internet. In addition to the tremendous growth of China-based internet giants like Huawei, ZTE, Tencent, Baidu, and Alibaba, the government has invested $173.73 billion in telecom and data infrastructures in Africa and Asia as part of the Belt and Road initiative (BRI), a development strategy of connectivity and cooperation between China and countries in Asia, Africa, and Europe.[57] Dubbing this a "Digital Silk Road," China aims to expand internet connectivity and digital economy across Eurasia and Africa while investing in next-generation network technologies like artificial intelligence, smart cities, and big data. By mobilizing both state-owned and private telecom and internet companies, the country hopes to "promote an internet-enabled inclusive globalization."[58] In addition to economic investments, China is also taking the lead in launching and setting standards for 5G, the next-generation wireless technology.[59] Even as China seems to be replicating the 1990s U.S. policy of internet expansion in Eurasia and Africa with the BRI, Silicon Valley companies are working hard to recapture the country; Facebook is aggressively courting Chinese leadership,[60] and Google recently opened a China-based research center devoted to artificial intelligence.[61]

It only took a decade for China, India, and Brazil to catch up with the United States and Europe in terms of internet penetration, and, by 2019, the first two led the world in internet users, with the United States just above Brazil.[62] As the consumer base expanded, these new hegemons gained sway over Silicon Valley, which still had money and know-how, but needed new markets. Emerging regional powers also funded and promoted entrepreneurial culture and built their capacity for tech innovation.[63] The growth of new internet billionaires across China and India is striking, while the European Union, Brazil, Russia, and Turkey contested U.S. dominance on the internet via infrastructure, regulation, and taxation. As of 2020, it is not clear what the future of the global internet will look like—free, decentralized, and open, or tightly controlled, balkanized, and regulated? But it will no longer be run by the decisions of Silicon Valley and U.S. policy makers. [64]

In 2013, Google's former chair and CEO Eric Schmidt coauthored *The New Digital Age* with Jared Cohen, then a director at Google and former advisor to then–secretary of state Hillary Clinton. The book ambitiously tried to showcase how the internet—"the largest experiment involving anarchy in history"—would transform social relations, states, and businesses.[65] The authors met in Baghdad in 2009 to figure out "how technology can be used to help rebuild a society,"—a society, they conveniently neglected to mention, wrecked by a U.S.-led war. They first "collaborated as writers of a memo to Secretary of State Hillary Clinton about lessons learned in Iraq," one of which was that there was no bridge between the people who understand technology and the people responsible for tackling the world's toughest political issues. Packed with anecdotes, assertions, and speculations, the book reads more like a superficial ode to the power of global connectivity than a thoughtful reflection on a digitally enabled collective future. Yet it epitomizes that moment when U.S. foreign policy–makers and tech executives explicitly cooperated to put the global internet at the heart of international liberalism as a means of regaining U.S. dominance.

The underlying assumption of *The New Digital Age* is that the global internet, a paragon of Western liberalism, had arrived at a crossroads by 2010. As the initial excitement about the Arab Spring ebbed, and the WikiLeaks and Snowden revelations shook the implicit trust between the public and tech companies with respect to surveillance and privacy, cyberspace called for a new governance framework. The authors' solution was clear: the global internet needed to be run by a coterie of liberal internationalists aligned with U.S. interests. Their obvious perception of the global internet as an exclusively Western, liberal, and democratic project overlaps with the evolution of Nye's soft power in the late 2010s—just as Nye repeatedly suggested that China could not truly have soft power because of its illiberal values, the authors could not imagine that repressive countries could participate in the governance of the internet.

Yet myriad civic groups, regular users, tech companies, and governments on the internet, each with their own values and agendas, are now so deeply entwined that these various networks cannot be simply separated into binary camps or their differences simply narrowed down to issues of freedom or democracy.[66] The economic, political, and even cultural relationships among states and peoples, on and over the internet, are tightly enmeshed, and while the United States still claims leadership over information and communication networks, it has been significantly challenged on many fronts over the last decade. It also became impossible for U.S. tech companies to avoid their political responsibilities, at home as well as abroad, when their business decisions and massive platforms have the potential to inflict harm on anyone, particularly already-marginalized populations around the world. States, civil society groups, tech companies, international organizations, and citizens all grapple with this "chained" connectivity, which sorely lacks a locus of responsibility and needs a plan for cooperation.[67]

This chapter has documented the evolving relationship between the global internet and soft-power internationalism since the 1990s. I argue that the intimate connection between soft-power internationalism and the global internet formed slowly and then let them proceed in lockstep. Just like soft power, the global internet started as an attempt to project a U.S.-led, liberal, and multilateral world. It immediately became a frontier to assert post–Cold War hegemony while propagating global trade, communication, and democracy. As happened with soft power, the global war on terror spurred the U.S. government's intentional investing in digital infrastructures, in Silicon Valley as well as abroad, while advancing a narrative of global connectivity as a public good. Silicon Valley companies soon joined this civilizing crusade, which converged neatly with their ambitions to create new markets. This synergy reached its logical conclusion with Hillary Clinton's smart power and internet freedom strategies. As the U.S. roots of the global internet became obvious—partly intentionally with Clinton's internet freedom agenda, partly due to the leaks and movements enabled by the internet—China, India, Brazil, Turkey, and the European Union ramped up their efforts to counter U.S. dominance in cyberspace.

According to legal scholar David Pozen, the internet freedom agenda was "fundamentally a national economic project, rather than an international political or moral crusade."[68] He argues that its failure was almost inevitable as U.S big tech became powerful around the world, and foreign governments had to push back. Internet critic Evgeny Morozov similarly suggests that it was American diplomats' explicit attempts to link Silicon Valley and the political interests of the U.S. government that provoked the ire of other countries.[69] What both authors overlook, however, is that the decline of U.S. dominance on the global internet is also the result of competitive counterhegemons that have explicitly challenged U.S. telecom and social media platforms over the last few years. China's state-supported tech companies not only undermine Silicon Valley's global order, but also embolden ties between Silicon Valley and the U.S. government.[70] As U.S. policy makers and big tech companies grapple with the reality that emerging hegemons will continue challenging the omnipotence of a U.S.-based internet, they converge around a newly visible tech nationalism complete with military partnerships and scaremongering about China. It remains to be seen whether the next generation internet will be more divided or will inspire a more internationalist cooperation, but the pretense of a postnational internet is over.

Notes

1. Miriyam Aouragh and Paula Chakravartty, "Infrastructures of Empire: Towards a Critical Geopolitics of Media and Information Studies," *Media, Culture, and Society* 38, no. 4 (2016): 559–75.
2. Joseph S. Nye Jr. and William A. Owens, "America's Information Edge: The Nature of Power," *Foreign Affairs* 75, no. 2 (March–April 1996): 20–36.

3. Nye and Owens, "America's Information Edge," 28.

4. Nye and Owens, 35.

5. Nye and Owens, 20.

6. Joseph S. Jr. Nye Jr., *Power in the Global Information Age: From Realism to Globalization* (New York: Routledge, 2004).

7. Esther Dyson, George Gilder, George Keyworth, and Alvin Toffler, *Cyberspace and the American Dream: A Magna Carta for the Knowledge Age* (Washington, DC: Peace and Progress Foundation, 1994).

8. Janet Abbate, *Inventing the Internet* (Cambridge, MA: MIT Press, 1999), 106.

9. Aouragh and Chakravartty, "Infrastructures of Empire."

10. Pamela Samuelson and Hal Varian, "The 'New Economy' and Information Technology Policy" in *American Economic Policy During the 1990s*, ed. Jeffrey A. Frankel and Peter R. Orszag (Cambridge, MA: MIT Press, 2002), 361–434; Ryan David Kiggins, "Open for Expansion: U.S. Policy and the Purpose for the Internet in the Post–Cold War Era," *International Studies Perspective* 16 no. 1 (2015): 86–105; Patrice Flichy, *The Internet Imaginaire* (Cambridge, MA: MIT Press, 2007).

11. Michael Jablonski and Shawn M. Powers, *The Real Cyber War: The Political Economy of Internet Freedom* (Urbana: University of Illinois Press, 2015). As Jablonski and Powers document, the Clinton administration announced the Defense Reinvestment and Conversion Initiative (DRCI) in 1993. It was a $24-billion program intended to shift the U.S. economy from investing in Cold War military missions to investing in new technologies that would drive the country's global economic expansion.

12. Jablonski and Powers, *Real Cyber War.*

13. Albert Gore Jr., "Remarks Prepared for Delivery by Vice President Al Gore," speech, World Telecommunication Development Conference, Buenos Aires, Argentina, March 21, 1994.

14. Janet Abbate, "Privatizing the Internet: Competing Visions and Chaotic Events, 1987–1995," *IEEE Annals of the History of Computing* 32, no. 1 (2010): 10–22.

15. Milton L. Mueller, *Ruling the Root: Internet Governance and the Taming of Cyberspace* (Cambridge, MA: MIT Press, 2002).

16. Milton L. Mueller, *Networks and States: The Global Politics of Internet Governance* (Cambridge, MA: MIT Press, 2010); Tim Wu, *The Master Switch: The Rise and Fall of Information Empires* (New York: Knopf, 2011).

17. Rick E. Yannuzzi, "In-Q-Tel: A New Partnership Between the CIA and the Private Sector," *Defense Intelligence Journal* 9, no. 1 (Winter 2000): 25–38, https://www.cia.gov/library/publications/intelligence-history/in-q-tel#copy (accessed September 22, 2020).

18. Linda Weiss, "Global Governance, National Strategies: How Industrialized States Make Room to Move under the WTO," *Review of International Political Economy* 12, no. 5 (2005): 723–49.

19. "In-Q-Tel: The CIA's Tax-Funded Player in Silicon Valley," All Things Considered, NPR, July 16, 2012, https://www.npr.org/sections/alltechconsidered/2012/07/16/156839153/in-q-tel-the-cias-tax-funded-player-in-silicon-valley.

20. Sandra Braman, *Change of State: Information, Policy, and Power* (Cambridge, MA: MIT Press, 2006), 315. Braman defines this shift with the concept of "informational state," wherein the traditional notion of panopticon-style surveillance is replaced with the "panspectron," in which information is gathered about everything, all the time.

21. Jeffrey Rosen, "Silicon Valley's Spy Game," *New York Times Magazine*, April 14, 2002, https://www.nytimes.com/2002/04/14/magazine/silicon-valley-s-spy-game.html.

22. Jablonski and Powers, *Real Cyber War*.

23. Pablo Accuosto and Niki Johnson, "Financing the Information Society in the South: A Global Public Goods Perspective," Association for Progressive Communications (APC), June 2004, https://www.apc.org/sites/default/files/financing_0.pdf (accessed September 22, 2020).

24. Yochai Benkler, *The Wealth of Networks: How Social Production Transforms Markets and Freedom* (New Haven, CT: Yale University Press, 2006).

25. Tim Jordan, *Cyberpower: The Culture and Politics of Cyberspace and of the Internet.* (London: Routledge, 1999); Arne Hint and Stefania Milan, "User Rights for the Internet Age: Online Policy According to 'Netizens,'" in *The Handbook on Global Media and Communication Policy*, ed. Robin Mansell and Marc Raboy (Oxford: Blackwell, 2011), 230–41.

26. Zeynep Tufekci, "As the Pirates Become CEOs: The Closing of the Open Internet," *Daedalus* 145, no. 1 (2016): 65–78.

27. Rebecca MacKinnon, *Consent of the Networked: The Worldwide Struggle for Internet Freedom* (New York: Basic Books, 2012).

28. Aouragh and Chakravartty, "Infrastructures of Empire."

29. Manuel Castells, *Communication Power* (Oxford: Oxford University Press, 2009).

30. James K. Glassman and Michael Doran, "The Soft Power Solution in Iran: Here's What a Serious Plan to Undermine the Regime in Tehran Would Look Like," *Wall Street Journal*, January 21, 2010, https://www.wsj.com/articles/SB10001424052748704541004575011394258630242?mod=WSJ_Opinion_LEFTTop Opinion.

31. Evan MacAskill, "U.S. Confirms It Asked Twitter to Stay Open to Help Iran Protesters," *Guardian*, June 17, 2009, https://www.theguardian.com/world/2009/jun/17/obama-iran-twitter.

32. Jack Goldsmith, "The Failure of Internet Freedom" (Emerging Threats Essay Series, Knight First Amendment Institute, Columbia University, June 13, 2018), https://knightcolumbia.org/content/failure-internet-freedom#/_ftn13.

33. Marion Wrenn, "Inventing Warriors: U.S. Philanthropies and the Postwar Reorientation of Foreign Journalists," PhD diss., New York University, 2008.

34. Helmi Noman and Jillian C. York, "West Censoring East: The Use of Western Technologies by Middle East Censors, 2010–2011," OpenNet Initiative, March 2011, https://opennet.net/west-censoring-east-the-use-western-tech nologies-middle-east-censors-2010-2011 (accessed October 22, 2020).

35. Hillary Rodham Clinton, "Remarks on Internet Freedom," Newseum, Washington, DC, January 21, 2010, https://2009-2017.state.gov/secretary/20092013 clinton/rm/2010/01/135519.htm.

36. Turkey completely shut down YouTube in May 2008 after a series of temporary bans the preceding year based on complaints from Turkish citizens about videos deemed insulting to Kemal Ataturk, modern Turkey's revered founding president.

37. "Google Calls for Pressure on Internet Censors," Reuters, September 8, 2010, https://in.reuters.com/article/us-google-trade-idINTRE6874UI20100908.

38. As of May 2019, Chelsea Manning had been sent back to jail after refusing to testify before a grand jury investigating WikiLeaks.

39. Mary Beth Sheridan, "Hillary Clinton: WikiLeaks Release an 'Attack on International Community,'" *Washington Post*, November 29, 2010, http://www .washingtonpost.com/wp-dyn/content/article/2010/11/29/AR2010112903231 .html.

40. Robert Mackey, "WikiLeaks Founder's Statement From Prison," *New York Times*, December 14, 2010, https://thelede.blogs.nytimes.com/2010/12/14/?scp =6&sq=tuesday%20%22december%2014,%202010%22&st=cse.

41. Sami Ben Gharbia, "The Internet Freedom Fallacy and the Arab Digital activism." Nawaat, September 17, 2010, http://nawaat.org/portail/2010/09/17/the -internet-freedom-fallacy-and-the-arab-digital-activism/.

42. "Hillary Clinton: Internet Repression 'Will Fail,'" BBC News, February 15, 2011, https://www.bbc.co.uk/news/world-us-canada-12475829.

43. Danielle Kehl, Robyn Greene, Robert Morgus, and Kevin Bankston, "Surveillance Costs: The NSA's Impact on the Economy, Internet Freedom, and Cybersecurity" (New America's Open Technology Institute Policy Papers, July 29, 2014), https://www.newamerica.org/oti/policy-papers/surveillance -costs-the-nsas-impact-on-the-economy-internet-freedom-cybersecurity/.

44. Jeevan Vasagar, Richard Waters, and James Fontanella-Khan, "Europe Strikes Back," *Financial Times*, September 15, 2014, https://www.ft.com/content/37e3 63c2-3cc9-11e4-871d-00144feabdc0.

45. Vasagar, Waters, and Fontanella-Khan, "Europe Strikes Back."

46. Vasagar, Waters, and Fontanella-Khan.

47. Dilma Rousseff, "Statement," Opening of the General Debate of the Sixty-Eighth Session of the United Nations General Assembly, September 24, 2013.

48. See "The Right to Privacy in the Digital Age," Office of the United Nations High Commissioner of Human Rights, https://www.ohchr.org/en/issues /digitalage/pages/digitalageindex.aspx (accessed September 22, 2020).

49. Ian Traynor, "Internet Governance Too U.S.-centric, Says European Commission," *Guardian*, February 12, 2014, https://www.theguardian.com/tech nology/2014/feb/12/internet-governance-us-european-commission.

50. Sarah M. West, "Searching for the Public in Internet Governance: An Examination of Infrastructures of Participation at NETmundial," *Policy & Internet* 10, no.1 (2018: 22–42.

51. Maria Farrell, "Quietly, Symbolically, U.S. Control of the Internet Was Just Ended," *Guardian*, March 14, 2016, https://www.theguardian.com/technology /2016/mar/14/icann-internet-control-domain-names-iana.

52. Burcu Baykurt, "Turkey's Twitter Ban Is Easily Bypassed, But There Are No Easy Answers to Erdoğan's Abuse of Power," LSE EUROPP, March 24, 2014, http://blogs.lse.ac.uk/europpblog/2014/03/24/turkeys-twitter-ban-is -easily-sidestepped-but-there-are-no-easy-answers-to-erdogans-abuse-of -power/.

53. Ivana Kottasová, "EU Slaps Google with Record $2.7 Billion Fine," CNN Tech, June 27, 2017, https://money.cnn.com/2017/06/27/technology/business /google-eu-antitrust-fine/index.html.

54. Nick Statt, "Apple Agrees to Pay Ireland $15.4 Billion in Back Taxes to Appease EU," Verge, December 4, 2017, https://www.theverge.com/2017/12/4/16736 114/apple-ireland-european-union-order-back-taxes-agreement.

55. Adam Satariano, "G.D.P.R., a New Privacy Law, Makes Europe World's Leading Tech Watchdog," *New York Times*, May 24, 2018, https://www.nytimes .com/2018/05/24/technology/europe-gdpr-privacy.html.

56. Satariano, "G.D.P.R."

57. "Chinese Firm Hopes to Wire Continent with Same Strategy that Boosted Internet Access Across China," *Global Times*, March 13, 2017, www.globaltimes .cn/content/1037500.shtml.

58. Hong Shen, "Building a Digital Silk Road? Situating the Internet in China's Belt and Road Initiative," *International Journal of Communication* 12 (2018): 2683–701.

59. Raymond Zhong, "China's Huawei Is at Center of Fight Over 5G's Future," *New York Times*, March 7, 2018, https://www.nytimes.com/2018/03/07/tech nology/china-huawei-5g-standards.html.

60. Zheping Huang, "An Idiom Uttered by Xi Jinping Perfectly Describes Mark Zuckerberg's Frustrating China Courtship," Quartz, October 31, 2017, https://qz.com/1115960/an-idiom-uttered-by-xi-jinping-perfectly-describes -mark-zuckerbergs-frustrating-china-courtship/.

61. Carlos Tejada, "Google, Looking to Tiptoe Back Into China, Announces A.I. Center," *New York Times*, December 13, 2017, https://www.nytimes.com/2017/12/13/business/google-ai-china.html.

62. "Top 20 Countries with the Highest Number of Internet Users," Internet World Stats https://www.internetworldstats.com/top20.htm (accessed September 22, 2020).

63. Anita Chan, *Networking Peripheries: Technological Futures and the Myth of Digital Universalism* (Cambridge, MA: MIT Press, 2013); Lilly Irani, *Innovators and their Others: Entrepreneurial Citizenship in Indian Development.* (Princeton, NJ: Princeton University Press, 2019).

64 Dwayne Winseck, "The Geopolitical Economy of the Global Internet Infrastructure," *Journal of Information Policy* 7 (2017): 228–67.

65. Eric Schmidt and Jared Cohen, *The New Digital Age: Reshaping the Future of People, Nations, and Business.* (New York: Knopf, 2013).

66. ShinJoung Yeo, "Geopolitics of Search: Google versus China?," *Media, Culture & Society* 38, no. 4 (2016): 591–605.

67. Henry Farrell and Abraham L. Newman, "Chained Globalization," *Foreign Affairs* 99, no. 1 (January–February 2020): 70–80.

68. David Pozen, "The De-Americanization of Internet Freedom," Emerging Threats Essay Series at Knight First Amendment Institute, Columbia University, 2018, https://knightcolumbia.org/content/de-americanization-internet-freedom (accessed July 14, 2018).

69. Evgeny Morozov, *The Net Delusion: The Dark Side of Internet Freedom* (New York: Public Affairs, 2011).

70. J. S. Tan, "Big Tech Embraces New Cold War Nationalism," *Foreign Policy*, August 27, 2020, https://foreignpolicy.com/2020/08/27/china-tech-facebook-google/.

PART TWO
Turkey

CHAPTER III

Turkey's "Soft Power"

A Conceptual Overreach and a Conversation in Multiple Concepts

DILEK BARLAS AND LERNA K. YANIK

Defining Soft Power and Its Relationship with Public Diplomacy à la Joseph Nye

Writing in February 2006, in "Think Again: Soft Power," Joseph S. Nye Jr. argued that "soft power is cultural power," and that "a country's soft power can come from three sources: culture (in places where it is attractive to others), political values (when it lives up to them at home and abroad) and its foreign policies (when they are seen as legitimate and having moral authority)."[1] Additionally, according to Nye, economic strength can be converted into hard or soft power. In the same article, Nye contends with a critic who complained that, like globalization, soft power is too elastic a concept to be useful; Nye says his critic fails to understand the difference between power resources and behavior. Then he adds: "Whether soft power produces behavior that we want will depend on the context and the skills with which the resources are converted into outcomes."[2] Nye has written elsewhere that a country's soft power is promoted by public diplomacy, which tries to attract others by drawing attention to potential resources "through broadcasting, subsidizing cultural exports, arranging exchanges, and so forth. But if the content of a country's culture, values, and policies are not attractive, public diplomacy that 'broadcasts' them cannot produce soft power."[3]

Two years later, in a 2008 article, Nye used Turkey as an example of a country under the influence of the European Union's (EU) soft power:

Turkey today is making changes in its human rights policies and domestic law to adjust to EU standards. How much of this change is driven by the economic inducement of market access, and how much by attractiveness of Europe's successful economic and political system? It is clear that some Turks are replying more to the hard power of inducement, whereas others are attracted to the European model of human rights and economic freedom.[4]

In Nye's conception, Turkey's attempt to harmonize its laws with the EU (as a condition of a potential membership in the EU) in the early 2000s was an example of the EU successfully using its soft power to influence and create a positive change in Turkey. But what about Turkey's own soft power? Can we evaluate Turkey not as the recipient, but as a potential disseminator of soft power? If so, how?

This chapter reviews and traces Turkey's "transformative power," or the uses of the phrase "soft power" and the like, that denote Turkey's capability to influence countries it came into contact with from the 1980s to the military coup attempt in July 2016.[5] A preliminary examination of these discourses reveals that even before Joseph Nye coined and defined the term "soft power" in the 1990s, as "the ability of a country to get what it wants through attraction rather than coercion or payments," terms like "neo-Ottomanism" and the "Turkish model" were employed in the context of Turkish foreign policy, denoting a similar transformative capability for Turkey. Second, the predominant trend among politicians in Turkey who referred to Turkey's transformative power has been to misapply or to misuse the terms that denote Turkey's transformative power—that is, the tendency has been to equate having the power of attraction and the channels to disseminate this power with the automatic realization of getting the outcomes that Turkey wants. Or, if rephrased through Nye's conception of soft power, presumed power resources of Turkey's transformative capabilities are automatically equated with a desired/positive outcome in foreign policy. Third, the Justice and Development Party (Adalet ve Kalkınma Partisi, JDP) era, from 2002 until the military coup attempt, has the most intriguing and elaborate reformulations of Turkey's transformative power. During this period not only the terms "neo-Ottomanism" and the "Turkish model" made a comeback, but the term "soft power" itself became one of the most frequently referred terms by Turkey's politicians, in addition to other concepts used in lieu of "soft power," such as "humanitarian diplomacy," or Turkey as the "virtuous power." What is more, this period is distinguished by the increase in the financial and institutional capabilities of Turkey's soft-power instruments. Finally, what sets this period apart is the insistence of subsequent JDP governments' wielding soft power as the condition for being or becoming a global power—a goal that is mentioned recurrently by subsequent JDP governments as the foreign policy goal of Turkey.

Neo-Ottomanism and Turkish Model: Soft Power à la Turca Avant la Lettre

Viewed from a foreign policy perspective,[6] neo-Ottomanism is the idea of formulating an effective foreign policy for Turkey by highlighting the capability of Ottoman-Islamic heritage as a presumed common and shared past, forming the basis of a presumed common future, especially with the countries that were once part of the Ottoman Empire or with which Turkey has ethnic, linguistic, and/or religious affinity.[7] Since it was first coined in the mid-1980s, the term "neo-Ottomanism" has gone in and out of favor two more times: immediately after the end of the Cold War in the 1990s, and after the rise of the JDP to power in 2002. Whenever it has come back to life internationally, the term has implied not only a change in the basis of engagement for Turkey with countries with which it had some linguistic/ethnic ties or shared historical past as a result of the Ottoman presence in these countries, but also Turkey's capability to transform these countries positively as a result of these presumed commonalities that resulted partially from being under the Ottoman rule—or, as was the case in the 1990s, for presumed common ethnic, cultural, and ethnic ties with the Turkic states. What is more, all these three periods that witnessed the emergence and reemergence of neo-Ottomanism coincided with a profound internal or external change that forced Turkey to recalibrate its power and identity internationally and domestically.

The first time the term "neo-Ottomanism" appeared was in 1985, when David Barchard used it in his monograph *Turkey and the West*.[8] In his conclusion, Barchard spoke of neo-Ottomanism as one of the potential paths that post–1980s military coup Turkey could take vis-a-vis the "Iberian model," "Korean Model," "Mexican Model," "Latin American Model," "Swedenization," and Marxism.[9] Writing five years after the 1980 military coup that had, to some extent, strained Turkey's ties with the West, Barchard argued that "consciousness of the imperial Ottoman past is a much more politically potent force in Turkey than Islam and as Turkey regains economic strength, it will be increasingly tempted to assert itself in the Middle East as a leader."[10] In the context of souring Turkey-Europe relations, for Barchard the most rational choice for Turkey would be to make its presence known in the Middle East rather be treated as a country in the periphery of Europe. But the partial souring of the relations between Turkey and the West was not the only reason for Turkey "asserting itself in the Middle East" by emphasizing a common imperial Ottoman past. Post-1980 Turkey had a more restrictive constitution; under the guise of the Turkish-Islamic synthesis, religion, seen as an antidote to communism and other leftist currents, had become more and more public. But, more important, a neoliberal, export-oriented growth program to revive the economy was in full swing. This new economy required Turkish businessmen to find new markets besides the already-saturated European ones. The Ottoman imperial past, but more so the presumed commonness that stemmed from that history, was expected to be able to open up Middle Eastern markets to Turkey and justify Turkey's Islamization under the name of Turkish-Islamic synthesis, thus "transforming" Turkey's immediate neighborhood to become more receptive to Turkish goods and services.[11]

The next time the term "neo-Ottomanism" started to recirculate was just after the collapse of the Soviet Union. It was brought to life in *Turkey's New Geopolitics: From the Balkans to Western China*, a 1993 work edited by Graham E. Fuller, Ian O. Lesser, Paul B. Henze, and J. F. Brown, Rand Corporation's Turkey experts.[12] In his article in the volume, Fuller argued that in contemporary Turkey "a broader re-examination of the Ottoman period seems to be under way today," yet added that this

> re-examination and revaluation of Ottoman history in no way implies the emergence of a new Turkish irredentism or expansionism. It does suggest, however, a renewed interest in the former territories and people of the empire, which includes Muslims who were part of that empire. It suggests that certain organic geopolitical,

cultural and economic relations that had been absent during the "abnormal" period of Cold War polarization may reemerge in the new "normal" regional environment. It suggests that the Turks may now come to see themselves once again at the center of a world reemerging around them rather than at the tail-end of a European world that is increasingly uncertain about whether or not it sees Turkey as part of itself.[13]

Interestingly, Fuller's chapter was called "Turkey's New Eastern Orientation," a nod to the fact that, for Turkey, the *new* "East" was not the Middle East, but post-Soviet space and the Balkans. He concluded his discussion of neo-Ottomanism by saying that, given the geopolitical transformations that happened around Turkey, these "new horizons of foreign policy cannot be ignored by any leader."[14] In addition to reviving neo-Ottomanism as a potential means for Turkish foreign policy, Fuller also argued that the collapse of the Soviet Union and the disintegration of Yugoslavia accordingly offered Turkey the chance to become a regional leader by providing some level of order in the post–Cold War disorder. Its ethnic, linguistic, and cultural affiliation with the Turkic republics and historical affiliation with the Balkans as a result of the Ottoman past, according to Fuller, justified Turkey's political and economic involvement in these regions.

Put differently, the early uses of neo-Ottomanism as a term by two well-known foreign Turkey observers in the 1980s and 1990s were about reshuffling the Turkish identity by taking the Ottoman past into consideration and transforming Turkey's immediate external environment by using this new identity for "the elimination of economic borders among the Balkans, Caucasus and the Middle East countries, but respecting the political borders of the ex-Ottoman space."[15]

Although neo-Ottomanism was repeatedly put back into circulation by scholars and Turkey observers, and, although references to the Ottoman Empire and Ottoman past frequently appeared in their speeches, Turkey's policy makers never pronounced the term "neo-Ottomanism" themselves. In fact, whenever possible, Turkish politicians rejected the idea of Turkey being neo-Ottomanist or having neo-Ottomanist ambitions, as they knew the term could have derogatory connotations. At the Foreign Policy Institute in Ankara, Turkey, in November 1994, for example, Süleyman Demirel argued that Turkish foreign policy "has never been in expansionist efforts," despite claims from some of Turkey's neighbors that "you are neo-Ottomanist, neo-Ottomanist expansionist, Turkey, during 71 years of existence, has never followed an expansionist policy."[16]

Interestingly, while adamantly refuting any linkage to a neo-Ottomanist foreign policy, Demirel and other leaders had no problem using the phrase "Turkish model," which essentially meant that Turkey, being a secular and a democratic country where the dominant religion was Islam, can be emulated by other countries where the predominant religion was Islam but not secular and democratic, hence hinting again at Turkey's presumed transformative power. In 1995, addressing the Turkish parliament, Demirel argued that the "Turkish model was a result of Turkey's special location," and "that Turkey was executing a foreign policy that was geared toward contributing to regional peace and security."[17] "History," according to Demirel, "has created new hopes and new responsibilities for Turkey that it needs to shoulder in the Balkans, in the Black Sea Basin, in the Caucasus, in the Middle East and in Central Asia."[18] Tansu Çiller, prime minister of Turkey and (for a short while) the minister of foreign affairs in the 1990s, was on the same wavelength with Demirel. While, for example, debating the government program in the Turkish parliament in June 1993, Tansu Çiller emphasized Turkey's importance as a model, stressing its location and values, which constituted its basis. Clearly, because of its geography and ethnic and linguistic affiliations with the newly independent Turkic states and the Balkans, as well as its status as a "democratic, secular and Muslim" nation, Turkish politicians saw it fit to export this model to its newly independent neighbors. Çiller said,

Turkey has a special role within Atlantic-Europe and Eurasian belts. . . . We are a country that has integrated with the Western world. We are a democratic, secular, contemporary member of the Islamic world [sic]. We are taken as a model by the newly independent states, especially those that speak Turkic languages. With our presence and success, we are living proof that Islam is compatible with democracy and that economic, social and cultural developments can only take place in a democratic environment.[19]

This rhetoric of helping "distant brothers" or being a "model" to these "newly discovered brethren"—or, put differently, transforming these newly independent countries through Turkey's transformative power—did not remain just rhetoric; it was turned into action by both state and nonstate actors. Türk İşbirliği ve Koordinasyon Ajansı (Turkish Cooperation and Coordination Agency or TIKA), for instance, was established in 1992 to coordinate development aid. Modeled on the Japanese International Aid Development Agency, TIKA's mission involved delivering development assistance to a variety of activities ranging from the restoration of Ottoman Turkish architectural heritage to the distribution of aid in kind in the Balkans and the former Soviet Union. While TIKA quickly became an instrument of Turkish foreign policy, the ever-changing coalition governments in the 1990s and economic crises that engulfed Turkey during those years turned the institution into a marginal one with a limited budget, professional staff, and impact.[20]

In addition to TIKA, educational exchange also became a way to extend the Turkish model, or Turkey's transformative power in the Balkans, to some degree, and more broadly in the former Soviet Union. Not only did the Turkish Ministry of National Education and the Gülen community[21] open schools in the newly independent countries of the Soviet Union and the Balkans (and later in Africa and North America), but both the Turkish government and the Gülen community invited students from those countries to study at Turkish universities,[22] making both education and the Gülen community important instruments of Turkish soft power.[23] Yet, while these efforts earned the Gülen community tacit approval from Turkish politicians such as Bülent Ecevit, the endorsement of these schools (and indirectly of the Gülen community) also drew the ire of members of the secular establishment.[24] During this period, Turkey did not ignore the Middle East, either. With the Paris Protocol of 1996, Turkey started granting development and humanitarian aid to the Palestinians,[25] and, in 1997, Turkey became part of the Temporary International Presence in Hebron, and its Foreign Ministry directed a Young Palestinian Diplomats' Training Program.[26]

However, despite elaborate formulations of the Turkish model and careful avoidance of the term "neo-Ottomanism," the limitations of Turkey's transformative power in education quickly became apparent. Budgetary issues, coupled with mismanagement and diplomatic faux pas, plagued the state-run educational exchange, decreasing the number of incoming students by the end of the 1990s.[27] Moreover, when it came to education, Turkey from day one had a fierce competitor: the West. Even as late as 2011 and 2014, a poll conducted among Muslim African students that the Gülen movement had sponsored to study in Turkish universities showed that the students would have preferred to pursue their education in western Europe or the United States.[28]

Turkey's transformative power in the 1990s was also limited in terms of execution and credibility, as Turkey was both economically and politically unstable. Until İsmail Cem's appointment in 1997, frequently changing coalition governments made the position of the minister of foreign affairs a revolving door, leaving the ministry without a stable leadership. Finally, the so-called low-intensity warfare that Turkey waged against Kurdish separatists in eastern Turkey and the resulting human rights violations challenged Turkey's claim to subscribe to the values its model and transformative power emphasized.

Overall, the appearance of the term "Turkish model" and the reappearance of "neo-Ottomanism" in the 1990s was not a coincidence. Both terms—the former owned by Turkish politicians and the latter disowned by them—denoted Turkey's presumed transformative potential in the Balkans and the newly independent Turkic states of the former Soviet Union to create secular, democratic countries run with a market economy. Turkey's presumed transformative potential was based on several pillars. First, Turkey touted itself—and the West agreed—as the only secular democracy and free market economy in the Muslim world. Second, because of its ethnic, linguistic, and historical ties to these former Soviet Union republics and the Balkans, coupled with its location, Turkey presented itself as uniquely qualified to transmit values of democracy, secularism, and a free market economy that were considered Western. In other words, presumed commonalities in religion, ethnicity, language, and history—or, per Nye's concept soft power, "culture"—were to be used to spread democracy, free market economy, and secularism ("values," in Nye's definition). The third motivation was Turkey's desire to prove its usefulness to the West in the face of the American belief that communism was all that had kept the former Soviet republics from becoming a free market economy and liberal democracy. Turkey's transformative power both in the form of neo-Ottomanism and its spin-off, the Turkish model, stemmed from Turkey's need to recalibrate itself in the changing international environment. To quote Çolak, neo-Ottomanism meant "rewriting Turkish history on the basis of a shared Ottoman past in a globalizing context."[29]

What distinguished Turkey's transformative capability in the 1990s was the fact that, unlike in the 1980s, there were institutions, programs, and nonstate actors that, albeit with limited impact, turned Turkey's discourse of its transformative power into action. As the 1990s came to a close, two more factors with the potential to increase Turkey's transformative power at the international level emerged, preparing the ground for the JDP's reformulation of Turkey's transformative power: the launch of the Alliance of Civilizations Initiative in February 2002 by the outgoing minister of foreign affairs İsmail Cem, and the introduction of series of reforms expanding civil rights and liberties in Turkey as part of Turkey's harmonization efforts with the EU. Using the 9/11 attacks as an opportunity to organize the Alliance of Civilizations Conference in February 2002, Cem stated that the

> September 11th attacks that targeted New York and Washington have further highlighted Turkey's strategic importance; an urgent need for Turkey's contribution function emerged and, from a Western perspective, it made Turkey indispensable. In an environment where a perception that the US and the Islamic world has come head to head in the context of civilizations has arisen, Turkey is the only country that can eliminate this fallacy. With its European and Asian identity, NATO membership, the EU and Islamic Conference (Organization) identity, at that point in time, Turkey was in a position to mend the ruptured dialogue and make up for the misunderstandings between East and West. And Turkey succeeded in this. In the aftermath of the attacks, Turkey announced that it has been in the frontlines of fighting against terrorism for years and that this would be its fight and it would support the US.[30]

With this, Turkey added the idea of "civilization" to its collection of transformative power tools. For Cem, Turkey had to be predominantly engaged with the West, but as a European and Asian country that synthesized all civilizations, as well as the East.[31] The Alliance of Civilizations Conference initiated by Cem would later be turned by the JDP governments into an initiative cochaired by Turkey and Spain and run under UN auspices.[32] The current website of Turkey's Ministry of Foreign Affairs states that the strong interest in the project "proves Turkey's lead role in providing dialogue, harmony and cooperation between nations, cultures and civilizations," underscoring the fact that Turkey remains interested in the idea of civilization as part of its transformative power.[33]

The reforms that extended the civil rights and liberties in Turkey in the late 1990s and early 2000s as part of Turkey's efforts to harmonize its laws and political system for the sake of a potential membership to the EU became part of its transformative potential toolbox. From October 2001 to August 2003, after gaining the EU candidacy status in 1999, the Turkish parliament reduced police powers of detention, lifted the ban on Kurdish-language broadcasts, adopted a new civil code that improved freedom of association and assembly, and outlawed the death penalty.[34] These reforms would later form the basis of JDP's "value-based" foreign policy, enabling the argument that Islam and democracy/democratization is possible, and that Turkey was a case in point. The idea that Turkey represented a culmination of multiple civilizational traditions that could bring different groups together, along with the human rights reforms, as Nye pointed out in his 2006 piece "Think Again: Soft Power," helped Turkish politicians redefine and reshape Turkey's transformative power in the early years of the JDP rule.

Talking About Turkey's Transformative Power During the JDP Period: Further Conversations in Multiple Concepts

The concept of civilization and the reforms that expanded civil rights and liberties in Turkey launched by the outgoing coalition were the key to early JDP rule, taking Turkey's transformative power debate to a new level after the party's arrival to power in November 2002. During this era, in addition to "neo-Ottomanism" and "Turkish model," more elaborate terms were used to denote Turkey's "transformative power," including the term "soft power" itself. The JDP government's frequent reference to the term was not an accident. This period coincided not only with the 2004 publication of Joseph Nye's *Soft Power: The Means to Success in World Politics*, but also with the JDP's ambitious foreign policy, which aimed to make Turkey a global player in world politics. In addition to "soft power," new terms entered Turkish foreign policy discourse to denote Turkey's transformative power, including "humanitarian diplomacy" and "virtuous power," both of which would have policy implications.

The "architect" of these policies was Ahmet Davutoğlu, an academic who would first be appointed ambassador at large and later become the minister of foreign affairs and prime minister in the subsequent JDP governments.[35] Davutoğlu's book *Strategic Depth: Turkey's International Position*, first published in 2001, gave the first clues about how Turkish foreign policy's transformative power and the display of Turkey's strength would look like in JDP-led Turkey. In his book, Davutoğlu claimed that the failure of Turkish rulers to make full use of its history and geography so far had inhibited Turkey from being a global power in world politics. Accordingly, Turkey needed to use its historical and geographic "depths"—that is, to emphasize and idealize Ottoman-era history and practices in its foreign relations as well as its "unique" geography.[36] This linkage to the Ottoman past meant more than revering Ottoman history; like the term "neo-Ottomanism" coined earlier, it not only meant that Turkey had to have a say in regional affairs because neighboring countries had been part of the Ottoman Empire, but it also was based on the assumption that these countries would have a positive view of Turkey as a result of their common past.

The discourse, as stated above, would not stay just discourse and would become the practice of expanding Turkey's power internationally and lead to the question of whether JDP was neo-Ottomanist or followed a "neo-Ottomanist foreign policy."[37] As in the 1990s, the politicians who ruled Turkey disowned the term "neo-Ottomanism," and never used it in their speeches or statements.[38] Yet they frequently referred to the Ottoman Empire and glorified this period, highlighting the empire's Islamic tone and paving the way for the Ottoman Empire to become an everyday phenomenon in areas from architecture to popular soap operas in addition to Turkey's foreign policy discourse and practice.[39]

The term "Turkish model" also made a comeback in the 2000s—not once, but three times. The first was in the immediate aftermath of the 9/11 attacks, preceding JDP's taking power in November 2002, when Turkey was touted as a model country that could combine democracy and a Muslim identity. The electoral victory of the JDP, which had its roots in Turkey's Islamist parties, paved the way to the term's second comeback. Because the rise of JDP to power further solidified the view of Turkey as a secular and democratic model for countries plagued with radical Islam, political instability, and authoritarianism. The JDP coming to power in Turkey meant that it was possible to successfully "reconcile" Islam and democracy.[40] Finally, "Turkish model" returned to circulation after 2010, with the Arab Uprisings that swept the Middle East and North Africa, again with the idea of Turkey's Islamist government as a potential role model for Arab countries.[41] Though "Turkish model" yet again indicated Turkey's potential transformative power in its immediate neighborhood, not all

Turkish politicians were happy with the term. Abdullah Gül, who was minister of foreign affairs before becoming president in 2007, realized that using the phrase "Turkish model" and pushing other countries to adopt democracy carried hegemonic connotations. He argued that "Turkey should not be a model country, but rather a country that inspires."[42] In addition to reformulating Turkey's transformative role as a "power that inspires," Gül argued that Turkey was a "virtuous power,"[43] because "the added value Turkey would bring does not only culminate from its unique geography, but also the policies it pursues. Turkey aspires to be a virtuous power for democracy, peace, stability and prosperity in its region and beyond."[44] According to Yohanan Benhaïm and Kerem Öktem, the idea that Turkey should not represent a model "may have been based on the determination not to repeat the mistakes made in Central Asia in the 1990s, when Turkish foreign policy failed to live up to its ambitions of regional leadership."[45] Yet they also point out that, regardless of the past failure of the Turkish model in the 1990s, from the mid-2012 on the notion of the "Turkish model" still dominated foreign policy discourses.[46]

Moreover, using the terms "the power that inspires" or "virtuous power" did not preclude the leaders of Turkey from using the term "soft power" and talking about it in various contexts. A quick look at how key actors of the period—namely, Recep Tayyip Erdoğan, Abdullah Gül, and Ahmet Davutoğlu—used the term is revealing. To begin with, this was virtually the first time Turkish politicians used the term openly, perhaps in response to the 2004 publication of Nye's *Soft Power*. Additionally, a quick glance at the three major figures of the JDP government until 2014 reveals that Gül and Davutoğlu used the term more often than Erdoğan. Interestingly, Gül and Davutoğlu's understanding of soft power comes with a twist: it goes hand in hand with hard power and the belief that Turkey's soft power does not work only externally, as the standard Nye definition would have it, but internally as well, to resolve Turkey's Kurdish separatism problem. At the opening speech of the Turkish parliament in 2009, Gül argued that

we have armed forces that have passed the test of history that are always ready under any and every circumstance to defend our nation and have scored important victories in our fight against terrorism. We are always proud of this. On the other hand, in today's world, "soft power" assets like diplomacy, energy policy and strong economic indicators go hand in hand with military power when it comes to achieving results that directly affect the welfare of the countries. Turkey should utilize its well-developed elements of soft power more effectively in defending its national interests. What lies at the heart of the elements of national power, consisting of hard power to soft power, is the ownership of a societal consensus, which is far from deep fault lines. Our great nation merges the idea of being a single nation with the notion of respect for differences.[47]

On another occasion, addressing Turkey's ambassadors, Gül said, "Today international relations is not only about national interests or political, economic and military power, but it is also about culture, history and shared universal values. As a result, reforms in the realm of democracy, human rights and rule of law as part of the universal values become a powerful chip card for our ambassadors."[48] Davutoğlu also agreed that soft power was an instrument that can be used internally to provide societal harmony, saying that "Turkey's most important soft power is its democracy." He added:

In the fall of 2007, the Turkish military pursued a military operation against terrorist formations in Iraq for several weeks, with no negative impact on liberties in Istanbul, Ankara, Diyarbakır, or Van. Normal life continues, even while Turkey wages a war against terror. This successful balance is a matter of political culture. Turkish authorities did not declare a state of emergency, elections were not postponed, and the election results did not influence the process in a negative way. These results support the notion that Turkey's most important soft power is its democracy.[49]

Davutoğlu was aware that Turkey's external projections of soft power made sense and were credible only when civil liberties and democracy were working internally. In the same article, he argued that "Turkey has made great strides in protecting civil liberties despite serious domestic political challenges to such freedoms over the past seven years. This required vigorously carrying out the struggle against terrorism without narrowing the sphere of civil liberties—a challenge Turkey successfully overcame. In the process, we've found that Turkish soft power has only increased as our democracy has matured."[50] What is more, Davutoğlu claimed that having "adopted a new discourse and diplomatic style has resulted in the spread of

Turkey's soft power in the region. . . . Although Turkey maintains a powerful military due to its insecure neighborhood, we do not make threats. Instead, Turkish diplomats and politicians have adopted a new language in regional and international politics that prioritizes Turkey's civil-economic power."[51] This statement is quite revealing of the JDP mindset regarding Turkey's transformative power, as it equates Turkey's civil-economic power with its soft power, an approach that contradicts the basic definition of soft power—that is, the idea of getting the desired outcomes *without* coercion or payment. With that, Davutoğlu also equates the presumed means to soft power with the presumed outcomes of soft power; in other words, civil-economic power is presumed to translate into soft power and achieve Turkey's desired outcomes immediately and automatically. With this statement, one can conclude that Davutoğlu takes Turkey's transformative power for granted. Put differently, soft power is associated with automatically getting the outcomes Turkey wants.

The final twist in JDP's conception of Turkey's "transformative power" can be seen in its understanding of Turkey as a "humanitarian power," and the role of state and nonstate actors in becoming its instruments. When Davutoğlu claimed that humanitarian diplomacy can overcome the dichotomy between soft and hard power or between realism and idealism, he essentially equated humanitarian power—or Turkey being a humanitarian actor—with Turkey's soft or transformative power.[52] In an article titled "Turkey's Humanitarian Diplomacy," Davutoğlu wrote that "Turkey's understanding of humanitarian diplomacy is multi-faced and multi-channeled, with contributions from Turkey's public institutions and NGOs, ranging from Turkish Airlines to TİKA, Kızılay (Turkish Red Cross), TOKI (Toplu Konut İdaresi-Housing Development Agency of Turkey) and AFAD (Afet ve Acil Durum Yönetimi Başkanlığı-Disaster and Emergency Management Presidency)."[53] He approved this kind of an approach in another article by saying, "Turkey's success is not only the result of state policies, but also the activities of civil society, business organization, and numerous other organizations, all operating under the guidance of the new vision."[54] Put differently, by equating soft power with humanitarian diplomacy and with a series of NGOs that reflected partially Turkey's economic capabilities, Davutoğlu indirectly equated Turkey's economic capabilities with Turkey's "soft" or "transformative" power.

Davutoğlu was not alone in enlisting various institutions, civil society groups, and organizations as instruments of Turkey's transformative power.

Gül, too, asked state institutions as well as civil society groups to help Turkey become a virtuous power and asked the Turkish ambassadors abroad to facilitate the workings of these groups in the countries in which they operate.[55] Zeynep Atalay argues that, because these Islamic civil society groups help fulfill JDP's goal of being first a regional and then a global power, a mutually symbiotic relationship exists between the Turkish state and these groups.[56] Among these groups, the Gülen community had a privileged position, until the fallout between the JDP government and the Gülen community in 2013. Having established a religious network, the Gülen community was complemented by a business network that also encompassed educational institutions at different levels around the globe. The level of symbiotic relationship between the Gülen community and JDP was such that, as Bayram Balcı argues, especially in the context of West Asia, it was very difficult to determine whether the Gülen movement was "the cause or effect of increasing Turkish soft power," thus gaining not only the praise of the JDP government but also a group of Turkish intellectuals.[57] In 2005, a group of Turkish intellectuals offered their praise for Gülen community schools around the world in an edited volume called *Barış Köprüleri: Dünyaya Açılan Türk Okulları* (The bridges of peace: the Turkish schools that open into the world).[58] The Gülen movement's business network was further expanded by TUSKON-Türkiye İşadamları ve Sanayicileri Konfederasyonu (Turkish Confederation of Businessmen and Industrialists).[59] In addition to having very close ties to the JDP government,[60] TUSKON, it is said, has started competing with TÜSİAD Türk Sanayiciler ve İşadamları Derneği (Turkish Industrialists and Businessmen's Association)—a business advocacy group with more secular tendencies—in sectors and fields that had once been TÜSİAD's sole fiefdom.[61] However, the fallout between JDP and Gülen after 2013, coupled with the coup attempt of 2016, for which Gülenists have been held responsible, has, of course, removed the Gülen movement from being a potential source of Turkey's transformative power.[62]

Compared to the 1990s, the most important difference in Turkey's transformative power was not only the shifting rhetoric around it but also how Turkey exercised it. One change was the amount of the humanitarian/development aid that Turkey provided internationally. Since JDP's rise to power, Turkey's humanitarian aid has increased to such levels that Turkey has now become one of the most important donors in the world.[63] According to the Organization for Economic Cooperation and Development

Statistics (OECD), since the end of the Cold War, the official development aid distributed by Turkey to developing countries has gone from a meager 113 million USD in 1991 to 6.2 billion USD in 2016 (constant prices, 2016). Much of that increase took place during the JDP period. According to OECD, in 2003, while Turkey's Official Development Aid (ODA) distribution to developing countries was 35.9 million USD, this number increased almost six times within a year of JDP's taking power and in 2004 was 335 million USD (constant prices, 2016).[64] To put it differently, in the JDP period, Turkey's rhetoric of transformative power was backed up financially.

This marked increase in financial support for Turkey's transformative power also "transformed" the institutions that helped Turkey wield this power. As humanitarian aid increased during the JDP years, the institutions and organizations that delivered it were also reorganized, reshuffled, and reinforced. An overhauled TIKA became one of the main engines of aid distribution, first in the Balkans and Caucasus, and, after 2004, in the Middle East and Africa,[65] as a result of the foreign policy elite's converging "strategies of material interests and normative ideas."[66] The Diyanet (Directorate of Religious Affairs) of Turkey in the Balkans opened religious service offices charged with "maintaining rapport with the counsels and embassies, as liaisons between them and the targeted public."[67] The semi–state-owned Turkish Airlines became the "airline flying to most destinations" and was thus considered one of Turkey's soft-power tools.[68] In 2007, the Yunus Emre Foundation was established to teach Turkish language and culture abroad. A 2010 Yunus Emre Foundation bulletin quoted Davutoğlu saying that "foreign policy is not carried out solely with diplomacy but also with cultural, economic and trade networks. . . . This will enable us to place our historical-cultural richness in our current strategy," thus pointing out the foundation's place as part of Turkey's transformative power in Turkey's foreign policy.[69] What is more, in May 2016 Turkey hosted the First Humanitarian Summit under the auspices of the UN, prompting questions about whether Turkey was using this summit and the UN to project its soft power.[70] Most important, in 2010 the JDP government established the Office of Public Diplomacy and initiated "a new public diplomacy" with the aim of "telling the story of new Turkey to a wide ranging audience across the globe."[71] This office was immediately linked to Turkey's soft power by İbrahim Kalın, then an advisor to Prime Minister Erdoğan, now the presidential spokesperson. In an article titled "Soft

Power and Public Diplomacy in Turkey," Kahn wrote, "Public diplomacy, which is a platform for the implementation of soft power, is a new concept in Turkey."[72] In this article, Kalın linked the Ottoman past to Turkey's soft power while neatly rejecting claims of "neo-Ottomanism" yet again. He argued that

> In the larger Euro-Asian landmass, the common denominator for Turks, Kurds, Bosnians, Albanians, Circassians, Abkhazians, Arabs, Azeris, Kazakhs, Kyrgyzs, Uzbeks, Turkmens, and other ethnic groups, as well as Armenian, Greek, Jewish, and Assyrian communities, is the Ottoman experience they have shared and built together. It is this Ottoman heritage that brings together these diverse groups and enables them to relate to a shared experience in time and place. Today, Turkey represents the pivotal point of this heritage. This is not a new imperial adventure, termed by some as "neo-Ottomanism." Rather, this is a process whereby Turkey's new geopolitical imagination and the new possibilities in the global political system allow the people of the region to reconcile with their history and geography. Remembering this experience plays an important role in defining the spheres of soft power in Turkey.[73]

Overall, during the JDP period, Turkey's transformative power manifested itself in a variety of ways. First, the number of the concepts that came to denote it increased. Prior to JDP, the terms "neo-Ottomanism" and "Turkish model" were used to denote Turkey's transformative power, as Turkish politicians disowned the term "neo-Ottomanism," but still referred to Turkey's Ottoman past to justify its foreign policy and right and ability to wield regional influence. During the JDP period, Turkish leaders, like their predecessors, did not utter the term "neo-Ottomanism," but references to the Ottoman past further increased, now with an Islamist tone and an anti-Western tint.[74] Unlike neo-Ottomanism, "Turkish model" was used, along with "humanitarian diplomacy," "value-based foreign policy," "virtuous power," and direct references to "soft power." One marked difference of the JDP period was that the rhetoric of Turkey's transformative power had financial power behind it, as Turkey became one of the world's most important providers of official assistance. Along with this financial support for Turkey's transformative power came a better use of domestic and international institutions and platforms. Finally, the support of the

Gülen community in expanding Turkey's transformative power, which had already begun in the period preceding JDP's arrival to power, reached new highs during this period, followed by new lows beginning in December 2013 and ending with a total fallout with the JDP government after the military coup attempt of July 2016. In other words, the subsequent JDP government's rhetoric of making Turkey a regional and a global power went in tandem with the marked increase in a variety of versions of Turkey's transformative power.

This chapter surveyed the debates regarding Turkey's soft power—or, as we put it, Turkey's transformative power in the post–Cold War period. It argued that, even before the term "soft power" came into full use in the early 2000s, terms like "neo-Ottomanism" and "Turkish model" were used in the 1980s, and increasingly in the 1990s, to depict Turkey's transformative power in the Balkans, the former Soviet Union, and the Middle East. In the 1990s, the term "neo-Ottomanism" was disowned by Turkey's politicians. Yet this did not preclude them from frequently referring to a perceived common Ottoman past as the potential basis for conducting Turkey's foreign relations, especially with the regions where Turkey had either ethnic, linguistic, and/or religious commonalities, thereby transforming these regions. The term "Turkish model," on the other hand, was based on the assumption that, as a secular yet predominantly Muslim and democratic country, Turkey could be emulated by other countries that were authoritarian but where the predominant religion was Islam. While neo-Ottomanism, references to the Ottoman past as a way to a potential future, or the Turkish model justified increased Turkish involvement in these regions, they also hinted at Turkey's potential to transform regions. What is more, making the claim to own this transformative power helped Turkey to argue for its usefulness in the international system, especially as part of the Western alliance, and created more markets for Turkish goods both in the 1980s and the 1990s.

JDP's rise to power in November 2002 and the JDP governments' frequently repeated "desire" to make Turkey not just a regional but a global power changed the ways in which Turkey's potential transformative power was discussed, understood, and practiced. The most marked difference between the 1990s and the 2000s was the addition of the term "soft power" to the existing terminology to describe Turkey's transformative power—an obvious reflection of Joseph Nye's 2004 book *Soft Power*. The entry of "soft power" into the lexicons of Turkey's politicians were accompanied by other terms such as "virtuous power" and "humanitarian diplomacy," to further denote Turkey's transformative power. What is more, in the 2000s, Turkey was more committed to its use of soft-power instruments, finally creating and financially backing the institutions and civil society links needed to make Turkey's much-spoken and less-practiced transformative power a reality. As noted by Benhaim and Öktem, for the JDP leadership Turkey's soft power, once it was separated from the idea of being a model, made for a cultural and political atmosphere in which Turkey declared itself independent from U.S. interests.[75] In earlier decades, regardless of which term was used to denote Turkey's transformative power, this power was instrumentalized to solidify Turkey's position in the international system, as Turkey was regarded as an actor extending Western interests into the East. Put differently, in the 1990s Turkey's soft or transformative power was the manifestation of Turkey trying to prove itself in the international system, whereas, for the subsequent JDP governments, having or exerting Turkey's transformative power was the sine qua non of being a global power and pursuing Turkey's very own national interests at the international level. Finally, one other distinguishing practice of Turkey's transformative power in JDP-led Turkey was the use of hard power—internally in southeastern Turkey against Kurdish civilians and separatists, and externally in Syria during the Syrian Civil War—alongside the discourse and practice of soft power.

However, even when members of the JDP government were sure of Turkey's transformative power, as early as 2008 scholars had warned that this power depended on Turkey's credibility and its ability to create harmony both internally and externally and thus had limits,[76] especially when democracy promotion had become the focus in Turkey's foreign policy vis-à-vis its Eastern neighbors.[77] What is more, the recent authoritarian turn in Turkey, Turkey's willingness to engage with radical forces in Syria, JDP's fallout with the Gülen community—once seen as a key aspect of Turkey's soft power—[78] have raised further doubts about Turkey's transformative power.[79] Nonetheless, Turkey continues to appear—albeit sporadically—in the yearly list of the thirty countries with the greatest soft power. While the "Soft Power 30: A Global Ranking of Soft Power" issued in 2018[80] by the Portland Strategic Communications firm and the USC Center on Public Diplomacy no longer placed Turkey in the top-thirty list, as late as in 2017 Turkey was number thirty.[81] Turkey was off the list in 2016, but was twenty-eighth in 2015.[82] If these rankings can be considered accurate, and if Turkey continues to appear on these kinds of indices, it means that JDP's conceptually overreaching version of soft power and thus Turkey's transformative power has a taken on a new and internationally recognized life of its own.

Notes

1. Joseph S. Nye Jr., "Think Again: Soft Power," http://foreignpolicy.com/2006/02/23/think-again-soft-power/ (accessed September 30, 2017).
2. Nye, "Think Again."
3. Joseph S. Nye Jr., "Public Diplomacy and Soft Power," *Annals of the American Academy of Political and Social Science* 616 (March 2008): 95.
4. Nye, "Public Diplomacy," 95.
5. We use the phrase "transformative power" to cover a variety of terms that hint at Turkey's presumed power of attraction as well as to denote a range of concepts and terms used in lieu of the term "soft power."
6. Neo-Ottomanism is also used as a tool of identity management at the domestic level—an issue on which we do not elaborate here, as our focus is foreign policy.
7. Yılmaz Çolak, "Ottomanism vs. Kemalism: Collective Memory and Cultural Pluralism in 1990s Turkey," *Middle Eastern Studies* 42, no. 4 (2006): 587; M. Hakan Yavuz, "Social and Intellectual Origins of Neo-Ottomanism: Searching for a Post-National Vision," *Die Welt des Islams* 56, nos. 3–4 (2016): 443.
8. David Barchard, *Turkey and the West* (London: Royal Institute of International Affairs, 1985), 91; Yavuz, "Social and Intellectual Origins of Neo-Ottomanism," 443; Lerna K. Yanık, "Bringing the Empire Back In: The Gradual Discovery of the Ottoman Empire in Turkish Foreign Policy," *Die Welt des Islams* 56, nos. 3–4, (2016): 438–65. Kemal Karpat has argued that the Greeks used the term for the first time in the aftermath of Turkey's Cyprus Intervention in 1974. Kemal Karpat, "Civil Rights of the Muslims in the Balkans," in *Studies on Ottoman Social and Political History* (Leiden: Brill, 2002), 524.
9. Barchard, *Turkey and the West*, 89–93.
10. Barchard, 91.
11. See Yanık, "Bringing the Empire Back In," 438–65. This trend of referring to history to justify certain discourses and actions in Turkey's foreign policy, of course, did not start in the 1980s. Its origins can be traced to the aftermath of World War II, and it becomes more pronounced in the 1960s. Yet what needs to be underlined here is that emphasizing commonalities with the Middle East

coincides with the coining of the term "neo-Ottomanism," and the 1980s is a period in which Turkey's economic interests began to take precedence over its political ones.

12. Graham Fuller and Ian O. Lesser, with Paul B. Henze and J. F. Brown, *Turkey's New Geopolitics: From the Balkans to Western China* (San Francisco: Westview, 1993).
13. Fuller, "Turkey's New Eastern Orientation," in Fuller et al., *Turkey's New Geopolitics*, 47–48.
14. Fuller, "Turkey's New Eastern Orientation," 48–54.
15. M. Hakan Yavuz, "Turkish Identity and Foreign Policy in Flux: The Rise of Neo-Ottomanism," *Critique: Critical Middle Eastern Studies* 7, no. 12 (1998): 40.
16. "Cumhurbaşkanı Sayın Süleyman Demirel'in Dış Politika Enstitüsü Tarafından Düzenlenen '21'inci Yüzyılın Eşiğinde Türk Dış Politikası' Konulu Konferansta Yaptıkları Konuşma," in *Cumhurbaşkanı Süleyman Demirel'in Söylev ve Demeçleri*, ed. Cengiz Ergen (Ankara: Ataturk Research Center, 2002), 685.
17. "Cumhurbaşkanı Sayın Süleyman Demirel'in Türkiye," 25–26.
18. "Cumhurbaşkanı Sayın Süleyman Demirel'in Türkiye," 43.
19. İrfan Neziroğlu and Tuncer Yılmaz, eds., *Hükümetler-Programları ve Genel Kurul Görüşmeleri*, 9 Kasım 1989–30 Ekim 1995 (Ankara: TBMM Basımevi, 2013), 8:6739.
20. See, for example, Pınar İpek, "Ideas and Change in Foreign Policy Instruments: Soft Power and the Case of the Turkish International Cooperation and Development Agency," *Foreign Policy Analysis* 11, no. 2 (2015): 180; and Güner Özkan and Mustafa Turgut Demirtepe, "Transformation of a Development Aid Agency: TIKA in a Changing Domestic and International Setting," *Turkish Studies* 13, no. 4 (2012): 649–50.
21. For a detailed analysis of Fetullah Gülen and the emergence and development of the Gülen community since the 1960s, see Bayram Balcı, "The Gülen Movement and Turkey's Soft Power in the South Caucasus and the Middle East," in Mehran Kamrava, ed., *The Great Game in West Asia* (London: Hurst, 2017), 183–91.
22. Lerna K. Yanık, "The Politics of Educational Exchange: Turkish Education in Eurasia," *Europe-Asia Studies* 56, no. 2 (March 2004): 293–307.
23. Bayram Balcı, "Gülen Movement and Turkey's Soft Power," 183–201.
24. Önder Yılmaz, "Ecevit Gülen'e 'Siper,'" *Milliyet* (Istanbul), March 1, 2000, http://www.milliyet.com.tr/2000/03/01/siyaset/siy05.html.
25. Meliha Benli Altunışık, "The Possibilities and Limits of Turkey's Soft Power in the Middle East," *Insight Turkey* 10, no. 2 (2008): 51.
26. Altunışık, "Possibilities and Limits," 51.
27. Yanık, "Politics of Educational Exchange," 295–98.

28. Gabrielle Angey-Sentuc, "Challenging the Soft Power Analysis," *European Journal of Turkish Studies* 21 (2015): 9.
29. Çolak, "Ottomanism vs. Kemalism," 588.
30. Ismail Cem, *Türkiye, Avrupa, Asya: Strateji, Yunanistan, Kıbrıs* (İstanbul: İstanbul Bilgi Üniversitesi Yayınları, 2004).
31. Cem, *Türkiye, Avrupa, Asya*, 56.
32. "Medeniyetler İttifakı Girişimi," Republic of Turkey, Ministry of Foreign Affairs, http://www.mfa.gov.tr/medeniyetler-ittifaki-girisimi.tr.mfa (accessed September 22, 2020).
33. Selcen Öner, "Soft Power in Turkish Foreign Policy: New Instruments and Challenges," *Euxeinos* 10 (2013): 8.
34. Altunışık, "Possibilities and Limits," 43.
35. Just to cite two, "Davutoglu: Architect of Turkish Foreign Policy to be New PM," Middle East Eye, February 12, 2015, http://www.middleeasteye.net/news /davutoglu-architect-turkish-foreign-policy-be-new-pm-2142298220); and Bülent Aras, "The Davutoğlu Era in Turkish Foreign Policy," *Insight Turkey* 11, no. 3 (2009): 127.
36. Ahmet Davutoğlu, *Stratejik Derinlik* [Strategic depth] (Istanbul: Kure Yayınları, 2009).
37. Soner Çağaptay, "The JDP's Foreign Policy: The Misnomer of 'Neo-Ottomanism,'" Washington Institute, https://www.washingtoninstitute.org /policy-analysis/view/the-akps-foreign-policy-the-misnomer-of-neo -ottomanism (accessed September 22, 2020); Suat Kınıklıoğlu, "The Return of Ottomanism," *Zaman* (Istanbul), March 20, 2007, https://www.armenianclub .com/2007/03/28/return-of-ottomanism/; Yasin Atlıoğlu, "Davos Krizi Sonrası JDP'nin Yeni Osmanlıcılık Politikası," BILGESAM, February 2, 2009, http:// www.bilgesam.org/incele/1335/-davos-krizi-sonrasi-akp'nin-yeni -osmanlicilik-politikasi/#.XjdgIS2ZOv4; Ömer Taşpınar, "Turkey's Policies in the Middle East: Between Neo- Ottomanism and Kemalism," Carnegie Endowment for International Peace, October 7, 2008, https://carnegieendowment.org/2008/10/07/turkey-s-middle-east-policies-between-neo-ottomanism-and-kemalism-pub-22209; Einar Wigen, "Turkish Neo-Ottomanism: A Turn to the Middle East," NUPI Security Policy Library Report, 2009. For a comparison of Özal era neo-Ottomanism to JDP era neo-Ottomanism, see İlhan Uzgel and Volkan Yaramış, "Özal'dan Davutoğlu'na Türkiye'de Yeni Osmanlıcı Arayışlar," *Doğudan* 16 (March–April 2010): 3–31.
38. See, for example, "Neo Osmanlı Değiliz," *Takvim* (Istanbul), November 11, 2012, http://www.takvim.com.tr/siyaset/2012/11/11/neoosmanli-degiliz.
39. Hakan Övünç Öngür, "Identifying Ottomanisms: The Discursive Evolution of Ottoman Pasts in Turkish Presents," *Middle Eastern Studies* 51, no. 3 (2015): 416–32.

40. Emel Parlar Dal and Emre Erşen, "Reassessing the 'Turkish Model' in the Post-Cold War Era: A Role Theory Perspective," *Turkish Studies* 15, no. 2 (2014): 268.

41. Dal and Ersen, "Reassessing the 'Turkish Model,'" 269–70.

42. Abdullah Gül, "Küresel Sistemin İşlevi, Yükselen Güçlerin de Katılımıyla Yeniden Değerlendirilmeli," December 9, 2011, http://www.abdullahgul.gen .tr/haberler/170/81488/kuresel-sistemin-islevi-yukselen-guclerin-de -katilimiyla-yeniden-degerlendirilmeli.html?c=584.

43. Abdullah Gül, "Turkey, A Regional Powerhouse," in *Diplomaside Erdemli Güç* (Ankara: Presidential Publications, 2014), 111.

44. Abdullah Gül, "Turkey's Vision for the Future of Europe," in *Diplomaside Erdemli Güç*, 363.

45. Yohanan Benhaïm and Kerem Öktem, "The Rise and Fall of Turkey's Soft Power Discourse," *European Journal of Turkish Studies* 21 (2015): 10–11.

46. Benhaïm and Öktem, "Rise and Fall of Turkey," 11.

47. Abdullah Gül, Speech Delivered by H. E. Abdullah Gül, President of the Republic of Turkey, on the Occasion of the Commencement of the New Legislative Year of the Turkish Grand National Assembly, October 1, 2009, http://www.abdullahgul.gen.tr/speeches-statements/344/56250/speech -delivered-by-he-abdullah-gul-president-of-the-republic-of-turkey-on-the -occasion-of-the-comme.html.

48. Abdullah Gül, "Yurtta Sulh, Cihanda Sulh İlkesini 21. Yüzyıla Uyarlarken," *Diplomaside Erdemli Güç: Dış Politika Konuşmaları* (Ankara: Cumhurbaşkanlığı Yayınları, 2004), 86.

49. Ahmet Davutoğlu, "Turkey's Zero Problems Foreign Policy," *Foreign Policy*, May 20, 2010, http://foreignpolicy.com/2010/05/20/turkeys-zero-problems -foreign-policy/.

50. Davutoğlu, "Turkey's Zero Problems Foreign Policy."

51. Davutoğlu.

52. Ahmet Davutoğlu, "Turkey's Humanitarian Diplomacy: Objectives, Challenges, and Prospects," *Nationalities Papers: The Journal of Nationalism and Ethnicity* 41, no. 6 (2013): 866.

53. Davutoğlu, "Turkey's Humanitarian Diplomacy," 867.

54. Ahmet Davutoğlu, "Turkey's Foreign Policy Vision: An Assessment of 2007," *Insight Turkey* 10, no. 1 (2008): 83.

55. Abdullah Gül, "Yurtta Sulh, Cihanda Sulh İlkesini 21. Yüzyıla Uyarlarken," in *Diplomaside Erdemli Güç*, 87.

56. Zeynep Atalay, "Civil Society as Soft Power: Islamic NGOs and Turkish Foreign Policy," in *Turkey Between Nationalism and Globalization*, ed. Riva Kastaryano (New York: Routledge, 2013), 165–86.

57. Balcı, "Gülen Movement and Turkey's Soft Power," 192.

58. Toktamış Ateş, Eser Karakaş, and İlber Ortaylı eds., *Barış Köprüleri: Dünyaya Açılan Türk Okulları* (İstanbul: Ufuk Kitapları, 2005).

59. Yelda Ataç, "İş Dünyasında Gülen'li Örgütlenme," *Milliyet* (Istanbul), March 21, 2006, https://www.haber3.com/guncel/is-dunyasinda-gulenli-orgutlenme-haberi-58745.

60. Ayşe Buğra and Osman Savaşkan, "Yerel Sanayi ve Bugünün Türkiye'sinde İş Dünyası," *Toplum ve Bilim,* no. 118 (2010), 92–123, quoted in Altay Atlı, "Businessmen as Diplomats: The Role of Business Associations in Turkey's Foreign Economic Policy," *Insight Turkey* 13, no. 1 (2011): 124.

61. Aydın Ayaydın, "ABD ile ekonomik ilişkilerde TÜSİAD-TUSKON Arasında Güç Mücadelesi Yaşanıyor," *Vatan* (Istanbul), October 17, 2010, n.p.

62. Çağıl Kasapoğlu, "Gülen Okulları: 'Yumuşak Güç'ten 'Terör Örgütü' Suçlamasına," BBC News, September 23, 2016, http://www.bbc.com/turkce/haberler-turkiye-37446728.

63. Cemalettin Haşimi, "Turkey' Humanitarian Diplomacy," *Insight Turkey* 16, no. 1 (2014): 127–45.

64. For OECD statistics, see http://stats.oecd.org/Index.aspx?DataSetCode=TABLE2A# (accessed September 22, 2020).

65. Özkan and Demirtepe, "Transformation," 647–64.

66. İpek, "Ideas and Change," 173–93.

67. Alexander Rapis, "Turkish Pillars of Soft Power in Southeastern Europe," master's thesis, University of Macedonia, 2012, 11.

68. Orçun Selçuk, "Turkish Airlines: Turkey's Soft Power in the Middle East," *Akademik Orta Doğu* 14 (2013): 175–99.

69. Elen Huijgh and Jordan Warlick, *The Public Diplomacy of Emerging Powers, Part 1: The Case of Turkey* (Los Angeles: Figueroa, 2016), 23.

70. Bruce Mabley, "Is the World Humanitarian Summit Part of Turkey's Soft Power Strategy?," Open Canada, May 13, 2016, https://www.opencanada.org/features/world-humanitarian-summit-part-turkeys-soft-power-strategy/.

71. İbrahim Kalın, "Soft Power and Public Diplomacy," *Perceptions* 16, no. 3 (2011): 5.

72. Kalın, "Soft Power," 7.

73. Kalın, 10.

74. Yavuz, "Origins of Neo-Ottomanism," 440.

75. Benhaïm and Öktem, "Rise and Fall of Turkey," 30.

76. Benli Altunışık, "Possibilities and Limits," 53.

77. Senem Aydın-Düzgit and E. Fuat Keyman, "Democracy Support in Turkey's Foreign Policy," Carnegie Endowment for International Peace, March 25, 2015, https://carnegieendowment.org/2014/03/25/democracy-support-in-turkey-s-foreign-policy-pub-55096.

78. Balcı, "Gülen Movement," 183–201.

79. Kemal Kirişçi, *Turkey and the West: Fault Lines in a Troubled Alliance* (Washington, DC: Brookings Institution, 2017), 151–80.

80. "The Soft Power 30: A Global Ranking of Soft Power," Portland Communications, 2018, http://www.aalep.eu/global-ranking-soft-power-2018 (accessed October 21, 2020).

81. "The Soft Power 30: A Global Ranking of Soft Power," Portland Communications, 2017, http://publicdiplomacypressandblogreview.blogspot.com/2017/07/a-global-ranking-of-soft-power-2017.html (accessed October 21, 2020).

82. "Soft Power 30," 2017.

CHAPTER IV

Turkey as "Trading State"

The High Hopes for Commerce from the
Boom Years to the Arab Spring

MUSTAFA KUTLAY

F oreign policy activism during the Justice and Development Party
(Adalet ve Kalkınma Partisi, AKP) era has become one of the
intensely debated topics among students of Turkish politics.[1] The
role of trade and investments in Turkish foreign policy is a central aspect
of these debates, as Turkey adopted new policies to use economic linkages to deepen bilateral relations in its neighborhood. With respect to
the role of economy in the foreign policy making process, we can divide
the AKP era into three periods.[2] First come the "consolidation years"
(2002–7); the second we can call the "recalibration years" (2007–11); and
the third the "turbulent years," which broadly coincide with the Arab
upheavals.

In all three periods, Turkish government pursued an ambitious regional
power strategy intended to upgrade its status among its neighbors, particularly in the Middle East and North Africa (the MENA region). This activist foreign policy was built on both structural factors and on choices made
by Turkish policy makers. At the structural level, the relative decline
of the U.S. hegemony and the rise of non-Western powers in a shifting
international order opened up new opportunities for regional powers to
shape their respective regions. In fact, the global diffusion of power and
accompanying rise of emerging economies like BRICS (Brazil, Russia,
India, China, and South Africa) and near-BRICS (Mexico, Indonesia,
Turkey, and South Korea) increasingly rendered the prior international

order void. In a "world of regions,"[3] the "multiregional system of international relations" has become the main level of analysis.[4] As an assertive near-BRICS power, Turkey has pursued multifaceted regional power strategies to increase its influence over the last two decades.

This chapter discusses Turkey's economic engagement policies in the MENA region intended to promote "gradual regional integration" with its neighbors based on economic transactionalism and cultural affinity.[5] Turkey's foreign policy activism, as suggested above, can be partially explained as the functional outcome of structural transformations in a changing international order. As Sandra Destradi points out, however, structure-induced dynamics alone cannot explain divergences in the foreign policy behavior of regional powers.[6] Agency-related factors also need to be taken into account in order to see the main causal mechanisms operating beneath the surface. The AKP ruling elite, in this sense, wanted to reformulate Turkey's regional role in relation to Middle Eastern countries, which, drawing on ideological affinities along with market opportunities, became the main focus of the Turkish foreign policy.

Turkey's conception of its regional role has been framed within the context of economy-driven integration policies—so much so that some scholars have utilized the concept of "Turkish trading state" in analyzing this trend.[7] Richard Rosecrance suggests that states opt to be either a "trading state" that prioritizes wealth through commerce and economic integration or a "territorial state" that relies on military expansion and territorial control.[8] Rosecrance argues that current conditions compel states to develop trading strategies because wars are too costly and the marginal benefit from military expansion has decreased. Trade, in contrast, can be beneficial to all parties, and, in an increasingly interdependent world, the incentives to engage in conflict decreases while those to engage in free trade increase. From an economic interdependence perspective, increasing density of trade networks restrains state aggression, as leaders look for new opportunities to increase the wealth and prosperity of their nations.[9] Thus, the argument goes, a trading mode targeting market integration and economic engagement is likely to be more beneficial than a security-focused, coercive foreign policy strategy.

Kemal Kirişçi has used the concept of trading states in the context of Turkish foreign policy analysis to emphasize the increasing centrality of economic rationales in Turkey's external relations. Kirişçi argues that the transformation of the Turkish economy provided infrastructural power for its foreign policy activism such that a trade-oriented engagement mentality replaced a security-oriented hard power approach.[10] He added to this later by exploring how nonstate actors and transnational economic relations boosted Turkey's foreign economic capabilities.[11] Kadri Kaan Renda built on this work, emphasizing "the significance of the interplay between domestic and regional dynamics and the effects of the unprecedented level of economic interdependence in contemporary Turkish foreign policy" in the context of "complex interdependence."[12] Mustafa Kutlay, on the other hand, problematized the transformation of Turkish political economy in line with the fiscal and financial reforms launched in the aftermath of the 2001 economic crisis. He stressed the restructuring of state-business relations and the increasing impact of the new bourgeoisie emerged in the inner circles of the country as the key explanatory factors in the foreign policy making process.[13]

The relevant literature, however, is silent on a number of crucial questions regarding the properties, limits, and sustainability of Turkey's regional economic integration strategies, especially in the changing regional and domestic landscape following the Arab upheavals.[14] This chapter analyzes the achievements and limitations of the economic instruments as a soft-power tool in Turkish foreign policy. It offers a political economy account that links trading state debates with the Turkish state's capacity to manage ever-changing regional affairs. I argue that regional security dynamics have dramatically changed post–Arab upheavals, and that this means there are imminent impediments to utilizing economy as a problem-solving mechanism in Turkish foreign policy. My premise here is that an in-depth study of the Turkish case might be useful to determine the conditions that shape the enablers and limits of trading state policies. Drawing from the Turkish case, the chapter argues that domestic economic structures and regional security environment jointly determine the success and failure of economy-driven regional integration strategies.

Economic Dimensions of Turkey's Regional Integration Strategy

Several studies appraise Turkey's economic performance during the first decade of the AKP rule (2002–12).[15] A World Bank report published in 2014 asserts that "Turkey's economic success has become a source of inspiration for a number of developing countries, particularly, but not only, in the Muslim world. The rise of Turkey's economy is admired, all the more so because it seems to go hand in hand with democratic political institutions and an expanding voice for the poor and lower middle classes."[16]

The transformation of the Turkish economy in the twenty-first century started with the 2001 economic crisis, which represented a watershed in Turkish politics and economy, not only because it was the worst in the country's history, but also because of the changes it allowed. The ruling coalition government used the crisis to initiate a major restructuring of state-market relations as part of a comprehensive reform package, the aim of which was to "fundamentally [transform] the functioning of the state."[17] The reform program that ensued was both wide-ranging and long-lived; the coalition government that legislated the reform program, in contrast, quickly collapsed, but the incoming AKP government, which took power in November 2002, implemented the reform template in its first term in office without any major deviations.[18] Strengthened by the extraordinarily favorable global liquidity conditions and availability of cheap foreign capital prior to the 2008 global economic crisis, the Turkish economy expanded considerably.[19] In current US$ values, GDP increased from $233 billion in 2002 to $851.5 billion in 2017. In the same period, Turkey's total trade went from $114 to $390.8 billion. As a result, per capita GDP rose to $10,404 in 2014, a threefold increase. Even in constant prices, a more accurate calculation, real GDP rose by 74 percent and per capita GDP by 50 percent—still remarkable growth.[20]

Turkey's economic expansion laid the foundations for a more assertive foreign economic policy. Its strong growth boosted exports and imports, nearly quadrupling its trade volume, and its economic relations with its neighbors thrived. Not content with the transformations in the global order, Turkey looked for new markets beyond Europe. In 2002, almost 53 percent of Turkey's total trade was with the European Union, but by 2017 this figure had declined to 41 percent. Turkish exports to the Middle East, meanwhile, increased from just $3.4 billion in 2002 to $42.4 billion in 2012, declining to $35 billion in 2017.[21] Turkey's trade relations with MENA countries became an aspect of soft power, contributing to its attractiveness in the Middle East in the pre–Arab upheaval period.

Turkey's regional integration strategy in the MENA region relied on two main pillars. First, increased trade connections expanded common interests and created motivation to utilize material gains to help solve regional problems.[22] The underlying functionalist idea was straightforward: even if deadlocks in the field of high politics could not be solved, dialogue mechanisms could still be kept open via the cooperation networks found in low politics (i.e., trade and investments).[23] The idea echoed the main propositions of the trading-state paradigm: trade interdependence was expected to shift regional interstate relations from military competition to a commercial relationship as parties began acknowledging and exploiting their increasing prosperity. As connections intensified and national welfare improved, the assumption was that countries with a trade advantage would be able to project soft-power elements onto other countries and employ mechanisms to inform the preference functions of peer states. Second, the functionalist logic sees nonstate actors such as the business elite and civil society representatives as actors who create new channels of cooperation and potential spillover effects.[24] Their involvement is expected to help overcome decades-long political and ideological disconnect. In this way, a sense of "regional community" could be created, the ultimate goal of which would be to level the political playing field for deeper sociopolitical integration.[25]

Turkish-Syrian relations are a case in point. Syria became a prototype country for Turkey's foreign policy strategy, which was formulated as "zero problems with neighbors."[26] After taking power in 2002, the AKP government planned to use regional integration to create a zone of stability and prosperity, expending great effort to improve relations with Syria. The Turkish political elite urged the Assad regime to gradually liberalize the Syrian economic and political system. The two countries had arrived at an unprecedented level of economic integration in their history just before the Arab upheavals. They had, for instance, signed a free trade agreement, reciprocally lifted visas, and encouraged cross-border movements. Bilateral trade increased from just $773 million in 2002 to a threshold of $2.5 billion in 2010. This went hand in hand with improved political relations, to the extent that the countries created a High Level Strategic Council, modeled on Turkey's relations with other MENA and Balkan countries, that had paved the way for the deepening of Turkey's economic relations with neighboring zones.[27] And then came the Syrian civil war.

Emerging Stateness Problems in Regional
Security Architecture

In the post-2011 period, the regional and domestic political economy offered many challenges to the trading state argument and related economy-oriented explanations. Following the derailment of the Arab Spring, the relatively benign regional security environment in the MENA region was replaced by violent conflicts. State structures collapsed spectacularly, leading to deterioration of bilateral trade and investment ties. At the same time, the Turkish economy faced limitations on its ability to use the economy as a practical hand in foreign policy. The double challenge at the domestic-regional nexus led to a new suboptimal equilibrium that undermined Turkey's regional power credentials.

One issue dominating Middle Eastern politics post-2011 was the stateness problem. The term "stateness" is used to discuss a state's ability to perform its core functions. According to comparative politics scholars, strong states have control over their territory and maintain government authority everywhere—including the sparsely populated and mountainous areas within their borders.[28] Territorial control of a state includes its ability to prevent other states and nonstate armed groups from claiming authority and using force across its borders.[29] A state should also ensure that its citizens are safe and secure from domestic and external threats. Weak or failed states, according to this perspective, cannot maintain these functions.[30] Stateness, as Francis Fukuyama asserts, has two components: first, the scope of state activities—that is, the "different functions and goals taken on by governments;" and, second, the strength of state power, or the "ability of states to plan and execute policies and to enforce laws cleanly and transparently."[31]

Stateness or state capacity is crucial to sustain economic-driven regional power strategies as well. And, after the Arab uprisings, Turkey's regional security environment changed radically: the tumultuous instability that resulted from the upheavals was so great that it seriously jeopardized the stateness of some key MENA countries. Turkey's major economic partners were at the epicenter of these state failures. The protests that erupted in Tunisia in 2010 led to an uncontrollable blaze in Syria, Libya, Egypt, and Iraq, throwing the MENA region into violence and conflict. The growing strength of the Islamic State of Iraq and Syria (ISIS) and several other nonstate violent groups disrupted regional order and political stability. In addition, the protracted nature of the bloody civil war in Syria led to a greater power vacuum and security challenges in the region.

The events in Turkey's neighborhood make clear the extent to which stateness has been undermined, unseen for decades. The catastrophic civil war in Syria led to the collapse of the Syrian state, with almost half a million people dead and almost 11 million fleeing the country. The Syrian economy was also devastated: the World Bank says that "from 2011 until the end of 2016, the cumulative losses in GDP have been estimated at $226 billion, about four times the Syrian GDP in 2010."[32] According to a 2014 UNWRA report, "Even if the conflict ceased now and GDP grew at an average rate of five per cent each year, it is estimated that it would take the Syrian economy 30 years to return to the economic level of 2010."[33] The havoc in Syria, formerly the oft-cited case of Turkey's transformative role as a benign regional power, has had dramatic spillover effects on the Turkish political economy. The once-quiet Turkey-Syria border has seen mass bombings in Reyhanlı and Akçakale, the main trade gates linking the two economies.[34] In addition, according to official figures, more than 3.6 million Syrian refugees are now in Turkey, which will likely have long-lasting sociopolitical and economic consequences.[35] At the same time, Turkey has faced security threats from the expanding power vacuum in Iraq, where violent nonstate actors proliferated and began controlling more territory.

The acute state capacity problems among Turkey's neighbors render previous assumptions partially invalid, as the economic integration policies rely on bilateral cooperation, which requires a certain level of stability and rule-based order. In this new regional security structure post-2011, the ontological underpinnings of Turkey's foreign policy have shifted from *economy-oriented integration* to *military-driven security supply*. The decline in Turkey's trade performance with its regional partners is a clear indication of this trend: Turkey's total trade volume with MENA countries declined to $47 billion in 2018 from around $63.9 billion in 2012 (see table 4.1). The deepening civil war in Syria severely diminished economic activity in Turkey's inner southeastern cities, once seen as the homeland of emergent "Anatolian tigers."[36] Similarly, in Iraq, the expanding power vacuum and rising ISIS threat pushed Turkish-Iraqi economic relations into "total chaos."[37] ISIS militants forced Turkish truck drivers to pay bribes, posing an insurmountable challenge for the more than two thousand Turkish firms operating in the region, as Turkish trucks could not transfer their products

TABLE 4.1

Regional Breakdown of Turkish Foreign Trade (in Millions of Dollars)

	2002	2004	2006	2008	2010	2012	2014	2015	2016	2017	2018
TOTAL EXPORTS	36,059	63,167	85,535	132,027	113,883	152,462	157,61	143,839	142,53	156,993	167,921
TOTAL IMPORTS	51,554	97,540	139,576	201,964	185,544	236,545	242,177	207,234	198,618	233,8	223,047
TOTAL TRADE	87,613	160,707	225,111	333,991	299,428	389,007	399,787	351,073	341,148	390,793	390,968
EU (28)											
Export	20,458	36,699	48,149	63,719	52,934	59,398	68,514	63,998	68,344	73,906	83,954
Import	25,698	48,131	59,448	74,513	72,391	87,657	88,784	78,681	77,501	85,205	80,813
Share in Total Trade	52.68	52.79	47.80	41.39	41.85	37.80	39.35	40.64	42.75	40.71	42.14
OTHER EUROPE											
Export	2,564	4,389	7,748	15,349	11,124	14,167	15,184	14,141	9,736	9,805	11,700
Import	7,478	15,722	25,635	44,091	30,101	37,206	36,367	28,112	21,907	31,381	29,391
Share in Total Trade	11.46	12.51	14.83	17.80	13.77	13.21	12.89	12.04	9.28	10.54	10.51
AFRICA											
Export	1,697	2,968	4,566	9,063	9,283	13,357	13,754	12,449	11,406	11,674	14,451
Import	1,239	2,598	3,910	5,596	4,824	5,922	5,938	5,099	5,356	7,177	7,048
Share in Total Trade	3.35	3.46	3.77	4.39	4.71	4.96	4.93	5.00	4.91	4.82	5.50

(continued)

TABLE 4.1 (CONTINUED)

	2002	2004	2006	2008	2010	2012	2014	2015	2016	2017	2018
AMERICAS											
Export	3,914	5,733	6,328	6,532	6,078	9,623	10,083	9,225	9,345	12,166	12,822
Import	4,065	6,595	9,401	17,224	16,799	20,233	18,894	16,771	16,99	21,009	22,920
Share in Total Trade	9.11	7.67	6.99	7.11	7.64	7.67	7.25	7.40	7.72	8.49	9.14
MIDDLE EAST											
Export	3,440	7,921	11,316	25,430	23,295	42,451	35,384	31,086	31,304	35,337	29,457
Import	2,321	4,269	8,641	13,145	13,011	21,41	20,48	13,575	13,761	19,786	17,858
Share in Total Trade	6.58	7.59	8.87	11.55	12.13	16.42	13.97	12.72	13.21	14.11	12.10
OTHER ASIA											
Export	1,790	2,544	3,942	7,074	8,581	10,575	11,591	10,307	9,684	11,271	12,351
Import	6,530	15,500	25,658	37,616	40,343	49,602	56,162	53,339	54,257	57,168	51,518
Share in Total Trade	9.50	11.23	13.15	13.38	16.34	15.47	16.95	18.13	18.74	17.51	16.34

Source: Turkish Statistical Institute.

to the southern parts of the country—the main transport route for Turkish exporters to Middle Eastern and Gulf countries.[38]

The deterioration of bilateral ties with other regional players has also impeded market potential and thus Turkey's trading state policies. Turkey-Egypt relations are a case in point. In the wake of the Arab upheavals, Turkish policy makers developed a close relationship with the Morsi government and the Muslim Brotherhood—which, following the removal of Hosni Mubarak, started ruling Egypt for the first time in decades. Indeed, the relative success of Islamist actors in elections all around the MENA region made political Islamists believe a new Middle East was about to be born. The overreliance on political Islam as a unifying ideology arguably led Turkish ruling elite to overlook the complex dynamics of Egyptian politics. Bilateral relations reached a new low in 2013 when Abdel Fattah el-Sisi's military coup ousted the Morsi government. Turkey harshly criticized the incoming Sisi rule, denouncing the coup and adopting a much more normative stance than the Western powers, which followed an antidemocratic appeasement policy. The Turkish government ended all diplomatic relations with Egypt and harshly criticized the Sisi regime. Not surprisingly, this die-hard anti-Sisi stance pushed Turkey-Egypt relations to the brink of collapse, with devastating consequences, as Turkey lost its only remaining trade route to the MENA region.[39]

During the Morsi years, Turkey had signed a transit transport agreement with Egypt to bypass conflict-ridden lands; the agreement was later canceled by the Sisi administration.[40] Similarly, the Libyan government "decided to exclude Turkish firms from operating in Libya."[41] Turkish construction firms were projected to lose more than $15 billion as ongoing projects were halted, with no prospect of being recompensed.

Emerging Capacity Problems in Domestic Political Economy

With Turkey's trade relations with neighboring countries suffering, European markets became ever more important for Turkish exporters. However, the crisis in the Euro area and the more aggressive penetration policies of non-Western great powers like China meant that, compared to the precrisis era, Turkey had more competition in Europe. To remain competitive in European markets and compensate for its losses in the

MENA region, Turkey needs to develop industrial policies that improve its production capacity and export performance.

In a changing geoeconomic environment, the second dimension of the state capacity concept, drawing from comparative political economy literature, offers a useful analytical tool to explore the domestic challenges to Turkey's trading state policies. In this regard, states with high capacity, called "transformative states," have the infrastructural power to transform domestic industrial relations in a way that ensures high value-added production that sustains export performance.[42] Transformative states have the capacity to organize their finance capital as part of a comprehensive industrial upgrading closely linked to foreign economic policies. Thanks to the state's market-enhancing role and the institutionalized relationship between bureaucratic actors and economic interest groups, in these political economies the reformation of prevailing institutional arrangements takes place within the context of carefully designed and patiently implemented industrial policies.[43] Because of institutional complementarities, these states are more capable of developing export-oriented industries that let them remain competitive in global markets.[44] Leading trading states such as Germany and South Korea are examples of this high institutional capacity and multidimensional state-market complementarity.

Following the 2001 economic crisis, Turkey developed a robust regulatory framework compatible with the fundamental principles of the post–Washington Consensus.[45] The banking system was placed under strict supervision and surveillance by independent regulatory institutions.[46] The regulatory policies were implemented so successfully that Turkey was one of the few countries whose banking system did not have to be bailed out during the 2008 financial crisis.[47] This shift in its financial system and public finance, however, was not complemented by an industrial transformation strategy.[48] This is where the flawed nature of the trading state argument can be seen, as mainstream debates on the Turkish case have typically been framed within the contours of the regulatory state paradigm. In a benign regional security environment, the government's commitment to fiscal and financial discipline ensured robust economic growth that undergirded the economy-led regional integration strategy. In the post-2008 global financial crisis, however, the Turkish economy has reached a threshold called the "middle-income trap," and thus it seems to exhaust the existing version of trading state policies.

The middle-income trap is defined as the tendency of fast-growing economies to slow down after their per capita income has reached a threshold.[49] Economies that have reached the middle-income plateau find it daunting to achieve high income levels. The World Bank research estimates that only 13 of the 101 countries defined as middle income in 1960 had reached high income status by 2008.[50] The quasi-consensus among pundits is that Turkey has fallen into the middle-income trap.[51] GDP per capita in current prices was stuck around $10,500 during 2010–15 and declined to $9,632 in current prices due to the deprecation of Turkish lira vis-à-vis foreign currencies in the second half of 2018.[52]

Both the middle-income trap and declining growth and trade performance are related to the structural problems of the Turkish economy. The recalcitrant current account deficit illustrates the major flaw in Turkey's economic structure.[53] In the post-2000 period, high current account deficits—which increased from 2.5 percent of GDP in 2003 to a record 7.9 percent in 2013—have become one of the Turkish economy's major structural weaknesses.[54] In fact, the current account deficit is closely linked to the critique offered in this chapter, since it reveals the critical role of industrial upgrading policies in ensuring a sustainable trade performance in global markets.

There are two aspects to this argument. First, the foreign trade deficit constitutes the largest component of the current account deficits in Turkey. Turkey exports mainly consumption goods and imports investment and intermediary products.[55] Since its exports depend heavily on imported intermediate goods, Turkish foreign trade and its energy imports contribute to the current account deficit.[56] In this way, the inadequate export performance is closely related to the poor technological composition of Turkey's manufactured exports. Despite an increase in the share of medium-technology exports from 43.5 percent to 52.5 percent and a decline in the share of low technology exports from 51.8 percent to 45.7 percent during 2003–14, the percentage of high technology exports in Turkey's total manufactured exports is 2.3 percent as of 2017, which is significantly lower than the world average. Thus, a structural change through industrial upgrading is required to break up Turkey's dependence on imported goods and sustain its trading performance in Europe and beyond.

Second, the weak technological composition of foreign trade makes it very difficult to overcome the middle-income trap. Richard F. Doner and Ben Ross Schneider argue that a middle-income country typically "reflects a slowdown in productivity growth as economies exhaust the gains from moving into middle-income status."[57] This suggests that Turkey needs a comprehensive research and development (R&D) strategy to upgrade the production base of the domestic economy, one that goes beyond diversification into new sectors and efficient allocation of resources. The technological upgrading, however, requires not only economic reforms, but also the consolidation of inclusive political institutions that promote power sharing, rule of law, and more and higher quality education to ensure high value-added production.[58] The literature suggests that overcoming the middle-income trap necessitates some degree of political inclusivity and rule-based state-business collaboration, which is critical in the Turkish case.[59] Otherwise, it appears that the Turkish trading state has reached its limit, as it will be very difficult for it to remain competitive and sustain its economy-led foreign policy strategy, given the widespread stateness problems in the region.

The relevant literature supports this argument. According to Håvard Hegre, the trading state approach is especially valid for developed countries, since "there is a clear negative relationship between trade and conflict. However, this relationship is basically restricted to dyads consisting of two developed dyads."[60] It is fair to suggest that Turkey's trading state potential is restricted by developmental concerns as well as difficult regional circumstances. Because Turkish economic interdependence is based on low and medium technology products, partner countries can cut trade ties and obtain these products from new partners with relative ease. It is no coincidence that leading trading states like Germany and South Korea are home to well-known firms that produce and export high value-added products. Thus the debate about Turkey's future trajectory as a regional economic power is closely correlated with its developmental capacity in the coming years.

This chapter offered a political economy account of Turkey's regional integration strategy, with particular reference to trading state discussions. It maintained that Turkey used its economy as part of its foreign policy repertoire to increase its leverage in the MENA region and beyond, particularly during the first two terms of the AKP. The expansion of the Turkish economy post-2001 and the accompanying intensification of Turkey's trade relations with neighboring countries enabled Turkish policy makers to rely more on economy-oriented soft-power instruments. Given this, some scholars have defined Turkey as a trading state in the making, but these arguments in the Turkish context differ from established examples on two grounds.

First, trade relationships in the region tend to be less important than identity concerns and geopolitical rivalries. Turkey's relations with its neighbors in the Middle East and the Balkans clearly demonstrate the role of collective identity. Turkey has traditionally played a dual role in this regard, as the legacy of the Ottoman Empire has informed perceptions toward Turkey—sometimes positively, sometimes negatively. Therefore, trading state debates in the Turkish context must be placed in the context of its cultural boundaries. Second, in terms of its main macroeconomic indicators, Turkey is still a middle-income country with state capacity problems, which makes it difficult to compare it with developed states such as Germany, Japan, or South Korea. Also, the literature suggests that trade bonds among developed countries have a better chance of restraining aggressive state behavior. Turkey and the other regional actors are mainly developing economies, which limits the pacifying impacts of deepening trade ties, especially since the level of institutionalization in the MENA region is rather thin. The shifts in the region following the Arab upheavals have demonstrated that trade relations are just one of the factors that inform leaders' preferences.

Recent developments in the region and Turkey's domestic political economy shifts present insurmountable challenges to this approach. This chapter links trading state debates with state capacity literature to contextualize the potentials and limitations of Turkey's regional economic power. It therefore proposes that for Turkey to revitalize its foreign trade performance as part of a sustainable regionalization strategy, it must introduce an economic framework that emphasizes high value-added production and export structures.

Notes

1. This chapter is a substantively revised and significantly expanded version of a short policy brief: Mustafa Kutlay, "Whither the Turkish Trading State? A Question of State Capacity" (GMF on Turkey Series, February 5, 2016). I would like to thank Ziya Öniş, H. Emrah Karaoguz, and O. Bahadır Dinçer for the opportunity to exchange ideas and collaborate on related topics. Also,

many thanks to Burcu Baykurt and Victoria de Grazia for their valuable editorial comments. For a working paper-length analysis on some of the main arguments about Turkey's domestic political economy dynamics discussed in this chapter, see Mustafa Kutlay, "The Turkish Economy at a Crossroads: Unpacking Turkey's Current Account Deficit" (IAI Working Paper no. 10, April 2015).

2. Ziya Öniş, "Monopolizing the Center: The AK Party and the Uncertain Path of Turkish Democracy," *International Spectator* 50, no. 2 (2015): 22–41.

3. Peter J. Katzenstein, *A World of Regions: Asia and Europe in the American Imperium* (Ithaca, NY: Cornell University Press, 2005); Amitav Acharya, "The Emerging Regional Architecture of World Politics," *World Politics* 59, no. 4, (2007): 629–52.

4. Andrew Hurrell, "One World? Many Worlds? The Place of Regions in the Study of International Society," *International Affairs* 83, no. 1 (2007): 127–46.

5. Ziya Öniş, "Turkey and the Arab Spring: Between Ethics and Self-interest," *Insight Turkey* 14, no. 3 (2012): 52.

6. Sandra Destradi, "Regional Powers and Their Strategies: Empire, Hegemony, and Leadership," *Review of International Studies* 36, no. 4 (2010): 903–30.

7. Kemal Kirişçi, "The Transformation of Turkish Foreign Policy: The Rise of the Trading State," *New Perspectives on Turkey,* no. 40 (2009): 29–57.

8. Richard Rosecrance, *The Rise of the Trading State: Commerce and Conquest in the Modern World* (New York: Basic Books, 1986), 13–25.

9. Robert O. Keohane and Joseph S. Nye Jr., *Transnational Relations and World Politics* (Cambridge, MA: Harvard University Press, 1973); Robert O. Keohane, *After Hegemony: Cooperation and Discord in the World Political Economy* (Princeton, NJ: Princeton University Press, 1984).

10. Kemal Kirişçi, "The Transformation of Turkish Foreign Policy: The Rise of the Trading State," *New Perspectives on Turkey,* no. 40 (2009): 29–57.

11. Kemal Kirişci, "Turkey's Engagement with Its Neighborhood: A 'Synthetic' and Multidimensional Look at Turkey's Foreign Policy Transformation," *Turkish Studies* 13, no. 3 (2012): 319–41.

12. Kadri Kaan Renda, "Turkey's Neighborhood Policy: An Emerging Complex Interdependence?," *Insight Turkey* 13, no.1 (2011): 89.

13. For details of this argument, see Mustafa Kutlay, "Economy as the 'Practical Hand' of 'New Turkish Foreign Policy': A Political Economy Explanation," *Insight Turkey* 13, no. 1 (2011): 67–89.

14. For a critical review of the literature upon which this section is built, see Mustafa Kutlay, "'Yeni Türk Dış Politikası'nın Ekonomi Politiği: Eleştirel Bir Yaklaşım," *Uluslararası İlişkiler* 9, no. 35 (2012): 101–27; and Ziya Öniş and Mustafa Kutlay, "Rising Powers in a Changing Global Order: The Political Economy of Turkey in the Age of BRICs," *Third World Quarterly* 34, no. 8 (2013): 1409–26.

15. See, for instance, Erdal Tanas Karagöl, "The Turkish Economy During the Justice and Development Party Decade," *Insight Turkey* 15, no. 4 (2013): 115–29.

16. World Bank, *Turkey's Transitions: Integration, Inclusion, Institutions* (Washington, DC: World Bank, 2014), 3.

17. Undersecretariat of the Treasury, *Strengthening the Turkish Economy: Turkey's Transition Program* (Ankara: TCMB), 34.

18. For an extensive discussion, see Mustafa Kutlay, *The Political Economies of Turkey and Greece: Crisis and Change* (Basingstoke: Palgrave Macmillan, 2019).

19. Ziya Öniş and İsmail Emre Bayram, "Temporary Star or Emerging Tiger? The Recent Economic Performance of Turkey in a Global Setting," *New Perspectives on Turkey*, no. 39 (2008): 47–84.

20. Mahfi Eğilmez, "Kişi Başına Gelirimiz Gerçekte Ne Kadar Arttı?" *Kendine Yazılar*, October 21, 2015, http://www.mahfiegilmez.com/2015/10/kisi-basna -gelirimiz-gercekte-ne-kadar.html. Due to the rapid deterioration of the Turkish lira vis-à-vis the U.S. dollar in the second half of 2018, the GDP per capita decreased to $9,632 in 2018 in current prices.

21. Data retrieved from the Turkish Ministry of Economy and calculated by the author.

22. For an extensive discussion on this topic, which also forms the basis of this section, see O. Bahadır Dinçer and Mustafa Kutlay, "Turkey's Power Capacity in the Middle East: Limits of the Possible, an Empirical Analysis," *International Strategic Research Organization*, Report no. 12-04, June 2012, pp. 20–21. Also see Mustafa Kutlay, "Economy as the 'Practical Hand' of 'New Turkish Foreign Policy': A Political Economy Explanation," *Insight Turkey* 13, no. 1 (2011): 67–89.

23. Robert O. Keohane and Joseph S. Nye Jr., "An Introduction," in R. O. Keohane and J. S. Nye, eds., *Transnational Relations and World Politics* (Cambridge, MA: Harvard University Press, 1973).

24. Ernst B. Haas, *The Uniting of Europe: Political, Social, and Economic Forces, 1950– 1957* (Stanford, CA: Stanford University Press, 1968).

25. For the concept of "regional community," see also Mohammed Ayoob, "From Regional System to Regional Society: Exploring Key Variables in the Construction of Regional Order," *Australian Journal of International Affairs* 53, no. 3 (1999): 247–60.

26. Ahmet Davutoğlu, *Stratejik Derinlik* (Istanbul: Kure Yayinlari, 2012). Davutoğlu, the former minister of foreign affairs, formulated the "zero problems with neighbors" policy.

27. Ozlem Tur, "Economic Relations with the Middle East Under the AKP: Trade, Business Community, and Reintegration with Neighboring Zones," *Turkish Studies* 12, no. 4 (2011): 589–602.

28. Robert I. Rotberg, *When States Fail: Causes and Consequences* (Princeton, NJ: Princeton University Press, 2003), 2–3.

29. Rotberg, *When States Fail.*

30. James D. Fearon and David D. Laitin, "Ethnicity, Insurgency, and Civil War," *American Political Science Review* 97, no. 1 (2003): 75, 80, 88; Ann Hironaka, *Neverending Wars: The International Community, Weak States, and the Perpetuation of Civil War* (Cambridge, MA: Harvard University Press, 2005).

31. Francis Fukuyama, *State Building: Governance and World Order in the 21st Century* (London: Profile, 2004), 9.

32. World Bank, *The Tool of War: The Economic and Social Consequences of the Conflict in Syria* (Washington, DC: World Bank, 2017), i.

33. Aryn Baker, "Syria's Economy Will Take at Least 30 Years to Recover, Says the U.N.," *Time*, April 3, 2014, https://time.com/48294/syria-economy-30-years -unrwa.

34. Kareem Fahim and Sebnem Arsu, "Car Bombings Kill Dozens in Center of Turkish Town Near the Syrian Border," *New York Times*, May 11, 2013, https:// www.nytimes.com/2013/05/12/world/middleeast/bombings-in-turkish -border-town.html; "Turkey Blames Syria for Border Gate Attack," *Hurriyet Daily News* (Istanbul), March 11, 2013, https://www.hurriyetdailynews.com /turkey-blames-syria-for-border-gate-attack-42749.

35. The UNHCR data are from March 21, 2019, https://data2.unhcr.org/en /situations/syria/location/113.

36. For an in-depth discussion, see Kutlay, "Economy as the 'Practical Hand,'" 67–89.

37. Eniş Şenerdem, "IŞİD'in İlerleyişi Türkiye'yi Tehdit Ediyor," BBC Türkçe, June 13, 2014, https://www.bbc.com/turkce.

38. Ceyhun Kuburlu, "İhracat İçin IŞİD Haracı," *Hürriyet Daily News* (Istanbul), August 8, 2014, https://www.hurriyet.com.tr/ekonomi/ihracat-icin-isid-haraci -26963163.

39. This section is based on Mustafa Kutlay, "Whither the Turkish Trading State? A Question of State Capacity," GMF on Turkey Series, February 5, 2016.

40. "Transporters Worried About Egypt's Decision not to Renew Ro-Ro Deal with Turkey," *Hurriyet Daily News* (Istanbul), March 1, 2015, https://www .hurriyetdailynews.com/transporters-worried-about-egypts-decision-not-to -renew-ro-ro-deal-with-turkey--79015.

41. "Libyan Gov't to Exclude Turkish Companies from Contracts," *Hurriyet Daily News* (Istanbul), February 23, 2015, https://www.hurriyetdailynews.com/libyan -govt-to-exclude-turkish-companies-from-contracts--78718.

42. Linda Weiss, "Globalization and the Myth of the Powerless State," *New Left Review* 1, no. 225 (1997): 3–27; Linda Weiss, *The Myth of Powerless State* (Ithaca, NY: Cornell University Press, 1998). The "transformative state" concept is only relevant to the subset of states that meet the basic criteria of stateness. Stated

differently, in comparative political economy literature these states meet the Weberian template of having the "monopoly of the legitimate use of physical force within a given territory." See Max Weber, "Politics as a Vocation," in H. H. Gerth and C. Wright Mills, eds., *From Max Weber: Essays in Sociology* (London: Routledge, 1948), 78.

43. Ha-Joon Chang, "Breaking the Mould: An Institutionalist Political Economy Alternative to the Neoliberal Theory of the Market and the State," *Cambridge Journal of Economics* 26, no. 5 (2002): 539–59.

44. Alice H. Amsden, *Asia's Next Giant: South Korea and Late Industrialization* (Oxford: Oxford University Press, 1992); Ha-Joon Chang, *Globalization, Economic Development, and the Role of the State* (London: Zed, 2002).

45. Öniş and Kutlay, "Rising Powers," 1409–26.

46. Caner Bakır and Ziya Öniş, "The Regulatory State and Turkish Banking Reforms in the Age of Post-Washington Consensus," *Development and Change* 41, no. 1 (2010): 77–106.

47. Ziya Öniş and Ali Burak Güven, "Global Crisis, National Responses: The Political Economy of Turkish Exceptionalism," *New Political Economy* 16, no. 5 (2011): 585–608.

48. Erol Taymaz and Ebru Voyvoda, "Marching to the Beat of a Late Drummer: Turkey's Experience of Neoliberal Industrialization since 1980," *New Perspectives on Turkey*, no. 47 (2012): 83–113; Mustafa Kutlay, "Internationalization of Finance Capital in Spain and Turkey: Neoliberal Globalization and the Political Economy of State Policies," *New Perspectives on Turkey*, no. 47 (2012): 115–37.

49. Barry Eichengreen, Donghyun Park, and Kwanho Shin, "When Fast Growing Economies Slow Down: International Evidence and Implications for China" (NBER Working Paper 16919, National Bureau of Economic Research, March 2011), https://www.nber.org/papers/w16919; Barry Eichengreen, Donghyun Park, and Kwanho Shin, "Growth Slowdowns Redux: New Evidence on the Middle-Income Trap" (NBER Working Paper 18673, National Bureau of Economic Research, January 2013), https://www.nber.org/papers/w18673.

50. World Bank, "China 2030: Building a Modern, Harmonious, and Creative High-income Society," Washington, DC, World Bank Group, March 23, 2013, https://www.worldbank.org/content/dam/Worldbank/document/China -2030-complete.pdf, 13.

51. Güven Sak, "Turkey Trapped in the Middle," *Hurriyet Daily News* (Istanbul), December 15, 2012, https://www.hurriyetdailynews.com/opinion/guven-sak /turkey-trapped-in-the-middle-36894; Kemal Kirişci, "Getting Out of the 'Middle-Income Trap,'" *Hurriyet Daily News* (Istanbul), February 18, 2015, https://www.hurriyetdailynews.com/getting-out-of-the-middle-income -trap-78488; Sadık Ünay, "Smart Economic Planning and New Turkey," *Daily*

Sabah (Istanbul), June 6, 2014, https://www.dailysabah.com/columns/sadik
_unay/2014/06/07/smart-economic-planning-and-new-turkey.

52. The depreciation in Turkish lira was the outcome of a political rift between
Turkish government and the United States, which imposed sanctions against
two high-profile Turkish government officials after the Turkish government
refused to release an American pastor who was detained in Turkey. Relations
between the two countries were already souring, however, due to "Turkey's
irritation over American support for Kurdish forces in neighboring Syria that
Ankara views as part of a terrorist group." Adam Goldman and Gardiner Har-
ris, "U.S. Imposes Sanctions on Turkish Officials Over Detained American
Pastor," *New York Times*, August 1, 2018, https://www.nytimes.com/2018/08
/01/world/europe/us-sanctions-turkey-pastor.html.

53. For an extensive discussion, see Mustafa Kutlay, "The Turkish Economy at a
Crossroads: Unpacking Turkey's Current Account Deficit" (IAI Working Paper
no. 10, April 2015).

54. Turan Subaşat, "The Political Economy of Turkey's Economic Miracle," *Journal of Balkan and Near Eastern Studies* 16, no. 2 (2014): 152. Turkey's current
account deficit was 5.4 percent and 4.5 percent of GDP in 2015 and 2016.

55. Aysu İnsel and Fazıl Kayıkçı, "Evaluation of Sustainability of Current Account
Deficits in Turkey," *Modern Economy* 3, no. 1 (2012): 45.

56. Daniel Gros and Can Selçuki, "The Changing Structure of Turkey's Trade and
Industrial Competitiveness: Implications for the EU" (Global Turkey in Europe
Working Paper 03, Instituto Affari Internazionali, November 1, 2013), https://
www.iai.it/en/pubblicazioni/changing-structure-turkeys-trade-and-industrial
-competitiveness.

57. Richard F. Doner and Ben Ross Schneider, "The Middle-Income Trap: More
Politics than Economics," *World Politics* 68, no. 4 (2016): 608–44.

58. Daron Acemoğlu and James Robinson, *Why Nations Fail: The Origins of Power,
Prosperity, and Poverty* (London: Profile, 2012).

59. For state-business relations in Turkey, see Ayşe Buğra and Osman Savaşkan,
New Capitalism in Turkey: The Relation between Politics, Religion, and Business
(Cheltenham: Edward Elgar, 2014).

60. Håvard Hegre, "Development and the Liberal Peace: What Does It Take to
Be a Trading State?," *Journal of Peace Research* 37, no. 1 (2000): 5–30.

PART THREE
Brazil

CHAPTER V

Bridge Builder, Humanitarian Donor, Reformer of Global Order

Brazilian Narratives of Soft Power Before Bolsonaro

OLIVER STUENKEL

This chapter analyzes and critically assesses Brazil's soft-power narratives that have, until recently, informed the way it projected itself to the rest of the world. Since it is too early to make any conclusive statements about foreign policy under the Bolsonaro government, this analysis will focus on the concepts that dominated Brazil's soft-power discourse from the early 1990s until the end of the Temer administration (2016–18). In the first section, I describe how Brazil interpreted the end of the Cold War, and the contrast between policy makers' profound ambivalence and the optimism and euphoria that shaped the 1990s in the West. In the second section, I describe how Brazilian policy making elites have embraced and adapted the soft-power narrative to domestic circumstances. In the third and final section, I show how Brazil's attempts to engage globally as a humanitarian donor can best be understood in the context of what it believes its principal sources of soft power were, and how that ended up limiting the impact and sustainability of Brazil's role as a donor country.

When the Berlin Wall fell and the Soviet Union collapsed, more than four decades of great power confrontation—and all the dangers this scenario implied for third parties—came to a sudden end. A new era loomed, and the international space seemed to no longer be shaped by traditional geopolitics, but by global governance made up of a sophisticated web of rules and norms creating greater predictability and platforms to discuss how to jointly address global challenges. Western democracies that adopted a liberal cosmopolitan discourse infused by the specter of the end of history hoped they could help enlighten the few remaining backward societies in the world.[1]

Yet, while the 1990s are often seen as a time of great freedom, triumphalism, and optimism, this overlooks the reality that policy elites in countries around the non-Western world—including democratic ones like Brazil—reacted to the end of the Cold War with hesitation, wariness, and some unease about what an unrestrained U.S. policy across the world would mean for them. Why, Western elites ask, would a country like Brazil not be more enthusiastic about the end of the Cold War, considering its firm belief in democracy and international law? What would a country like Brazil have to worry about, given its long tradition and firm commitment to multilateralism—a commitment that Brazil itself constantly emphasized? The reasons for Brazil's hesitation and doubts in the early 1990s had little to do with nostalgia or appreciation for the Soviet Union or the benefits Brazil obtained in a world divided along ideological lines. Rather, policy makers in Brasília were uneasy partly due to the uncertainty the transition would bring and the cost of adapting to a new global dynamic with a struggling economy shaped by high inflation and the government's recent suspension of foreign debt payments. A still-fragile transition to democracy further complicated matters. More important, however, this wariness reflected a profound skepticism about the capacity of rules and norms to constrain a hegemonic power with clearly articulated plans to reshape global politics in ways that could affect weaker countries' sovereignty and that now conceived of itself as having both the legitimacy and the material capabilities to do so. Located in a region where the United States had actively sought to influence internal politics for more than a century—by no means always to promote democracy and the rule of law—Brazil adopted a cautious wait-and-see approach. The 1823 Monroe Doctrine, originally a U.S. policy of opposing European colonialism in the Americas that was later used to legitimize regular U.S. interference in Latin America, still made close cooperation with the United States a politically risky enterprise for governments in the region, including Brazil. Initiatives that could have provided the United States with greater influence in Latin America, such as the Free Trade of the Americas (FTAA), presented by president Bill Clinton in 1994, were officially welcomed but diplomatically kicked into the long grass by Brazil, even at a time when personal ties on the presidential level were excellent. Fernando Henrique Cardoso and Bill Clinton held remarkably similar worldviews and frequently shared ideas about the so-called third way. However, projects that could have had benefits for Brazil, including greater coordination with the U.S.-American and Colombian governments in the fight against Revolutionary Armed Forces of Colombia (FARC) guerillas, were blocked because they were seen as a dangerous precedent. Brazil's support would have implicitly legitimized U.S. military presence on South American soil in the context of Plan Colombia—a more abstract, but ultimately more important, strategic concern for Brazilian foreign policy makers than instability and lawlessness along its northwestern border.

Outside observers may criticize Brazil's reluctant stance and point out, correctly, that Brazil ultimately benefited from global dynamics in the 1990s, with external developments—the U.S. economic boom, double-digit growth in China, and the absence of the risk of great power wars—helping to consolidate its economy and democracy sufficiently for president Henrique Cardoso to articulate a regional leadership strategy vis-à-vis South America. In 2000, Cardoso organized the first gathering of the region's heads of state. Since most of them had been elected democratically, their meeting symbolized not only greater regional cooperation, but also the beginning of a meaningful conversation about how to strengthen and defend democracy. Debates about Brazil's regional leadership peaked in 2004, when Cardoso's successor Lula da Silva used the somewhat vague concept of "nonindifference" in the context of Brazil's leadership in the UN peacekeeping mission in Haiti. This, the closest Brazil ever came to developing a regional foreign policy doctrine, has its origins in 1995, when President Cardoso successfully overcame hyperinflation and began to discuss ways to deepen regional integration and cooperation on Brazil's terms. Yet, interestingly, successive Brazilian governments did not frame their decade-long leadership of the United Nations Stabilisation Mission in Haiti (MINUSTAH) as promoting democracy. Rather, the Lula government sought to underline its contributions of global public goods at a time when it was intensifying its push for UN Security Council reform, seeking to become a permanent member. Lula's successors, Dilma Rousseff and Michel Temer, only rarely mentioned Brazil's troop presence on the Caribbean island, and Temer decided in 2018 not to accept UN Secretary General Guterres's invitation to send peacekeeping troops to the Central African Republic. Even at the time, the public regarded the mission either neutrally or negatively, and the popular slogan "Haiti is here," frequently shared online, suggested that many Brazilians would have preferred troops to protect citizens at home, rather than in a country few had heard of. Brazil's rise and confident strategy of projecting itself abroad fizzled out in 2013, when large-scale protests and subsequent economic collapse eliminated governments' capacity to focus on anything but political survival.

Yet, even during the golden years before 2013, Brazil never fully bought into the Western-led global liberal narrative inspired either by a Kantian democratic peace or Francis Fukuyama's "end of history." The West's cultural attraction to Brazil was and remains powerful, and the United States (and Europe, to a lesser degree) continues to serve as Brazilian society's cultural reference point. Still, other important narratives—such as the belief that globalization can pose a threat to national interests, and that the state should play a relevant role in the economy (ideas supported by the well-connected and protected economic elite)—made Brazil's experience of the wave of economic liberalization in the 1990s far less disruptive than those of other countries in the region, where in Mexico, Argentina, and across Central America, economic policy makers trained in the United States eagerly embraced recommendations related to the "Washington Consensus."

The negative impact of the Asian financial crisis in the late 1990s reinforced the notion that greater economic interdependence reduced Brazil's capacity to defend itself against global dynamics it did not control. As a consequence, the commonly shared belief in the West that the world was witnessing an irreversible transformation of global order was never fully felt in Brazil. Democracy promotion was never part of a greater Brazilian liberal narrative or an important element of Brazil's mission. Rather, Brazil was and remains suspicious of any pursuit of ideological convergence among states; indeed, the U.S.-led liberal narrative looked strikingly simplistic and dangerous to Brazilian eyes.[2] Brazil did not develop any kind of *mission civilisatrice* or interest in expanding its particular ideological narrative across the world, and it rarely elevated its own success into an ideological basis for foreign policy—even though, as I seek to show below, it did use its temporary success in reducing poverty to justify its humanitarian aid strategy. It also sought to gain international recognition as a contributor of public global goods and to be rewarded for it—for example, by gaining more voting rights at the World Bank or the IMF, or being invited to Middle East peace negotiations, as happened in 2007, when President

Lula was invited by U.S. President Bush to an important conference in Annapolis about the future of the Middle East.

As a consequence, talk of U.S. soft power in the context of a liberal order was always overshadowed by skepticism about the hegemon's actual commitment to these very rules, and cases like the U.S. intervention in Iraq or perceived double standards when dealing with U.S. allies such as Israel or Saudi Arabia made the liberal rhetoric used in Washington, DC, seem disingenuous to policy makers in Brasília. Seen from Brazil, the difference between legitimacy and coercion was never as clear-cut as many Western scholars like to believe, and the United States' swift and sometimes violent reaction to governments embracing alternative models, particularly in Latin America, seemed to confirm doubts about the liberal narrative and its rhetoric regarding democracy promotion.

While the case of Cuba is perhaps most emblematic, Latin Americans also closely followed events in 2009 in Honduras, when the United States did not insist on Manuel Zelaya's return to power after his illegal ouster in a military coup d'état. That, reasoned observers across the region, was partly due to Zelaya's friendliness to Venezuela's Hugo Chávez. While most agreed that Honduras's military had acted alone, a more pro-American president, Brazilian diplomats privately argued, would have had far more support in Washington to return to Tegucigalpa to finish his mandate. This, to them, showed that global rules and norms did not apply evenly across the board. That understanding seemed to be confirmed when the United States was willing to turn a blind eye to the erosion of democracy in Latin America as long as leaders like Peru's Alberto Fujimori in the 1990s or, more recently, Honduras's Juan Orlando Hernandez were firmly committed to aiding the United States' war on drugs.[3]

It often surprises Western analysts when they hear that Brazilian policy makers across the political spectrum, when asked over the past decades about the greatest threat to international stability, pointed not to North Korea, Iran or China, but to the United States. They would agree with Simon Reich and Richard Ned Lebow, who argue that "the United States has violated the responsibilities and roles assigned to a hegemon . . . constituting as much a threat to global order and stability as it is a possible pillar of its preservation."[4] That explains why Venezuela and Cuba, two countries with little soft power in the West but who stood up to hegemonic pressure, enjoyed considerable recognition across Latin America for a long time despite their failing economic models and systematic human rights abuses. How, Brazilian diplomats ask, can we count on global rules and norms when the United States openly considers itself the indispensable nation that saw further than the rest and therefore could break the rules when it deemed necessary? It is because of worries like these that terms like "democracy promotion" remain almost taboo in Brazil until today, and why Western concerns about Chinese "sharp power" are not shared in Brazil. How, if not sharp, did U.S. power feel to Latin Americans during most of the twentieth century? Even President Bolsonaro, who promised closer ties to the United States in a radical departure from traditional foreign policy, early on encountered strong resistance among the generals, who occupy key posts in the government and who were less inclined to align with the Trump administration. While the antiglobalist pro-Trumpian faction spoke about creating an unconditional alliance, with ideas ranging from allowing a U.S. military base on Brazilian soil to supporting a possible U.S. military engagement in Venezuela, both traditional foreign policy elites and the armed forces rejected these ideas.

The demise of the spirit of the 1990s, shaped by Clintonian and Blairite optimism and assertiveness in areas such as trade liberalization, democracy promotion, and nation-building therefore did not lead to the same disappointment in Brazil as it did in many Western capitals—even though many are aware that the United States' retreat from the global stage under Donald Trump also poses significant risks to Brazil's national interest. To some extent, even U.S. scholars themselves recognize that soft power does not, in any way, eliminate traditional hard power considerations. Quite the contrary, soft power serves as a supporting narrative for U.S. hegemony, one that may help make hard power less blatant: "The US is certainly not above using force. It has been at war with one country or another for much of the past century. But soft power has provided a narrative. Many people—though certainly not all—believe America acts out of decent intentions and is basically a benign power. That is quite a trick. China by contrast has had few wars in recent decades. Yet it is generally held in suspicion."[5]

Despite all that, the readiness of virtually all countries around the world to accept the idea of soft power is notable. Hillary Clinton has been called the "soft-power Secretary of State" for fully embracing the concept, and India's former minister of external affairs Shashi Tharoor frequently used the idea to frame India's place in the world.[6] The Chinese government has made soft power a central theme of its foreign policy. Consulting firms have established soft-power indexes to rank countries.[7] Even Russia, seen by many in the West as a country without soft power, has frequently used the concept. In 2014, Russia outlined a new soft-power doctrine called "Integrated Strategy for Expanding Russia's Humanitarian Influence in the World." The plan, according to foreign minister Sergey Lavrov, was to counter "unprecedented measures to discredit Russian politics and distort Russia's image."[8] While Joseph S. Nye Jr.'s initial concept of "soft power" was intimately tied to the emergence of a post–Cold War, U.S.-led liberal order, several countries using the term did not necessarily support that system. Governments in Beijing and Moscow, for instance, may simply have started referring to some of their preexisting foreign policy strategies as soft power, or they have set up a soft-power unit, given the relatively low cost of these strategies, compared to traditional investments in hard power. Russia's attempt to improve its international image makes use of Western tools: it hired Ketchum, a U.S. agency, to design what President Putin officially calls a soft-power strategy. While opposing the West, Russia nevertheless frames its own demands in the Western language of democracy. These acts of mimicry are signs of normative dependency on the West and the inability to come up with any distinct ideological platform.[9] Irrespective of these considerations, it suggests that even countries critical of the liberal order recognized the attractiveness of the narrative soft power helped create. In the same way, embracing the idea of soft power did not necessarily imply seeking to emulate or compete with the United States. Rather, each country sought to loosely associate existing policies with the idea of soft power to improve their image, often directed as much at their own population as at an international audience.

Brazilian Narratives of Soft Power

Brazil was similarly eager to make soft power work for its purposes, and Brazilian foreign policy makers, particularly since the Lula government (2003–10), made the idea one of the trademarks of its foreign policy strategy, adapting it, like other countries, to Brazil's own peculiarities.[10] This implied providing the greatest possible visibility to the country's positive aspects and hiding negative aspects—its extreme levels of inequality, poverty, and violence. Yet, even before that, the foreign ministry adroitly sought to project a positive image of the country to the rest of the world, including during the dictatorship, when Brazilian diplomats attempted to shift international attention away from the regime's systematic human rights abuses by promoting the country's soccer prowess. That said, the term "soft power" translates awkwardly into Portuguese, and it remains an elite concept known only to scholars and diplomats.

In Brazil's official discourse and imaginary before the Bolsonaro election, the country's soft power was, above all, based on its vibrant democracy, multiethnic society, and cultural diversity. In addition, its large size, developing-country status, and ambiguous role vis-à-vis the West allowed Brazilian diplomats to build rapport with or attempt to speak for a remarkable number of different groups. Indeed, no other country was comfortable among fellow G77 members the BRICS, the G4 (made up of aspiring permanent members of the UN Security Council), and the Organisation for Economic Co-operation and Development (OECD), which Brazil now seeks to join.[11]

These elements help explain the vague but persistent belief among Brazilian elites that the country—unlike other large Latin American nations such as Mexico or Argentina—could make a unique contribution to global affairs. That was no recent phenomenon: Brazil not only insisted in being an active participant in the Hague Convention of 1907, where it defended the principle of legal equality of nations, but also played a visible role in the League of Nations in the 1920s. It sees its thwarted attempt to be a permanent UNSC member from the start as one of its great disappointments of the twentieth century. Brazilian foreign policy makers believe the country deserves a seat at the high table not because of what it does, but of who it is—a notion that is so explicitly visible only in China, Russia, India, and the United States, which all believe their exceptionality translates into a capacity to offer a unique perspective on the world. The understanding that Brazil is a "giant by nature"—a phrase found in the country's national anthem—is self-evident to any Brazilian and is rarely the subject of scrutiny; affirmations to the contrary generate an outcry. In 2014, for example, Israeli prime minister Benjamin Netanyahu called Brazil a "diplomatic dwarf," producing a strong public response. The flip side of this conviction, of course, is a degree of provincialism present among the elites, who tend to be unaware of the many similarities that exist between Brazil and, say, Mexico, Nigeria, South Africa, or Indonesia.

To officials in Brasília, particularly of the Lula administration, the idea of soft power and Brazil sounded like a match made in heaven—after all,

Brazil had projected soft power for so long without even trying. This suggests that while the United States may have been the country that most successfully instrumentalized the soft-power narrative (and that, given its material capabilities, may be most closely associated with the concept), other countries, including Brazil, made use of it and, just like policy makers in Washington, sometimes believed their own hype. Brazil's remarkable success produced unforeseen consequences, as when African diplomats visiting Brazil for the first time were taken aback by the overt and structural racism present in Brazil's daily life.[12] They had been convinced by the official soft-power narrative of Brazil being a post-racial, color-blind society.

The conviction that Brazil has significant power of attraction also stems from its profound skepticism of the use of military force, its tireless defense of a particular type of multilateralism—one that is egalitarian in principle, rule-based in practice, and universal in reach—and its conviction that reciprocity is the foundation of international society.[13] Indeed, rather than projecting its influence through military might, foreign policy makers have long sought to define Brazil's role in the world by its embrace of international law.[14] This strategy was born out of necessity: despite its dominant size in South America, the guiding principle of Brazilian diplomacy through most of the nineteenth and twentieth centuries was managing its military vulnerability and weakness.

In South America, this weakness required avoiding the emergence of a regional counterhegemonic alliance. It is no coincidence that Brazilian foreign policy makers actively sought to avoid the fate of Germany, a regionally dominant actor who, prior to unification in 1871, faced neighbors working together against its rise. This explains why, to many foreign policy makers and intellectuals, the closest Brazil has to a national hero is the Baron of Rio Branco, a diplomat who successfully negotiated the demarcation of several of the country's borders in the early twentieth century, and why, despite the limited role international issues play in the domestic debate, Brazil's diplomats are still the country's most revered bureaucrats, and the foreign ministry entry exam is the country's most competitive. Agreeing on the final borders with its ten neighbors without resorting to conflict, along with South America's near-absence of interstate wars in more than a century, continues to sustain the overall narrative of Brazil's diplomatic prowess. Unlike other BRICS members, Brazil's investments in hard power are negligible; while it has the biggest army in the region, it cannot be remotely compared to the large military investments made by countries like Russia, India, and China.

On a broader level, rules and norms-based global governance are often seen as a shield against transgressors. Indeed, the few times that realpolitik trumped Brazil's traditionally principled support for international law—such as when President Rousseff decided not to condemn Russia's annexation of Crimea in 2014—a debate ensued about the damage such exceptions would do to Brazil's reputation and soft power, and to the rules-based system on which Brazil depends. This is relevant because, to Brazilian diplomats, the country's strong support for international law gave more credence to its voice abroad and provided it with additional legitimacy in multilateral fora. While the Bolsonaro government has adopted a different rhetoric vis-à-vis global rules and norms, multilateralism is unlikely to disappear entirely from Brazilian foreign policy making—after all, given its lack of military power, the fundamental logic that international institutions offer the best way for Brazil to project power remains.

This perceived moral high ground historically gave Brazil the confidence to regard itself as a legitimate player on issues that at first glance seem of little interest to it, be it emerging as a major humanitarian donor in Africa in times of plenty (starting around 2005), attempting to take the lead in negotiating a nuclear deal with Iran (2010), or organizing a global summit on internet governance (2014). Brazil's normative entrepreneurship in the aftermath of the Libya intervention in 2011, when Foreign Minister Patriota proposed the concept of "Responsibility while Protecting" (RwP), is a case in point, as it sought to build a consensus between what Brasília saw as an overly aggressive NATO and an excessively uncooperative China and Russia.[15] Even though Brazil ultimately pulled back from the issue, as President Rousseff preferred to focus on domestic challenges, the foreign policy establishment felt reassured by the positive reception of Brazil's initiative.[16] All these examples are notable because they usually were not tied to a specific Brazilian interest (for example, Brazil traded little with the countries it sent humanitarian aid to), but rather symbolized attempts to move up the international hierarchy. Being a participant in Middle East peace negotiations—an issue usually reserved for major powers—was seen as a proxy for being a recognized actor on the international stage. That mattered more than specific strategic or economic interests in the Middle East, which were unlikely to be affected by being a participant in negotiations.

The same is true regarding the RwP. It is not that Brazil had a specific policy interest in Libya during the military intervention in 2011, but that the topic had traditionally been reserved for major powers.

Brazil Donates

Brazil's temporary role as a significant humanitarian donor, from 2005 to about 2011, serves as a useful case study for Brazil's conceptions of soft power.[17] The financial crisis began in 2013 and led to a dramatic reduction of Brazil's activities in this realm, allowing us to assess the rise and fall of the country's humanitarian engagement more objectively, without the excessive optimism that shaped so many of the analyses at the time. The distribution of Brazil's humanitarian aid among different regions varied substantially, even during the years analyzed here. Variations are explained mostly by a small number of big donations to specific countries in a given year. For example, a substantial donation of around $10 million to Palestine in 2007 pushed the Middle East to the top of the table, yet this number fell considerably in 2008 and 2009.[18] The same happened in 2010, when the earthquake in Haiti led Brazil to make a series of big donations, including 40 million USD for the Haiti Reconstruction Fund and 15 million USD. as budget support for the Haitian government. However, the numbers for Central America and the Caribbean quickly fell again the next year. Such volatility was explained by the program's relative infancy, lack of institutionalization and experienced staff, and relatively small size. In 2009, Brazil briefly ranked as Somalia's second largest donor of humanitarian aid, although Brazil has no relevant relationship with Somalia.

In addition to assuming a far larger role in its neighborhood, assertively assuming regional leadership in an unprecedented way—as described above—emergent Brazil identified Africa as a strategic priority. President Luiz Inácio Lula da Silva (2003–10) traveled to Africa more often than all of his predecessors combined, and Brazil has now more embassies in Africa than do established powers such as the United Kingdom. Although Dilma Rousseff, Lula's successor, visited Africa much less frequently, both Brazilian public and private investments in Africa increased substantially during her tenure, with Brazil's Development Bank (BNDES) playing an important role in both.[19] Brazil's focus on Africa served three purposes. Firstly, it provided important business opportunities (and, compared to most of the world's other regions, less competition) for Brazilian companies keen to globalize. Secondly, it helped strengthen Brazil's soft-power narrative as a multiethnic and supposedly color-blind melting pot with strong African elements—a uniqueness that, officials claimed, allowed Brazil to engage with Africa in a more egalitarian way than Western powers could.[20] Finally, the Brazilian government regarded Africa's more than fifty votes in the UN General Assembly as crucial to achieving its greatest strategic goal: a permanent seat on the UN Security Council—a calculus that proved ill conceived, since Moscow, Beijing, and Washington, whose support would have been necessary, demurred.

As its economic and strategic interests around the world expanded, Brazil became a vocal advocate for reform of the international system, while also seeking to obtain more responsibility within the institutions it often criticized for being overly exclusive and lacking legitimacy because they did not provide emerging actors with sufficient space.[21] Particularly during the Lula years, the economic crises in the United States and Europe in the face of rising actors such as China and India helped Brazil develop a narrative in which it was an important element in reforming global order and transferring power to new actors to increase both legitimacy and effectiveness of international institutions, even though the period ended up producing far fewer reforms that many in Brasília had hoped. Brazil's decision to assume more international responsibility on issues like international development and humanitarian politics must thus be understood in the context of this broader argument that current structures of global governance were seen as unjust and that emerging powers such as Brazil desired and deserved a greater say.[22]

Brazil's role in the international development system very much exemplified this transformation. Brazil had turned—along with other rising powers such as India and China—into a donor, even though, remarkably, it still received aid throughout this period. Yet, rather than fully integrating into the system dominated by the OECD's Development Assistance Committee (DAC), Brazil was seeking to engage with other donors and recipient countries on its own terms. Like other "emerging donors," many Brazilian decision makers in the Lula years considered existing structures to be dominated by established donors, which were, they argued, despite claims of universality, fundamentally designed in accordance with U.S.-American and European interests.[23]

This did not mean that Brazil had divorced itself completely from engagement with DAC members and established development institutions.

In many instances it signed trilateral cooperation agreements with established donors (most of them only for technical cooperation) and coordinated with major donors and UN system institutions for the delivery of humanitarian assistance in complex emergencies. More significantly, it joined multilateral initiatives like the Good Humanitarian Donorship (GHD) that it regarded as broad enough in scope and principles to allow for differences between Brasília and traditional donors to be bracketed.

But reasons for not joining went beyond normative considerations and also involved very concrete interest and power calculations. Many in Brasília feared that by adhering to more established institutions the country would be tied by commitments not of its making, and with what was still a relatively small humanitarian program they feared Brazil would lose the freedom to allocate resources where it pleased, reducing the potential soft-power gains of thinking out of the box. For example, as a fully integrated yet second-rate donor, Brazil would have had to follow larger donors' lead and, in times of crisis, the stream of established donors' resource flow. Put differently, signing up to the existing agreements would have limited Brazil's capacity to use its aid program to project itself as a different kind of power, one less concerned with strategic interests than its industrialized peers in the North—a vague and ultimately self-serving connotation common to the concept of "South-South cooperation."

Yet, aside from global governance considerations, the domestic transformation in Brazil—both the fight against poverty and inequality and the emergence of a new middle class—strongly informed Brazilian policy makers' ideas about international development and humanitarian issues. These policy makers viewed the country's own experience—prior to the economic downturn that began in 2014—as a success story that proved that its trajectory contained useful lessons for actors facing similar challenges. In addition, successfully tackling development issues at home (for example, through cash-transfer programs like Bolsa Família) provided Brazil with the legitimacy to engage in the international development debate. According to Brazilian policy makers, this was in stark contrast to OECD countries, who possessed little firsthand domestic experience, and whose policy makers could not relate to the challenges developing countries faced because their countries had overcome poverty long ago. From Brazil's viewpoint, this undermined the usefulness of Western powers' expertise regarding what produces growth (not to mention that their success stories often overlooked colonialism or highly exploitative trade practices).

At the time, this led to criticism abroad. Some argued that Brazil was keen to export its own policy experience but was not receptive to other ideas. The World Food Program (WFP) and some European donors ran joint operations with Brazil, hoping for cooperation in other types of humanitarian projects, but Brazil was often seen as unresponsive to their proposals.

The Brazilian government often framed its engagement as "humanitarian cooperation" rather than "humanitarian assistance," underlining its desire to respect national sovereignty and local norms and rules and avoid a donor hierarchy. This pointed to their belief in the need for reform in the current global governance of development—such as more voting rights in the World Bank for developing countries—and their insistence in avoiding what they perceived as the interventionist undertones of traditional donors' rhetoric. Yet, while Brazil's rhetoric pointed in this direction, Brazil was never, not even under Lula, interested in undermining global order as such. As the Brazilian historian and columnist Matias Spektor rightly pointed out at the time, "The Brazilian establishment does not see itself as a challenger of the global order, even if in its eyes the world remains a nasty place dominated by a handful of powerful nations that will do what they can to keep the likes of Brazil in their place. The solution, it says, lies in piecemeal reforms to mitigate existing inequalities of power. Nobody in Brasília wants to rock the boat—just to make it bigger and more balanced."[24]

The key reason, then, for Brazil's discontent was that it rightly saw itself as having little voice in the system. Why, Brazilian policy makers asked, would we join organizations whose rules we have had little say in making and that we will have little say in shaping in the future? This factor explained far more than did the often-mentioned inefficiency of the system—after all, Brazil's aid project often proved less organized and less predictable for recipient countries than those of established donors.

The notion that Brazil was in a position to avoid the mistakes of established donors was deeply rooted in decision-makers' view of the country's development and relation to the world order after 1945. For many of those charged with setting aid policy in Brasília, the post–World War II order is not an open, inclusive system rooted in multilateralism, but a system defined by big powers who often impose their will on the weak through force, using strict and often arbitrary rules and international institutions that all too often adapt to please their most powerful masters.

It was no coincidence that Brazil emerged as a humanitarian player at a time of great disaffection with the regime's practices and trajectory. In the eyes of policy makers in Brasília, humanitarian grants were a great opportunity. For them, it was not Brazil that was challenging the established international regime, since the regime itself, and norms about sovereignty (with new concepts such as R2P), have changed enormously. In this regard, compared to the conditionalities that at times struck recipient countries as cumbersome and interventionist, Brazil was quite conservative: it wanted to advance human development goals while keeping sovereignty norms in place. Aware of the difficulties that highly asymmetrical relationships cause for weak countries, it packaged its aid in a language of sovereign equality, nonintervention, and mutual respect—a hugely appealing discourse to countries across the developing world.

Brazil's Motives for Humanitarian Assistance: More Soft Power Than Specific Economic or Strategic Gains

Why did Brazil, at the peak of its emergence, become a provider of humanitarian assistance? Because of its new role in global order—and because the government identified providing humanitarian assistance as a means to develop its soft power. This is not to say that it did not seek to use other means to burnish its image, including leading a peacekeeping mission in the Caribbean or organizing large sporting events such as the World Cup and the Olympic Games. The humanitarian aid strategy, however, is particularly striking, given its novelty in Brazilian foreign policy at the time and the missing connection between it and concrete, measurable foreign policy interests.

This becomes obvious when we compare Brazil to other, more traditional humanitarian aid providers. Security is typically relevant for traditional providers of humanitarian assistance, but this did not apply to Brazil. Natural disasters, droughts, or other kinds of disasters can create large-scale refugee streams, which in turn can destabilize surrounding regions. Humanitarian assistance by the United States in Haiti, for example, is at least partially aimed at preventing Haitian refugees from coming to the United States. Brazil, however, was and is unlikely to be affected by instability in any of the places it engages in as a humanitarian actor: it is located relatively far from the trouble spots that were Brazil's largest recipients from 2005 to 2009—Cuba (21.59 percent), Haiti (19.21 percent), Palestine (12.84 percent), and Honduras (10.07 percent),[25] and the number of refugees coming to Brazil has historically been low.[26] Regarding Haiti, however, the opposite may be true. It was largely after Brazil's decision to send peacekeepers and provide humanitarian aid that Haitians began to consider migrating to Brazil (about fifty thousand live there today).

Brazil's humanitarian donor strategy served to project a narrative that Brazil was not only another emerging power, but one that could have a supposedly unique impact, even if that meant implementing an uneven and somewhat unpredictable aid program that was always unlikely to create a lasting legacy, and even when compared to other developing countries such as Cuba, which specialized in sending doctors abroad. The priority was to benefit those places where officials believed they could make a positive contribution while also demonstrating global reach and enhancing Brazil's soft power. This shows that Brazilian policy makers saw soft power as something inherently relational, and Brazil was aware that some audiences would be more receptive to its ideas than others. Brazil, China, and other emerging countries' development model may seem attractive to several African countries, while their low GDP per capita and profound socioeconomic challenges are unlikely to appeal much to Europe.

The BRICS grouping, consisting of Brazil, Russia, India, China and South Africa, is another useful example in this context. While it is seen as an odd phenomenon of little consequence in the rich world, the opposite is true in poorer countries, and many governments—including Turkey, Mexico, Sudan, Iran, Egypt, Argentina, Nigeria, and Indonesia—have expressed interest in joining the group, a clear sign of its attractiveness.[27] From a Brazilian or Chinese perspective, enjoying soft power in its neighborhood and other developing countries may be equally or more important than European or U.S. opinions on the matter, as policy makers in both countries know that it is almost impossible for a poor country to be admired or emulated by rich countries. In the same way, Western analysts often confidently assume that China will never be as attractive as democratic regimes, yet populations in Africa or other parts of the world may not necessarily agree. As Trevor Moss points out, "In many states, China probably is wasting its time and resources when it tries to get people to watch CCTV, piles newsstands with English versions of *China Daily,* or part-funds its Confucius Institutes. These initiatives are doomed to fail in certain contexts. But these same activities can work beautifully elsewhere."[28]

Yet, while the target of the Brazilian government's soft-power initiative was evidently the developing world, Brazil's humanitarian strategy also sought, at least in theory, to have an impact in the West. At the time of economic growth, the country's ambitions to eventually play a central role in international debates shaped much of its policy and served as the main argument diplomats used to secure key resources in domestic debates. This soft-power initiative can be divided into two areas: regionally, Brazil used humanitarian aid to reduce regional fears of an overbearing Brazil, particularly in neighboring countries such as Bolivia and Paraguay, where fears that Brazil can develop into a bully and a regional hegemon had and continue to be visible. Globally, Brazil's goal was to be recognized as an emerging power with influence beyond its neighborhood and, ideally, as a representative of its region, a claim contested by almost all countries in South America and not taken seriously in Central America or Mexico. In several instances, the decision to provide humanitarian aid symbolized Brazil's attempted strategic entry into a given region or market, even though it rarely materialized. This applied to the decision to provide humanitarian aid worth $182,000 after a cyclone in Bangladesh in 2007 or a year later to Myanmar and Afghanistan.[29] Such moves were often largely symbolic, meant to prove Brazil's global engagement, and did not lead to any systematic follow-up. As Andrea Binder and Claudia Meier pointed out at the time, "Rapid economic growth of the past years has given emerging powers new opportunities to contribute to global public goods and thereby establish their countries' leadership—on the world stage, in their own region, with respect to disaster-affected countries, and domestically. Humanitarian donorship is a soft-power instrument that, as many non-established donors started to discover, is an ideal tool for staking a claim in this way."[30]

Providing technical support and helping other countries develop better public policies also legitimized specific domestic policies in areas such as health and agriculture. The Brazilian government systematically touted both "Fome Zero" (Zero Hunger) and "Bolsa Familia" (Family Stipend) as examples that deserved wide-scale emulation abroad.[31] As Brazil's then–foreign minister Antonio Patriota argued, "The success of Brazilian social policy under the Zero Hunger Strategy, which has lifted 28 million men and women out of poverty in recent years, has transformed the country into a global leader in the fight against hunger and poverty. All of Brazil's humanitarian strategy adhered to the same quality standards as its domestic social policy."[32]

When it comes to pursuing tangible economic interests, there was little evidence of any connection between aid and trade or investments. Brazil had identified great political and commercial opportunities in the agricultural expansion in Africa and other regions and considered itself to be in a privileged position to benefit from this moment. At the same time, most aid went to places where there was very little commercial interest. Data on trade and investment support the idea that financial ties with countries receiving humanitarian aid did not increase significantly, and that countries with good trade relations did not get more aid. While this has sometimes been depicted as a genuine altruistic attempt to help countries with development challenges by providing economic resources, critics rightly point out that, in retrospect, the aid program was untransparent and hastily implemented and could have had a much greater impact.

Finally, coexisting with considerations of reputation and material power, there was a genuine moral vision underpinning the move toward the provision of development and humanitarian aid. Brazil sees an unjust international system and an exaggerated concentration of institutional and economic power in the rich world as important causes of poverty and suffering in the Global South. The Brazilian government had a broad notion that new policies could make a difference in terms of development, and that Brazil's situation created an obligation to help reform the system and create a world in which poverty could be tackled more effectively. Given its expertise in agriculture and humanitarian assistance, the Brazilian government argued that it was uniquely qualified to offer "sustainable humanitarian aid," helping countries in the South prepare for future emergency situations. According to official documents, Brazil's overall development policy was "demand driven, untied from conditionalities and non-profit-oriented."[33]

In general, however, it was evident that Brazil's definitions, motives, and principles around humanitarian assistance were in much more flux than those of established humanitarian donors. This also applied more generally to Brazil's role as an emerging donor. Considering that Brazil's Interministerial Working Group for Humanitarian Assistance was only created in 2006, this ought not be surprising.[34] The lack of an institutional framework complicated the articulation and implementation of a clear strategy and partly explains the seemingly random and quickly changing list of countries and projects. Indeed, anecdotal evidence suggests that policy makers were sometimes forced to pick projects very quickly to avoid losing access to available financial resources. A similar logic led Brazil's foreign ministry to rapidly expand its diplomatic missions, though diplomats privately acknowledged that lack of planning would cause organizational difficulties later. This also explains why, despite frequently mentioning Brazil's humanitarian engagement in speeches and debates, the government remained (and remains to this day) remarkably reluctant to share data and has hardly ever implemented any systematic, transparent, and independent impact assessments of its aid projects. As a consequence, very few academic analyses about the effectiveness of Brazil's humanitarian strategy exist.

The ad hoc nature of Brazil's humanitarian engagement explains the high fluctuations of Brazilian contributions in situations that otherwise seem very similar—a violation of one of the most basic rules for humanitarian aid, as recipients need, above all, predictability in addressing the emergencies they face.[35] Brazil also preferred to provide humanitarian aid through multilateral channels, arguing that "this is what recipient countries prefer."[36] Considering the high benefits of multilateral cooperation in terms of aid effectiveness, how can one explain this? As mentioned above, Brazil feared that by cooperating it would lose its independence and capacity to develop its own approach. Given the small size of its aid program, engaging with others automatically meant, to Brazil, engaging on their terms—Brazilian decision makers talked routinely about their fear that participating in multilateral arrangements would lead to being absorbed and becoming insignificant players. Diplomats from established donor countries often responded that Brazil would not have lost its independence, and that UN organizations would have done whatever it took to please Brazil. While this fear may be difficult to understand from an established donor perspective, new players often feel overwhelmed by the complex webs of established rules and norms that leave little room for an independent role in the development debate. From the Brazilian government's view, vast concentration of power on the part of the traditional donors inevitably leads to a system of global aid and assistance that—despite its multilateral guise—is marked by the hegemonic presumptions of the most powerful countries in the international system.

Starting in the 1990s, soft power became one of the most important new concepts in international affairs, intimately tied to the rise of U.S.-led liberal hegemony. The crisis of this project, symbolized by the financial crisis of 2008, the rise of Donald Trump, and the end of unipolarity, diminished its role. While many other countries embraced the concept, as this analysis of Brazilian uses of the idea of soft power shows, and though the concept is still associated with U.S. foreign policy and the creation and defense of the international liberal order, other countries are using it to develop and project their own narratives. And these are not necessarily related to sustaining the liberal order. From a rigorously analytical point of view, this may be problematic. The concept's meaning has become far too broad, denoting different things to different actors. Yet the fact that it has been used by non-Western and anti-Western powers also points to a broader change in the normative debate about global politics, one that goes beyond West vs. non-West debates. The idea of soft power suggests that, irrespective of regime type, there is a broadening consensus that economic and military strength are not the only types of power that matter, and that states must dedicate time and energy to building narratives that make sense to a broader number of actors, both state and nonstate, inside and outside its borders. We see this idea in Yan Xuetong's "moral realism," his argument that China can only become a global hegemon if it can provide "higher-quality moral leadership" than the United States.[37] In Brazil, the government's decision to provide humanitarian aid to countries abroad was not only a means to convince the world of Brazil's ambitions: it was also a way to legitimize and consolidate domestic support for antipoverty measures that were transforming society and that initially did not enjoy unanimous support. The government sought to show that its policies were so well thought out that other developing countries wanted to learn from Brazil—no small thing in a country eager to obtain international recognition and admiration.

The case of Brazil as a humanitarian donor for a relatively brief period of time—after 2013, it practically ceased donations, barring occasional symbolic gestures—allows us to understand how the soft-power concept was interpreted outside the West, and how an ambitious regional power sought to operationalize it. Rather than integrating into a sophisticated international system of rules and norms of humanitarian aid, as Western observers would likely have expected, Brazil sought to engage on its own terms. Established donors often saw this strategy as confrontational, and they readily challenged emerging actors on aid effectiveness and transparency, accusing them of pursuing substandard practices. Yet Brazil's decision not to embrace existing institutions was not really about a fundamental disagreement regarding norms and values. Rather, as a new donor of humanitarian aid with few institutionalized structures in place,

Brazil not only believed it had little to gain from adhering to a complex set of rules that would straightjacket it, but wanted to be able to instrumentalize its policies to build its global narrative. Possibly stupefied by its success (however short-lived), the government genuinely believed that its experience as a developing country that was finally making economic progress gave it a different perspective, one that it could not project through established platforms.

Some criticize Brazil as opportunistic, saying that, rather than making a meaningful contribution, it destabilized the international regime and complicated aid efforts by briefly pouring considerable resources into a few countries in an uncoordinated way. Others respond by saying that Brazil's decision not to embrace the established rules and norms shows how, from the outside, the liberal order does not look "easy to join and hard to overturn," as G. John Ikenberry claims, but exclusive, rigid, hierarchical, and ultimately impractical for new actors.[38] It is highly questionable, however, whether Brazil's approach served it well. Roughly a decade after Brazil's entry into the much-hyped group of "emerging donors" and a commodity boom–fueled economy, a deep political crisis and the worst recession in the country's history dramatically reduced its international role. Brazil's role as a donor remains underinstitutionalized, and the country still lacks adequate training for bureaucrats managing foreign aid projects. If successful, the Temer government's recent decision to apply for OECD membership status implies Brazil's adherence to DAC standards, even though Brazil's economic plight makes it unlikely that it will play a relevant role in humanitarian aid anytime soon. The antiglobalist faction in the Bolsonaro government, which seeks to emulate the Trump administration, is keen to implement a profound rupture by rejecting global governance, but both bureaucrats and the military will seek to contain change. For example, Brazil's participation in the BRICS grouping remains, despite Bolsonaro's fear of China. As in the past, the attempt to build a close alliance with the United States will be complex, because it requires Brazil to help Washington address geopolitical challenges like the rise of China in Latin America and the crisis in Venezuela, two areas where even Bolsonaro's Brazil is unlikely to deliver. In the long term, Brazil's soft-power narrative will continue to be guided by the overarching principle that the country's uniqueness—partly Western, partly BRICS, perhaps soon partly OECD—allows it to make an exceptional contribution on the global stage.

Notes

1. Rahul Rao, *Third World Protest: Between Home and the World* (Oxford: Oxford University Press, 2010), 22.
2. Mehta makes a similar observation about India: P. B. Mehta, "Do New Democracies Support Democracy? Reluctant India," *Journal of Democracy* 22, no. 4 (2011): 102.
3. Oliver Stuenkel, "It's Not Just Venezuela. Central American Democracies Are Under Threat, Too," *Americas Quarterly*, August 30, 2017, https://www .americasquarterly.org/content/its-not-just-venezuela-central-american -democracies-are-under-threat-too.
4. Simon Reich and Richard Ned Lebow, *Good-Bye Hegemony! Power and Influence in the International System* (Princeton, NJ: Princeton University Press, 2014), 37.
5. David Pilling, "China Needs More Than a Five-Year Charm Offensive," *Financial Times*, November 9, 2011, https://www.ft.com/content/12ff0d6e-0abc -11e1-b9f6-00144feabdc0.
6. Michael Hirsh, "The Clinton Legacy: How Will History Judge the Soft-Power Secretary of State?" *Foreign Affairs*, May–June 2013, https://www.foreignaffairs .com/articles/united-states/2013-04-03/clinton-legacy; Shashi Tharoor, "Why Nations Should Pursue Soft Power" (Lecture, TEDIndia, November 2009), https://www.ted.com/talks/shashi_tharoor_why_nations_should_pursue _soft_power (accessed September 23, 2020).
7. See, for example, a study conducted by Ernst and Young, "Rapid-Growth Markets Soft Power Index—Spring 2012," https://www.ey.com/Publication /vwLUAssets/Rapid-growth_markets:_Soft_power_index/$FILE/Rapid -growth_markets-Soft_Power_Index-Spring_2012.pdf (accessed September 23, 2020); and Victoria Berry, ed., *Country Brand Index 2012–13* (London: Future Brand, 2013), https://mouriz.files.wordpress.com/2013/02/cbi-future brand-2012-13.pdf (accessed September 23, 2020).
8. Matt Robinson, "In Fight for Influence, Russia Can Play Good Cop Too," Reuters, November 30, 2014, http://www.reuters.com/article/2014/11/30/us -europe-russia-influence-insight-idUSKCN0JE07I20141130.
9. Viatcheslav Morozov, *Russia's Postcolonial Identity: A Subaltern Empire in a Euro-centric World* (London: Palgrave 2015), 119.
10. Celso Amorim, "Hardening Brazil's Soft Power," Project Syndicate, July 16, 2013, https://www.project-syndicate.org/commentary/a-more-robust-defense -policy-for-brazil-by-celso-amorim?barrier=accesspaylog.
11. Oliver Stuenkel, "Brazil's Foreign Policy Isn't Dead. It's Just Hibernating," *Americas Quarterly*, November 9, 2017, http://www.americasquarterly.org /content/brazils-foreign-policy-hibernating.
12. Interviews conducted with African diplomats in Brazil, 2015–18.

13. Oliver Stuenkel and Marcos Tourinho, "Regulating Intervention: Brazil and the Responsibility to Protect, Conflict, Security & Development," *Post-Western World*, June 30, 2014, 379–402.

14. This does not mean Brazil's foreign policy is more principled than that of other countries. For example, it strategically decided not to criticize Russia after the annexation of Crimea in 2014 and remained neutral during growing tensions between Russia and the West in the aftermath of the poisoning of Sergei and Yulia Skripal in Salisbury, UK, in 2018.

15. Marcos Tourinho, Oliver Stuenkel, and Sarah Brockmeier, "'Responsibility while Protecting': Reforming R2P Implementation," *Global Society* 30, no. 1 (2016): 134–15.

16. While the concept influenced global debates about norms of intervention for several months, there were virtually no repercussions at home, as the public generally pays little attention to foreign policy, unless it directly influences Brazil in a visible way—for example, the refugee crisis in Venezuela.

17. Some of the analyses presented here are based on research conducted with my colleague Eduardo Achilles Mello on Brazil's role as a humanitarian donor.

18. See Claudia Meier and C. S. R. Murthy, "India's Growing Involvement in Humanitarian Assistance" (Global Public Policy Institute [GPPi] Research Paper no. 11, March 2011, 1–47), https://www.alnap.org/system/files/content/resource/files/main/meier-murthy-2011-india-growing-involvement-humanitarian-assistance-gppi.pdf (accessed September 23, 2020); and Khalid Al-Yahya and Nathalie Fuster, "Saudi Arabia as a Humanitarian Donor: High Potential, Little Institutionalization" (GPPi Research Paper no. 14, March 2011, 1–35), https://www.gppi.net/media/al-yahya-fustier_2011_saudi-arabia-as-humanitarian-donor_gppi.pdf (accessed September 23, 2020). Compared to other countries, Saudi Arabia donated 21 million USD to Palestine in 2005, $3 million in 2006, and $26 million in 2009; and India donated 2.5. million USD in 2006, $2 million in 2008, and $1 million in 2009.

19. *Balanço de Política Externa: 2003–2010* (Brasília: Brasília Ministry of External Relations, 2011).

20. The fact that Brazil's diplomatic corps is overwhelmingly white, reflecting the profound racial inequality in Brazilian society, made that claim somewhat less convincing.

21. Andrew Hurrell, "Brazil and the New Global Order," *Current History* 109, no. 724 (2010): 60–68.

22. Hurrell, "Brazil and the New Global Order," 60–68.

23. Veronique de Geoffroy and Alain Robyns, "Emerging Humanitarian Donors: The Gulf States," Humanitarian Aid on the Move #3, Group URD, September 2009, https://www.urd.org/en/review-hem/emerging-humanitarian-donors-the-gulf-states/ (accessed September 23, 2020).

24. Matias Spektor, "A Place at the Top of the Tree," *Financial Times*, February 22, 2013, https://www.ft.com/content/9c7b7a22-7bb9-11e2-95b9-00144feabdc0.

25. Marcos Antonio Macedo Cintra, ed., "Cooperação brasileira para o desenvolvimento internacional: 2005–2009," Institute of Applied Economic Research (IPEA), December 22, 2010, http://www.ipea.gov.br/portal/images/stories/PDFs/Book_Cooperao_Brasileira.pdf.

26. Oliver Stuenkel, "Temer and Refugees in Brazil: Off the Mark," *Americas Quarterly*, September 29, 2016, https://www.americasquarterly.org/article/temer-and-refugees-in-brazil-off-the-mark/.

27. Oliver Stuenkel, *The BRICS and the Future of Global Order* (Lanham, MD: Lexington, 2015), 37.

28. Trefor Moss, "Soft Power? China Has Plenty," *Diplomat*, June 4, 2013, http://thediplomat.com/2013/06/soft-power-china-has-plenty/.

29. *Relatório de Assistência Humanitária Coordenação-Geral de Ações Internacionais de Combate à Fome, 2006–2009* (Brasília: Ministry of External Relations, 2010), 17–23.

30. Andrea Binder and Claudia Meier, "Opportunity Knocks: Why Non-Western Donors Enter Humanitarianism and How to Make the Best of It," *International Review of the Red Cross* 93, no. 884 (2012): 1135–49.

31. While there is no clear consensus about the success of Fome Zero, Bolsa Familia is still largely seen as a highly effective cash-transfer program.

32. *International Humanitarian Cooperation*.

33. Ruy Nogueira, "South-South and Triangular Cooperation: The Brazilian Experience" (presentation at ECOSOC High-Level Symposium, Cairo, January 19–20, 2008), http://www.un.org/en/ecosoc/newfunct/pdf/brazil_ssc_cairo.pdf. It must be noted here, however, that Western humanitarian aid is also generally free of conditionalities.

34. *International Humanitarian Cooperation*.

35. See, for example, Oya Celasun and Jan Walliser, "Predictability of Aid: Do Fickle Donors Undermine Economic Development?" (paper presented at the Forty-Sixth Panel Meeting of Economic Policy in Lisbon, October 19–20, 2007), http://siteresources.worldbank.org/INTPRS1/Resources/Thematic-Workshops/Celasun_Walliser_AidPredictability.pdf.

36. *International Humanitarian Cooperation*.

37. Yan Xuetong, "How China Can Defeat America," *New York Times*, November 20, 2011, https://www.nytimes.com/2011/11/21/opinion/how-china-can-defeat-america.html.

38. John Ikenberry, *Liberal Leviathan: The Origins, Crisis, and Transformation of the American World Order* (Princeton, NJ: Princeton University Press, 2011), 9.

CHAPTER SIX

Lula's Assertive Foreign Policy

Soft Power or Dependency?

FERNANDO SANTOMAURO AND JEAN TIBLE

Peripheral Condition and Brazilian Power:
Soft and Hard

Since the mid-1990s, Brazil, the largest country in Latin America, has made sporadic attempts at regional leadership. However, under the Lula government (2003–10), these efforts were ramped up as Brazil became much more vocal in advocating for the regional interests of South America in international organizations, regularly contributed to humanitarian efforts outside the region, and took on a more active role in global policy overall. Brazil's newly found capacity to effect change in international affairs together with its rising prominence in global markets stood in stark contrast to its previous history, which was largely defined by its peripheral status, as a so-called underdeveloped country at the mercy of the North.

500 Years of Periphery, by Brazilian career diplomat Samuel Pinheiro Guimarães, is one of the most striking works on Brazil's international relations.[1] Published in 1999, the book argues that Brazil's peripheral condition is a five-century-old phenomenon. Guimarães's thesis echoes many debates arising in the second half of the twentieth century about how to characterize the country's connections with the world .[2]

As the country went through a series of political, economic, and social reforms in the late 1990s, it seemed to move away from the periphery, not that it was at all clear where it was headed. Was Brazil now a semi-industrialized,

[153]

mid-size power, an emerging country? Or only an intermediate one? Would it be only a large peripheral state with a wide, but not deep, emerging market, or would it emerge as a leading regional power? [3]

This chapter examines Brazil's rising reputation in international affairs from the perspective of what looked like its transition from periphery to core. It then analyzes in what ways Brazil's international liberalization was marred by what we call the country's hovering illiberal clouds, such as ongoing dependency on international financial markets, the influence of oligarchical families inside the political establishment, and lingering corruption in Brazilian bureaucracy.

Whereas Brazil's industrialization only haphazardly reduced its overall dependency on international capitalism over most of the twentieth century, what we call a multilateralization of Brazil's international relations took place with a certain systematicity. Political leaders began to question the automatic alignment with the United States, searching for new regional and institutional spaces beyond traditional relationship, especially by participating more and more in international organizations. In spite of having been economically dependent, technologically uncompetitive, and militarily weak, Brazil had employed soft power in foreign policy strategy since its independence in 1822. Indeed, the country was in many respects a "permanent diplomatic state," operating according to a set of norms and attitudes: since independence (except in the 1850–70 period), it was notable for its pledge to maintain peace among peoples, its noninterventionism and nonviolent conflict resolution, its defense of the sovereign equality of nations, and its respect for international law.[4] Having become intrinsic to the country's international behavior, these practices remained constants despite changes and inflections in foreign policy. And they became tenets of diplomatic practice: both to foster "improvement in diplomats' training and negotiating capacity" and in the "effort to construct the singular image of the country as . . . a bridge between the richer and the poor."[5]

According to official narratives, the diplomat Baron di Rio Branco was the first incarnation of this diplomatic tradition, a soft power avant la lettre.[6] Before he came on the scene, from the time of the Treaty of Tordesillas, which defined the lands of the new world between Portugal and Spain, the territorial space of Brazil had been gigantic but ill-defined Luso-Brazilian geoimaginary imperialism.[7] His youth saw the War of the Triple Alliance (1865–70), which banded together the empire of Brazil with Argentina and Uruguay against Paraguay in Latin America's bloodiest war. But it was his negotiation over Acre with Bolivia, which required both troops and diplomatic skill, that eventually won for Brazil 300,000 km^2 of territory, four times the size of Portugal, and while minister of foreign affairs from 1902–12, he oversaw Brazil's "peaceful expansion," prevailing in international disputes against Argentina, Bolivia (playing the interests of U.S. citizens and corporations during the rubber boom), and Peru. To argue that Brazil only used its negotiating skills in Latin America would be far from the truth. During the military dictatorship between 1964 and 1985, ideologues put forward the idea of "Brazil as a power."[8] As the recent Truth Commission revealed, Brazilian diplomats actively supported the coup that toppled Chilean president Salvador Allende in 1973.[9]

The "Brazilian prestige diplomacy" tradition, which consisted of searching for a noninterventionist international posture and using dialogue and partnerships as the main tools for achieving international interests, prevailed once the twenty-one years of a military dictatorship (1964–85) ended.[10] Brazil's search for a foreign policy image consistent with redemocratization in domestic affairs was consolidated formally in the 1988 Constitution, which framed Brazilian foreign policy as peace-seeking, embracing the active pursuit of global human rights, settling negotiations in multilateral forums, and prioritizing Latin American integration. Nuanced differences aside, this new agenda continued through the Nova República governments (those following the end of the civil-military dictatorship in 1985) and gained a new impetus from the government of Luiz Inácio Lula da Silva (2003–10).

An Assertive Foreign Policy for an Emerging Power

The presidential victory in 2003 of Luiz Inácio Lula da Silva, a former factory worker, brought about a new domestic politics that combined a prudent economic policy with a minimum welfare state, promising unprecedented economic growth and a decrease in social inequality. It also offered a new frame for foreign policy, boldly proposing new Global South alliances via cooperative and solidarity initiatives while simultaneously supporting the growth of Brazilian corporations abroad. This significantly changed the way the country was perceived internationally: since 2003 and Lula's election, Brazil has begun to be perceived as an emerging power. This was a stark departure from the previous Cardoso government, when minister of foreign affairs Luiz Felipe Lampreia said that "Brazil cannot want to be more than it is . . . , Brazil has a role adequate to its size . . . , it cannot be more than it is, not least because it has a number of limitations, the main one being its social deficit."[11] More dependency than development: Lampreia's tenure was marked by an endless pursuit for credibility with the United States and other major economic actors, with special attention to the financial markets. The privatization of strategic sectors including the world's largest mining company (Vale do Rio Doce), the core steel industry (Companhia Siderúrgica Nacional), and telecommunications all took place in that era, in perfect alignment with the Washington Consensus economic playbook.

The tone drastically changed with the Lula government, which reinterpreted the autonomist policies of the twentieth century, including the independent foreign policy (1961–64) that was interrupted by the 1964 civil-military coup, and the "Ecumenical and Responsible Pragmatism" foreign policy (1974–79). The latter, developed during the dictatorship by minister Azeredo da Silveira, asserted that a country's power does not originate from material wealth, but is rather an act of creation.[12] In a democratic context with a commitment to fighting social inequalities, the foreign policy of the Lula da Silva government recaptured those motivations. Celso Amorim, the foreign minister during the Lula years, defined this policy as active and unsubmissive, while Lula declared the creation of a new economic and political geography.[13]

The influence of Samuel Pinheiro Guimarães, who became Lula's foreign affairs general secretary in 2006, can easily be seen in the changes in Brazilian foreign policy. The international system's main characteristic is the military, technological, economic, and ideological disparity between countries. Brazil was now perceived to be a country of extraordinary potential. In the early twenty-first century only three countries appeared on the lists of largest countries by population, territory and GDP: the United States, China, and Brazil. A tapestry reproduction in Amorim's office at the time showed a radically different world map: Africa and Brazil were displayed in the north, while countries traditionally called Northern were in the south. The map symbolized a country fighting for a new world order and a new narrative. This rebellious perspective created new political spaces for action, as Brazil was no longer going to accept its intended and subordinated place within the traditional postcolonial global arrangements.

Between the changes in domestic politics (social policies, support for the internal market, new alliances) and economic growth (commodity boom in line with China's rising), Brazil gained a new kind of prestige based on its reduction of inequalities in the world's most unequal country, growth in social mobility, and a substantial reduction in Amazon rain forest devastation. We should also mention the unique trajectory of President Lula, who came from rural poverty and became a metalworker, then a union leader, and eventually the founder of an important political party, inspiring a kind of "Brazilian dream." His main policy agenda, "Bolsa Família," or family fund, lifted more than thirty-five million people out of poverty in just the seven years from 2003 to 2010. Other inclusive social policies included the biggest popular housing program in the country's history, an unprecedented proliferation of public universities, a new kind of economic micropolitics (rural and urban credits for the poor and working class), and cultural policies. All of these changes produced a symbolic revolution, in which a new subjectivity began taking shape. Lulismo, as it came to be known, produced or contributed to an expansion of possibilities of life, perspectives in struggle, and even existential horizons.[14]

It was within this context that the country's "assertive foreign policy" emerged.[15] Its innovation came from prioritizing South American regional integration and the diversification of Brazil's relationships. Another inventive aspect was the protocol of autonomy and development, in which Brazil acted as a South American regional power, thereby inserting itself into international debates in a propositional, independent way. In 2005, in Mar del Plata, Argentina, a decisive shift took place: an alliance of Brazil, Venezuela, and Argentina defeated a U.S. proposal for a Free Trade Area of the Americas (FTAA). This victory paved the way for Brazil's foreign policy priority: South American integration with the support of the Mercosur and the creation of the Union of South American Nations (UNASUR) and the Community of Latin American and Caribbean States (CELAC), which sought to build and consolidate a new integration model for the region—economically, financially, politically, and even physically, via infrastructures and energy. These principles also manifested themselves in new bilateral relations with Bolivia and Paraguay. After the nationalization of Bolivian refineries, the government renegotiated gas sales contracts with the Brazilian market, resulting in relatively fairer conditions for Bolivian and Paraguayan energy sales from the Itaipu hydroelectric plant. The creation of the Mercosur Structural Convergence Fund (FOCEM) was another example of the country's efforts for regional cooperation, with Brazil and Argentina making major contributions to finance projects that mainly benefited Paraguay and Uruguay, in an effort to correct internal asymmetries between its members.

Brazil also showed greater political engagement beyond the region by building innovative alliances and prioritizing South-South relations. The main milestone of this new assertive policy was Brazil's public posture when it refused to participate in the Iraq War in 2003. Lula instead launched his proposal for a global war against hunger and called attention to the creation of an international fund to combat misery and hunger (with support from France and other countries).[16]

These actions propelled Brazil into an active role in multilateral forums such as the creation of the G-20 at the WTO (to tie issues of development to trade decisions) and the upgrade of the financial G-20, which became, for a while, the main forum for global macroeconomic coordination and debate. In April 2010, Brazil hosted the IBSA (India, Brazil, and South Africa) Dialogue Forum, and BRIC (Brazil, Russia, India, and China) meetings in Brasília. These meetings marked how much had changed in a short time, and the fact that, "for the first time in its history, Brazil regards itself, and is internationally regarded, as not only an emerging or rising regional power (in South America, if not Latin America), but also an emerging or rising global power—or at least a regional power with global influence and aspirations."[17] Those actions helped the country participate in and create new spaces and multilateral forums and redesign international organizations that had traditionally been dominated by the central powers, from the small changes in the IMF to the participation in humanitarian operations, such as the United Nations Stabilisation Mission in Haiti (MINUSTAH).

A discursive shift in South-South cooperation took place with Brazil's increased interest in the African continent, based on the belief that "for each African problem, there is a Brazilian solution."[18] Focusing on three areas—agriculture, health, and education—Lula sent thirty-three official missions to the African continent between 2003 and 2010, including the opening in Ghana of an Embrapa office (agricultural research company) and in Mozambique of a Fiocruz office (public health agency) office. Nineteen embassies were opened or reopened, trade increased sevenfold, and the continent absorbed 60 percent of the Brazilian Cooperation Agency (ABC) budget during this time period. This bigger political and diplomatic representation had immediate commercial results, as Brazilian-African commercial relationships increased by 410 percent.[19] This happened concomitantly—provoking tensions—with a process of internationalization of Brazilian companies in oil, mining, infrastructure, and agriculture. The Brazilian discourse mixed "moral duty" (solidarity) with "strategic necessity" (interests) in these relations and brought a critical perspective based on demand-driven principles and principles of horizontality and nonconditionality to traditional forms of aid.

The country also opened unprecedented fronts for Brazilian soft power via technical and humanitarian cooperation by joining the Food and Agriculture Organization of the United Nations (FAO-UN) to implement food security programs in Africa via its own office, Embrapa. Brazil financed technical cooperation programs on urban planning, solid waste management, and participatory budgeting in African and Haitian cities, moving from being a receiver country to being a donor (even as it still received funding). Brazilian funding for development skyrocketed from $158 million in 2003 to $923 million in 2010, covering a wide range of technical, educational, technological, and humanitarian cooperation projects, peace operations, and contributions to international organizations.[20] Humanitarian cooperation leapt from $488,000 in 2005 to $161 million in 2010.[21] Brazil also "accelerated its engagement with South-South cooperation activities, even if the size and scale of Brazilian IDC are not large by OECD's Development Assistance Committee standards."[22] Added to that are Brazilian National Development Bank (BNDES) loans (for the activities of Brazilian companies, mainly in Angola), cooperation by subnational entities, and the cancellation of debts (of Mozambique, for example).[23]

According to Barbosa, Narciso, and Biancalana, Lula's foreign policy in Africa had three immediate goals: conducting South-South diplomacy to strengthen his global leadership, getting Brazil onto the UN Security Council, and advancing its biodiesel agenda (especially ethanol as an alternative to oil).[24] According to APEX and the Ministry of Development, Industry, and Foreign Trade, in 2000, Brazil exported goods and services worth close to $1.3 billion to Africa, while in 2015, under president Dilma Rousseff, Brazilian exports to the African continent were worth $8.2 billion.[25] Imports also rose significantly during this period. In 2000, the country imported close to $2.9 billion worth of products from the African continent, raising these imports to over $17 billion in 2014.[26] Even more impressive is the overall growth of Brazilian exports during the 2000s, especially compared with the 1990s, plus the percentage of this growth attributable to Africa. The main growth in Brazilian exports to Africa was in the sugar (cane, beet, and sucrose), meat, and grain sectors. The products imported from Africa in the same period were either petroleum derivatives or related to the petrochemical industry overall.

After Lula left office, Brazil's humanitarian cooperation was discontinued without having produced demonstrable or lasting results; henceforth, the political legacies were limited to issues like lack of transparency, demands for greater social participation, a growing popular disbelief in political institutions, and the absence of specific legislation about cooperation. Still, the Brazilian rhetoric gave rise to some enduring concepts of diplomacy based on ideas of mutual benefit and solidarity that mobilized social imaginaries of a shared history of colonialism, the slave trade, common ancestors and language, and commitment to liberation and democracy—horizontal and demand-driven cooperation as an alternative to the traditional one-way North-South cooperation model. Yet this new model had its own contradictions. The ProSavana project, for instance, managed by Brazil, Mozambique, and Japan since 2009, and the Mais Alimentos program, both aimed at boosting the productive capacity of smallholder farmers in Mozambique. While the Mozambican government actively supports such projects, some members of the local civil society of Mozambique, particularly the National Union of Farmers (UNAC), have had doubts about the impact of these programs on social inclusion and environmental sustainability. Some Brazilian associations also lent their solidarity to African initiatives, as they faced similar difficulties in Brazil in confronting the political and economic strength of agribusiness.[27] Beyond those local challenges, Brazil's volume of resources is very low compared to China and other countries. Further, despite significant increases during the Lula da Silva government, the country still lacks a coherent diplomatic structure and a sufficient number of diplomats around the world. Brazil earned an unprecedented position internationally between 2003 and 2010, but its new reputation also revealed a significant gap between the country's rhetoric—of a new commercial expansion, for example—and concrete possibilities, say, for regularizing relations with the African continent or an effective South American regional integration.

An Assertive Foreign Policy Inhibited

Perhaps the height of Brazilian soft or possible power was when the country was picked to host the 2014 World Cup and the 2016 Olympics. These events symbolized Brazil's new position as a country with one of the best reputations and highest prestige in the international community.[28]

It is within this context that we should examine Brazil's and Lula's insistence on seeking UN reform along with demanding a permanent seat for Brazil on the Security Council and victories in the World Trade Organization (WTO) panels on issues such as U.S. cotton subsidies and FAO and WTO elections. One of the key actors in this period, then–foreign minister Celso Amorim, refers to Brazil as the "crossover—of an inhibited 'mid-size power' confined to its own region—to the status of a global actor, recognized and encouraged by a great variety of countries that interact with us."[29] Other experts define Brazil as an "emerging power,"[30] or an "atypical global power," since the country lacks nuclear power and a strong conventional arsenal.[31] But, in Amorim's eyes, it is a country that is friendly toward all. Under Amorim, Brazil made three daring moves. First, along with Turkey, it played an active role in the Tehran Declaration, "the first time [Brazil] intervened in a negotiation far away from its immediate regional zone of interest, involving a nuclear agenda and all the world's great powers. The message was clear: Brazil wants to be a global power and will use its influence to help shape the world."[32] The Tehran Declaration of May 17, 2010, cosigned by Turkey and the Islamic Republic of Iran, provided for the exchange of enriched uranium to promote peaceful nuclear activities. True, this was completed according to the terms stipulated by the Vienna Group, which comprised the United States, Russia, France, and the International Atomic Energy Agency (IAEA). However, it overcame the impasse in negotiations that had begun the previous year and was interrupted by the Iranian government.

How did Turkey and Brazil achieve what the Vienna Group failed to do? Celso Amorim explains that the two—both countries of the "developing world"—already had good relations with Iran, and neither of them possessed nuclear weapons. On several occasions, Lula stated that what he advocated for Iran was what he wanted for Brazil: the right to nuclear energy for civilian purposes. Thus, Brazil did not accuse Iran of having a priori belligerent intentions and defended Iran's right to enrich uranium as well as the IAEA inspectors' right to ensure that regulations were being complied with. The decisive feature was restoring trust, which, in turn, would ensure future discussions.

Brazil's second daring attempt to join the A-Team of international politics took place in the context of the Responsibility to Protect principle adopted by the UN in 2005 when Brazil proposed the concept of "Responsibility while Protecting" (RwP). Brazil, one of the most assiduous members of the UN Security Council, was known for being critical of foreign intervention in humanitarian crises, fearing the excessive use of force and questioning its legitimacy within the framework of the UN Charter and international law. Brazil's RwP aimed to improve the criteria for intervention made under UN auspices. Though Brazil had evaded some norms during the military period, after redemocratization it came to accept them, and had now become a proponent of R2P.[33]

It was the NATO intervention in Libya in 2011 that provoked Brazil's interest in improving accountability for such actions None of the BRICS had voted against Resolution 1973. Like Germany, they had abstained for supporting the measure.[34] However, NATO's mission to protect citizens, in keeping with the resolution, had quickly escalated into a regime change mission, with the result that it breached the terms of the UN mandate to help overthrow Kaddafi's regime. The resolution was also violated by supplying weapons to the opposition. Proposing the RwP sought to address some of R2P's frailties. RwP, too, was not sufficiently clear, or far-sighted enough, to deal with all of the issues involved in such interventions, as the civil war in Syria demonstrated. In spite of the terrible human rights violations alleged against the Syrian government, Brazil's position moved closer to that of China and Russia, to oppose outright intervention.

The third attempt was the proposals for global internet regulation and the removal of the United States from its primary role in internet governance. In the aftermath of the National Security Agency (NSA) espionage scandal, which caused president Dilma Rousseff to cancel a state visit to the United States, Brazil approved a civil framework for the governance of the internet. The proposal included the idea of digital rights and extensive public participation and was proposed in the UN (with Germany's support) as a global internet regulation to move toward a more democratic process in governing the global infrastructure.

Amorim claimed that, in this period, "Brazil's role in the world has undeniably attained new heights. Our voice is heard with greater attention not because we scream louder, but because we are more respected. That has a lot to do with the growth of our economy, the vibrancy of our democracy and the example of our social policies. But some of the success can also be credited to our foreign policy."[35] Brazilian foreign policy also reinforced its hard power themes, insisting on South America's energy infrastructure integration, purchasing nuclear submarines from France and military aircraft from Sweden (including technology transfer), and continuing its satellite program with China. On balance, Brazil accumulated much more soft than hard power. Yet Brazil could not sustain its new protagonism, finding itself limited by the power relations built into the international system. The failure of these three propositions indicated its lack of hard power and its limited armed forces and experience in international conflicts.

The negotiation with Iran, the RwP concept, and the new internet governance proposals, however daring and inspirational, all ended in failure. Right after the agreement between Iran, Turkey, and Brazil, which was encouraged by then–U.S. president Barack Obama, a new round of sanctions was imposed on the Islamic Republic by the UN Security Council with broad support, including from Russia and China. This was functionally a veto against two emerging powers playing a prominent geopolitical role in the Middle East, an area where the traditional large powers routinely failed. Turkey and Brazil voted against these sanctions. It was the first time that Brazil opposed a resolution that ended up being approved. The RwP initiative and the new internet ruling—both of which were commendable and pertinent—followed a similar trajectory, as Brazil lacked implementation power or even the power to continue debates.

The limitations on Brazil's assertive foreign policy were not solely external. An internal limitation can be seen in the government's alliances with big Brazilian companies and the bourgeoisie. Although Brazil's foreign policy seemed to reject traditional alliances with powerful social groups and oligarchies, it adopted certain protocols typical of central powers. It promoted native capitalism in new fields by using the country's growing soft power. For example, Brazil's hosting of megaevents such as the Olympics and the World Cup, both of which involved big communication corporations and corporate sponsors such as MasterCard, Visa, Nike, and McDonald's, plus its heavy influence in the politics of international sporting associations, was possible due to the massive support from African, Latin American, and Asian countries, all members of the southern political cooperation alliance led by Brazil in other fields.[36]

Despite its emancipating speeches about humanitarian programs and technical and political cooperation, the new global Brazil was also a product of new businesses that benefited from the same old dependent, national capitalism of the Brazilian state. As Brazil diversified its partnerships and national interests, reinforced regional integration, and solidified its role as a relevant interlocutor on important issues, its foreign policy discourse seemed consistent with its rank as a newly emergent power.[37] But that image could not last. The World Cup and the Olympics were intended to project the definitive version of a new assertive Brazil. However, they also symbolized the country's structural contradictions. As Brazil moved forward with its political, cultural, and humanitarian projects, its dependent native capitalism was in no way curbed—indeed, it prospered—creating illiberal clouds in the way of conflicting economic interests, clientelism, and corruption. In the eight years that he governed, Lula was also a "hawker for Brazilian companies" overseas, with commercial policies sponsored by the National Bank for Economic and Social Development (BNDES) and promoted by the Brazilian Agency for Exports Promotion (APEX).[38] Large Brazilian multinationals grew as never before. The traditional holders of economic power in Brazil profited from the large-scale infrastructure projects in African, Asian, and Latin American countries, condensing illiberal clouds in the South.

Paradoxically, while the governments led by the leftist Workers Party (PT) reproduced and leveraged long-standing arrangements between the state, construction companies, and big overseas agribusinesses, they also moved to control corruption. They strengthened the federal police, made the public prosecutor more self-sufficient, and appointed independent attorneys general and Federal Supreme Court (STF) justices, many of whom were publicly anti-Lula. It is important to emphasize that the Brazilian model for expanding its native capitalist sector is no different from the way traditional powers have always handled such expansion: by associating political actions with national economic interests and marrying cultural, technical, and humanitarian cooperation with the expansion of its multinationals in new countries. To this end, it is worth mentioning that southern countries similar to Brazil were fertile ground for Brazilian companies, which began fighting for inroads against the northern companies that had traditionally dominated there. In this way, the "assertive foreign policy" reproduced the internal economic-political plot. Even as it advanced unprecedented alliances, commitments, and themes, it also perpetuated—and even deepened—the profit-seeking movements of Brazilian capital overseas, especially in the Global South.

An Assertive Foreign Policy Defeated

At the end of 2010, the confluence between *virtù* and *fortuna* that went into the making of Lulismo ended. At the international level, the end of the commodities boom and the effects of the 2008 crisis put pressure on the public budget and created a distributive conflict that in 2013 caused protests and popular demand for better public services, more democracy, and stronger policies against inequalities. Lulismo peaked at the end of Lula's time in office, in December 2010, when he enjoyed an almost 90-percent popularity index, and confidence in his government was at the 80-percent mark.[39] That was about to change drastically, however.

Lula's successor, Dilma Rousseff, tried to counter these emerging critical voices, but she chose the wrong actors to cooperate with, and the country's bet on megaevents and construction like the Belo Monte dam project[40] in the name of a Big Brazil proved mistaken.[41] Despite trying to sustain continuity with the Lula government, Rousseff quickly lost influence and power. Earlier political experimentation was discarded, and the government's priorities shifted away from foreign policy. There was a noticeable decline in areas from human rights to security, agrarian policy to environment, and even popular culture. But the highly questionable decisions to create megacompanies with public money did not start with the Rousseff government.[42] There were long-standing issues with telecommunications (the judicial recovery of the Oi telephone company), the concentration of the meat market (JBS Friboi and its worldwide role as a food processor), and the bankruptcy of Eike Batista's Group EBX (Batista was a successful entrepreneur and a symbol of the Lula years). One might say the tensions between a single big Brazil and one that championed plurality, notable during the Lula years, faded during Rousseff's government as what we can call "smaller politics—that is, policies for culture, agrarian reform, community support, indigenous issues, and human rights—were deemphasized.

That took on new meaning after June 2013, in the face of widespread outrage against the difficulties of life in major cities, particularly corruption, police brutality, the low quality of public services, and the limits of a representative democracy believed to be bought by major corporations. There was a desire for high-intensity democratic participation. Initially Rousseff and the PT party welcomed some of the protests and tried to offer solutions—for instance, the "More Doctors" health program, a referendum on an exclusive constitutional amendment proposal, through a presidential decree to be approved by the Congress, that aimed at renovating the political system and using petroleum income for education. However, they never actually established a real dialogue, and they certainly did not disarm the repressive apparatus. The June protests opened a space for democratic radicalization that the government did not seize—a space that could have extended the openings of Lulismo. The reasons for the failure to act included international conditions, since the world was still recovering from the 2008 global economic crisis, and falling commodity prices that affected Brazilian exports. There were national considerations as well, such as the deepening of the redistributive conflict and Rousseff's inability to deal with the traditional political elites and their successive attempts to prevent the continuation of her second mandate.

In her second term, Rousseff tried to form a political alliance with center and right-wing parties, though her reelection campaign had skewed left. She assumed a neoliberal economic position; for example, she assigned an executive of Brazil's largest private bank to the Ministry of Finance, who advocated for cutting expenses and public services. Her government quickly lost social and political support. Rousseff's eventual impeachment is now widely known. In addition to the irresponsibility of political and economic elites, what was key to the impeachment process was popular discontent with the economic crisis and the anticorruption judicial processes (with support from street demonstrations) that daily linked the PT governments, construction companies, and Petrobras, along with the leakage of these processes to Globo Network, which disclosed witnesses' immunity reports the very day they were issued.

The alliances between the vice president and the opposition and between the Lava Jato (or "Car Wash") anticorruption operation and the country's main communication conglomerate, along with the blessing of the Federal Supreme Court, made for the perfect scenario to overthrow the newly elected president within supposedly legal parameters. In other words, it was a media-judicial-parliamentary coup. With no criminal responsibility proven and no direct evidence connecting Rousseff to any unlawful act, the National Congress went ahead with the impeachment and nominated her vice president to take over the government. Vice President Temer assumed his new role in August 2016 and adopted the government program of the previous election's losing candidate, which included privatizing Brazilian public companies, discontinuing the country's international projects (Mercosul, CELAC, UNASUR, IBSA, and BRICS) and stifling labor and pension legislations. As in the 1964 military-civilian coup, one of the main causes of discontent—and the fall of the constitutional president—was foreign policy.

At the same time, proximity between former president Lula and figures from the national business community who had benefited considerably while he was in office was judged mainly by inference and witness immunity plea bargains. Despite the evident shared political approach and interests among the PT and the national champions, the Lava Jato operation and chief investigator Judge Moro condemned, based on the judge's previous beliefs and a biased and punitive justice, the close relationships between the former president and leaders of the national economy. While there are indications of a not-so-republican relationship between Lula and an entrepreneurial class interested in using him to facilitate public contracts under PT governments (a relationship inherent to capitalism in so-called liberal democracies), there is no specific material evidence to date.

In sum, a perfect storm of economic, political, and social crises ended these assertive foreign policy and domestic policies that highlighted income distribution and featured unusual support for the poor, women, Blacks, workers, and small farmers. In opposition to this project, a vast oligarchic coalition emerged consisting of Brazil's main industry federation, the Federation of Industries of the State of São Paulo (FIESP), Globo Network, right-wing politicians, middle-class and upper-class "anticorruption" (in fact, anti-PT) protestors, judges, and a public prosecutor with not-so-tacit Supreme Court and military support and international connections.

Hard Power Pressures

The geopolitical context that underlines the ruling class's illegitimate deposing of an elected president and a party's national-regional project is crucial. Various investigations of Brazilian companies started and were supported by legal cooperation among the United States, Switzerland, and Brazil in a way that jurist Joaquim Falcão has described as a "unilateral expansion of the laws and North American judicialization, through international agreements such as the Anti-Corruption Act and the Anti-Terrorism Act."[43] These investigations were covered favorably by the Globo Network, the biggest Brazilian communication company and a major force in mobilizing the urban middle class to get involved in anti-corruption protests. The anticorruption movement, supported by the big media companies, focused on rejecting the PT —specifically, Lula and Rousseff—and had the Lava Jato operation, which was investigating corruption in Petrobras, as its role model.[44] During public manifestations, a significant part of this movement's supporters asked for military intervention as a way to, as they saw it, clean up politics. The anti-PT media coverage built up the political figure of the federal judge Sérgio Moro as the leader of this national anticorruption movement, positioning him as bringing rapid justice against the powerful, using legal or even illegal procedures to achieve this end. The judge became the vigilante.

Lava Jato focused on Brazilian companies from internationally competitive sectors, particularly oil and engineering companies that operated in Africa and Latin America, and Brazil's biggest food and agricultural export company, the JBS Group, which was involved in producing and exporting Brazilian meat.[45] A U.S. Justice Department report presented evidence that Odebrecht, Brazil's biggest civil engineering company, paid Angolan authorities to secure public contracts for construction there, which became evidence for the Brazilian investigation of the company.[46] It is worth mentioning that this international legal effort did not investigate other foreign companies and their lobbying methods or public-private relationships in and with Brazil. This form of systemic corruption—the expected outcome of international capitalist interests in all representative democracies—was selectively and partially investigated. The focus was on sectors that were at the forefront of Brazilian expansion into the Global South and on events that occurred when the PT was in charge. Companies such as Embraer,[47] Odebrecht, Petrobras, and JBS were all prosecuted by the U.S. Justice Department and had to go along with pleas and fines and/or acts of leniency that were not always transparent.[48] The same rigor has yet to be seen in investigations of the U.S., French, German, or Chinese companies operating in Latin America and Africa that became the main beneficiaries of these anticorruption judicial task forces in Brazil.

In this context, it is worth mentioning the 2013 WikiLeaks scandal, which found that the U.S. National Security Agency (NSA) was bugging the phones of Rousseff's staff; some ministers; the presidential plane; Brazilian diplomatic missions, including the one at the UN; and Petrobras.[49] State Department cables indicated that the North American interest in oil and pre-salt oil was the link between Brazilian political sectors and the

American embassy. José Serra, Romero Jucá, and Michel Temer, all key players in the parliamentary coup against Rousseff, were revealed to be the sources by the American embassy in Brasília. In what was perhaps the most symptomatic moment, Temer's former chancellor and presidential candidate José Serra said that, if he won the 2010 election against Rousseff, he would change the existing "oil sharing law" by making the new reserves more accessible to foreign companies.[50]

The petrochemical sector had always been geopolitically sensitive. Until 1960, it was dominated by the "seven sisters": seven oil companies supported by their respective national governments (the UK, the United States, and Holland). That changed with the foundation of OPEC in 1960, and the rise of new countries and a new seven sisters, all state-owned, from Russia, Saudi Arabia, China, Brazil, Venezuela, and Malaysia.[51] An "oil sharing law" was approved during the final phase of the Lula government after the discovery of pre-salt oil fields, giving the Brazilian state and Petrobras greater control of these new reserves (which were the property of the state), with the obligatory participation of the company in 50 percent of the exploitation of the reserve. At the time, Lula described this as a "passport to the future."[52] But Petrobras's monopoly on exploiting the new reserves and the approval of constitutional amendments that directed profit from the pre-salt oil into a national fund intended to support the country's education and health did not last long.

The intersection of domestic and geopolitical tensions was bluntly on display in the international cooperation of the judiciary and the public prosecutor. Lava Jato was clearly inspired by the 1990s Italian anticorruption operation Mani Pulite, which judge Sérgio Moro had earlier analyzed in an article.[53] According to journalist Luis Nassif, the two operations had in common a "pro-internationalization, ideological vision of the economy, intent on criminalizing all promotion policies of the internal economy."[54] The closed-off Italian economy made it easy for corrupt actors to manipulate it, and, in the context of Cold War debates, opening the economy seemed like a good solution. A similar logic appeared in Brazil of 2010, which explains why "a group of prosecutors visiting the United States, led by the country's own Attorney General of the Republic, supplied North American justice and its shareholders with the elements necessary to sue Petrobras."[55] The belief that free trade interests were disguising themselves in anticorruption actions gained strength regarding the Brazilian oil company. If, in other situations, companies were accused of corrupting authorities, in this specific case "the prosecutors transformed the company from victim into co-author of the frauds, advocating against the Brazilian state itself in favor of the interests of North American stakeholders."[56]

It is not far-fetched to think of an independent country asking the U.S. Justice Department to investigate important companies such as Petrobras and Odebrecht, the construction company. But would the opposite be possible? Would U.S. authorities ask Brazil to investigate Chevron or another American company? Further, the fact that the national prosecutor at TCU (Brazil's audit court) decreed, on his own, the unfeasibility of the pre-salt oil public management is not crime suppression, but an action that could be inspired by external figures in geopolitical disputes.[57] Another journalist, Jânio de Freitas, asked why Lava Jato spared foreign companies that had acted in Brazil and elsewhere in the same corrupt, antidemocratic way that the legal international cooperation on which the operation based itself had behaved.[58]

Defense issues added to the equation. The offensive against contractors spread to the Eletronuclear company and retired Admiral Othon Luiz Pinheiro da Silva, considered one of the authors of the Brazilian nuclear program, the founder of the Cycle of Nuclear Fuel and Propulsion for submarines, and the former director of IPEN (Institute of Energy and Nuclear Research). This investigation, which resulted in Othon's arrest, started "with information passed to the Brazilian Attorney General by the North American Justice Department," an unequivocal demonstration that the United States actively used international legal cooperation as one of its geopolitical strategies.[59] Moro (along with other judges and prosecutors) completed two training courses in the United States and was named one of the most important people in the world by *Time* magazine in 2016, which fed into the perceptions of conspiracy.[60]

The pertinent issue here is realizing that the Brazilian judiciary and public prosecutor, unlike the United States, lacked any geopolitical perspective. That may be one of the decisive limits of Brazilian power in international affairs. And all this occurred amid an American offensive against corruption, observable in the FIFA scandal and the work of the U.S. prosecutor. Brazil's entire politics, internal and external, came under attack: BNDES, the Mariel port in Cuba, and business on the African and Latin American continents. While social movements were calling for transparency and discussing the social and environmental requirements for Brazilian companies working overseas, prosecutors seemed to follow the road to criminalization for commercial promotion and export funding, two notable features of Lula's foreign policies. Our analysis does not suggest that the coup in Brazil was born in the United States, nor do we draw a direct parallel with the 1964 Brother Sam Operation, in which there was outright North American interference.[61] This coup came from within the country. But the United States contributed to it by destabilizing Brazilian capitalism's model of income distribution during Lula's government and working against what it saw as audacious efforts in three strategic sectors: Petrobras, the construction industry, and agribusiness. Also involved were the Koch brothers, who had their own oil interests,[62] and new conservative groups that advocated for ultra-neoliberal economic reforms and privatizations and became important in the street protests against Rousseff.[63]

Illiberal Liberals, at Home and Abroad

When it came under attack, the Lula model could not sustain itself because it could not shape a domestic project coherent with the geopolitical process. Brazil lacked the foundation to sustain its role as a new regional and global power, a BRICS member, a peacemaker in the Iranian nuclear debate, and a leader in regional integration and model of social politics for the South. Instead, the declining popularity of Rousseff's government converged with a selectively targeted anticorruption operation, and a coup by the ruling class, with support from U.S. actors, to destroy this new Brazilian protagonism.

The Brazilian elites have always faced a dilemma between supporting internal markets and the consequent movements and changes (and risks for traditional rule) and maintaining a submissive project for the country. In the end, they did not even accept a soft reformist project, preferring an irresponsible political adventure: first, in the figure of the traditional Brazilian (corrupt) politician embodied by former vice president Michel Temer, then in the figure of Jair Bolsonaro, in spite of all that was known about him, from his terrible record as a parliamentary deputy to his well-known homophobic, racist, antipoor, and macho posturing.

The initial outcome of these confrontations left Lula in prison after a Kafkaesque process. In the run-up to the 2018 elections, he was the popular favorite, but the electorate couldn't vote for him because he was in jail. Other former Latin American presidents are facing similar situations, including Rafael Correa in Ecuador and Cristina Kirchner in Argentina. Alan Garcia, the former president of Peru, who was also involved in Odebrecht's corruption, committed suicide before being arrested. Brazil's government now has more than one hundred members of the military cadre in top positions (ironically, the most important ones are at MINUSTAH in Haiti, one of Lula's cherished initiatives) but lacking a national project and advocating (as in 1964) total alignment with the United States—not to the country, but, in a rupture of Brazilian diplomatic tradition, to its president, Donald Trump.

Finally, Lava Jato superstar Sérgio Moro, after arresting Lula, abandoned his judgeship and became the justice minister for Bolsonaro, the person who benefited the most from Lula's arrest. After just a hundred days of Bolsonaro's government, already faced with corruption scandals linking the Bolsonaro family with Rio de Janeiro militias, Moro is on the defense, focusing on proposals like facilitating gun ownership and lowering taxes for the tobacco industry. After multiple public disputes with President Bolsonaro, Moro left the government in April of 2020, during the biggest economic and pandemic crisis in Brazil, accusing Bolsonaro of attempting to use the government to protect his family from corruption allegations. Moro then began to work at the American consultancy firm Alvarez & Marsal, which was hired for the corporate restructuring of Odebrecht. Brazil is facing a huge social, economic, and political crisis combined with a continuing loss of its international prestige, and it's not clear how it will end.[64]

How to interpret the decline of Brazilian soft power between the early 2000s and now? On one hand, it can be understood as the result of a deep political dispute in a country marked by the most extreme inequalities and violence. On the other, it can also be seen as the aftermath of a new (hybrid) war waged not against one political or ideological project, but against a country and its people. Either way, this experience reaffirmed Brazil's peripheral and dependent condition as a structural element in its foreign policy. The effort to gain international prestige and become an emerging Global South power through assertive foreign policy failed because of a lack of a balancing and sustainable hard power and the fragility of political institutions. But it also offered a glimpse of what was possible for Brazil in the international arena under the best of conditions.

It takes a great leap of faith to imagine the renewal of state, society, and political system that would be capable of challenging the current ruling-class mediocrity, overcoming the internal social and political barriers, building new domestic and global connections, and rising up once more to dream of Brazil's capacity to act independently and in the name of global equity.

Notes

1. Samuel Pinheiro Guimarães,*Quinhentos anos de periferia* (Porto Alegre: Editoria da UFRGS, 1999), 1:455. Pinheiro Guimarães took over as general secretary of the Ministry of Foreign Affairs (also known as Itamaraty) after Luiz Inácio Lula da Silva became president in 2003.
2. *Dependency and Development in Latin America*, by Chilean sociologist Enzo Faletto and the future president of Brazil (from 1995 to 2002) Fernando Henrique Cardoso, took up similar questions. So did Ruy Mauro Marini in *La Dialéctica de la Dependencia* [Dialectics of dependency] (Argentina: Ediciones Ungs, [1973] 2017), 115.
3. Maria Regina Soares de Lima, *The Political Economy of Brazilian Foreign Policy: Nuclear Energy, Trade, and Itaipu* (Nashville: Vanderbilt University Press, 1986), 732; Paulo Gilberto Fagundes Vizentini, *A política externa do regime militar brasileiro* (Porto Alegre: Editoria da UFRGS, 2004), 409; Samuel Pinheiro Guimarães, *Desafios brasileiros na era dos gigantes* (Rio de Janeiro: Contraponto, 2005), 455.
4. Guimarães.
5. Daniel Flemes and Miriam Gomes Saraiva, "Potências emergentes na ordem de redes: o caso do Brasil," *Revista Brasileira de Política Internacional* 57, no. 2 (2014): 215.
6. See, for example, Alvaro Lins, *Rio Branco*, 2 vols. (Rio de Janeiro: José Olympio, 1945); and later approaches like E. Bradford Burns, *The Unwritten Alliance: Rio Branco and Brazilian-American Relations* (New York: Columbia University Press, 1966).
7. Luiz Alberto Moniz Bandeira, *O expansionismo brasileiro, e a formação dos Estados na Bacia do Prata* (Brasília: UnB, 1998), 254.
8. Golbery Do Couto e Silva, *Geopolítica do Brasil* (Rio de Janeiro: José Olympio, 1967), 633.
9. In the internal realm, Brazil has experienced and continues to experience extremely high levels of violence (genocide of indigenous peoples, slavery, huge urban and rural violence).

10. Amado Luiz Cervo and Clodoaldo Bueno, *História da Política Exterior do Brasil* (Brasília: Instituto Brasileiro de Relações Internacionais/Editora da Universidade de Brasília, 2002), 146.

11. Marco Aurelio Garcia, *O lugar do Brasil no mundo a política externa em um momento de transição*, in *Brasil entre o passado e o futuro*, ed. Marco Aurelio Garcia and Emir Sader (São Paulo: Perseu Abramo, 2010), 200.

12. Matias Spektor, *Azeredo da Silveira: um depoimento* (São Paulo: FGV, 2010), 373.

13. Luiz Inácio Lula da Silva, "O Brasil no mundo: mudanças e transformações," in *2003–2013: Uma nova política externa*, ed. Gilberto Maringoni, Giorgio Romano Schutte, and Gonzalo Berron (Tubarão: Editoria Copiart, 2014), 244.

14. André Singer, *Os sentidos do lulismo: reforma gradual e pacto conservador* (São Paulo: Companhia das Letras, 2012), 209.

15. Celso Amorim, *Acting Globally: Rethinking Global Democracy in Brazil* (Lanham, MD: Hamilton, 2017), 489.

16. Lula da Silva, *O Brasil no mundo*, 244.

17. Leslie Bethell, "Brazil: Regional Power, Global Power," Open Democracy, June 8, 2010, https://www.opendemocracy.net/leslie-bethell/brazil-regional-power-global-power.

18. Carlos R. S. Milani, Enara Echart Muñoz, Rubens de S. Duarte and Magno Klein, *Atlas da Política Externa Brasileira* (Rio de Janeiro: CLACSO, 2014), 112.

19. Based on data from the Brazilian Ministry of Industrial Development and Commerce, in Natalia da Luz, Brasil-África, "A importância da representaçao e da cooperaçao com o continente africano," Por Dentro da África, June 6, 2016, http://www.pordentrodaafrica.com/brasil-africa/brasil-africa-importancia-da-representacao-diplomatica-e-da-cooperacao-com-o-continente-africano.

20. Milani, *Atlas*, 112.

21. Milani, 112.

22. Carlos R. S. Milani, "Educational Cooperation as Soft Power: The Case of Brazil's Foreign Policy" (paper presented at ISA/Global South Caucus, Singapore, January 8–10, 2015), https://pdfs.semanticscholar.org/3690/11ce35c5e8eb1cfbff73eac54ca68ba2862f.pdf.

23. See Thomas Cooper Patriota, "Le Brésil, un partenaire de l'Afrique qui s'affirme: Les relations Brésil/Afrique sous les gouvernements Lula (2003–2010)," Institut français des relations internationales (IFRI), 2011, 72, https://www.ifri.org/sites/default/files/atoms/files/bresilafriquethomaspatriota.pdf (accessed September 24, 2020). Furthermore, successful social policies have influenced public policies throughout the world, including in Pakistan, which hosted the Brazil-Pakistan International Seminar on Food Security and Poverty Eradication in Islamabad.

24. Alexandre de Freitas Barbosa, Thais Narciso, and Marina Biancalana, "Brazil in Africa: Another Emerging Power on the Continent," *Politikon: South African Journal of Political Studies* 36, no 1 (2009): 59–86.

25. Barbosa et al., "Brazil in Africa," 59–86.

26. Barbosa et al., 59–86.

27. Thomas Cooper Patriota and Francesco Maria Pierri, "Brazil's Cooperation in African Agricultural Development and Food Security," in *Agricultural Development and Food Security in Africa: The Impact of Chinese, Indian and Brazilian Investments*, ed. Fantu Cheru and Renu Modi (London: Zed, 2013), 280.

28. "Brazil must be the world's least hated country," Timothy J. Power suggested. "It is a country that has the instinctive trust of several different actors, who can be on opposite sides of some very problematic issues. For example, both the U.S. and Iran see Brasília as an important interlocutor. If you have Tehran's and Washington's trust, it's because you've done something right." Interview by Silio Boccanera, Globo News, September 29, 2010, http://www.conjur .com.br/2010-nov-26/entrevista-timothy-power-brasilianista-americano.

29. Celso Amorim, *Teera, Ramalá e Doha*: *memórias da política externa ativa e altiva* (São Paulo: Benvirá, 2015), 11.

30. Maria Regina Soares de Lima, "Introdução," in Milani, *Atlas da Política Externa*, 5.

31. Peter Dauvergne and Déborah B. L. Farias, "The Rise of Brazil as a Global Development Power," *Third World Quarterly* 33, no. 5 (2012): 904.

32. Jose Luís Fiori. *História, estratégia, e desenvolvimento: para uma geopolítica do capitalismo* (São Paulo: Boitempo, 2014), 245.

33. Oliver Stuenkel, "Brazil as a New Global Agenda Setter?," in *Shifting Power and Human Rights Diplomacy*, ed. Thijs van Lindert and Lars van Troost (Amsterdam: Amnesty International Netherlands, 2014), 104.

34. That justified military foreign interventions in order to "protect" the Libyan civil society.

35. Celso Amorim, "Brazilian Foreign Policy under President Lula (2003–2010): An Overview," *Revista Brasileira de Política Internacional* 53 (2010): 214–40.

36. The "Global South" is understood here to mean the socioeconomic and political point of view of the developing countries, according to the postcolonial approach of authors like Theotônio dos Santos and Boaventura de Sousa Santos.

37. Oil, arms, and construction, among others. The strong presence of the Brazilian contractor Odebrecht in African countries such as Angola is part of that. See Fábio Zanini, *Euforia e fracasso do Brasil grande: política externa e multinacionais na era Lula* (São Paulo: Editoria Contexto, 2017), 78.

38. President Lula defined himself this way during his commercial missions abroad: see Mair Pena Neto, "Lula quer ser 'mascate' do Brasil para combater

crise," *O Estado de S. Paulo*, September 18, 2008, https://politica.estadao
.com.br/noticias/geral,lula-quer-ser-mascate-do-brasil-para-combater-crise
,244103.

39. See Carlos Luís Duarte Villanova, *Diplomacia pública e a imagem do Brasil no século XXI* (Brasília: Editoria FUNAG, 2017), 357.

40. The tragically misguided Hydroelectric Plant of Belo Monte, at the bay of the Xingú River (one of the main rivers of the Amazon region,) in the Brazilian State of Pará, was built despite strong opposition from civil society and the region's indigenous nations. The environmental impact is still incalculable. The plant was built by a consortium of enterprises: the National and Public Energy Corporation Eletrobrás, major Brazilian construction companies such as Queiroz Galvão, and the National and Public Brazilian Bank of Development (BNDES).

41. See Leonardo Souza and Bruno Villas Bôas, "Dilma deu R$458 bilhões em desonerações," *Folha de S. Paulo,* September 6, 2015, https://m.folha.uol.com
.br/mercado/2015/09/1678317-dilma-deu-r-458-bilhoes-em-desoneracoes.

42. Known in Brazil as the "national champions," they were the most competitive Brazilian corporations abroad, including Petrobrás, JBS-Friboi, Odebrecht, and Embraer, and received diplomatic and commercial support from the national government to expand their businesses abroad.

43. Joaquim Falcão, "JBS e a globalização da Justiça americana," *Folha de S. Paulo,* June 15, 2017, 1.

44. Petrobrás and other small oil Brazilian companies also expanded in African countries—for example, Namibia—during the governments of Lula and Dilma. See Zanini, *Euforia e fracasso*, 69, 224.

45. After the company's president took a plea bargain on charges of having financed several schemes of lobbying, kickbacks, and political donations in Brazil, JBS is preparing to move its head offices to the United States (where almost 80 percent of its operations—comprising more than fifty-six meat processing factories and millions of workers—are already located). The company has had several high records on the New York Stock Exchange. See Fernando Brito, "A Delação que veio de longe," *Requaio Senador do paraná*, May 30, 2017, http://www.robertorequiao.com.br/a-delacao-que-veio-de-longe-por
-fernando-rosa/.

46. According to Zanini, *Euforia e fracasso*, 82, an investigation of the U.S. Justice Department revealed that "between 2013 and 2016, Odebrecht paid more than 50 million USD to government authorities in Angola to assure contracts in public works" as the biggest hydroelectric plant in Angola, with partial financing from the Brazilian Public Bank of Development (BNDES).

47. Falcão, "JBS e a globalização."

48. Odebrecht's entry into Angola began in 1975 during the Brazilian military regime, after Brazil became the first country to recognize Angola's independence. See Zanini, *Euforia e fracasso*, 85.

49. Natalia Viana, "NSA espionou assistente pessoal de Dilma e avião presidencial," *Agência Pública*, July 4, 2015; Natalia Passarinho, "Dilma diz na ONU que espionagem fere soberania e direito internacional," *G1 Globo*, September 24, 2013, n.p.The revelation of the NSA espionage led to the canceling of a scheduled Brazilian State visit to the United States. In perhaps one of her finest moments as president, Dilma Rousseff later made a poignant UN speech saying that the espionage was not motivated by terrorism or safety, but was serving the economic and strategic interests of the United States, Brazil, and Germany. She then suggested that the internet be regulated internationally instead of by the United States, in the hopes that this would keep the internet from becoming a means of espionage, sabotage, and infrastructure attacks.

50. Juliana Rocha and Catia Seabra, "Petroleiras foram contra novas regras para pré-sal," *Folha de S. Paulo,* December 13, 2010, n.p.

51. Ildo Luiz Sauer, "O pré-sal e a geopolítica e hegemonia do petróleo face às mudanças climáticas e à transição energética," in *Recursos Minerais do Brasil: problemas e desafios*, ed. Adolpho José Melfi, Aroldo Misi, Diogenes de Almeida Campos, and Umberto Giuseppe Cordani, 308–22 (Rio de Janiero: Academia Brasileira de Ciências, 2016).

52. Luiz Inácio Lula da Silva, "O pré-sal é um passaporte para o futuro," *O Globo*, August 31, 2009, n.p.

53. Sérgio Fernando Moro, "Considerações Sobre a Mani Pulite," *Revista Centro de Estudos Judiciários* 26 (2004): 56–62.

54. Luis Nassif, "As implicações geopolíticas da Lava Jato," *GGN Jornal,* October 15, 2015, https://jornalggn.com.br/coluna-economica/as-implicacoes-geopoliticas-da-lava-jato/.

55. Nassif, "As implicações geopolíticas."

56. Nassif.

57. Nassif,

58. Janio de Freitas, "Jatos desiguais," *Folha de S. Paulo*, November 8, 2015, n.p.

59. Freitas, "Jatos desiguais."

60. On the possible relations between the cooperation and training of Brazilian judges (like Moro) in the United States, the relative weakening of the Brazilian national champions, and possible geopolitical impacts, see Luiz Alberto Moniz Bandeira, *A desordem mundial: o espectro da dominação: guerras por procuração, terror, caos e catástrofes humanitárias* (Rio de Janeiro: Editoria José Olympio, 2016), 644.

61. Luiz Alberto Moniz Bandeira, "1964: Os generais sob a estratégia Americana," Outras Palavras, March 31, 2014, https://outraspalavras.net/sem-categoria/1964-os-generais-sob-a-estrategia-americana/.
62. Marina Amaral, "A nova roupa da direita," *Agência Pública* (São Paulo), June 23, 2015 n.p.
63. The nontransparent involvement of some movements organized by NGOs, think tanks, and foreign interests was visible in market liberalization initiatives and antileft political groups in Latin America such as the Atlas Network, the Millennium Institute, the Liberal Institute, and the "Free Brazil Movement" (Movimento Brasil Livre), all of which had hidden funding sources. See also Lee Fang, "Esfera de influência: como os libertários americanos estão reinventando a política latino-americana," *Intercept*, August 11, 2017, n.p.
64. The British consulting enterprise Portland has taken note of the fall of Brazilian international prestige in its study "The Soft Power 30," in which Brazil has fallen five notches since 2016. In 2017, it occupied the twenty-ninth position out of thirty.

PART FOUR
China

CHAPTER VII

China's Soft Power in Africa

Promoting Alternative Perspectives

MARTINA BASSAN

C hina's use of soft power in international relations developed far before Joseph S. Nye Jr.'s coinage of the phrase in the 1990s and its ensuing appearance in China's official and academic discourse. In fact, China's soft-power practices can be traced back to the first years after the establishment of the People's Republic of China, when cultural exchanges with other countries and development aid began to be used as political tools.[1] China's aid program was first formulated in the 1950s, with the transfer of food, medicines, and cotton to North Korea after the invasion of the South and the American embargo.[2] China also signed its first formal cultural agreement with a foreign country early in that decade.[3] Since then, China's use of soft power practices has evolved along with its foreign policy priorities, in lockstep with an effort to reinterpret Nye's original concept on the basis of specific Chinese features—or, as it is often called, "soft power with Chinese characteristics."

As China's economic situation has improved, its soft-power diplomacy has intensified, especially on the African continent, to the point that Africa has become the symbol of China's soft-power success. The main argument of this chapter is that, since the beginning of the twenty-first century, China's soft-power strategy toward Africa has not only been used to protect China's economic interests on the continent, but as an instrument for Beijing to advance alternative views on global issues under the rhetoric of a renewed Afro-Asian identity. In other words, China's practice of soft power in Africa should be seen as evidence of a new phase in its foreign policy, one that is characterized by the desire to elaborate norms that offer an alternative to Western ones. For Beijing, Africa is a territory in which China can test its foreign policy practices and refine its approach in order to demonstrate that it is a responsible great power. The evolution of China's soft-power policy strategy and its discourse about Africa demonstrate China's overall perceptions of the international relations system and approaches to global governance. This chapter is organized as following: I will first give a short overview of the beginning of China's soft power in Africa in the Maoist era. Then I will analyze how soft power has evolved along with the Chinese economy in ways that support China's development and its global aspirations in international relations. Finally, I will conclude by discussing China's current soft-power strategy and its conception of the international system.

"The 'Poor Help the Poor':' The Roots of China's Soft Power in Africa in the Maoist Era

China's soft-power strategy in Africa can be traced back to the Bandung Conference of 1955, a time of anticolonial wars across the Global South, and to the Afro-Asian People's Solidarity Organization, whose first conference in 1957 shaped the approach and spirit of the nonaligned movement.[4] The two conferences created a sense of solidarity across the Global South based on a shared struggle against Western hegemony, imperialism, and neocolonialism.[5] Their common experiences provided a foundation on which to build a new international force[6] that would act according to the "Five Principles of Peaceful Coexistence" and respect territorial sovereignty.[7] In this process, the Chinese government initially elaborated cultural diplomacy as a political tool to introduce African countries to the great success of the Chinese Revolution and facilitate the establishment of diplomatic relations. Starting in the mid-1950s, the Chinese government began sponsoring a number of cultural events in Africa, mostly in the north.[8] At that time, there were changes in the official discourse, as shown by articles that appeared in the late 1950s and early 1960s. Chinese scholar Liu Haifang quotes from *People's Daily* of April 1956, which used the expression "to have cultural contact with friendly countries,"[9] as well as from articles in *Ever Bright Daily* from September 1959 and *Shijie Zhishi* (*World*

Affairs) from 1964, which both use the phrase "to have cultural exchange" with the outside world instead.[10] According to Liu Haifang, this was a clear sign of the Chinese government gaining confidence in its foreign policy practices, while at the same trying "to avoid any potential foreign cultural influence."[11] This shift in the official language can therefore be regarded as the starting point of a conscious strategy of cultural diplomacy. Such an approach rapidly proved effective. In 1956, Egypt became the first African country to establish diplomatic relations with China, and four more African countries recognized the People's Republic of China before the decade ended: Morocco and Algeria in 1958, and Sudan and Guinea in 1959.[12] Diplomatic recognition continued in the following two decades, with fourteen African countries establishing diplomatic ties with China in the 1960s and twenty-two in the 1970s.[13]

In the 1960s, Africa was a contested ideological terrain, with China competing not only with the United States and remaining European influences, but with Taiwan, which needed political support to remain in the United Nations (UN), and the Soviet Union. In an effort to overcome Taiwan's international influence and compete with the Soviets, the Chinese government increased the number of cultural and diplomatic exchanges and launched an aid program in Guinea.[14] Chinese medical assistance to Africa also began in this period: the first medical team left Beijing for Algeria in April 1963.[15] In December of the same year, Zhou Enlai's famous seven-week African tour marked a milestone in China–Africa relations. In Ghana, Zhou confirmed China's support for African struggles against imperialism and established principles for aid and cooperation between China and Africa.[16] This was followed by a series of new agreements with a number of African countries, ranging from communications to economic aid and technical assistance. China's African aid at that time was mainly a mixture of technical training and projects in industry and agriculture, reflecting China's domestic ideas about development: centrally planned interventions to boost production and self-reliance, to be carried out throughout low-interest or interest-free loans.[17] Along with aid, China also offered military training and financial support in southern Africa to liberation movements that were ideologically committed to Maoist China rather than the Soviet Union[18] such as the Uniao National para a Independencia Total de Angola (UNITA),[19] the Zimbabwe African National Union (ZANU), or the Algerian Front de la Liberation Nationale (FLN).[20]

Ideology, Afro-Asian Solidarity, and a Multipolar World

As we have seen, until the late 1970s the primary purposes of China's extensive cultural exchanges with and aid and military support to African countries were ideology and political strategy. China's African policy was driven by strategic diplomacy, aimed at countering the influence of the West and the Soviet Union and, more important, at wresting diplomatic recognition from Taiwan. Cultural exchanges were conceived as political tools to "prepare African public opinion for the establishment of formal relations with China," "increase the level of affinity in the relationship," and create "a greater sense of international proletariat solidarity."[21] Aid and military support, in contrast, were seen as geopolitical tools against Taiwan

Figure 7.1 W. E. B. Du Bois shaking hands with Mao Tse-Tung, ca. 1959; W. E. B. Du Bois Papers (MS 312), Special Collections and University Archives, University of Massachusetts Amherst Libraries

and the USSR that would show the limitations of its rivals' capacities. This period saw an intensification of narratives that used history—specifically, the idea of a shared past experience of colonization and a common future of political liberation through revolution—to legitimize China's foreign policy practices in Africa. Bandung in this phase was "a symbol of Afro-Asia as a viable political concept,"[22] despite the fact that at the time of the conference China had no real interest in the African continent, with the possible exception of Egypt.[23] The idea of an Afro-Asian solidarity that could compete with the United States and the USSR was further reinforced through the cultivation of transnational intellectual networks with African American intellectual activists. The discourse of W. E. B. Du Bois, who visited China and met Mao Zedong in 1959, helped legitimize the idea of solidarity among—as Du Bois said—"colored people" against imperialists.[24]

China's foreign policy engagements and discourse toward Africa under Mao Zedong reflected China's vision of the international order during the revolutionary era: it called developing countries to rise up against capitalist countries and create a multipolar world. This world would be defined by alliances that could restrain all forms of hegemony and build an international order in which major countries would have roughly equal influence. This perspective changed in the years that followed, and evolutions in China's soft-power practices toward Africa can be useful in understanding how.

Changes in China's Soft-Power Practices Toward Africa Since the Economic Reform Period: Toward a Post-Western Approach to Global Issues?

The Revival of China's Traditional Culture and the Rise of New Cultural Practices

Along with the opening up of China in the 1980s came the rediscovery of China's traditional culture. During the Cultural Revolution, Chinese traditional arts and ideas had been publicly attacked by Mao as feudal and bourgeois.[25] After his death in 1976, Deng Xiaoping's Open Door policy officially put an end to an ideology-driven foreign policy and the revolutionary era and shifted the country toward a more pragmatic diplomatic approach aimed at sustaining China's economic growth. The Chinese government's efforts to revive Chinese culture in this period had both political and economic motivations. Mao Zedong's idea of a cultural policy "in which literature and art must serve the workers, the peasants and soldiers" was replaced by a new one where cultural diplomacy was meant to attract overseas Chinese with the same language and cultural roots to build a platform for investment and business.[26] In fact, as China focused on a diplomatic approach toward the West that would attract investments, it began to see Chinese culture as a way to develop a cultural industry that would aid the country's economic development.[27] China's relations with Africa were then formally reconfigured on the basis of mutual benefits, practical results, and common development.

The new source of national modernization, the "Chinese culture-building movement," initially promoted during the Deng-Xiaoping era, became more important politically in the following decade as part of the official discourse of China's soft power.[28] After the Tiananmen Square protests, China found itself isolated by the international community and decided to place even greater emphasis on its traditional culture, hoping it would help rebuild its international status. Since then, a new concept of China's soft power has emerged. The 1993 publication of "Culture as a Form of National Power: Soft Power" by Wang Huning, a major advisor to Jiang Zemin, marked the beginning of Chinese academics' effort to distinguish between China's soft power and that of the United States. Chinese intellectuals began to describe China's soft power, using aspects of the traditional Chinese cultural vocabulary such as Confucianism. This process continued into the 2000s, culminating under Hu Jintao's administration (2003–12), when cultural diplomacy was connected to the "harmonious world" theory. In 2005, harmony (he 和, one of the major components of traditional culture) was described in a white paper on peaceful development as the ultimate goal of China's development; two years later, the Chinese government officially endorsed cultural soft power. Since then, traditional values have been inseparable from China's foreign policy aims, including economic diplomacy, multilateralism, and noninterventionism. Both Chinese leaders and Chinese scholars believe that these values are China's main asset in shaping its image on the international stage.

From the 1990s on, China's cultural diplomacy has moved into many new channels, particularly in Africa. After Tiananmen, China prioritized the African continent as a territory in which it could counter Taiwanese influence, realign its international position, and prevent its isolation. On one hand, African countries were the only political actors on the international stage that did not turn down China after the Tiananmen Square protests. On the other, the conjunction of the failure of the structural adjustment programs (SAP) imposed by Bretton Woods institutions and the pressure placed on African regimes by Western donors for political liberalization and human rights gave China a unique opportunity to reaffirm its position on the continent on the basis of a solidarity derived from a common striving against "rich and powerful countries that use the politics of power," as Deng Xiaoping put it. In this new phase of Chinese-African relations, besides the traditional forms of cultural diplomacy used in the 1960s—performing troupes, academic exchanges—a number of joint conferences and projects were implemented. The first, held on October 24, 2000, after the first Forum on China-Africa Cooperation (FOCAC), was the New Century China-Africa Cultural Exchange Symposium. The proliferation of Confucius Institutes, established to promote China's culture and language worldwide (the first in Nairobi, in 2005) along with the expansion of the Chinese media presence, particularly since 2006, were intended to influence African perceptions of China.[29] The overall goal was to use direct bilateral communication to build the image of China as a "strong but gentle country" in opposition to the idea of a "China threat,"[30] likely to destabilize regional security as well as the international liberal order.[31] The Chinese government has also stressed "cultural intellectual exchanges" such as the China–Africa Think Tanks Forum (CATTF) or the China-Africa Joint Exchanges Initiative, both launched in the framework of the fourth FOCAC in 2009. These new platforms of "dialogue, cooperation, and exchange" are intended to shape China–Africa economic and political cooperation. During the 2015 CATTF forum, for example, the discussion focused on coming development trends in Africa and China's industrial cooperation with African countries, bilateral investments, and trade, including the "One Belt, One Road" initiative.[32] At the same time, increasing intellectual exchanges on questions like poverty reduction and development strategies signal the Chinese government's effort to influence African elites' perceptions.[33] Events such as the Africa-China Poverty Reduction and Development Conference, held regularly since 2010, explicitly provide policy guidelines and action for poverty reduction in Africa and China while strengthening connections between key African and Chinese actors (e.g., ministries, research institutions, universities) engaged in development discourses.[34] By establishing a "community of common knowledge and philosophy" through an approach reminiscent of the Afro-Asian solidarity of the 1950s, events like these help build a new perspective on issues such as development or security, an alternative to the Western model that, as China likes to say, is rooted in a common historical experience, common struggles, and a "common future."[35]

Aid, Political Rhetoric, and China's Development Model

Efforts to promote Chinese culture notwithstanding, it is often described as the weak link in China's foreign policy and soft-power influence. However, if Chinese culture has not been as influential as expected, China's economic power surely has. China's development assistance to Africa, which has continued relatively uninterrupted from the Cultural Revolution to the present day, despite ups and downs in relations between China and Africa, is a central element of its soft engagement there. In the last fifty years, however, the modalities and principles underlying this assistance have changed drastically, along with China's perception of opportunities on the African continent. In the 1980s, when China was mainly focused on attracting investments from the West, its relations with African countries were reconfigured on the basis of mutual benefits, practical results, and shared development. For the first time, Chinese economic assistance modalities began to include preferential loans, debt-equity swaps, and the possibility of creating aid-related Chinese-African joint ventures.[36] This new model of linking Chinese assistance to investments was intended to serve China's own modernization goal by helping its companies move in new markets, while at the same time letting the recipient country earn foreign exchange and technology.

In the 1990s, China's development assistance to Africa further intensified, thanks to the establishment of special funds for medium-to-long-term loans at low interest to support joint venture projects in Africa and the 1994 creation of the China Exim Bank, intended to provide financial policy support and assist Chinese companies in their offshore contract projects and outbound investment. Finally, after China's integration in the world economy—having joined the World Trade Organization in 2001—and the implementation of the Go Out policy (走出去战略, Zǒuchūqū Zhànlüè),[37] China's development assistance to Africa has taken many forms: loans, direct economic support, health, agriculture, education, vocational and technical training, and infrastructure construction.[38] During the Mao era, these initiatives were completely under state control; starting from the 1980s, a plethora of provincial and private actors have become involved in a sort of partnership in which the state retains a strategic role in agenda setting. Another difference is that in the 1960s, China focused mainly on East Africa, less on the North and the West.[39] This changed in the decades that followed, with the creation of new diplomatic relations and the diversification of aid projects and exchanges. While East African countries still received the most loans from China in the 2000s—mainly because of their geostrategic situation and the region's dynamism in terms of regional economic integration—starting in the 1990s, Western African countries (especially Nigeria, Africa's largest oil producer and most populous country) began to attract Chinese loans. Finally, francophone countries such as Guinea and Côte d'Ivoire have received significant funding from China, mainly for infrastructure projects, in recent years.[40]

An increasing number of investments, facilitated by the China–Africa Development Fund (CADF) founded in 2007, have come to support what J. Kurlantzick has labeled a "charm offensive."[41] As Kurlantzick states, in China's view soft power includes "not only popular culture and public diplomacy, but also more coercive economic and diplomatic levers like aid and investment and participation in multilateral organizations."[42] Changes in China's method of providing aid and its growing economic presence in Africa have not only blurred the boundaries between what could be considered hard and soft power, but also empowered nongovernmental actors whose actions have not always been in concert with the state or official foreign policy.

Consequently, as China's success on the continent has grown, its development assistance has become the focus of criticism and debates in the West, especially after 2004, when China expert Joshua Cooper Ram offered the concept of the "Beijing Consensus" as an alternative to the Washington Consensus.[43] There was also growing criticism of the "Angola model," a term coined to describe China's linking of cash with natural resources— that is, its habit of providing low-interest loans to nations who rely on commodities, such as oil or mineral resources, as collateral.[44]

China's approach is a complete break with the donor-recipient model of development dominant among OECD countries. Deborah Bräutigam, a leading expert on China's development aid in Africa, points out that the differences are primarily in content and implementation of aid.[45] In China's funding program, infrastructure is central:[46] grants and zero-interest loans from the Ministry of Commerce are usually used to finance politically friendly projects such as ministries or stadiums, while concessional loans (from Exim Bank) are directed to projects with potential economic return.[47] This approach is often paralleled by the rehabilitation of China's past projects, such as the 1976 Tazara railway or the 1917 French-built Addis Ababa-Djibouti railway. This modus operandi helps sustain a smooth translation of China's economic capital into symbolic power and cultural capital. China's aid model explicitly connects aid with business, replicating what China learned from its experience with other donors, especially Japan. Another point is that, except for One China policy,[48] there is no conditionality on China's aid; also, finally, unlike the World Bank, China does not usually deposit aid funds into accounts controlled by the host government.[49]

The success of China's development model in Africa, however, rests not only on its differences but, more important, on the recognized failures of Western approaches. The persistent low economic growth in developing countries following the implementation of the Structural Adjustment Program (SAP) in the 1980s has moved Western academic research to a more deterministic understanding of African economic stagnation.[50] In the last decade, some scholars have pointed out that Eurocentric models like modernization theory and the neoliberal development model embraced by international financial institutions have limited African access to alternative strategies and local development of technologies.[51] Economist William Easterly, for example, suggests that conventional aid undermines recipients' incentives to develop their own economies, and that the West might be more effective in Africa if it played a less intrusive role.[52]

China's development model is also distinctive because of the way it intertwines with strong political rhetoric that emphasizes South-South credentials, reflecting what is seen as a "win-win" development equation, based on a "partnership of equals."[53] With regard to this point, the idea of an "African Dream" has recently become part of the rhetoric supporting China's foreign relations with African countries. Such an idea explicitly recalls the "Chinese Dream," a concept coined in 2013 by Xi Jinping to link China's reforms to both national unity and the promotion of individual aspirations.[54] As it has rapidly become the slogan of China-Africa development, its use represents a further development in China's soft-power narrative toward Africa, as China tries to draw additional parallels with African countries by combining the rhetoric of a common past with that of a shared and glorious future.[55] As Chris Alden and Daniel Large suggest, the attempt to build a historically informed framework defined by equality, mutual respect and benefit, sovereignty, and noninterference—the principles of peaceful coexistence that have officially guided China's foreign relations since the Bandung Conference—is essential for China's foreign policy toward Africa as it allows China to use its exceptionalism to build relationships.[56] According to these scholars, "The moral basis of China's power in Africa is in itself a form of 'exceptionalism' . . . informed by a discourse of difference and similitude."[57] China emphasizes its unique understanding of Africa's economic dilemma and empathy for its economic challenges, while, perhaps more important, contributing to its development with an alternative to the Washington Consensus. In fact, China has succeeded in both its own development and its contributions to Africa, while other powers have repeatedly failed, thereby "proving that a country can successfully pursue an endogenous development plan tailored to its own context and achieve results, rather having to accept Western doctrine."[58] In a way, China's own reform experience "offers a powerful counter-narrative to Western-based norms of development."[59] Chinese scholars support this discourse of difference and similitude, using terminology that reveals the different perspectives on development (see table 7.1).

Beijing's attempt to connect China-Africa developmental initiatives to a broader global perspective and to offer a realistic alternative to the North-South patterns that have dominated the economic governance

TABLE 7.1
Main Differences Between China and the West in
Terms of Development Assistance, According to
China's Africa's Watchers

China	West
Blood transfusion	Blood injection
Partnership of equals (win–win)	Donor/recipient
Livelihood aid	Hegemonic aid
Gradual reform	Shock therapy
Pragmatism	Idealism

model since colonial times has become increasingly evident with the launch of the BRICS development bank and, more recently, of the "One Belt, One Road" initiative (OBOR)[60] and the Asian Infrastructure Investment Bank (AIIB).[61] In a 2015 article, Justin Yifu Lin, former chief economist of the World Bank and honorary dean of the National School of Development at Peking University, has explicitly related Africa to the OBOR, arguing that the OBOR initiative should evolve into "a One Belt, One Road and One Continent strategy [that] can help developing countries break the bottleneck of their development by introducing a 'blood-making' mechanism to help them develop on their own."[62] Examples of this initiative are the recent Chinese-invested rail plans for Kenya and Tanzania, which are intended to unlock intra-Africa by better connecting them to nearby landlocked economies such as Uganda, South Sudan, Rwanda, and Burundi.[63] In the process, these projects would also contribute to promoting broader international trade opportunities. The linking of OBOR to African development possibilities shows Africa's central role in China's more active international approach. Scholars outside China have increasingly been looking at this new model of South–South cooperation based on infrastructure-led development, preservation of a recipient country's ideology, and a focus on technology transfer via human resource development that ensures the sustainability of development projects as a way of advancing a post–Washington Consensus that implicitly challenges the neoliberal approach to international development.

TABLE 7.2
Different Perspectives on Development

Standard Western Recipe for Development	China's Alternative Recipe for Development
Economic and political freedoms go hand in hand	Economic development leads to political development
Democracy is necessary for economic growth	Preservation of the recipient country's ideology
Limited government and deregulation	Central role of the state
Assistance	Investment cooperation

The shift in China's security role in Africa and its evolving position on UN peacekeeping provides an insight into China's evolving views on intervention and sovereignty and its commitment to international norms.[64] For a long time, Beijing was reluctant to play a security role on the continent, but, after the end of the Cold War, it increased its engagement in African security as it built its economic and human presence in Africa. This was at the time of intense criticism from the West about human rights abuses (through arms transfers) and China's no-strings approach to economic ties. A "significant metamorphosis"[65]in its foreign and security policy was marked by China's deployment in 1989 of civilian observers in Namibia.[66] In 1992, China supported a Security Council vote for a peacekeeping operation in Somalia.[67] More significant changes came near the end of the Hu Jintao era (2002–12). In 2006 postwar reconstruction was mentioned in the FOCAC III Action plan for the first time, marking an explicit shift toward integration of peace-building into China's Africa policy.[68] In 2011, right after the Arab Spring and the regime change in Libya, which required a massive evacuation of Chinese citizens, Chinese leadership became more conscious of the risks Africa's political instability posed to Chinese economic interests. This led China to declare the protection of Chinese overseas interests as a foreign policy priority and to establish, in July 2012, on the occasion of FOCAC IV, a China–Africa Cooperative Partnership for Peace and Security.[69]

Under Xi Jinping's leadership, the Chinese government has moved further in this direction: Xi has made cooperation with Africa on peace and security an explicit part of Beijing's foreign policy.[70] In 2013, China dispatched security forces to Mali, marking the first time that the Chinese army was responsible for the security of other countries' forces. A battalion of combat troops was sent to South Sudan in 2014, and, in February 2016, China began constructing a "logistical support facility" in Djibouti[71] to assist navy antipiracy patrols in the Gulf of Aden. China has also begun contributing to the UN Peace-Building Fund.[72] In September 2015, Xi Jinping told the UN General Assembly that China would provide $100 million in military assistance to the African Union over the next five years to support the establishment of an African standby force and boost its capacity for crisis response. It also pledged $1 billion to establish the UN Peace and Development Trust Fund.[73]

The primary motivation for China's rise as a global security provider in Africa is, of course, economic factors: Beijing believes that a stable African political situation will make Chinese investments safer. But there are also political reasons behind it. As the idea of soft power has become increasingly intertwined with China's "peaceful rise," China has begun to increase its influence and promote its international image through participation in UN peacekeeping missions and involvement in African security. These are meant to prove China's benign intentions and project its image as a responsible power and cooperative global player. Of course, the blue-helmet deployments give the People's Liberation Army a chance to gain field experience abroad, which increases China's legitimacy and lets it negotiate on the basis of its field experience, thus buttressing its "right of discourse" (*huayuquan*) in UN Security Council debates and policy circles. This is particularly important, since "whereas peacekeeping aims to reduce armed conflict, peace-building is a far more encompassing term that focuses on the longer-term developmental aspects of post-conflict societies."[74] In other words, China's increasing engagement as a security provider will eventually allow Beijing to advance legitimate alternative views on global security issues.

This raises another important point. China's rise as a global security provider in Africa has put Beijing into the difficult situation of having to reconcile its noninterference policy with the responsibilities of being a global power.[75] China's increased participation in international institutions has therefore led Chinese academics to use terms like "creative interference" or "developmental peace" to provide a framework for China's evolving approach.[76] These terms seem to indicate an "aspirational commitment to a more institutionalized form of involvement" that does not totally renounce the country's traditional position on national sovereignty and noninterference in states' internal affairs.[77] This can be seen as the basis of a new normative alternative, where liberal prescriptions and Chinese perspectives converge in a sort of hybrid[78]—that is, an "illiberal peace-building approach" that emphasizes political stability rather than democracy, indigenous agency rather than universalism, the prioritization of economic modernization as a means of overcoming structural conflict, and the state's central role in peace-building.[79]

TABLE 7.3

Different Perspectives on the Implications of Peacebuilding

Industry Sector	Western (or Traditional) Perspective	China's Perspective
Objective/ Priority	Liberal democracy	Development
Focus	Good governance	Good government
Strategic Culture	Preemptive	Reactive
Method	Top-down and bottom-up (i.e., prepare for new constitution, hold national elections, build multiparty system, and/or strengthen civil society)	Top-down (i.e., strengthen state capacity, enhance national identification and national reconciliation, and/or promote economic recovery)
Challenges to	Local ownership	Public participation

Source: L. Zhao, "China's influence on the future of UN peacekeeping," in *Beyond the "New Horizon:" UN Peacekeeping Future Challenges*, Norwegian Institute of International Affairs and Geneva Centre for Security Policy Seminar Proceedings, Geneva, June 23–24, 2010, 86–98.

Focus on the Forum on China-Africa Cooperation (FOCAC)

Since 2000 FOCAC has become an important part of China's soft power. According to one Chinese Ministry of Foreign Affairs official, FOCAC is now the brand in China–Africa relations. Inspired by French–African summits and those between Japan and Africa (TICAD, begun in 1993), a number of African countries suggested the idea of the forum in the late 1990s as a way of consolidating and advancing multilateral Sino-African interaction. Convened every three years, either in Beijing or an African capital, the forum is regarded as a new political framework for "collective consultation, dialogue and cooperation" and described as "a quasi- institutionalized collaborative mechanism, designed and intended to advance Sino-African cooperation in the context of a rapidly globalizing world and expanding South-South cooperation."[80] It encompasses assistance, economic development, trade, investment, and political partnerships. Apart from developing a system for Sino-African collaboration, FOCAC has become the most important platform for the promotion and implementation of the Chinese perspective on economic and political governance issues. It is also, of course, a platform to advance China's strategies in the current international order. This has been clear since the first FOCAC conference in 2000, which focused on two questions: "How should we further strengthen Sino-African economic cooperation and trade under the new circumstances?" and "In what way should we work toward the establishment of a new international political and economic order in the 21st century?"[81]

China watchers have recently suggested that China's increased dealings with African countries through multilateral institutions like the FOCAC have opened new opportunities for China's role in global governance.[82] These scholars have pointed out that, by assuring regular exchanges between African and Chinese leaders and the former's feedback on cooperation projects, the meetings have helped Beijing adapt its policies and respond to emerging problems (such as corporate social responsibility). In addition, multilateral-sponsored projects "give an opportunity to Chinese-led development alternatives to be tested on African contexts and hence tuned/adjusted as necessary."[83] From this perspective, the FOCAC process not only embodies China's ability to adapt its Africa engagement (as we have seen, important decisions in foreign policy toward Africa have always been announced in a FOCAC summit or conference), but, more important, the initiatives launched under FOCAC represent China's attitude toward global governance issues. The important political and economic decisions made within this framework should be considered an expression of China's views on economic and political governance issues and its intention of providing an alternative mode of approaching global issues.

FOCAC forums have provided a platform for China to present solutions to global issues through the African case, much as the BRICS forums represent a platform for non-OECD leaders to discuss global challenges and coordinate their actions inside and outside existing global institutions. The forums are concrete examples of new alternative platforms that allow the Global South to stand up to the economies that still dominate the global system simply because they were the founders of the post–Bretton Woods global order. There are many similarities between decisions made at FOCAC and more recent initiatives such as the AIIB and the OBOR[84] that are seen as a more nuanced exercise of soft power and that offer further indication of Beijing's readiness to assume a more global role.[85] In other words, the creation of FOCAC and the implementation of other institutional initiatives, especially since 2000, are additional evidence of the beginning of "a new phase of China's foreign policy making which lends itself more to norm making rather than norm following."[86]

Since the post-Mao era, Beijing has focused on a multidimensional soft-power strategy aimed at protecting its growing economic interests and sustaining China's desire to have what it considers a legitimate place in the international system. Despite being undermined in the 1960s and 1970s, Chinese culture was reintroduced as an essential source of China's soft power in the 1980s. It was celebrated as one of China's distinctive features in the 1990s and, in the 2000s, creatively connected to China's peaceful development. More recently, however, China has faced a number of situations that have challenged its soft-power strategy in Africa, where its economic interests have been jeopardized and its reputation as a peaceful rising power repeatedly, as China sees it, attacked or tainted by the West. China's soft-power strategy toward Africa has therefore had to evolve, as evidenced in initiatives taken under Hu Jintao and Xi Jinping. Africa is now an emblem, a risk, and an opportunity for China: an emblem of its soft-power success, a risk of undermining its image as a benevolent country, and an opportunity to gain legitimacy as a global power by showing effective alternative methods of resolution of global issues.

China's evolving soft-power practices and discourses also reveal much about the differences between the liberal and illiberal international orders' view of Africa and China's evolving views of the international system and its place within it. China's soft-power strategy in Africa emphasizes anti-hegemonic narratives and an Afro-Asian identity. This rhetoric has been shaped into new slogans such as the "African Dream" to further support South-South cooperation and what China likes to call, in contrast to the Western model, a partnership of equals. This rhetoric is also an attempt to reverse an orientalist perception of the international order in which Africa is generally marginalized and managed and to move Africa into a more prominent position.[87] This in turn suggests a substantial difference between China and the West in the way the two conceive of the African continent's role in international relations.

In recent years, China has increased its multilateral engagements to mitigate the challenges of operating in volatile environments. China's willingness to adopt a multilateralist approach to solve Africa's security and development problems[88] indicates that it has moved past its vision of a multipolar system, where different poles compete for supremacy.[89] China's move toward greater respect for the international order and its institutions, even when it calls for their democratization, may be read as a new willingness to cooperate in addressing global problems. At the same time, it suggests the need to overcome the widespread idea that China's increasing intervention in global affairs can have only two mutually exclusive scenarios: China as a "responsible stakeholder," or China as engaged in a "struggle for mastery."[90] In fact, China could become more involved in global issues without either imposing its perspective or conforming to the existing one; its participation in global governance is not incompatible with the preservation of its cultural differences. According to a China scholar, this is the reason why the battle between China and the West will be a "serious cultural debate":

> What China wants now is an offer of cultural compromise from the Western order, for it has been successfully free-riding it, even though many painful adjustments and accommodations have been made to the system. But China's priority is to strive for international recognition of an alternative governance model through its cultural restoration. In this sense, it will continue to resist any infringement upon national sovereignty in the name of universal values.[91]

This point brings us to a final aspect of China's soft-power strategy, which has to do with the idea of a possible ideological debate between China and the West. According to Lanxin Xiang, "A new ideological debate over what it perceives to be the Western double-standard against the rights of nation states has already been started in China and it will be a defining Chinese theme for years to come."[92] But, for this debate to become concrete, China will have to better define and explain the theoretical basis of its foreign policy—a task, perhaps, for China's intellectual class. If this happens, a real cultural debate can take place, and we will be able to see if the story China tells through its soft diplomacy represents a genuine alternative to the Western model.

Notes

1. Deborah Bräutigam, *The Dragon's Gift: The Real Story of China in Africa* (Oxford: Oxford University Press, 2009), 15.
2. Bräutigam, 31.

3. Liu Haifang, "China-Africa Relations Through the Prism of Culture: The Dynamics of China's African Cultural Diplomacy," *Journal of Current Chinese Affairs* 37, no. 3 (2008): 9–44, 14. In 1951 with the Polish government, later with all other socialist countries.

4. Chris Alden and Daniel Large, "China's Exceptionalism and the Challenges of Delivering Difference in Africa," *Journal of Contemporary China* 20, no. 68 (2011): 21–38, 28.

5. I call it "neocolonialism" (instead of "colonialism") since it is intended not only as a form of economic and political independence, but also as a form of cultural dominance. This idea was at the basis of the Pan-Africanist movement, as well as the Bandung Conference (Asian-African Conference, 1955), which led to the Non-Aligned Movement (1961). So the focus was not on direct colonization—i.e., the establishment, exploitation, maintenance, acquisition, and expansion of territories (or colonies) in one geographic area by people from another area—but on a coordinated effort by former colonial powers and other developed countries to block growth and independence in developing countries and retain them as sources of cheap raw materials and labor.

6. George Yu, "Sino-African relations: A Survey," *Asian Survey* 5, no. 7 (1965): 321–32, 324.

7. The Five Principles, as stated by the Panchsheel Treaty signed on April 29, 1954, are: mutual respect for each other's territorial integrity and sovereignty; mutual nonaggression; mutual noninterference in each other's internal affairs; equality and cooperation for mutual benefit; and peaceful coexistence.

8. Liu "China-Africa Relations," 19. In 1956, the Chinese government sent cultural and arts delegations to four countries in north Africa, plus Ethiopia, and in 1957 an acrobatics delegation was dispatched to North Africa and Ghana.

9. Liu, 14.

10. Liu, 14.

11. Liu, 14.

12. Pippa Morgan, "The Truth Behind China's Aid Ambitions in Africa," Sixth Tone, February 16, 2017, http://www.sixthtone.com/news/myths-behind -chinese-aid-africa#. Egypt was also the first African country to receive aid from China: in 1956, China donated agricultural and manufacturing machinery, money, and relief supplies to the Egyptians to assist victims of the Suez Crisis.

13. Chris Alden and Cristina Alves, "History and Identity in the Construction of China's Africa Policy," *Review of African Political Economy* 35, no. 115 (2008): 43–58, 47.

14. Bräutigam, *Dragon's Gift*, 31.

15. Anshan Li, "Chinese Medical Cooperation in Africa: With Special Emphasis on the Medical Teams and Anti-Malaria Campaign" (discussion paper no. 52, Nordiska Afrikainstitutet, 2011), 7.

16. Philip Snow, *The Star Raft: China's Encounter with Africa* (London: Weidenfeld & Nicolson, 2008).

17. Bräutigam, *Dragon's Gift*, 32–34.

18. George Yu, "Africa in Chinese Foreign Policy," *Asian Survey* 28, no. 8 (1988): 849–62, 851.

19. With regard to China's support to UNITA, see Steven F. Jackson, "China's Third World Foreign Policy: The Case of Angola and Mozambique, 1961–93," *China Quarterly*, no 142 (June 1995): 388–422.

20. With regard to China's support to the FLN, see Donovan Chau. "The French Algerian War, 1954–1962: Communist China's Support for Algerian Independence," in *Military Advising and Assistance: From Mercenaries to Privatization, 1815–2007*, ed. D. Stoker (New York: Routledge, 2007), 111–26.

21. Liu, "China-Africa Relations," 20.

22. Bruce D. Larkin, *China and Africa, 1949–1970: The Foreign Policy of the People's Republic of China* (Berkeley: University of California Press, 1971), 28.

23. Larkin, *China and Africa*, 19. The Bandung Conference indeed marked the beginning of Chinese initiatives in Africa; nevertheless, as Larkin points out, "there is no evidence that China foresaw this with clarity."

24. Du Bois, one of the founders of the National Association for the Advancement of Colored People (NAACP) in 1909, is famous for his sociological theorization of the idea of the "color line." This idea of Africa and China "being colored" was reiterated in a speech Du Bois gave in China and was published in the *Peking Review*, March 3, 1959.

25. The Cultural Revolution (1966–69) was meant to be a political move against China's intellectual elite, as Mao decided to get rid of the "Four Olds"—namely, old ideas, old customs, old culture, and old habits. Criticism of feudal and bourgeois cultures was followed by the banning of Western arts and music accused of carrying "feudal" and "bourgeois" ideas.

26. Werner Meissner, "Cultural Relations between China and the Member States of the European Union," *China Quarterly*, no. 169 (2002): 181–203, 185.

27. After the Cultural Revolution, Deng Xiaoping initiated China's recovery to revive traditional culture. This move was intended to emphasize Chinese identity and foster nationalism, as well as to generate new forms of economic profit. From the 1980s on, the Chinese government slowly began to restore monuments, cultural sites, and art artifacts. Universities and schools were renovated and given more autonomy. In 1985, China signed the UNESCO Convention on World Heritage and established a state bureau to preserve Chinese culture and heritage in 1988.

28. Liu, "China-Africa Relations," 18.

29. Catie Snow Bailard, "China in Africa: An Analysis of the Effect of Chinese Media Expansion on African Public Opinion," *International Journal of Press/*

Politics 21, no. 4 (2016): 1–26, 2. After the call in the Beijing Action Plan (published as part of the 2006 FOCAC summit), initiatives were taken to increase the presence and relevance of Chinese media in Africa, including the transfer of the Xinhua news service's overseas headquarters from Paris to Nairobi in 2006; China Radio International's (CRI) first foreign-based radio station, inaugurated in Nairobi in 2006; and Africa-specific programming by China Central Television (CCTV) from 2012 on.

30. Yun Sun, "China-Africa Think Tanks Forum: China Broadens Soft Power Campaigns in Africa," Brookings Institute, October 1, 2015, https://www.brookings.edu/blog/africa-in-focus/2015/10/01/china-africa-think-tanks-forum-china-broadens-soft-power-campaigns-in-africa//

31. See Denny Roy, "The China Threat Issue: Major Arguments," *Asian Survey* 36, no. 8 (August 1996): 758–71.

32. Sun, "China-Africa Think Tanks Forum."

33. See, Bob Wekesa, "A Review of FOCAC Side-Events 2015," Africa-China Reporting Project, February 9, 2016, http://africachinareporting.co.za/2016/02/a-review-of-focac-side- events-2015/. The last one was on December 8–9, 2015 at the Gallagher Convention Centre in Johannesburg. The key drivers of this important subconference were the United Nations Development Programme (UNDP-China), the Department of Rural Development and Land Reform of South Africa, the International Poverty Reduction Centre in China (IPRCC) and the Finance Centre for South-South Cooperation. Significantly, the sub-forum was themed "Towards Post-2015 Africa-China Sustainable Cooperation on Poverty Reduction and Development," thus connecting Africa-China development initiatives to the broader UN transition from Millennium Development Goals (MDGs) to the Sustainable Development Goals Agenda 2030 and African Union Agenda 2063.

34. On the impact of China's development model in Africa based on the theory of lesson-drawing, see Elsje Fourie. "L'Éthiopie et le Kenya face au 'modèle chinois' de développement. Une nouvelle carte pour l'Afrique?," *Afrique contemporaine* 253 (2015): 87–103.

35. Jinping Xi, "Open a New Era of China-Africa Win-Win Cooperation and Common Development" (discourse at the Opening Ceremony of the Johannesburg Summit of the Forum on China-Africa Cooperation, December 4, 2015), http://www.fmprc.gov.cn/mfa_eng/zxxx_662805/t1321614.shtml.

36. Deborah Bräutigam and Xiaoyang Tang, "China's Engagement in African Agriculture: Down to the Countryside," *China Quarterly*, no. 199 (September 2009): 686–706, 694.

37. Bräutigam, *Dragon's Gift*, 74. The Go Out Policy is a Chinese government policy of internationalization of large state-owned enterprises, initiated in 1999 and further developed during the 2000s, intended to promote Chinese

investments abroad. Throughout the 1980s, the Chinese government encouraged state-owned enterprises to bid on contracts and form joint ventures abroad; during the 1990s, it created additional tools and instruments to promote trade and investments.

38. For instance, between 2010 and 2012, China provided technical and on-the-job training for almost fifty thousand people from poorer countries, including the provision of nearly three hundred training programs for around seven thousand agricultural officials.

39. After Zhou Enlai's visit to some African countries in 1963–64, he was convinced that Arab nationalism and China's competition with the West and the Soviet Union on aid might limit China's influence in this part of the continent. This explains the readjustment of China's diplomacy toward Africa in the months following his visit.

40. As some scholars have underscored (e.g., Juliette Genevaz and Denis Tull, "Les Financements chinois dans le secteur des transports en Afrique: un risque maîtrisé," *Étude* no. 67, Institute for Strategic Research at the Military School (IRSEM), June 2019, https://www.irsem.fr/data/files/irsem/documents /document/file/3124/Etude_IRSEM_n672019.pdf (accessed October 20, 2020); Sun, "China's 2018 Financial Commitments to Africa"), the omnipresence of China in Africa goes hand in hand with the fragmentation of the decision-making process in Beijing. The Ministry of Foreign Affairs does not deal with Africa as a whole, but rather from two regional angles: North Africa is grouped with West Asia, sub-Saharan Africa with the countries of the Indian Ocean.

41. Joshua Kurlantzick, *Charm Offensive: How China's Soft Power Is Transforming the World* (New Haven, CT: Yale University Press, 2007).

42. Kurlantzick, *Charm Offensive*, 6.

43. Former *Time* foreign editor Joshua Cooper Ramo coined the term "the Beijing Consensus" to define the Chinese political and economic policies since the death of Mao Zedong and to frame China's economic development model as an alternative to the Western Washington Consensus model of market-friendly policies promoted by Bretton Woods institutions and the developed countries.

44. In 2004, China offered Angola $2 billion in cheap credit, backed by Angolan oil. The gesture attracted wide international attention and was the source of the derogatory phrase "the Angola model." The money was to be used for infrastructure projects, similar to the oil-for-infrastructure loan model used by the Japanese when they provided assistance to China during the early decades of China's reform and opening-up.

45. Bräutigam, *Dragon's Gift*, 133, 134.

46. Of the US$60 billion of lending China promised to African countries in late 2015 at the FOCAC summit in Johannesburg, more than half will be spent to build infrastructure.

47. Bräutigam, *Dragon's Gift*, 161.

48. Genevaz and Tull, *Financements chinois*, 38. This point has received criticism in recent years. In fact, while China has always distinguished its policy from OECD-led Western aid and supported the principle of an aid "untied" from any conditions (no strings attached), Chinese loans to African countries to finance infrastructure construction projects can be said to be linked economically, since the contracts require Chinese construction companies as prime contractors.

49. Bräutigam, *Dragon's Gift*, 142.

50. William Easterly and Ross Levine, "Africa's Growth Tragedy: Policy and Ethnic Divisions," *Quarterly Journal of Economics* 112, no. 4 (1997): 1203–50. Starting from these reflections, Easterly and Levine focused on the link between Africa's endogenous features, such as ethnic fragmentation and heterogeneity and its economic development.

51. See, for example, Michael Clemens, Steven Radelet, and Rikhil Bhavnani, "Counting Chickens When They Hatch: The Short-Term Effect of Aid on Growth," Center for Global Development Working Paper no. 44 (2004), https://www.files.ethz.ch/isn/35677/2004_07_22.pdf (accessed September 24, 2020); Doris A Oberdabernig,"The Effects of Structural Adjustment Programs on Poverty and Income Distribution," Vienna Institute for International Economic Studies, 2010, https://wiiw.ac.at/the-effects-of-structural-adjustment-programs -on-poverty-and-income-distribution-paper-dlp-2017.pdf (accessed September 24, 2020); William Easterly, Ross Levine, and David Roodman, "Aid, Policies, and Growth: Comment," *American Economic Review* 94, no. 3 (2004): 774–80; and William Easterly, *White Man's Burden: Why the West's Efforts to Aid the Rest Have Done So Much Ill and So Little Good* (Oxford: Oxford University Press, 2007).

52. William Easterly, "Can Foreign Aid Save Africa?" (Clemens Lecture Series no. 17, Saint John's University, Collegeville, Minnesota, December 2005), 22.

53. Ron Matthews, Ping Xiaojuan, and Ling Li, "Learning from China's Foreign Aid Model," Diplomat, August 25, 2016, http://thediplomat.com/2016/08 /learning-from-chinas-foreign-aid-model/.

54. Paul Tembe, "The Temptations and Promotion of 'China Dream': Calling for Africa's Home-Grown Rhetoric" (Policy brief, Centre for Chinese Studies, Stellenbosch University, August 2015, 1–4, 2), http://hdl.handle.net/10019.1 /99157 (accessed September 24, 2020).

55. Asha-Rose Migiro, "Chinese Dream, African Dream: Achieving Common Development," *China Daily*, August 28 2013, http://usa.chinadaily.com.cn

CHINA'S SOFT POWER IN AFRICA [203]

/china/2013-08/28/content_16927233.htm; Qizheng Zhao, "Chinese Dream and African Dream Fly Hand in Hand," Center for Chinese Studies, July 11, 2016, https://ccs-ng.org/chinese-dream-and-african-dream-fly-hand-in-hand-by-zhao-qizheng/.

56. Alden and Large, "China's Exceptionalism," 21–38.

57. Alden and Large, 27.

58. Lucy Corkin, "China's Rising Soft Power: The Role of Rhetoric in Constructing China-Africa Relations," *Revista Brazileira de Politica Inernacional* no. 57 (2014): 49–72, 63.

59. Yuen Yuen Ang, "How China's Development Story Can Be an Alternative to the Western Model," *South China Morning Post*, February 3, 2017, http://www.scmp.com/comment/insight-opinion/article/2067512/how-chinas-development-story-can-be-an-alternative-western.

60. In 2013, on a visit to Kazakhstan, Chinese president Xi Jinping announced a proposal for a "Silk Road Economic Belt." In South East Asia later that year, Xi proposed a "21-Century Maritime Silk Road." The combination is now commonly known as the OBOR initiative.

61. The BRICS Development Bank's membership is limited to developing countries; the AIIB's is not.

62. Justin Yifu Lin, "Industry Transfer to Africa Good For All," *China Daily*, January 20, 2015, http://usa.chinadaily.com.cn/epaper/2015-01/20/content_1935 7725.htm.

63. Lauren A. Johnston, "Africa, and China's One Belt, One Road Initiative: Why Now and What Next?," *International Centre for Trade and Sustainable Development* no. 15 (September 2016), https://minerva-access.unimelb.edu.au/bitstream/han dle/11343/241261/Africa%2c%20and%20China%e2%80%99s%20One%20Belt %2c%20One%20Road%20initiative%20-%20Why%20now%20and%20what %20next.pdf?sequence=2&isAllowed=y (accessed October 20, 2020). Kenya has been designated as the African hub for the OBOR initiative; with regard to neighboring and coastal Tanzania, in July 2016 its government signed a US$7.6 billion loan agreement with the Export-Import Bank of China (China EXIM Bank), aimed at the construction of a standard-gauge rail corridor that will link the country with neighbors Uganda, Rwanda, Burundi, and Congo.

64. Bates Gill and Chin-Hao Huang, "China's Expanding Role in Peacekeeping," Sipri Policy Paper no. 25 (November 2009): https://www.sipri.org/sites/default /files/files/PP/SIPRIPP25.pdf (accessed October 20, 2020).

65. Gill and Huang.

66. Twenty Chinese military observers took part in the UN Transition Assistance Group (UNTAG) monitoring elections in Namibia.

67. It justified the vote by stressing the "exceptionality" of the circumstances and "the present lack of a Government in Somalia": United Nations Document

S/PV.3145, Security Council Meeting 3145, December 3, 1992, cited in Christopher Holland, "Chinese Attitudes to International Law: China, the Security Council, Sovereignty, and Intervention," *NYU Journal of International Law & Politics*, online forum, July 17, 2012, https://www.nyujilp.org/chinese-attitudes-to-international-law-china-the-security-council-sovereignty-and-intervention, 27. This trend has continued: in 2006, China noted that while it had not "pressed its objections" on Security Council Resolution 1679 on the Sudan, its abstention and the passage of the resolution "should not be construed as constituting a precedent for the Security Council's future discussion and adoption of new resolutions on the Sudan." Finally, in 2011, after emphasizing the regional support for the resolution, Ambassador Li Baodong stressed the "special circumstances" in Libya that underlay China's abstention on Resolution 1973 (29).

68 Alden and Large, "China's Exceptionalism," 131.

69. The China-Africa Cooperative Partnership for Peace and Security was established to provide financial assistance, capacity building, and other forms of institutionalized support for Africa's efforts to foster peace and security on the continent. These trends were reinforced by the financial and diplomatic commitments made in early December 2015 at FOCAC VI in Johannesburg.

70. The Forum on China-Africa Cooperation Johannesburg Action Plan (2016–18), Forum on China-Africa Cooperation, December 25, 2015, http://www.focac.org/eng/ltda/dwjbzjjhys_1/t1327961.htm.

71. Djibouti is strategically located at the southern entrance to the Red Sea on the route to the Suez Canal. The country hosts both U.S. (Camp Lemonnier) and French bases. Since 2011, a Japanese Self Defence Force contingent of 180 troops has occupied a twelve-hectare site as a base from which to operate maritime patrol aircraft as part of an international antipirate force in the Gulf of Aden and off the coast of Somalia. Following China's decision to build a base in Djibouti, the White House announced a twenty-year lease renewal that doubled its annual payments for Camp Lemonnier to $63 million, as well as a plan to invest more than $1 billion to upgrade the installation. Japan also decided to expand its military presence as a counterweight to the growing Chinese influence in the region.

72. China began to finance peacekeeping in 1982.

73. Michael Martina and David Brummstrom, "China's Xi Says to Commit 8,000 Troops for U.N. Peacekeeping Force," Reuters, September 28, 2015, http://www.reuters.com/article/us-un-assembly-china-idUSKCN0RS1Z120150929/.

74. Romain Dittgen, Aditi Lalbahadur, Elizabeth Sidiropoulous, and Yu Shan Wu, "On Becoming a Responsible Great Power: Contextualizing China's Foray into Human Rights and Peace Security in Africa," *SAIIA Policy Insights* no. 37 (September 2016): 6.

75. One example is China's ambiguous response to the UN-sanctioned intervention in Libya (China abstained from voting in the UNSC), which unambiguously highlighted the difficult terrain China is negotiating between respecting the principle of noninterference and ensuring stability in countries where it has substantial economic interests. Sudan is another example: prior to South Sudan's 2011 vote for independence from the Sudan, Beijing, along with Russia, usually defended Khartoum at the UN. In 2006, it stopped a vote to authorise UN deployment in Darfur because of the regime's opposition to it, before taking a leading role in rallying Khartoum to a hybrid option, with the deployment of a joint UN-AU operation in 2007. After the independence vote in 2011, China changed tack—cooperating closely with the United States to manage some crises and letting Moscow do the hard work of defending (northern) Sudan in border conflicts between the recently divided states, so as not to alienate South Sudan. When divisions within South Sudan led to its implosion in December 2013, China—which already had troops under UN command there—strongly advocated strengthening the UN mission.

76. Xuejun Wang, "Developmental Peace: Understanding China's Policy towards Africa in Peace and Security," working paper, Institute for Africa Studies, Zhejiang Normal University, September 12, 2014, http://ias.zjnu.cn/_upload /article/files/95/ba/fcea02bc47efa26eca2eb5fe7815/47c9883a-8b33-45b7-bb23 -f2e92198757e.pdf.

77. Chris Alden, "Seeking Security in Africa: China's Evolving Approach to the African Peace and Security Architecture," Norwegian Peacebuilding Resource Center (NOREF) Report no. 221, March 2014, 1–2.

78. Chris Alden and Daniel Large, "On Becoming a Norms Maker: Chinese Foreign Policy, Norms Evolution, and the Challenges of Security in Africa," *China Quarterly* no. 221 (March 2015): 138.

79. Alden and Large.

80. Garth Shelton and Farhana Paruk, "The Forum on China-Africa Cooperation: A Strategic Opportunity" (monograph, Institute for Security Studies, December 1, 2008), https://www.files.ethz.ch/isn/103618/MONO156FULL .pdf, 18.

81. Guijin Liu, "All-Weather Friends in Need and in Deed: China-Africa Relations Seen from the Eye of a Chinese Diplomat," in *Africa in China's Global Strategy*, ed. Marcel Kitissou (London: Adonis & Abbey, 2007), 79.

82. For example, Nicola P. Contessi, "Experiments in Soft Balancing: China-led Multilateralism in Africa and the Arab World," *Caucasian Review of International Affairs* 3 (2009): 404–34; and Lina Benabdallah, "Towards a Post-Western Global Governance? How Africa-China Relations In(form) China's Practices," *Rising Powers Quarterly* 1, no. 1 (2016): 135–45.

83. Benabdallah, "Towards a Post-Western Global Governance," 139.

84. OBOR emphasizes five areas of cooperation: (1) coordinating development policies; (2) forging infrastructure and facilities networks; (3) strengthening investment and trade relations; (4) enhancing financial cooperation; and (5) deepening social and cultural exchanges. See Geoff Wade, "China's 'One Belt, One Road' Initiative," Parliament of Australia, August 2016, https://www.aph .gov.au/About_Parliament/Parliamentary_Departments/Parliamentary _Library/pubs/BriefingBook45p/ChinasRoad (accessed October 20, 2020).

85. Antonio Villafranca, "At the Crossroads of New Global Governance, China's AIIB and the Western World," *ISPI Analysis*, no. 304 (September 2016), https:// www.ispionline.it/sites/default/files/pubblicazioni/analisi304_villafranca_02 -09-2016.pdf (accessed October 20, 2020).

86. Benabdallah, "Towards a Post-Western Global Governance," 140.

87. Marcus Power and Giles Mohan, "The Geopolitics of China's Engagement with African Development" (paper presented at the POLIS- and BISA-supported workshop "New directions in IR and Africa," Open University, London, July 9, 2008), 4.

88. The successful signing of the Memorandum of Understanding on U.S.-China Development Cooperation (2015) is another sign that Chinese foreign assistance and assistance from DAC member countries are becoming increasingly aligned. Also significant: since 2012, along with the legitimate FOCAC members (i.e., all the African countries except those that still recognize Taiwan), the African Union has been admitted as a member on an ad hoc basis, paving the way for closer collaboration, and this collaboration was expanded in May 2015 when China officially opened its permanent mission to the AU.

89. Leif Eric Easley, "Multilateralism, Not Multipolarity Should/Be Goal," *China Post*, March 29, 2008, http://www.chinapost.com.tw/commentary/the-china -post/leif-eric-easley/2008/03/29/149402/Multilateralism-not.htm.

90. Lanxin Xiang, "China and the International Liberal (Western) Order," in *Liberal Order in a Post-Western World*, ed. Trine Flockhart, Christina Lin, Patrick W. Quirk, Bartlomiej E. Nowak, Charles A. Kupchan, and Lanxin Xiang, German Marshall Fund of the U.S., May 5, 2004, 109, http://www.gmfus.org/publica tions/liberal-order-post-western-world.

91. Xiang, "China and the International Liberal (Western) Order," 119.

92. Xiang, 119.

CHAPTER VIII

The Evolution of China's Soft–Power Quest from the Late 1980s to the 2010s

ZHONGYING PANG

China's quest for soft power has evolved in interesting ways since Joseph S. Nye Jr. originated the concept. This chapter reviews the progress, problems, and prospects of that quest and offers a brief assessment of China's soft-power status. I proceed as follows: first, I provide background for the complex course of the "reform and opening up" (改革开放), introduced by Deng Xiaoping in 1978. In 2018, the People's Republic of China (PRC) under the rule of the Chinese Communist Party (CCP), grandly commemorated the fortieth anniversary of "reform and opening up." I argue that we can see these forty years (1978–2018) as two distinct periods: the rise *and* decline of China's "reform and opening up," or as two stories, the "rise of China" and the "fall of China." China's rise has been overresearched, but its fall is less studied, and even less noticed. China's employment of the concept of soft power may have been helpful in accelerating the "reform and opening up" that has made China part of the existing international order.[1] But its "reform and opening up" is an unfinished business. The lack of "modernization of politics"—or at least the "modernization of the ruling system"—has led to the end of China's much-heralded rise and perhaps even to the beginning of its fall.[2] If we say China's understanding and learning of soft power helped its economic modernization, we can also say that its misunderstanding of soft power and its actions based on that misunderstanding may cause problems in China's future relations with the world. China's shift from being a soft-power learner to a soft-power exporter reflects a form of soft power from that is different from the American type, both conceptually and in terms of its policies and instruments.

Next, this chapter analyzes the evolutional changes in the official "principles" or "guidance" of China's foreign policy, because they represent the ways that China's soft-power pursuit has evolved from import to export.[3] Then, in assessing the evolution of China's soft power, this chapter contends that China's relationship with the United States is key. Once a student of American soft power, China is now its challenger. Soft power has always been a positive factor in Sino-U.S. relations, aiding in cooperation, but now the two countries may be entering into competition around their different models of development (the "China model" and the "American model") and the different picture of the future world order. Riskily, this kind of competition could deteriorate into a new Cold War, or even what members of the Trump administration have called a "clash of civilizations."[4]

For the assessment of China's soft power, I focus on a few key questions: Why is China's soft power not necessarily soft but getting sharp? Why does China regard non–soft-power elements such as money (in international development assistance or cooperation) and state propaganda or publicity as instruments of soft power? Why in certain situations does soft power degenerate into sharp power? Finally, this chapter mentions (but does not elaborate on) related key institutions such as the Confucius Institutes and the Belt and Road Initiative and key policy slogans such as the "China Solution" (中国方案) for global governance in the evolution of China's soft-power quest.

The Learning/Importing Stage

In the early 1990s, just as the concept of soft power was born in the United States, not only to rebut those who saw U.S. world power declining, but also to explain how the United States had triumphed over the Soviet Union, China began to reopen after the Tiananmen Square protests in 1989 and the 1991 Soviet collapse.[5] China's initial opening up was marked by the establishment of diplomatic relations between the PRC and the United States on January 1, 1979. At this historic crossroads, China witnessed the birth of the soft-power concept and showed great interest in it. Chinese scholars in international studies and international politics who came to the United States for training or exchange quickly brought the concept back to China.

The scholars who originally introduced the concept of soft power in 1993 and 1994 included Wang Huning, then a professor of international politics at Fudan University and now a standing member of the politburo of the CCP Central Committee. He published two journal articles on soft power in China ("Culture as a National Capability: Soft Power" and "Cultural Expansion and Cultural Sovereignty: The Challenge to the Concept of Sovereignty"), both of which understood culture as a major component of soft power. Mingjiang Li, an associate professor at Singapore's Nanyang Technological University, summarized the soft-power debate in China[6] and Hongying Wang, a Chinese American political scientist, investigated the ways that Chinese scholars introduced Nye's concept of soft power into China.[7] I have also been a contributor to work on these early introductory efforts.[8] One question to consider: What is the relationship between the efforts to introduce soft power and the campaign of reopening that Deng Xiaoping launched in 1992?

Between 1989 and 1992, Deng Xiaoping offered 28 words to guide China's post–Cold War foreign policy, literally: "calmly dealing with international changes by hiding our capacities, biding our time, and doing something selectively in order to survive" (冷静观察、稳住阵脚、沉着应付、韬光养晦、善于藏拙、决不当头、有所作为). This is the famous "Tao Guang Yang Hui" (韬光养晦).[9] What is the true essence of the Tao Guang Yang Hui? Since Deng coined this teaching doctrine, there have been multiple interpretations at home and abroad, but they can be classified into two schools: China's interpretation or official explanation of a low-key foreign policy and that of the rest of the world, which has largely understood Deng's words to mean that China will hide its capacities and bide its time in the era of the United States as the dominant superpower.

Unsurprisingly, some in China have seen foreign interpretations as flawed or even wrong. Guangkai Xiong, former director of the People's Liberation Army General Staff Intelligence Department, for one, thought international interpretations were distorted and inaccurate.[10] General Xiong is one of few insiders within the Chinese foreign policy establishment to respond to the question of how to better interpret the Tao Guang Yang Hui.

I believe that the differences between the two schools can be understood by looking carefully at how China has presented its foreign policy principles across the greater Deng Xiaoping period (from the 1980s to 2012, with four party secretaries, Hu Yaobang, Zhao Ziyang, Jiang Zemin, and Hu Jintao). From this perspective, we can easily demythologize the doctrine of Tao Guang Yang Hui. I have found that almost all of China's statements of foreign policy principles are prefaced by either "no" (不), "not" (不), or "non" (不). A shortened list of the key "不" (bu) ideas includes:

- "Noninterference," which China has advocated since the Bandung Conference (the 1955 Afro-Asian Conference in Indonesia). Notwithstanding, China intervened heavily during the 1960s and 1970s in some Southeast Asian nations. After 1978, Deng Xiaoping stressed "noninterference" (不干涉), and China has reemphasized it since 1989.
- "Not challenging" (不挑战) U.S. power primacy or its actions in the world. In order to manage and improve relations with the United States, Deng Xiaoping warned that, even with inevitable tensions and frictions, China must avoid a collapse of relations between the countries (斗而不破).
- "Nonhegemonic": before the 1980s, China repeatedly spoke out against hegemony (反霸)—particularly the idea of a bipolar world dominated by the United States and the USSR. After 1978, as it became a rising power, it continued to assure or reassure the world that Beijing "does not seek a U.S.-like hegemony" (不称霸).
- "No leadership in international affairs": according to Deng Xiaoping's teaching, China has no intention of or interest in taking leadership in international crises or global challenges (不带头 or 不当头).
- "No seeking an alternative foreign order": when it was established in 1949, the People's Republic of China vowed to overturn the post–World War II international order (at that point the Republic of China occupied China's seat at the United Nations (UN) and on the Security Council) and, in the 1950s, it sought an alternative international order, allying militarily with the Soviet Union in 1950 (一边倒) and revolutionizing its ministry of foreign affairs (另起炉灶). China's 1982 Constitution stated that China adhered to an "independent foreign policy," and since then, as China sought to join existing intergovernmental organizations, it has repeatedly said it no longer wants to overturn the existing international order—"to seek an alternative order" (不另起炉灶).
- "Nonalliance" (不结盟): since the collapse of the China-Soviet Union alliance in the early 1960s, China has maintained the principle of nonalliance. The "independent foreign policy" rules out alliances with

others in the world. Nonetheless, China has maintained its alliance with North Korea since the 1950s.

- "Nonexport of ideologies": Deng Xiaoping stopped the export of China's political ideologies to others (不输出).
- "No strings": China claimed that its development assistance to third world/developing countries was given without political strings attached (不附加任何政治条件)

These are the most important of China's "no," "not," and "non" policies, but there are many others that are similar—for example, China's proposal of "new great power relations"(新型大国关系) with the United States: "No conflict, no confrontation, mutual benefits, and mutual respect" (不冲突，不对抗，相互尊重，平等互利). Collectively, these precepts shape China's foreign policy discourse. For this reason, it is possible to use them to interpret the Tao Guang Yang Hui; in other words, it is already footnoted by China's "no," "not," and "non" statements.

China's "no"s, "not"s, and "non"s began in 1989 and the early 1990s. In the early 1980s, when China established its new Constitution and in 1982, when it concluded the PRC- UK Joint Declaration for the return of Hong Kong to China in 1984, Deng Xiaoping offered the formula of "one country, two systems." This not only meant that China committed to nonintervention in Hong Kong's "high autonomy," and that "Hong Kongers govern Hong Kong," but it also implied that China had ended interventionism for its domestic development causes, or "four modernizations," in industry, agriculture, military, and science and technology. In 1978, Deng Xiaoping visited Singapore to promise prime minister Lee Kuan Yew that China no longer supported the antigovernment communists in Malaysia and Indonesia. In 1964, when China became a nuclear power, it immediately declared that it would "not be the *first to use* at any time or under any circumstances." Given this and the original non-intervention policy in 1955 at Bandung, we can say China's "no," "not," and "non" foreign policy doctrine has lasted more than six decades.

The "no"s, "not"s, and "non"s weren't just negative: they also suggested many positive things. China conducted a pragmatic diplomacy to manage its differences and discords with the United States more effectively, and the PRC-U.S. normalization of diplomatic relations in January 1 1979, sparked China's opening up. China concluded its key negotiation with the United States over China's membership in the World Trade Organization (WTO) on November 15, 1999, the twentieth anniversary of the start of diplomatic relations. China's accession to the WTO in 2001 marked the moment that China fully became part of the existing international order, particularly the post–Cold War U.S.-led liberal international order.

An interesting question is whether China's embrace of the U.S.-born idea of soft power played an implicit and important role in promoting China's "reform and opening up" and managing Sino-U.S. relations. My answer is yes. Deng Xiaoping's thought and policy was that, to achieve its modernization plan, China had to learn from others who have advanced knowledge and technology.[11]

Premier Zhu, Rongji, who led China's successful entry in the WTO, wrote: "Binding international agreements like China's WTO Agreement inevitably and effectively help promote China's future reforms."[12] Chinese scholars and policy makers later summarized China's gaining WTO membership as "opening up promotes reform," or "Daobi" (倒逼).[13] Since acceding to the WTO, China has achieved a massive transformation from a Stalinist Soviet Union–style, centrally planned economy to one that is modern and market-oriented, although the process is far from finished.

It is widely argued that China has created an alternative development model: the "Beijing Consensus," which acts as a competitor to the "Washington Consensus." I think this is a serious misunderstanding. If there is in fact a "Chinese development model," it is a variant of the "American development model." However, some in China have endorsed the "Beijing Consensus" in order to help strengthen its "confidence doctrine"—Xi Jinping's statement of confidence in the Chinese system, path, and theory. The confrontation between the two consensuses, is arguably, a case of a self-fulfilling prophecy of China-U.S. conflict.

China learned a lot about soft power from the United States, and it used that knowledge to modernize its economic system. There are two main examples: first, China introduced American macroeconomic policy instruments, including monetary policy, during the "reform and opening up" period. Today, although China is still not fully recognized by its peer members at the WTO as a market economy, its economic system looks like one. The People's Bank of China, its central bank, implements monetary policy much as its counterparts in other states do. China is a charter member of the world's top twenty economies—the G20—that coordinate and cooperate macroeconomically with each other and that have a Mutual Assessment Process, or MAP. Second: China's national plan of building "world-class universities" (世界一流大学), which began in 1998 when Peking University celebrated its centenary, and Chinese president Jiang Zemin called for China to have a number of global research universities in the twenty-first century. American universities are China's major models of "world class universities," and China has experienced an Americanization of its universities.

The Transitional Stage

In China's politics, foreign policy and economics, the 2002–12 period was a watershed. China's membership in the WTO helped liberate China's economic potential. It overtook Japan as the world's second-largest economy (after the United States) in 2010. Beijing organized China's first Olympics in 2008 and used it to display its soft power—something the United States clearly understood.[14]

However, several key things happened in this decade as China's learning of soft power from the United States gradually faded:

- In 2007, for the first time, China declared its own soft-power strategy (中国的软实力战略), which it called "socialist cultural soft power" (社会主义文化软实力), or soft power "with Chinese characteristics" (有中国特色). Hu Jintao's political report to the Seventeenth CCP National Congress in 2007 is widely regarded as the CCP's first documented use of the term "soft power."[15]
- In 2004, China created its first Confucius Institute, to project its "cultural soft power."[16] China began using its traditional resources, including the thoughts of Confucius and Sun Tzu and other aspects of what it called "Chinese traditional culture" (中国传统文化) to start spreading its soft power. China conducted its soft-power campaign, which outsiders called "China's charm offense," worldwide.[17] But China's soft-power dilemma emerged: it did not have enough cultural soft power to support the campaign. As I have pointed out (and Nye has cited), there is a "poverty of thought" among China's leaders.[18]
- Although China's economic growth was still rapid, China's reform toward becoming a market economy gradually slowed.
- Officially and unofficially, China coined the term "peaceful rise" to offer an unprecedented narrative of its rise to power. The "peaceful rise"

signified that China, unlike other countries, would continue to rise by soft power.[19] The building of soft power was closely linked to China's "external strategy," particularly in Africa, which became a major recipient of China's soft-power projection.[20] China organized its first China-Africa Cooperation (FOCAC) summit, which was attended by the majority of African heads of state, in 2006. It was like a UN conference, except that it took place in Beijing, not New York. Since then, the question of China's soft power in Africa has become a global theme. To deal with it, the European Union organized the Trilateral Cooperation among Africa, China, and itself.[21] In Europe, I offered several observations on China's soft-power role in Africa. At Turin University, I helped organize a volume with two European colleagues to talk about China in Africa.[22] At the University of Frankfurt, I delivered a keynote address on China's cultural diplomacy in Africa.[23].

At this transitional stage, it seemed that China did not abandon the Tao Guang Yang Hui, but began to revise it by adding new principles to the "no"s, "not"s, and "non"s, suggesting that its foreign policy was on the verge of change. But the coexistence of the new proactive principles and the old pragmatics led to contradictions and dilemmas. First, while maintaining its old idea of "noninterference," China began to seek to intervene "conditionally" or "constructively."[24] It hosted the Six Party Talks on North Korean nuclear weapons from 2003 to 2007 and was involved in the Joint Comprehensive Plan of Action ("Iran Nuclear Deal") in 2015.

Then China, despite its principle of "not taking the lead," began to do just that. One of the legacies of Hu Jintao's foreign policy (2002–12) is China's tentative and cautious international leadership. During the Tao Guang Yang Hui years of the 1990s, it was hard to imagine that China would begin to explore leadership, especially, in multilateral systems and forums. On June 15, 2001, China became a leader of a post–Cold War Eurasian regional organization, the Shanghai Cooperation Organization.[25] And, after Hu, Jintao, in the "new era" or "Xi Jinping's era" (习近平新时代), which started in 2013, there came the possibility of a big change in China's foreign policy—the end of the Tao Guang Yang Hui, and the beginning of a more assertive approach, At that time, the future of China's soft-power quest was discussed at several important conferences.[26]

The Projection Stage

The report that Xi Jinping delivered to the Nineteenth CCP National Congress on October 18, 2017 proclaimed that China was entering a "new historical position" (新的历史方位). This declaration of a new era signifies the third stage of China's soft-power quest—the projection of soft power, a transformative shift in China's approach.

The Nineteenth CCP conference announced that, over the past nearly seven decades since 1949, China had obtained a level of ruling and developmental experience that Xi Jinping summarized as "The Governance of China" (治国理政).[27] In the first stage of China's soft power, what China could project was mainly Chinese traditional culture—for example, Chinese language-training programs (via the Confucius Institute). In the "new era," what China has to export is its governance. This shows China moving beyond its "no export" model, by which it meant that it did not export its political ideology and ruling methods—although, of course, in the 1960s Mao Zedong exported or wanted to export China's revolution to Asia and Africa and even Latin America.

China has been constructing a number of platforms to project its soft power, of which the Belt and Road Initiative (BRI) formally outlined in 2015, is perhaps the most important because of its global reach.[28] Internationally, the BRI is often compared with the U.S. postwar Marshall Plan, but China does not accept this comparison. Why not? The reasons are complex. For one thing, although China has already pursued a more assertive foreign policy, the denial reflects its desire to show that the essence of the Tao Guang Yang Hui remains. But the main reason for the denial is that the Marshall Plan is too small to compare to the BRI.

The United States once urged China to assume greater international responsibilities, hoping that it would become a "responsible stakeholder."[29] However, with its foreign policy of keeping a low profile, China had not done this. In the era of the BRI, though, China has greatly surpassed being a "responsible stakeholder," taking on extensive international responsibilities. While the United States withdrew from the UN-orchestrated climate change governance (UNFCCC), China is a leading signatory of the Paris Accord. In 2015, China took the lead in the UN-led Sustainable Development Goals (SDGs).[30] It established the Institute of South-South Cooperation and Development (ISSCAD) at Peking

University and the national Center for International Knowledge on Development (CIKD).

China only accepted the concept of global governance at the G8-plus-China summit in Italy in July 2009, when Dai Bingguo (standing in for president Hu Jintao, who opted not to attend) spoke about the concerted efforts to deal with the then ongoing global financial crisis. In the "new era," by contrast, China very closely links its soft power with its role in global governance,[31] presenting the BRI and other China-led international projects as new approaches to solving global challenges.[32] It sees the BRI as a new type of global governance,[33] one that can offer "Chinese Solutions" (中国方案) to what it calls the "global governance deficit" and thus contribute to global governance.[34]

China also sees the AIIB, a new China-led international institution for financing development in infrastructure, founded in 2015 in Beijing, as an example of its soft power.[35] The AIIB not only provides an alternative in financing development (money), but also acts as a complement to the World Bank development approach.[36] And its attractions are potent: in 2019 it had more than one hundred state members.[37] There is no doubt that Africa is the center of China's soft-power projection. In the 2018 Beijing Summit of the Forum on China-Africa Cooperation, Xi Jinping repeated China's old five "no"s (五个不) to reassure African governments: "No intervention in African countries' pursuit of development paths that fit their national conditions; no interference in African countries' internal affairs; no imposition of China's will on African countries; no attachment of political strings to assistance to Africa; and no seeking of selfish political gains in investment and financing cooperation with Africa." But after the five "no"s, he offered "Ren Lei Ming Yun Gong Tong Ti" (人类命运共同体) to Africa. In China's greater "Wai Xuan" (大外宣), or international publicity, Ren Lei Ming Yun Gong Tong Ti is translated as "A Shared Future." For this "Shared Future" with Africa, Xi announced "another" $60 billion in aid and loans to Africa.[38]

In the future, however, China's soft-power pursuit faces several challenges: the first is that many international observers feel that China's soft power relies too heavily on its hard power, particularly its economic might.[39] As one of the world's two economic superpowers (along with the United States), China uses its economic success—the so-called Chinese development model—to underscore its soft power. China's economic success requires a real reform toward a market economy and rule of democratization–based law. But China's progress toward these goals is zigzag, not straight, and in the "new era," in fact, these reforms are on the retreat, as the CCP strengthens its "absolute leadership"(党是领导一切的).[40] China wants to have a "complete opening up" (全面对外开放)—that is, a "new globalization" (新的全球化) that will support its next economic growth spurt, but the United States, its largest trading partner, is in a trade war and wants to decouple from China. It is for these reasons that we can now envision the fall of China after many years of discourse about its rise. How sustainable is China's state power? If China's economy (including its education, science, and technology sectors) really enters a downturn, its hard power–based soft power will decline.

Another possibility is that China's soft power will mutate into "sharp power,"[41] to use the term that is now a focal point in the United States' current debate on China.[42] But there are two schools of "sharp power." The first is extremely political, in that it criticizes China's sharp power while neglecting its continuous soft-power efforts and soft-power learning process and equates that soft power with sharp power.[43] The other school, led by Nye, sees the issue differently. Nye says that "it is a mistake to prohibit Chinese soft power efforts just because they sometimes shade into sharp power." He opposes efforts to shut down "legitimate" "Chinese soft power tools" such as the Confucius Institute as a way of dealing with a "sharp power threat" from China.[44]

When a spokesperson from China's Foreign Ministry responded to the sharp power question, she rejected the term sharply, calling it a Cold War mentality or zero-sum mindset. She suggested that China's development should be seen more objectively.[45] Scholars in China—for instance, professor Xie Tao at the Beijing Foreign Studies University, point out that there is also American "sharp power" even if America prefers to call it "democracy promotion." He warns of the danger of "double standards" in dealing with "sharp power" in the world.[46]

The reality is that all three concepts—"soft power," "hard power," and "sharp power"—are necessary to assess China's soft power and help prevent Chinese soft-power efforts from shading into "sharp power." China's grand projects such as the Confucius Institute or the BRI are expressions of its hard power. The fact that China overtook the World Bank as the world's largest development bank is proof of China's soft power.[47] Meanwhile, when China uses rhetoric like "common development" or "for a shared future" to appeal to what it calls its "peer" countries in the "developing world," we see China's sharp power. And China uses its hard power sharply when it pretends that hard power is soft power, as when its public relations arm uses money and other "hard" resources to "better narrate China's stories" (讲好中国故事).[48]

This chapter has sought to evaluate China's soft power and show how China's soft-power efforts have evolved since 1989. To assess this evolution, it has been necessary to understand China's foreign policy changes. Chinese foreign policy, like that of other countries, has internal contradictions and dilemmas. Over the three decades from 1989 to the present, there have been three stages, each with its own version of soft power. China's learning of the concept from the United States in the post–Cold War era represented its positive efforts to present itself to the world as a rising power via its "reform and opening up." Only later did China's hard power begin to emerge, but the question we must ask is why China's soft-power efforts mutated into sharp power. At the same time, we must recall that China's foreign policy has been able to support multilateral solutions to global common challenges—global governance—even amid the era of America or Europe first. This contributes to China's soft power.

It is impossible to say whether China will return to its soft-power quest. Perhaps China's soft power will be strengthened not only by sharp power in the guise of soft power, but by China's larger role in addressing ungovernable global issues and its ability to steer clear of a soft power Cold War with others, particularly the United States.

Notes

1. Fu Ying, "Putting the Order(s) Shift in Perspective" (speech at the Munich Security Conference, February 13, 2016), https://securityconference.org/mediathek/asset/panel-discussion-doubling-down-china-and-the-international-orders-1400-13-02-2016/.
2. See the Nineteenth CCP National Congress in 2017, particularly its fourth plenum statement in Beijing on November 1, 2019. China wanted to modernize its "ruling or governance system" (治理体系现代化).
3. See Men Honghua, *China: Soft Power Strategy* (Hangzhou: Zhejiang People's Publishing House, 2007). Chinese researchers like Men Honghua conducted the first assessments of China's soft power.

4. Paul Musgrave, "John Bolton Is Warning of 'Clash of Civilizations' with China: Here Are Five Things You Need to Know," *Washington Post*, July 18, 2019, https://www.washingtonpost.com/politics/2019/07/18/john-bolton-is-warning-clash-civilizations-with-china-here-are-five-things-you-need-to-know.

5. Joseph S. Nye Jr., *Bound to Lead: The Changing Nature of American Power* (New York: Basic Books, 1990).

6. Mingjiang Li, ed., *Soft Power: China's Emerging Strategy in International Politics* (Lanham, MD: Lexington, 2009).

7. Hongying Wang and Yeh-Chung Lu, "The Conception of Soft Power and Its Policy Implications: A Comparative Study of China and Taiwan," *Journal of Contemporary China* 17, no. 56 (August 2008): 425–47.

8. Zhongying Pang, "Soft Power in International Relations and Other Issues" (《国际关系中的软力 量及其它》), *Strategy and Management* (《战略与管理》) 2 (1997): 49–51.

9. See *Selected Works of Deng Xiaoping*, vol. 3 (1982–1992) (《邓小平文选》第三卷) Beijing: People's Press, 1994), 321. On September 4, 1989, Deng Xiaoping resigned as the chairman of the Central Military Commission with these twenty-eight words to the Politburo known as "Tao Guang Yang Hui."

10. Guangkai Xiong, "The Diplomatic and Strategic Implications for the Translation of 'Tao Guang Yang Hui' from Chinese Into English" (《中文词汇"韬光养晦"翻译的外交战略意义》), *Public Diplomacy Quarterly* 2, (2010): 55–59.

11. Deng Xiaoping, "Talking Points in Wuchang, Shenzhen, Zhuhai, Shanghai, etc. (January 18–February 21, 1992)," in *Selected Works of Deng Xiaoping*, 3 vols. (Beijing: People's Press, 1994), 373.

12. *Zhu Rongji on the Record* is a book based on Zhu's *Volumes of Speeches* (《朱镕基讲话实录》) published by Beijing-based People's Press in 2011. It is difficult to find this English book. See https://www.brookings.edu/book/zhu-rongji-on-the-record-2/ (accessed October 20, 2020).

13. Yao Yang, "Daobi Reform: China's Changing Approach to Finance," in *The Harmonious Superpower?: China's Role in a Multipolar World* (Berlin: Alfred Herrhausen Society, 2013), 17–19.

14. Zhongying Pang, "Beijing Olympics and China's Soft Power," Brookings Institution, September 4, 2008, https://www.brookings.edu/opinions/the-beijing-olympics-and-chinas-soft-power/.

15. Jintao Hu, "Hold High the Great Banner of Socialism with Chinese Characteristics and Strive for New Victories in Building a Moderately Prosperous Society in All Respects," report at the 17th National Congress of the Communist Party of China, Beijing, October 15, 2007, http://english.qstheory.cn/resources/party_congress/201109/t20110930_114421.htm.

16. "Sun Tzu and the Art of Soft Power," *Economist,* December 17, 2011, https://www.economist.com/christmas-specials/2011/12/17/sun-tzu-and-the-art-of-soft-power.

17. Lucian W. Pye, review of *Charm Offensive: How China's Soft Power is Transforming the World,* by Joshua Kurlantzick, *Foreign Affairs,* September–October 2007, https://www.foreignaffairs.com/reviews/capsule-review/2007-09-01/charm-offensive-how-chinas-soft-power-transforming-world (accessed September 28, 2020).

18. Joseph S. Nye Jr., "What China and Russia Don't Get About Soft Power," *Foreign Policy,* April 29, 2013, https://foreignpolicy.com/2013/04/29/what-china-and-russia-dont-get-about-soft-power/.

19. Zheng Bijian, "China's 'Peaceful Rise' to Great-Power Status," *Foreign Affairs,* September–October 2005, https://www.foreignaffairs.com/articles/asia/2005-09-01/chinas-peaceful-rise-great-power-status (accessed October 20, 2020).

20. Yu Xintian, "The Role of Soft Power in China's Foreign Strategy," *Guoji Wenti Yanjiu* (Beijing), March 13, 2008, 13–22.

21. European Commission Directorate-General Development and Relations with African, Caribbean and Pacific States, *Report on the Public Consultation on the Communication of the European Commission on "The EU, Africa, and China: Towards Trilateral Dialogue and Cooperation on Peace, Stability and Sustainable Development"* (Brussels: European Commission, 2008), https://eur-lex.europa.eu/LexUriServ/LexUriServ.do?uri=COM:2008:0654:FIN:EN:PDF (accessed October 20, 2020).

22. Luca Castellani, Zhongying Pang, and Ian Taylor, eds., *China Outside China: China in Africa* (Torino: CASCC, 2007).

23. Zhongying Pang, "China's Cultural Diplomacy in Africa—Recent Developments," (opening Lecture, Confucius Institute-AFRASO-February 14, 2013, Frankfurt) http://www.afraso.org/en/content/confucius-institute-afraso-lecture-opening-china%E2%80%99s-cultural-diplomacy-africa-%E2%80%93-recent.

24. Zhongying Pang, "China's Non-intervention Question," *Global Responsibility to Protect* 1, no. 2 (March 2009): 237–52.

25. Jia Qingguo, "The Shanghai Cooperation Organization: China's Experiment in Multilateral Leadership," in Akihiro Iwashita, ed., *Eager Eyes Fixed on Eurasia: Russia and Its Eastern Edge* (Hokkaido: Slavic Research Center, 2007), 113–23.

26. Zhongying Pang, "Does China Need a New Foreign Policy," presentation, SIPRI Conference, Hu Jintao Decade in China's Foreign and Security Policy 2002–12, Solna Sweden, April 18, 2013.

27. *Xi Jinping: The Governance of China,* vols 1. and 2 (Beijing: Foreign Languages Press (外文局), 2014, 2017).

28. See Belt and Road Initiative, https://www.beltroad-initiative.com/belt-and -road (accessed October 20, 2020).

29. National Committee on U.S. China Relations, "Robert Zoellick's Responsible Stakeholder Speech," https://www.ncuscr.org/content/robert-zoellicks -responsible-stakeholder-speech (accessed September 28, 2020).

30. Xi Jinping, "Strive for Common and Sustainable Development as a Win-Win Partner for Cooperation, speech, UN Development Summit, September 12, 2015, http://www.xinhuanet.com/world/2015-09/27/c_1116687809.htm.

31. Timo Kivimäki, "Soft Power and Global Governance with Chinese Characteristics," *Chinese Journal of International Politics* 7, no. 4 (Winter 2014): 421–47, https://doi.org/10.1093/cjip/pou033.

32. Zhongying Pang, "China and the Struggle for the Future of International Order," in *The Rise and Decline of the Post-Cold War International Order*, ed. Hanns W. Maull (Oxford: Oxford University Press, 2018).

33. Xi Jinping, "Developing Wisdom and Strength for Building a Better Earth Home," China-France Global Governance Forum, Paris, March 26, 2019, http://www.gov.cn/gongbao/content/2019/content_5380351.htm.

34. Wang Linggui, Wang Jinbo, and Xie Laihui, eds., *A Brief Introduction to the Belt and Road Initiative* (Beijing: China Intercontinental, 2019).

35. Kenneth Rapoza, "With New Bank, China Shows U.S. It's Got Soft Power," *Forbes*, March 23, 2015, https://www.forbes.com/sites/kenrapoza/2015/03/23 /with-new-bank-china-shows-u-s-its-got-soft-power/.

36. "AIIB Complementary to ADB, World Bank," State Council, People's Republic of China, March 21, 2015, http://english.www.gov.cn/state_council/minis tries/2015/03/21/content_281475075114012.htm.

37. Jun Xie, "AIIB Powered with 100 Members," *Global Times*, July 14, 2019.

38. Christian Shepherd and Ben Blanchard, "China's Xi Offers Another $60 Billion to Africa, But Says No to 'Vanity' Projects," Reuters, September 3, 2018, https://www.reuters.com/article/us-china-africa/chinas-xi-offers-another -60-billion-to-africa-but-says-no-to-vanity-projects-idUSKCN1LJ0C4.

39. See, e.g., Nye, "What China and Russia Don't Get."

40. "Absolute leadership" was written into the CCP's new constitution for the "new era" in 2017.

41. Rory Medcalf, "China's Influence in Australia Is Not Ordinary Soft Power," *Australian Financial Review*, June 7, 2017, https://www.afr.com/opinion/chinas -influence-in-australia-is-not-ordinary-soft-power-20170606-gwli1m. This is seen as the first use of the phrase "sharp power."

42. Joseph S. Nye Jr., "How Sharp Power Threatens Soft Power," *Foreign Affairs*, January 24, 2018, https://www.foreignaffairs.com/articles/china/2018-01-24 /how-sharp-power-threatens-soft-power.

43. Christopher Walker and Jessica Ludwig, "From 'Soft Power' to 'Sharp Power': Rising Authoritarian Influence in the Democratic World," in *Sharp Power: Rising Authoritarian Influence*, National Endowment for Democracy/International Forum for Democratic Studies, 2017, https://www.ned.org/wp-content/uploads/2017/12/Sharp-Power-Rising-Authoritarian-Influence-Full-Report.pdf (accessed September 28, 2020).

44. Nye, "How Sharp Power Threatens."

45. "Foreign Ministry Spokesperson Hua Chunying's Regular Press Conference on June 6, 2018," Ministry of Foreign Affairs of the People's Republic of China, https://www.fmprc.gov.cn/mfa_eng/xwfw_665399/s2510_665401/2511_66 5403/t1566463.shtml (accessed September 28, 2020).

46. Xie Tao, "The Hegemonic Logic and Double Standards of 'Sharp Power,'" (《"锐实力"背后的霸权逻辑和双重标准》), Chinese Social Science News, April 24, 2018, http://www.cssn.cn/gj/gj_hqxx/201804/t20180425_4212593 .shtml.

47. Kevin P. Gallagher, "Opinion: China's Role as the World's Development Bank Cannot Be Ignored," National Public Radio, October 11, 2018, https://www .npr.org/2018/10/11/646421776/opinion-chinas-role-as-the-world-s-develop ment-bank-cannot-be-ignored.

48. See, for instance, Louise Lim and Julia Bergin, "Inside China's audacious global propaganda campaign," *Guardian*, December 7, 2018; and David Bandurski, "The Fable of the Master Storyteller," China Media Project, September 29, 2017. http://chinamediaproject.org/2017/09/29/the-fable-of-the-master-storyteller/.

CHAPTER IX

Global China and Symbolic Power in the Era of the Belt and Road

ANASTAS VANGELI

T he social forces that shape the interactions among the ever-growing number of Chinese diplomats, companies, intellectuals, and their counterparts from the ever-increasing number of partner countries around the world that have signed up for China's landmark Belt and Road Initiative (*yidaiyilu*) are complex, multilayered, and multi-directional.[1] These encounters between thousands of Chinese and non-Chinese actors are shaped by both the contexts and dynamics of the social fields in which the different actors operate (i.e., politics, economics, knowledge production), but also the context of Chinese national/regional developments and those of the partner countries. The interaction of these different stories, the (re)shaping of the narratives and positions of actors participating in the Belt and Road, and the material outcomes of these discursive adjustments are best captured by the concept of *symbolic power.* To put it simply, symbolic power is the power that reshapes thinking and practice without coercion, but not necessarily by relying on attraction: it is a form of productive and world- and worldview-making power that operates through language—or, rather, through the act of speaking from a position of authority.

Symbolic power helps explain the impact of a proactive, globally resonant Chinese foreign policy. Historically, the pursuit of economic interest amid a politically unfavorable climate required Chinese diplomats and other actors to behave cautiously on the global stage; as a consequence, from 1978 to the 2010s, they embraced modest and pragmatic rhetoric that served to advance commercial ties and integrate into the global order.[2] In the era of Xi Jinping, however, they have gradually embraced a new, more confident posture, engaging with their counterparts around the world actively and creatively.[3] The formal launch of the Belt and Road in 2013 unifies external and domestic policies pursued by the Communist Party of China (CPC), collectively aimed at rewiring the global political economy by moving China from the position of outstanding "game player" to "game maker."[4] While some Chinese actors were present worldwide before the Belt and Road, their role was constrained and pragmatically business-oriented; it is only with the Belt and Road that they are increasingly assuming the authoritative role of initiators of collective action in the global arena, in line with the CPC's shift in foreign policy from "keeping a low profile" toward "striving for achievement."[5] As these processes unfold, the multitudes of Chinese actors who now operate globally emanate symbolic power—even if some of them do not yet realize it.

Symbolic power stems from the context in which social relations take place. Over time, Chinese actors have capitalized on the rise of the narrative of "the rise of China"—that is, the mantras by foreign (usually Western) observers of China who speak admiringly and/or fearfully of China's rise as an inevitable and tectonic shift in the global field of power.[6] As Breslin has argued, "In many respects, the idea of a Chinese alternative to the West has been driven by foreign observers of China's global influence."[7] It is Western discourses of the rise of China—internalized by policy, business, and knowledge elites all over the globe—that have (inadvertently) helped position China to project its story, wisdom, and solutions to others, to make its rise, at least in the pre-2015, pre-Trump world, seem destined, inevitable.[8] Those global narratives of "rising China" have provided the reservoir of symbolic capital and power that enables all the processes I describe here.

A symbolic power analysis takes into account the complexity visible on the microlevel of both the interactions between Chinese actors and their overseas counterparts and their outcomes. The scope of work of Chinese policy makers, companies, and research institutes under the Belt and Road framework requires going out at an unprecedented pace and dealing with an unprecedented number of countries and regions. Often, the new China-led interactions provide sites for lively and somewhat competitive discussion and proliferation of particular classifications, or "vision[s] of the social world and of its division."[9] In other words, many of the social interactions that have helped implement and advance the Belt and Road have involved a particular discussion on the state of the global economy that takes up the roles of and implications for particular countries and regions, the economy's power relations and asymmetries, and the emergence of a transnational community of nations and people, circumventing or transcending (though not necessarily competing with) existing groupings and alliances.

Symbolic power is about a profound change that happens seamlessly. The Belt and Road espouses a global vision that originates in China. Socialization under the Belt and Road framework involves a dialogical process whereby the vision and practices espoused by Chinese actors—which originally seemed arbitrary or particular—have over time become recognized and localized by others, thus becoming acceptable or universal.[10] At the core of the Belt and Road vision is a particular understanding of economic development, which in turn then is translated into policy.[11] In the context of the Belt and Road, this means that both the geographic *and* policy components of this general worldview, originally deployed by Chinese actors, are now accepted as the foundation of all joint discussions and cooperation by all participants. This shift from particular to recognized, this normalization, constitutes symbolic power's work as a "world-making" power, the power "to impose and to inculcate *doxic* principles, and particularly to preserve or transform established principles of union and separation, of association and disassociation," along with the power "over words used to describe groups or the institutions which represent them."[12]

The notion of symbolic power can help us address the dynamics of change, particularly in three different aspects of the interaction:

1. *Symbolic power in the relationships between the Chinese and non-Chinese participants* in China-led events, whereby Chinese actors emerge as central to global and world affairs, leading to reproduction of asymmetry (China initiating/leading, non-Chinese participants responding/following);

2. *Symbolic power in the relationships between participants and their own contexts,* whereby, for instance, for non-Chinese actors, working on China itself becomes a source of prestige, relevance, and what we can call "cognitive authority," thereby motivating these participants to reproduce the discourse of China's centrality, while in the case of Chinese actors, working on the Belt and Road also can boost one's legitimacy and position in the system;

3. *Symbolic power of the geoeconomic imagination*—that is, the transformative potential of the various representations of the grand geoeconomic vision of the Belt and Road as well as the creative thinking on economic cooperation—stimulated through China-led interactions.

This chapter will unpack the three types of relations of symbolic power, the products of symbolic power, and the limits of symbolic power, by discussing the Belt and Road in global terms, as well as by drawing on China's engagement with Central, Eastern, and Southeastern Europe (CESEE).[13] While taking into account the abundant secondary literature on the Belt and Road, it also draws on substantial empirical work conducted from 2014 to 2018 that included participant observation and interviews with Chinese and non-Chinese actors involved in these interactions. Geographically, most of the original data upon which this chapter is based comes from CESEE.

Relations and Interactions Between Actors

The study of symbolic power in the relations between actors directly concerns the impact of China-led platforms on processes that are often invisible from the macro–point of view, but are felt, experienced, and lived at the level of human interactions and embodied experiences—and, as such, often overlooked in policy-oriented and more formalistic and technocratic analyses. These subterranean and essentially elusive processes, however, are shaped, and in turn themselves shape, the thinking and practices of China-led cooperation in the era of the Belt and Road and are thus some of the central elements of the work of symbolic power.

Setting Up the Encounter

Never before in history could Chinese and non-Chinese actors have gathered and discussed policy issues in the high-profile, relevant context that occurs in the era of the Belt and Road. The Belt and Road Forums in 2017 and 2019 have brought together twenty-nine and thirty-eight heads of governments, respectively.[14] The regional forums—the triennial Forum on China Africa Cooperation (FOCAC) and the Forum on the Cooperation between China and the Community of Latin America and the Caribbean States (CELAC); the annual meetings of the platform for cooperation between China and the CESEE Countries (16+1, called 17+1 as of 2019, after the inclusion of Greece); and the occasional dialogue between China and the Pacific Islands Forum (China-PIF)—as well as the conventions of the BRICS group (in which China plays a leading role), the Ancient Civilizations Forum (which China has co-coordinated with Greece), and many other high-profile diplomatic exchanges led by China—all serve to advance the Belt and Road vision.[15] Sectoral discussion platforms, ministerial meetings, forums of research and education institutions, and events featuring businesses and financial institutions have been convened in China and around the world with higher and higher frequency; day in and day out foreign delegations from Belt and Road countries flock to China, while Chinese delegations have been traversing the globe, coordinating events in fields including economic policy, security cooperation, health care, and folk dance. These are new spaces in which Chinese actors "project their worldview both visibly and invisibly, by conceiving new taxonomies, setting the rules, effectively channeling pragmatic offers" for various forms of cooperation to non-Chinese actors, all while creating an amicable spirit and a discourse of camaraderie among participants.[16]

These platforms, though developed with feedback from all the participating actors, are in essence China-centered.[17] As I have argued elsewhere, "The visible, and especially the invisible elements of structure and hierarchy, the language, concepts and underlying ideological assumptions of how the world works are built into documents, correspondence, the code of communication, the visual and cultural elements of the interaction, the agenda of the events, and in the social practices that constitute the institutionalized relationship."[18]

Even though the actual content of these events matters, it is their contextualization in the broader picture of the Belt and Road and their regular repetition that serve to naturalize them as an integral part of participants' thinking and practice and as constitutive to the *doxa* of the field of international cooperation. Through the routinization of symbolic practices, the Belt and Road and its associated China-led institutions and mechanisms facilitate the memefication of new concepts, ideas, and a worldview that can initially seem puzzling and alien to the recipients, and even more so to onlookers. Hence, while tropes such as "win-win cooperation," "mutual benefit," "common destiny," and the like may appear prosaic, their ritualistic repetition over time leads to their acceptance as legitimate principles by participating actors, who even begin using them in their own speech.

The encounter is conceptualized in a way that ascribes the non-Chinese participants an active role in the process. Non-Chinese actors are empowered *coperformers* of the new formats of cooperation, not mere extras who sit in the background, but the space for their expression and their possible impact on the direction of the cooperation is delimited by the words and actions of Chinese actors. Furthermore, a prerequisite for participation in these venues is the acknowledgment of China's centrality, or at least no open challenge to or confrontation with official Chinese discourse. Another requirement is the commitment to mutual learning, which underpins much of the interaction; non-Chinese participants thus simultaneously play the role of students of China and teachers of the Chinese actors about their own countries and regions (and vice versa, their Chinese counterparts are teachers about China and students of the world). Finally, it is important that much of this interaction happens in line with the etiquette of international cooperation; in that sense, there is nothing particularly qualitatively outlying about it compared to other similar global endeavors—except that the setup is distinctively China-centered.

Performing China's Centrality

As in the case of any other regularized international platform, the events under the Belt and Road framework follow a script. During ceremonial opening acts, keynote speeches by senior Chinese officials reiterate rather vague but friendly points about the importance of mutual respect and win-win cooperation. These are then followed by a more analytical discussion, as most of the speakers reflect on ongoing developments and provide practical recommendations about how to proceed with various facets of the cooperation. At the same time, debates can take a reflexive turn, with non-Chinese participants talking about their own experiences, interpretations, and expectations. Such discussions are often loaded with normative and other subjective claims, provide assessments of the current situation, and offer various takes about the future direction of the cooperation.

What unites all the various narratives emerging from non-Chinese participants—including those that are critical, skeptical, or uncertain—are the expectations, desires, and demands presented to their Chinese hosts. These demands can vary in terms of content and scope: there are suggestions of particular policy measures in various fields (e.g., economic cooperation, cultural exchange, technology), suggestions of how to proceed with the interaction formats, and so on. This type of discussion, whereby non-Chinese participants make demands of their Chinese hosts (but never vice versa!) is a direct outcome of both the (asymmetrical) division of roles and labor in the context and the consultative nature of Chinese-led deliberations. By acting as organizers, and, in the language of management, as "external coordinators" of these interactions, Chinese actors implicitly take on the responsibility for future outcomes (even though nominally it is all about joint efforts and shared outcomes). Chinese actors thus encourage the discussion, asking the questions and noting the answers; as the Belt and Road is initiated by China, they have decision-making power over its implementation. Here, what matters is not so much the questions and demands of the non-Chinese participants, the answers of the Chinese ones, or whether the issues raised are followed with policy measures, but, rather, the emergence of this very constellation itself, which speaks of the internalization of the asymmetrical roles. By perpetuating the asymmetrical relationship, even those non-Chinese actors who harbor skeptical attitudes toward the Belt and Road are affirming the authoritative position of the Chinese hosts. Symbolic power, in this sense, downplays or rather normalizes these asymmetries by creating what appears to be an inclusive setup.

Importantly, symbolic power—by definition invisible in the eyes of non-Chinese participants—is also often invisible in the eyes of Chinese representatives. It is, however, the Belt and Road setup rather than anything else that amplifies symbolic power. Outside of that setup, China's centrality is not visible or felt to the same extent.

Symbolic Power and Actors in Their Own Contexts

The Chinese and non-Chinese actors who take part in Belt and Road activities are all primarily rooted in their national sociopolitical contexts—that is, their thinking and behavior in the context of interacting with each other is shaped to a great extent by social forces pertinent to their own background and idiosyncratic context. What happens throughout the interactions themselves is largely motivated and driven by the developments in what we can call their "fields of origin," but the dynamics in those fields may be affected by the interaction processes as well.

With the extension of the field of China's foreign policy practice, there seems to be enough space for negotiations of various interests within the country, as the Belt and Road offers something for everyone and is open to everyone's input.[19] At the same time, the visions, objectives, and approach to the Belt and Road vary among the Chinese actors. While some have based their enthusiasm on normative convictions or seen the Belt and Road as a profitable opportunity, others are more cynical, getting involved simply because Belt and Road was trendy or because the cost of staying out seemed too high.

But, regardless of the motivation, the high stakes in being a Belt and Road implementer have led to an intranational competition between Chinese actors at various levels. Local governments race each other to establish partnerships abroad; state-owned enterprises compete for projects; research institutions scramble to influence policy discourse, partnerships, and research projects; and sometimes this competition even occurs within organizations, as different departments or individuals compete for the privileged position of being a Belt and Road implementer. Both material and symbolic incentives stimulate this competition. Importantly, Chinese actors do not face external competitors; they pursue close cooperation with all sorts of external actors, as one measurement of the success of Belt and Road implementation is establishing more partnerships with peers around the world. The extent of these linkages then generates symbolic capital for the Chinese actors in their own context.

At the same time, while various Chinese actors have (co)shaped the Belt and Road, it has in turn reshaped their work. The Belt and Road implies internationalization of their worldview and daily work, but it also means tying different economic, political, and cultural aspects of that work together into a comprehensive, holistic bundle of (im)material and symbolic labor. "Belt and Road" is in essence a boundary concept—in other words, it is being developed in the elusive "space between fields."[20] It is politics by economic means and economics by political means; it is both knowledge production and publicity work; it is about implementing a central vision in a decentralized manner and expanding contacts and networks in an increasingly restrictive Chinese domestic environment. In that sense, the Belt and Road—and the struggle for symbolic capital it inspires within the Chinese context—significantly restructures various professional fields in China.

Somewhat similar, albeit less substantial, developments occur in the context of non-Chinese Belt and Road participants. Non-Chinese participants do not engage with China passively, but develop and exercise their own agency, shaped by their dispositions, context, and interests. This also makes the milieus of non-Chinese actors engaged with China distinct and varied, driven by different motivations, conditioned by variegated social forces. Some have become Belt and Road participants by accident, others as a natural upgrade of their previous China relations; some more opportunistic participants saw the Belt and Road as a source of both material and symbolic capital.

What they share, however, is that being engaged with the Belt and Road as it and Global China become ever more relevant topics in the global (and national and regional) debates means that their work inevitably comes to carry a certain strategic load. Political cooperation with China is not regular politics, but work aimed toward a new world order centered on the New Silk Road's vision; economic cooperation is not just business as usual, but building up new transcontinental economic corridors and markets; and, in terms of knowledge production, "China watching" and Sinology become increasingly political, policy-oriented fields, the study of a rising global power of particular strategic importance.[21] Even actors who have never dealt with China before must increasingly incorporate China in their day-to-day tasks. And all these actors have a stake in maintaining China's importance.

For a number of China-focused actors, an important driver is the sense that Global China and the Belt and Road are important themes: the more their society talks about China, the more their symbolic capital increases. They are early adopters of the new trend of inside knowledge and firsthand experience—whether in politics, economics, or research—in dealing with China. At the same time, it is not only those with a constructive attitude toward China who have a stake in its rise; those holding various normative orientations, even China critics, do too. Policy makers, businesses, or knowledge actors who deal with China do not have to like China or be enthusiastic about its rise to benefit from the growing awareness of, interest in, and opportunities to shape national policies and public attitudes on China.

Symbolic Power of the Geoeconomic Imagination

The Belt and Road has a clear purpose and vision: to radically reshape the global political economy through the pursuit of linkages in all forms and directions: to establish policy coordination and development agenda alignment; to stimulate physical connectivity by boosting hard and soft infrastructure; to facilitate trade, investment, and financial cooperation; and to build up "people-to-people" exchanges. The end goal is not the creation of transportation corridors that simply link up point A to point B on the world map (as often suggested in Western media reports), but rather to create an integrated economic space covering Eurasia, Africa, and beyond.[22] At the same time, the Belt and Road does not follow a particular blueprint for achieving this endeavor; it sets out general parameters of thinking, discussion, and action that become subjects of proactive engagement by the multitudes of participating Chinese and non-Chinese actors.

One can therefore think of this geoeconomic vision of the Belt and Road as a collaborative form of storytelling that is shaped through political speeches and memorandums of understanding, policy documents, scholarly and think-tank conferences and publications, and various forms of media content—even children's songs and bedtime stories—all packaging the Belt and Road message differently for different audiences. It is in this sense a "web of interlocution" that "comprises meta-narratives that reveal linkages between a wide range of interactions, organizations, and institutions and/or help to make sense of whole epochs."[23] The geoeconomic narratives and the idea of economic cooperation are seen as ways to mitigate uncertainties and security concerns, defuse or neutralize other differences, or desecuritize the context in which the interaction takes place.[24]

The process of collective geoeconomic imagination has been open to participants even from some of the most peripheral countries. For many of them, the collective contemplation of economic progress has a therapeutic component. The example of China's success in the post-1978 era is a reminder that economic miracles are possible, especially when juxtaposed against the less stellar, if not outright poor, performance of (many of) the partner countries (at least in comparison with China), which tend to be developing, transitional, or crisis-struck.[25]

The extension of the geoeconomic imaginaries of non-Chinese actors has been helped by two significant components: the triangular temporal rhetoric (glorious past—problematic present—bright future), and the focus on connective infrastructure.

Triangular Temporal Rhetoric

As a story that mobilizes and inspires others, the Belt and Road starts with a narration of the present-day condition of uncertainties, inequalities, and conflict that creates an image of an impending dark age of sorts. It next contrasts this contemporary decay with the past "golden age": the ancient Silk Road, imagined as a metaphor of shared peace and prosperity. While this glorious past is lost, China issues a call to restore it, thus overcoming contemporary predicaments. The imagined golden age of the ancient Silk Road is a selective, embellished, and idealized version of the past, best captured by the official term "Silk Road Spirit," which is said to encompass "peace and cooperation, openness and inclusiveness, mutual learning and mutual benefit."[26]

What enables and creates the context for this rhetoric to succeed around the world is the way it addresses some of the most burning questions of the postcrisis global order. The global financial crisis (GFC) of 2008, in addition to its material consequences, triggered what can be called a state of "ontological insecurity," leading to a situation where "previously established self-understandings and external role conceptions were susceptible to challenge."[27] Crises, in this sense, create the fertile ground for rhetorical maneuvers like the Belt and Road.[28] The GFC brought about a "crisis of symbolic capital" of Western/American-led globalization of a previously unimaginable scale—and every subsequent major global economic crisis has contributed to this crisis.[29] The fact that China has suffered comparatively less in the present "(post) crisis era" puts it in a position to command symbolic power in shaping the postcrisis narratives.[30]

The Belt and Road vision uses the distant (and glorified) past and the uncertain present cleverly, but the future-oriented discourse put forward by Chinese policy makers is particularly important. One of the key normative concepts in China's foreign policy rhetoric under Xi is developing a sense of shared future of planetary scope and working toward the construction of a "community of common destiny" (CCD) for humanity.[31]

The concept of constructing CCD lets a globally responsible China lead by example and steer the development of global affairs under a particular set of principles.[32] The underlying message of the CCD discourse, however, is one of interdependence—while China aspires to lead, the CCD narrative serves to reassure and empower others to see themselves as being on an equal footing.

At the same time, the future that Chinese scholars propose with the Belt and Road is context-specific and not equally appealing to everyone. The developmentalist vision that underpins it is ultimately aimed at actors coming from developing countries, transitional economies, and developed countries ravaged by crises; it is not surprising that ideas of new corridors, belts, roads, industrialization, and modernization will not be as appealing to the most advanced economies—who have already experienced all that—even though Belt and Road has found some support among actors in California,[33] Scandinavia,[34] and the United Kingdom.[35]

The Symbolic Power of Infrastructure

The Belt and Road is centered on the ideal of the pursuit of national economic greatness, associated with the development of the "real," physical economy.[36] Its vision of globalization is based on the notion of economic activity and production as preconditions for consumption; it is about the pouring of concrete, the noise of factories, and the passage of cargo trains and container ships. This is not to say that Western (U.S.-centric) frames of globalization are omitted: the Belt and Road is also about finance, smart technologies, and consumer brands, but those are of secondary importance, at least in terms of narration or broader appeal. The Belt and Road, in essence, provides a road map for modernization. There is nothing particularly ground-breaking in its content; what is extraordinary is its (almost) planetary scope, and the boldness required to foresee prosperous futures for some of the Earth's least prosperous places.

Of the elements that comprise the metanarrative of the revival of the real economy, the development of connective transport infrastructure is particularly important. Of course, the importance of connective infrastructure for economic development is an established notion in the body of knowledge and public policy, but it is even more so for China. Chinese actors reinforce this idea by repeating the principle "If you want to develop, build a road first" and "Build a road, and they will come." Western observers have again inadvertently helped China make the case for its infrastructure-centered vision of development: as the adage goes, every few years China pours more concrete than the United States did in the entire twentieth century.[37]

Aside from its obvious economic importance, connective infrastructure carries symbolic power. It is associated with speed and thus with modernity, progress, and growth, synonymous with conquering nature, transcending distances, bridging the local and the global, and localizing global visions of modernity and prosperity.[38] Physical, connective transport infrastructure is central to the development of future-oriented Belt and Road narratives that motivate thinking and action in the present, "elicit[ing] powerful temporal imaginaries."[39] As Brian Larkin argues, infrastructure is "an 'enthusiasm of the imagination,'" as it can stimulate "feelings of promise": "Roads and railways are not just technical objects then but also operate on the level of fantasy and desire [and] encode the dreams of individuals and societies and are the vehicles whereby those fantasies are transmitted and made emotionally real."[40] This is why infrastructure has a tremendous mobilization potential and matters not only at the level of economic development, but also in terms of creating broader sociopolitical narratives, political platforms, and popular movements—like the Belt and Road.[41]

The symbolic power of infrastructure also stems from the lived, embodied experiences associated with it. This is particularly visible in the social, "people-to-people" interactions of the Belt and Road framework; for a number of participants, the involvement in China-led platforms for cooperation is also about the physical, bodily experience of China and its infrastructure (which is newer and usually considered better than that in the developing world, not to mention in many developed countries). A Belt and Road–themed trip to China is not only about a particular discourse and interaction: it is also about physical sensations and the stimulation of the senses, the most significant, of course, being the rides on Chinese high-speed trains that go 350 km an hour, making physical infrastructure a subject of "embodied experience" that potentially shapes a set of interpretations, conclusions, and lessons to be taken back from China.[42]

These takeaways do not necessarily have to be rational—sometimes, the feeling of being overwhelmed can determine the thinking and actions of others. After all, humans are not perfectly rational; their inherent biases, imperfect information flows, and the impact of their lived experiences contribute to their ideational trajectories.

Symbolic Power in Action: Reframing Postsocialist Europe 2011–2015

Symbolic power in action in the context of the Belt and Road is not only about the interaction among and interdependent transformation of different worldviews, but also the interaction of different self-conceptions of the various actors involved.[43] In other words, the way Chinese actors have perceived, addressed, and engaged with others is different than the way those other actors see themselves, and moreover, how these others have been framed by other hegemonic actors. This mismatch in positions stems from different systems of values and references.

One region where such classification struggles have occurred is CESEE. While Chinese policy makers paid special attention to the region starting from the reform and opening up to the fall of communist governments in Europe (1978–89), learning lessons on building market socialism from CESEE, the 1990s and early 2000s were followed by destruction of the bridges between the two sides, as most of the CESEE countries (except Yugoslavia) pursued anticommunist foreign policy that was confrontational toward China. As relations warmed up in the aftermath of the GFC in 2008, and high-profile figures including then–vice president Xi Jinping traveled to the region, Chinese diplomats prepared to launch a multilateral cooperation platform involving sixteen CESEE countries. The platform was launched in 2011 and institutionalized in 2012, serving among other things, as a laboratory for "One Belt, One Road," as it was called when, a year later, it was announced. The China-CESEE cooperation has been driven by policy coordination, quasi-institution building, and the launch of numerous people-to-people dialogues. Normatively, the new encounter meant that Sinified Marxism would have to engage with the plethora of postsocialist discourses that shape the views of their CESEE counterparts, making China's reading of CESEE as a region vastly different from the reading of other global actors (e.g., the United States, the European Union, Russia, or Turkey).

The intensified and deepened interaction, for all the ceremonial displays of cordiality and positive rhetoric, has produced some awkwardness between Chinese and CESEE actors, an awkwardness that is one of the constitutive parts of their new relationship. A major source of discomfort has been the inability of CESEE actors to come to terms with the fact that China had arbitrarily convened sixteen (and later one more) countries. But what the original sixteen CESEE countries have in common is that they are all former socialist states; even more important, they have been grouped together because of their relatively comparable transition processes and their adoption of a dependent capitalist model.[44] The fact that such reading has gone against the self-perception of a number of CESEE actors has given rise to the central classificatory dilemma about CESEE's position in the global economy: Chinese actors have repeatedly framed it as part of the Global South, eliciting confusion, disapproval, or even offense from some CESEE representatives.[45]

This understanding of CESEE has prompted Chinese actors to reimagine the region's economic geography in light of emerging Belt and Road cartographic statecraft. CESEE, in this sense, is no longer defined primarily by its integration in the common European market and Western European supply chains, but by its proximity to Russia, Belarus, Central Asia, Turkey, and the wider Mediterranean—areas that the various overland and maritime transport routes and economic corridors are envisioned to pass through. This vision of CESEE as a regional economy of scale, a market of more than a hundred million people, with access to four seas (Baltic, Black, Adriatic, and Aegean), is different from the mainstream regional sense of itself, though it potentially communicates/corresponds with some local—albeit fringe—ideas and imaginations.

Even more significant is the reimagination of CESEE's history. CESEE countries generally have a rather negative attitude toward their communist past and harbor some of the world's most fervent anticommunist positions. Nevertheless, as Chinese actors attempt to build a deeper relationship with the region, they have often referred to the shared communist past and the long history of bilateral relations, some established as far back in 1949, as important symbolic aspects that facilitate contemporary relations between the two sides. When discussing the historic linkages between China and CESEE—and the triangular relations with the Soviet

Union (USSR) within the global socialist community—they emphasize the Sino-Soviet split and the times when China supported CESEE governments in the struggle with Moscow. The Chinese version of this history recognizes 1989 as a critical juncture as well, but what is important here is the fall of the USSR as a hegemonic force in the (former) communist world, not the fall of communism as such, and the resulting opportunity to rekindle the friendship between China and CESEE. As far as the divergence goes, Chinese actors say they are "not mad" at the CESEE elites for the ideological choices made in the 1990s.[46]

The various instances of awkwardness can be theorized as "hysteresis,"[47] defined as a "mismatch between the dispositions agents embody and the positions they occupy in a given social configuration," whereby actors with different habitus (e.g., anticommunist from CESEE with a profound neoliberal and/or militant Atlantic orientation) suddenly face alien doxa of global politics (e.g., being guests in a room full of red flags and red stars where people discuss South-South cooperation coordinated by a Communist Party).[48] Hysteresis, and the embodied experience of awkwardness that accompanies it, in these cases is the reverberation of a deeper transformation taking place. What changes is the constellation of the field of power in which CESEE actors operate: before the intensification of China-led interactions, for them a particular set and limits of what is thinkable and sayable was firmly in place (e.g., the formal framing of CESEE as part of the West or the Global North, or the consensus that communism fell in 1989). However, the interaction with China has exposed CESEE actors to a different doxa that has transcended, extended, or even contradicted the old one (e.g., CESEE being a part of the Global South; with communism not only alive, but also marching forward well into the 2010s). The notion of "hysteresis" here denotes the particular situation in which CESEE actors are caught off guard, which creates the conditions for transformation in their own dispositions—not by literally embracing the views promoted by their Chinese counterparts, but rather by embracing and adapting to the new reality of the power asymmetry.

Frame (Re)Alignment

What makes the 16+1 experience profoundly relevant is that these classification struggles and paradoxical realizations have not led to any major conflict, fallout, or interruption in the China-led, Belt and Road interactions. Rather, the interaction has yielded processes of mutual adaptation and frame alignment that offset or transcend the awkwardness stemming from the mismatched positions; in other words, the relationship between Chinese and CESEE actors has continued despite the fact that rarely would someone in CESEE openly and wholeheartedly embrace the "Global South" label proposed by China, let alone the Chinese communist iconography. Yet, even though some of the CESEE actors resist the label, they still engage in South-South cooperation, mimicking modes of cooperation that China has with developing countries in Asia and Africa.[49] To what extent the South-South cooperation policies in the context of China-CESEE relations—and beyond—are successful is a question for a different project.[50]

Furthermore, even though on a societal level CESEE societies still tend to see China through the prism of (anti)communism, policy, business and knowledge elites rarely contradict their Chinese counterparts on historical issues and do not object to the narratives of common/shared history. At the same time, the contradiction between domestic anticommunism and the close relationship with China can lead to somewhat cognitively dissonant situations. For instance, as the "illiberal turns and swerves" in CESEE intensify across the entire region, replacing liberal democratic teleology with nationally framed ideology, some actors have taken China as an example to follow (at least rhetorically).[51] This does not mean that China has been a major reason behind the illiberal shift in some CESEE countries; in fact, the emergence of China as inspiration is rather surprising, given that it coincides with anticommunist ideology. Paradigmatic in this sense is Hungary, where the anticommunist ruling party Fidesz—which has also positioned itself as against liberal democracy—has championed "opening to the East," and prime minister Viktor Orban has cited China as a model to follow. Even more perplexing has been Poland, where for instance, prime minister Mateusz Morawiecki and other policy makers and intellectuals admired Justin Yifu Lin, the former chief economist of the World Bank, and his concept of "new structural economics" (an economic paradigm largely based on China's experience) before coming to power and implemented some of its principles when they were in power.[52] At the same time, in the changing geopolitical landscape, Poland's leaders have become more cautious and critical of China.

Post-2015: Limits of Symbolic Power?

In the early stages of the Belt and Road cooperation and the 16+1 platform, and in particular before 2015, by emanating symbolic power Chinese actors managed to "desecuritize" its relations with CESEE.[53] Reading the region as part of the Global South and its communist history as a shared past upon which the two sides could build did not generate any major friction, despite the fact that these positions are far outside the CESEE mainstream. At the same time, the volume of economic cooperation did not increase dramatically; therefore, the complacent attitude of CESEE actors can only be analyzed in the context of immaterial, symbolic relations and in light of the potential expectations for getting more out of the cooperation (as discussed above) as a result of embracing the authoritative role of Chinese actors.

The major changes in the dynamics of the relationship, however, occurred in the post-2015 period, due to external shocks and alterations in the broader political landscape. By advancing the Belt and Road agenda in CESEE, Chinese actors managed to become visible and relevant, making China a "European power," and attracting the response of other European actors.[54] After initially ignoring the emerging China-CESEE cooperation, the core EU countries and institutions have gradually taken a (re)securitization approach to the issue, trying both to confront China as a competitor and to reassert influence over the part of Europe that has historically been seen as an internal other. But Western European criticism of the growing China-CESEE ties faced one major impediment—the fact that the vast majority of the Europe-China interaction and economic exchange involves Western European countries—with CESEE having only a disproportionately small slice of the pie. Therefore, European criticisms of 16+1 have had a limited effect on the development of the cooperation.

At the same time, a much more formidable power has returned to the region: under the administration of president Donald Trump, the United States has framed CESEE as a battlefront against China's global advance, prompting regional actors to assume more vigilant positions toward the Chinese actors present in the region—especially Huawei—while also urging that the Belt and Road be contained. CESEE—or the "New Europe," as U.S. diplomats have called it in the post-1989 era, especially during and after the war on terror—has been closely allied with the

United States. As a result, some of the CESEE governments (e.g., Poland and the Czech Republic) have adopted a much sharper discourse on China and the Belt and Road, undoing much of the symbolic power work done by Chinese actors in previous years.[55] Knowledge networks and civil society infrastructures built by American actors, which their CESEE counterparts have historically been part of, have increasingly started to deal with perceived Chinese influence and interference around the world, including in CESEE. Importantly, however, these developments have not led to any CESEE government abolishing the 16+1 format; in fact, the format was enlarged to 17+1 in 2019 to include Greece. On the other hand, one can observe dampening of the enthusiasm of a number of actors in CESEE. In this sense, one may argue that the symbolic power of China—at least in the CESEE region—has been greatly conditioned by the inputs of other external actors. Just as some CESEE policy makers and intellectuals were first attracted to China by reading Anglophone literature on China's economic miracle and took experienced Western "China hands" such as Henry Kissinger as their role models, today they increasingly rely on the growing number of critical reports produced in Anglophone research institutes and media. While, for CESEE, before 2015, working with China was a way to gain legitimacy, become globally relevant, and Westernized—which also, of course, facilitated the work of China's symbolic power—in the post-2015 period, the context and content of China-CESEE relations overall have been greatly affected by the changes in the global constellations of power. If we extrapolate lessons for the Belt and Road as a whole, then we are facing competing symbolic powers, with the outcome far from clear.

Notes

In conducting this research, the author has in part benefited from a fieldwork grant awarded by the French Center on Contemporary China (2014); a Claussen-Simon PhD Fellowship of the Trajectories of Change Program, ZEIT-Stiftung Ebelin und Gerd Bucerius (2015–2018); a Civil Society Scholar Award of the Open Society Foundations (2018); and a doctoral dissertation completion grant of the Chiang Ching-kuo Foundation (2019).

1. "Six Years of 'Belt and Road,'" *Belt and Road Portal*, October 11, 2019, https:// eng.yidaiyilu.gov.cn/qwyw/rdxw/105854.htm. As of July 2019, there are 136 countries and 30 international organizations that have signed memorandums

of understanding or other documents on jointly working on the Belt and Road with China.

2. Gungwu Wang, "China and the International Order: Some Historical Perspectives," in *China and the New International Order*, ed. Gungwu Wang and Yongnian Zheng (Abington: Routledge, 2008), 21–31; Dongsheng Di, "Continuity and Changes: A Comparative Study on China's New Grand Strategy," *Historia Actual Online*, no. 12 (2007): 7–18; Satoshi Amako, "China's Diplomatic Philosophy and View of the International Order in the 21st Century," *Journal of Contemporary East Asia Studies* 3, no. 2 (January 2014): 3–33.

3. Jiemian Yang, "China's 'New Diplomacy' Under the Xi Jinping Administration," *China Quarterly of International Strategic Studies* 1, no. 1 (April 2015): 1–17.

4. Zhibo Qiu, "From 'Game Player' to 'Game Maker': New Features of China's Foreign Policy," *China Brief* 15, no. 14 (2015), http://www.jamestown.org/programs/chinabrief/single/?tx_ttnews%5Btt_news%5D=44174&cHash=5953f99bd5b663abf2bf57f8e823b7e3 (accessed September 30, 2020).

5. Xuetong Yan, "From Keeping a Low Profile to Striving for Achievement," *Chinese Journal of International Politics* 7, no. 2 (June 1, 2014): 153–84.

6. William Kirby, "China's Prosperous Age: A Century in the Making," *China Heritage Quarterly*, June 2011, http://www.chinaheritagequarterly.org/features.php?searchterm=026_kirby.inc&issue=026 (accessed September 30, 2020).

7. Shaun Breslin, "The 'China Model' and the Global Crisis: From Friedrich List to a Chinese Mode of Governance?," *International Affairs (Royal Institute of International Affairs 1944–)* 87, no. 6 (2011): 1323–43.

8. See Arif Dirlik, *Complicities: The People's Republic of China in Global Capitalism* (Chicago: University of Chicago Press, 2017). The complicity of Western political, business, and intellectual elites in encouraging China's rise has also been discussed in light of the destructive expansion of global capitalism.

9. Pierre Bourdieu, "What Makes a Social Class? On the Theoretical and Practical Existence of Groups," *Berkeley Journal of Sociology* 32 (1987): 13.

10. Matthew Eagleton-Pierce, "Introduction," in *Symbolic Power in the World Trade Organization* (Oxford: Oxford University Press, 2012), 4.

11. Ngai-Ling Sum, "The Intertwined Geopolitics and Geoeconomics of Hopes/Fears: China's Triple Economic Bubbles and the 'One Belt One Road' Imaginary," *Territory, Politics, Governance* 8, no. 4 (October 5, 2018): 1–25.

12. Bourdieu, "What Makes a Social Class," 13–14.

13. See Anastas Vangeli, "China's Engagement with the Sixteen Countries of Central, East, and Southeast Europe under the Belt and Road Initiative," *China & World Economy* 25, no. 5 (September 1, 2017): 101–24. In 2011 in Budapest, China assembled the leaders of sixteen countries: Albania, Bosnia and Herzegovina, Bulgaria, Croatia, the Czech Republic, Estonia, Hungary, Latvia, Lithuania, Macedonia, Montenegro, Poland, Romania, Serbia, Slovakia, and Slovenia.

The gathering was formalized in 2012 in Warsaw. In 2019 the platform was enlarged to include Greece. The 16+1/17+1 cooperation was advanced through annual summits of heads of governments, policy coordination, and the building up of a quasi-institutional framework.

14. "Six Years of 'Belt and Road.'"
15. The members of the forum are: Greece, China, Bolivia, Egypt, Iraq, Iran, Italy, and Peru, with the addition of Armenia.
16. Anastas Vangeli, "Global China and Symbolic Power: The Case of 16+1 Cooperation," *Journal of Contemporary China* 27 (2018): 674–87.
17. Jakub Jakóbowski, "Chinese-Led Regional Multilateralism in Central and Eastern Europe, Africa and Latin America: 16 + 1, FOCAC, and CCF," *Journal of Contemporary China* 27, no. 113 (2018): 659–73; Chris Alden and Ana Cristina Alves, "China's Regional Forum Diplomacy in the Developing World: Socialisation and the 'Sinosphere,'" *Journal of Contemporary China* 26, no. 103 (January 2, 2017): 151–65.
18. Vangeli, "Global China and Symbolic Power."
19. Jinghan Zeng, "Narrating China's Belt and Road Initiative," *Global Policy* 10, no. 2 (2019): https://onlinelibrary.wiley.com/doi/abs/10.1111/1758-5899.12662 (accessed September 30, 2020).
20. For the concept of space between fields, see Gil Eyal, "Spaces Between Fields," in *Bourdieu and Historical Analysis*, ed. Philip Gorski (Durham, NC: Duke University Press, 2013), 158–82.
21. For a case study on knowledge actors, see Anastas Vangeli, "Diffusion of Ideas in the Era of the Belt and Road: Insights from China–CEE Think Tank Cooperation," *Asia Europe Journal* 17 (2019): 421–36.
22. Bruno Macaes, *Belt and Road: A Chinese World Order* (London: C. Hurst, 2018).
23. Bob Jessop, "Narrating the Future of the National Economy and the National State? Remarks on Remapping Regulation and Reinventing Governance," in *State/Culture: State Formation after the Cultural Turn*, ed. George Steinmetz (Ithaca, NY: Cornell University Press, 1999), 397.
24. Małgorzata Jakimów, "Desecuritisation as a Soft Power Strategy: The Belt and Road Initiative, European Fragmentation, and China's Normative Influence in Central-Eastern Europe," *Asia Europe Journal* 17, no. 4 (2019): 369–85.
25. What is sometimes lost in the discussion on China, is, of course, the right timing of the reform and opening up, and the fact that China's rise was enabled by the developments in global capitalism in the late 1970s.
26. "Vision and Actions on Jointly Building Silk Road Economic Belt and 21st-Century Maritime Silk Road," National Development and Research Commission of the People's Republic of China, March 2015, https://reconasia-production.s3.amazonaws.com/media/filer_public/e0/22/e0228017-7463-46fc-9094-0465a6f1ca23/vision_and_actions_on_jointly_building_silk

_road_economic_belt_and_21st-century_maritime_silk_road.pdf (accessed October 21, 2020).

27. Stefano Guzzini, ed., *The Return of Geopolitics in Europe?: Social Mechanisms and Foreign Policy Identity Crises* (Cambridge: Cambridge University Press, 2012), 3.

28. Bob Jessop, "Critical Semiotic Analysis and Cultural Political Economy," *Critical Discourse Studies* 1, no. 2 (October 1, 2004): 167.

29. Christian Marazzi, *Capital and Language: From the New Economy to the War Economy* (Los Angeles: Semiotext(e), 2008), 136.

30. William H. Overholt, "China in the Global Financial Crisis: Rising Influence, Rising Challenges," *Washington Quarterly* 33, no. 1 (January 2010): 21–34; Brantly Womack, "International Crises and China's Rise: Comparing the 2008 Global Financial Crisis and the 2017 Global Political Crisis," *Chinese Journal of International Politics* 10, no. 4 (December 1, 2017): 383–401.

31. Denghua Zhang, "The Concept of 'Community of Common Destiny' in China's Diplomacy: Meaning, Motives, and Implications," *Asia & the Pacific Policy Studies* 5, no. 2 (May 1, 2018): 196–207; Zhenmin Liu, "Following the Five Principles of Peaceful Coexistence and Jointly Building a Community of Common Destiny," *Chinese Journal of International Law* 13, no. 3 (September 1, 2014): 477–80; Jacob Mardell, "The 'Community of Common Destiny' in Xi Jinping's New Era," *Diplomat*, October 25, 2017, https://thediplomat.com/2017/10/the-community-of-common-destiny-in-xi-jinpings-new-era/.

32. Nikhil Sonnad, "Read the Full Text of Xi Jinping's First UN Address," *Quartz*, September 29, 2015, https://qz.com/512886/read-the-full-text-of-xi-jinpings-first-un-address/. These principles can be found in the discursive practices of China's top leaders: for instance, talking in front of the UN General Assembly and presenting the idea of constructing CCD for humanity, Xi Jinping discussed the principles of developing international relations on an equal footing and developing a global security architecture based on "fairness, justice, joint contribution and shared benefits." He promoted open and inclusive development, boosted "inter-civilization exchanges," and spoke of the need to "build an ecosystem that puts mother nature and green development first" and engage in "mutual consultation and show mutual understanding."

33. Kimmy Chung, "California Tries to Harness Belt and Road to Help Fight Climate Change," *South China Morning Post*, April 25, 2019, https://www.scmp.com/news/china/diplomacy/article/3007704/california-signs-chinas-belt-and-road-forum-help-fight-against.

34. "Norway Expects to Promote Ties with China Within Belt & Road Initiative," *Xinhua News* (Beijing), May 10, 2017, http://www.xinhuanet.com/english/2017-05/10/c_136271199.htm

35. Jim Pickard, "Hammond to Seek UK Deals in China's Belt and Road Initiative," *Financial Times*, April 24, 2019, https://www.ft.com/content/9f054218 -66af-11e9-a79d-04f350474d62.

36. Bijian Zheng, "China's 'One Belt, One Road' Plan Marks the Next Phase of Globalization," *New Perspectives Quarterly* 34, no. 3 (July 2017): 27–30.

37. Amy Hawkins, "The Grey Wall of China: Inside the World's Concrete Superpower," *Guardian*, February 28, 2019, https://www.theguardian.com/cities /2019/feb/28/the-grey-wall-of-china-inside-the-worlds-concrete-super power.

38. Paul Virilio, *Speed and Politics* (Los Angeles, CA: Semiotext(e), 2006). It is also connected to the destructive nature of global capitalism and the contemporary way of life.

39. Dimitris Dalakouglu and Penny Harvey, "Roads and Anthropology: Ethnographic Perspectives on Space, Time, and (Im)Mobility," *Mobilities* 7, no. 4 (November 1, 2012): 460.

40. Brian Larkin, "The Politics and Poetics of Infrastructure," *Annual Review of Anthropology* 42, no. 1 (2013): 327–43.

41. This in turn makes infrastructure construction a spectacularly complex policy issue. For Western scholars, the emotions and indulgence of the various sublimes (technological, political, economic, aesthetic) often trump rationality when it comes to planning infrastructure projects: "Planners and project promoters make decisions based on delusional optimism rather than on a rational weighting of gains, losses, and probabilities. They overestimate benefits and underestimate costs." Bent Flyvbjerg, "Policy and Planning for Large-Infrastructure Projects: Problems, Causes, Cures," *Environment and Planning B: Urban Planning and City Science* 34, no. 4 (August 2007): 578–97, 583. The logic of Chinese planners, which is reflected in the Belt and Road, however, turns this argument around: embracing the uncertain and somewhat hazardous nature of the business of infrastructure megaprojects construction, it often starts with an idea and a belief, with practical details left to be negotiated later on. See Anastas Vangeli, "On Sino-Balkan Infrastructure Development Cooperation (Experiences with Chinese Investment in the Western Balkans and the Post-Soviet Space: Lessons for CEE?)," (policy paper, Center for European Neighborhood Studies and Friedrich Ebert Stiftung, Central European University, Budapest, 2018).

42. Xiong Wang, *China Speed: Development of China's High-Speed Rail* (Beijing: Foreign Languages, 2016). The cognitive impact of these rides is documented by ample anecdotal evidence. In the most high-profile one, the former California governor Arnold Schwarzenneger, for instance, referenced his high-speed trains experiences—including taking a Chinese high-speed train on a visit to

Shanghai—in his (unsuccessful) bid to push for high-speed train construction in the United States.

43. Self-conceptions and worldviews are, of course, inalienable from each other.
44. The inclusion of Greece, however, spoils this argument, even though Greece has been a country with historically strong communist tendencies.
45. Bartosz Kowalski, "China's Foreign Policy towards Central and Eastern Europe: The '16+1' Format in the South–South Cooperation Perspective. Cases of the Czech Republic and Hungary," *Cambridge Journal of Eurasian Studies* 1 (April 7, 2017): 1–16; Bartosz Kowalski, "Central and Eastern Europe as a Part of China's Global South Narrative," *Asia Dialogue*, August 27, 2018, http://theasiadialogue.com/2018/08/27/central-and-eastern-europe-as-a-part-of-chinas-global-south-narrative/; Jakóbowski, "Chinese-Led Regional Multilateralism."
46. This point was expressed during the Fifth High-Level China-CESEE Think Tanks Summit in Skopje, October 30, 2018.
47. Cheryl Hardy, "Hysteresis," in *Pierre Bourdieu: Key Concepts*, ed. Michael James Grenfell (Abingdon: Routledge, 2014), 131–50.
48. Iver Neumann and Vincent Pouliot, "Untimely Russia: Hysteresis in Russian-Western Relations over the Past Millennium," *Security Studies* 20 (2011): 109.
49. Jakóbowski, "Chinese-Led Regional Multilateralism," 671.
50. For example, Marcin Kaczmarski, and Jakob Jakóbowski, "Beijing's Mistaken Offer: The '16+1' and China's Policy towards the European Union," *OSW Commentary* (Warsaw: Institute for Eastern Studies, September 15, 2017), https://www.osw.waw.pl/en/publikacje/osw-commentary/2017-09-15/beijings-mistaken-offer-161-and-chinaspolicy-towards-european, have argued that the success of these policies in CESEE is limited—a point backed by other CESEE scholars, who mainly focus on the incompatibility of the South-South approach with the EU regulations; other authors, however, argue that China's major "export" to CESEE has been the model of the developmental state. See Csaba Moldicz, "A Few Words About China's New Role in the Central European Region," in *China's Attraction: The Case of Central Europe*, ed. Csaba Moldicz (Budapest: Budapest Business School, 2017), 13–30.
51. Lenka Bustikova and Petra Guasti, "The Illiberal Turn or Swerve in Central Europe?," *Politics and Governance* 5, no. 4 (December 29, 2017): 166–76.
52. Alojzy Zbigniew Nowak, Justin Yifu Lin, and Grzegorz Grątkowski, eds., *New Structural Economics for Less Advanced Countries: Nowa ekonomia strukturalna wobec krajów mniej zaawansowanych* (Warsaw: University of Warsaw Faculty of Management Press, 2017); Witold Gadomski, "The Prime Minister's Guru—A Man from the PRC," *Gazeta Wyborcza* (Warsaw), February 16, 2018, https://wyborcza.pl/7,75968,23034905,guru-premiera-czlowiek-z-chrl.html.
53. Jakimów, "Desecuritisation."

54. Emilian Kavalski, "China in Central and Eastern Europe: The Unintended Effects of Identity Narratives," *Asia Europe Journal* 17, no. 4 (December 2019): 403–19.

55. Anna Grzywacz, "Closer to a Threat Than an Opportunity: Polish Perception of China's Rise and International Engagement," *Asia Europe Journal*, April 29, 2019, https://link.springer.com/article/10.1007/s10308-019-00541-7; Jeremy Garlick, "China's Principal–Agent Problem in the Czech Republic: The Curious Case of CEFC," *Asia Europe Journal* 17 (2019): 437.

PART FIVE

Euro-Atlantic Perspectives

CHAPTER X

The End or the Beginning of Normative Power Europe?

Transcendence and the Crisis of European Foreign Policy

THOMAS DIEZ

The development of a stronger international society, well functioning international institutions and a rule-based international order is our objective.
—EUROPEAN COUNCIL, *EUROPEAN SECURITY STRATEGY*

The Tragedy of European Foreign Policy

EU foreign policy has long had the aim of fostering a transformation of international politics, defining itself against the classic notions of Realpolitik with a vision of a global future populated by actors driven by the greater common good. These actors would cooperate, invest in international institutions, and take seriously their responsibility for people suffering from hunger, diseases, war, catastrophes, or deteriorating environmental conditions—not merely at home, but globally. The 2003 *European Security Strategy* emphasized multilateralism and global institutionalism, in stark contrast, for instance, to the U.S. National Security Strategy.[1] Its successor, the 2016 *Global Strategy*,[2] talks more about pragmatism, yet still stresses the importance of principles—a "principled pragmatism" that may be better able to bring about a transformation of international politics than a hard-nosed insistence on norms and values that others may simply see as neocolonialism.[3]

That the European Union (EU) has pursued multilateralism and tried to contribute to at least a deepening of existing international organizations and law, from the support of the Rome Statute establishing the International Criminal Court (ICC) to pushing a global climate change regime and fostering regional integration projects around the world, is not disputed. Yet the signs are increasing that the EU is simultaneously following a traditional foreign policy driven by unilateral considerations, aimed at expanding spheres of influence and, consciously or not, involving policies that reinforce rather than transcend borders. These signs are troubling—even more so as they come at a time when other great powers, including the Unites States and populist regimes within the EU, have left the liberal moment of the immediate post–Cold War era behind and are returning to old habits of geopolitics and Realpolitik.

Two cases may illustrate how the EU's transformative power has found its limitations. In Ukraine, the EU's pushing of an association agreement, whether in the name of consolidating democratization and liberalization or expanding its influence on its neighbors, has made it part of the conflict, increased the rift with Russia, and helped reinsert a border in Europe.[4] I am not arguing that the EU is to blame for the events in Ukraine, but clearly it has not been able to overcome the division within the country, or its own rift with Russia.

In Turkey, the EU has not seriously negotiated accession, technically because Cyprus has blocked the opening of new chapters (the building blocks of EU enlargement negotiations) in response to Turkey closing its harbors to Cypriot ships because Turkey does not recognize the Republic of Cyprus, which EU member states (and above all Cyprus) see as a violation of the 1963 Association Agreement with Turkey. Yet underneath the legal arguments, the governments of member states either bowed to what they saw as public pressure not to let Turkey in because of fears of migration, or had principled objections against Turkish membership due to cultural reservations or the institutional effects of bringing in another large member state. Accession would have been a chance to really have an impact on Turkey's sustained democratization. Instead, EU politicians were eager to strike a deal with Turkey when the flow of refugees brought the Syrian war closer to home, while the Erdoğan government, unconstrained by the EU, turned into an autocratic regime that violated basic democratic rules.

These are but two illustrations of the failure of what Ian Manners has called "Normative Power Europe" (NPE).[5] Power, in Manners's terms, ultimately rests with the ability to "shape conceptions of the normal."[6] Like soft power, this ability does not require military means and, indeed, limits the use of such means.[7] But normative power goes beyond winning hearts and minds in the pursuit of national interest.[8] First, normative power cannot be controlled by a single actor, because shaping of what is considered normal is a discursive process. Single actors such as the EU may try to influence such discourse, but they do not wield the power to change it on their own. And, second, one of Manners's central claims is that normative power works even in the absence of obvious economic or strategic gains.[9] In that sense, normative power is much more radical than soft power.

Of course, an immediate criticism of such a conception is that it is hard to think of policies that states or state-like actors pursue against their interest. In fact, I have elsewhere argued that we may reconceptualize normative power as hegemony in recognition of the fact that shaping conceptions of the normal is an act of organizing the world in a particular way, independent of whether or not this explicitly works in the name of certain interests.[10] However, following Nathalie Tocci's threefold criteria of normative purpose, normative means, and normative impact, we may still distinguish between different purposes, with some purposes more in line with normative criteria such as human rights and global justice than others.[11] The main challenge for the EU as a normative power, therefore, is not the pursuit of its interests in the absence of hard power instruments, but the pursuit of a world order that is considered just not only by the EU itself, but also by outside actors, especially those who would otherwise be marginalized.[12]

This is a tall order. Against the successes of the ICC and Kyoto,[13] as well as the sustained promotion of human rights in the UN[14] and of regionalism,[15] critics have pointed to the failures of EU foreign policy in living up to this goal for some time. These failures include the pushing back of migrants to third countries presumed safe;[16] the signing of a fisheries agreement in disputed waters with Morocco despite the EU's nonrecognition of Morocco's claims to Western Sahara;[17] the pushing of free trade agreements in East Africa and elsewhere despite resistances and the willingness to act on a bilateral rather than truly interregional basis—and the list could easily be expanded.[18] Even international environmental policies, such as the promotion of green energy technology and objections to genetically modified food, at times have looked suspiciously as if the EU was moved by its economic interests rather than by genuinely normative concerns.[19]

How can we account for these failures of Normative Power Europe and the concomitant crisis of EU foreign policy? While not discounting explanations that focus on domestic pressures, the return of populist nationalism, or the incomplete socialization of European elites and publics into a genuinely new understanding of international relations, I suggest we need to place the debate about Normative Power Europe in the context of an

English school account of international society and its transformation. The EU's own ambitions clearly aim at what English school authors would call the solidarization of international society: the move away from a "pluralist" society of states in which sovereignty and nonintervention remain the only fundamentally agreed norms to a "solidarist" society of states in which states bear responsibilities not only to their own citizen but even toward "strangers."[20]

Indeed, taking normative power seriously would go even further and undermine the principle of territoriality and thus push a revolutionary agenda that would entail a radical transformation of the constituent units of international society.[21] Yet, early on, skeptics voiced two reservations about such a transformation, and in light of rising populism and the return of geopolitical strategizing, we need to take these reservations more seriously than the enthusiastic endorsements of Normative Power Europe in the literature of the 2000s did. Most notably, Hedley Bull in the 1970s raised the question of whether the structures of a pluralist international society would not force the EU either to become what he called a normal great power, or disintegrate—prospects that seem much more likely today than ten or twenty years ago.[22] Even earlier, at the inception of the European integration process, David Mitrany[23] opposed the idea of regional integration because regionalism inserted a territorial component into his vision of a "working peace system" based on global functionalism.[24]

Taking these objections seriously does not mean accepting the inevitability of the end of normative power. Indeed, I suggest in the following pages that Normative Power Europe implies a normativity that exceeds the constraints of the present—that functions as a kind of political theology, challenging EU politicians and citizens to take up the objections raised by Bull and Mitrany and bring the EU and its policies back in line with normative power. "Normative" here is conceived of as shaping a move toward a global order in which the exclusionary effects of territorial boundaries are at least mitigated, and global justice concerns have a more prominent role than they currently do. A commitment to Normative Power Europe is thus always an analytical *and* a political stance. It urges us to analyze the virtues and problems of EU foreign policy and explain them—but also to insist that "another Europe is possible."[25]

My argument rests on the assumption that this "other Europe," and, by extension, the other world it implies, both offers a horizon for the future of international society *and* is open to negotiation. I start by suggesting that one of the problems underlying the crisis of EU foreign policy is that traditional understandings of normative power have overemphasized the idea that Europe knows better. They have thus partaken in EU foreign policy as a "mission civilisatrice."[26] Yet the EU's transformative force cannot exist in a reductionist, Eurocentric vision of the world. The EU needs to offer visions of the future while accepting that these need to be negotiated and constantly developed. The current crisis of EU foreign policy is thus an invitation to rethink and appreciate the value of this ambiguity for foreign policy, rather than to erase it. It is the end of normative power as a *mission civilisatrice* and its beginning as a belief in the possibility of another Europe and another international society.

In the next section, I briefly revisit the debate about Normative Power Europe. I then elaborate on the conventional explanations of the failures of EU foreign policy. The heart of the chapter unfolds the argument that we need to see this debate in the context of international society. In the conclusion, I insist on the imperative of conceptualizing Normative Power Europe as a form of political theology and the possibility of transcending the present order of international society, while recognizing the limitations of our time.

Normative Power Europe

The idea that the EU is a great power that does not conform to the traditional characteristics of great powers goes back to François Duchêne's point that the presumed shortcomings of EU power should be seen not as weakness, but as strength.[27] In the context of the desire of the then–European Community (EC) member states to develop an international identity and of demands for a more united EU foreign policy, Duchêne suggested that it is best to understand the EC as a civilian power. In his view, the fact that the EC was characterized by the preponderance of "civilian ends and means, and . . . social values of equality, justice and tolerance" did not mean that the EU was not a great power.[28] Instead, he understood these characteristics to be the core of any European foreign policy that would not pursue a realist path, but would be aimed at a fundamental transformation of international politics.

A number of things are noteworthy here. First, a European foreign policy that simply pursued a realist agenda would lose its entire raison d'être.

Duchêne sees no point in such an approach, since foreign policy could then just be left to member states, as moving it to the European level would not significantly alter its nature. Second, the whole idea of European foreign policy is intimately tied to the transformation of international politics. The litmus test of its success is thus not whether it can generate sufficient capabilities to play the great power game, but whether it can change that game to move foreign policy away from pursuing geopolitical interests and focus on issues of global justice instead. Third—and implicit in these first two observations—is the belief that such an alternative understanding of foreign policy and international politics is possible. The familiar form of state-to-state relations is not a given: it can be changed.

This third claim, then, becomes the main theme of Ian Manners's revamping of the civilian power argument as Normative Power Europe.[29] Less worried than Duchêne about showing that being a civilian power is also in the interest of the EU and thus, as we have seen, moving beyond "soft power," Manners focuses on the idea that whatever its material interests, the EU "shapes conceptions of the normal" through its promotion of norms that are not exclusive to it.[30] At the core of these norms are peace, liberty, democracy, rule of law, and human rights, plus subsidiary norms such as sustainable development. Manners does not limit this idea of shaping to active EU foreign policy: his different paths of norm transfer include what one can call passive norm diffusion, which relies, for instance, on "contagion"—a reconceptualization of what counts as normal created by setting examples and socializing international actors into new way of doing things.

The idea of the EU as a normative power was met with immense success, both in academic and policy circles. Manners's piece is among the most cited in European studies, and the European Union Studies Association in 2007 voted to include it in the five articles given to then-commission president Manuel Barroso. It sparked a massive research agenda, mostly focused on the question of whether the EU actually was a normative power and thus on the descriptive aspect of Manners's argument. Evidence in favor was the EU's role in the development of the ICC and the Kyoto Protocol; its efforts to promote environmental and labor standards (for instance, in the so-called deep trade agenda of the World Trade Organization's current Doha Round); the promotion of regionalism and human rights; and EU enlargement as a means of democratic stabilization.

Yet there have always been skeptics. Some pointed to the plethora of counterevidence in the times that the EU promoted its own interests instead of norms. A particularly pertinent criticism was the export of weapons into countries with dubious human rights records, when, as Jennifer Erickson argues, "market imperative" beat "normative power."[31] Even authors who accepted that the EU looked as if it was engaged in norm transfer pointed out that these attempts to shape its neighborhood and international society at large could also be seen as in its own interest,[32] and that norm promotion went along with the construction of a European identity through the representation of others as dangerous or less civilized.[33]

Manners's response to these arguments has been twofold. First, he has pointed to the universality of the norms the EU promotes. This may seem odd, given that the EU is supposed to be changing norms, but the norms Manners refers to are not those of traditional great power politics, but of what the English school would describe as a solidarist international society or a global society of human beings, neither of which are the modus operandi of the traditional state system. In that sense, the EU is a regional organization that embodies universal norms. Manners also emphasizes the fact that, in contrast to traditional great powers, the EU also binds itself to global norms through its commitment to the UN Charter. But this remains ambiguous, as the charter combines the core norms of sovereignty and non-intervention that have always guided traditional international relations with norms based on a conception of humankind. (I will return to these problems later in the chapter, when discussing the transformation of international society.)

Second, Manners makes no claim that the EU is consistent in its actions. Indeed, his argument has been misconstrued as saying that the EU is always a normative power. My reading instead is that Manners operates with a Habermasian counterfactual assumption rooted in actual practice. In other words, just as in Jürgen Habermas's ideal-speech situation, even when the EU does not act like a normative power, we still can assume it is one, and that fact then has normative consequences for the EU's behavior. Thus examples like the ICC and Kyoto, or Manners's example of the campaign against the death penalty, demonstrate the empirical feasibility of Normative Power Europe and act as both a mirror in which the EU can be seen and a standard against which it can be judged.[34]

This points to a dimension of the normative power argument that is often overlooked in the endless debates about whether the EU is a normative power: its ethical claims. By articulating the idea of Normative Power Europe and demonstrating that it is rooted in actual policy,

Manners has made an intervention that is not limited to academic analysis of EU foreign policy. Instead, his work has enabled him and others to criticize current practices of EU foreign policy and demand its revisioning. Most prominently, such demands have been raised in relation to migration policy.[35] This demand to judge and revision (EU) foreign policy is the key justification for my claim that we need to understand normative power as a kind of political theology based on demands that exceed the constraints of the present world—a world it tries to transcend.

Such a claim to transcendence may seem at odds with the explanatory dimension of Manners's argument and the majority of current work on normative power, but this is exactly the point: the literature has largely ignored the multiple tracks of the NPE argument, which build on each other. To Manners, normative power is driven by constitutionalized norms. The EU acts the way it does because its genesis has led to an identity that is enshrined in its founding treaties and the *acquis communautaire*, which break with the rules of the classic international system. This has fundamentally transformed the European international society.[36] A foreign policy with this origin cannot follow the same principles as traditional foreign policy. This explanation is part of Manners's Habermasian mirror; it shows why the EU sometimes functions as a different kind of actor and thus reminds us that such an alternative foreign policy is possible. The explanation does not serve a positivist purpose, but rather underpins the ethical claims that the normative power argument makes.

Yet Manners's explanation becomes problematic in moments of crisis like the current one of Brexit, populism, and financial turmoil, which seem to undermine the EU's possibilities. We thus need to look for explanations of the resistance to the transformations that NPE envisages. In theorizing these resistances, often while questioning NPE as such, the literature has largely looked to the continued prevalence of interests over norms. There are three problems with this approach, however. It looks at actual behavior and seeks to explain it on the basis of ontological assumptions (states and state-like actors are simply interest-driven); it discounts the possibility of tensions and contradictions between the norms the EU embodies; and it assumes the neat separation of interests and norms. Yet many EU norms are also in its interest—from the promotion of free trade[37] to that of green technology.[38] Duchêne, in fact, thought that developing a civilian power was in the interest of the EC because the promotion of peace, multilateralism, and international law would benefit a region highly dependent for its economic success on an international framework conducive to trade. This insistence on interests is what Manners disliked about the civilian power argument, but I do not think Manners can escape the problem that the norms espoused by the EU work toward an international system that is in its favor. Equally, his critics are wrong to discount norms when they see interests. In part to overcome the norms/interest dichotomy, I have suggested seeing normative power as hegemony.[39]

Explaining the Failures of Normative Power

Apart from the claim that what matters are interests, there are two common explanations for the EU as a normative power, which also allow us to explain its failure. The first of these explanations is closely related to the work of Robert Kagan.[40] While Kagan does not make explicit reference to normative power, his diagnosis of EU foreign policy is not so different from that of Manners. Kagan likens the EU to both Venus, goddess of love, and paradise, while comparing the United States to Mars, the god of war, and power. There is no shortage of metaphors, and in them lies an alternative explanation for the EU's normative power: Venus is protected by Mars, and power (i.e., the United States) protects paradise (i.e., the EU). Thus, the EU can only play the part of the romantic heroine offering an alternative vision of international politics because the United States and its military might allow it to do so. In other words, without NATO and U.S. military presence in Europe and the United States' willingness to take on global military responsibilities, the EU would have to engage more with the hard realities of warfare and military intervention and thus have to abandon its focus on norm promotion, international law, and multilateral agreements. This is in line with the U.S. government's insistence that European member states must invest more in military development in order to meet NATO standards.

In this light, the failure of normative power would arise from the United States deciding it no longer wanted to play that part, and the EU being pushed to, or wanting to, become a real international actor. Absent Mars, given the realities of the international system, Venus would either arm herself or die. In the current context, the United States has no interest in dealing with the refugee crisis, and while it has stakes in Ukraine, they are far weaker than that of the EU. After the end of the Cold War, the United

States reoriented itself to the Pacific and turned to Asia as its focal point in foreign policy. While the United States is still the most important power on the global stage, it is questionable whether the current international system can still be characterized as unipolar, if it ever could. This all would mean that the EU needs to take its fate into its own hands—and abandon its normative power ambitions.

Kagan's argument bears some similarity to those, like Bull's, that build on the structure of international society, which I will discuss in the next section. However, unlike Kagan, I do not treat international structures and imperatives as inevitable. While accepting that pressures arise out of specific historical configurations, I agree with Alexander Wendt that there is also room for agency to change these configurations.[41] We need to take structural obstacles more seriously than the normative power debate has done so far, but without treating them as eternal transhistorical realities. Instead, in the spirit of the transcendental reading of NPE offered here, the transformation of these obstacles is always a possibility, however unlikely. Indeed, international society and its core norms are continuously challenged and transformed—a point usually written out of realism's grand historical narratives. Building on this fact requires actors not to simply succumb to the pressures of what is presumed to be normal. Venus, after all, is a goddess with powers of her own. The fact that ancient gods embodied different, often conflicting, values and virtues does not make one of them the master.

A second explanation of the EU's foreign policy failures is the liberal-intergovernmentalist one, which sees the EU primarily as the sum of its member states, and thus emphasizes the importance of member state interests for EU policies. We see this argument at work, for instance, in Robert Falkner's treatment of EU opposition to genetically modified food.[42] Falkner argues that this opposition does not arise out of any values ingrained in the EU's body politic, but rather out of strategic domestic considerations. The EU does not share the enthusiasm for genetically modified food, in this account, because European consumers, for cultural and historical reasons, are more skeptical about it than those in the United States. They are thus less inclined to buy such food or allow its production on EU member states' soil, putting EU companies at a disadvantage on the global market. Thus, it is domestic interest groups that shape EU policy primarily via the member states.

This argumentation works to explain the failures of EU policy in both Ukraine and Turkey. The Ukraine policy was influenced, at least in part, by central and eastern European member states, including the Baltic States[43] and Poland,[44] which supported the West-leaning parts of the population in Ukraine and retained strong anti-Russian sentiments from the days of the Soviet Union. In the same vein, holding Turkey at bay can be seen as the consequence of electoral considerations in member states with large Turkish immigrant populations that feared being overrun by new migrant inflows merging with Cypriot objections to Turkish membership in light of the ongoing conflict on the island.

This liberal-intergovernmentalist account cannot be discounted. It makes sense of the wrangling among member states about refugee quotas and the increasing questioning of EU principles by EU member states with rising nationalist populism. Yet this account is not complete. It does not reflect the ways domestic interest formulation is embedded in broader transnational conceptualizations of what constitutes normal politics. In addition, it turns a blind eye to the global structures involved in what one may call, paraphrasing Robert D. Putnam, a multilevel game. I propose that we need to integrate this global level, just as Kagan does, but without his ontological misconceptions about international politics. An English school conception of international society allows us to do just this.

Normative Power and the Structure of International Society

The core conception that the discipline of international relations owes to the English school is that of an international society. Following Hedley Bull's famous definition in his *Anarchical Society*, an international system exists "when two or more states have sufficient contact between them, and have sufficient impact on one another's decisions, to cause them to behave—at least in some measure—as parts of a whole."[45] Relations in such a system thus emerge mechanically from interaction. In contrast, "a society of states (or international society) exists when a group of states, conscious of certain common interests and common values, form a society in the sense that they conceive themselves to be bound by a common set of rules in their relations with one another, and share in the working of common institutions."[46] Bull thus provides a constructivist reinterpretation of international politics in which the structure of the global level is important, but does not arise from quasi-natural laws of interaction, but from institutions. These institutions in turn—while relatively sticky, as social institutions tend to be—are subject to change through the actions of the states that form them.

In contrast to, and alongside, international society, world society in this thinking refers to a global society of humankind. Because of the organization of the world in states, the current configuration of world society is even more rudimentary than that of international society. For Bull, it emerges primarily in human rights claims, which show the tensions between international and world society. Because they take humans rather than states as their referent, they are in tension with the core state interest of nonintervention, enshrined in the classic institutions of international society. This has meant that even though human rights claims in international society have been guaranteed through states, they are claims of humankind—a basic contradiction that has prevented the emergence of an effective global human rights regime. Yet this example also shows the degree to which European international society has moved away from the classic model of international relations, and not just with the EU. In the European international society, individuals can bring claims in front of the European Court of Human Rights, which acts independently of the states that have signed the European Convention of Human Rights.

This transformation of European international society remains contested, and in recent years revisionist forces have increasingly challenged it. One could, therefore, argue that the illiberal state and its representatives are on the rise in Europe, from France to Hungary and from the UK to Poland, as they are elsewhere. Most of them are not opposed to every kind of international cooperation or the idea of international society as such, but their vision of such a society is clearly at the opposite end of the spectrum from that envisioned by the EU. U.S. President Trump's 2017 speech at the United Nations General Assembly is exemplary in this respect: "Strong, sovereign nations let diverse countries with different values, different cultures, and different dreams not just coexist, but work side by side on the basis of mutual respect."[47] Whatever the virtues of such a stance, it contrasts starkly with the integrationist ethos of deepening multilateralism and international law and overcoming the nation state.

The U.S. president is not alone in his populism and nation–state-centrism; these ideas have strong support within the EU as well, though at present they are still the minority view. This is a challenge to the persistence of the transformation brought about by integration, but it does not invalidate claims about the nature of integration as such. As I have argued, European integration thus inherently implies the transformation of international society and its normative claims—if these falter, so does integration.

The international society that Bull describes and that Trump and the populists, in a benevolent reading of their policies, pursue, is pluralist in the sense that one of its main aims is the preservation of diversity organized in states. Its normative foundations are thus similar to those of classical realism, which sees the safeguarding of national identity in states as a core feature of the state system. This means that sovereignty and nonintervention are not only the main interests of states—they are the main norms of this international society, guaranteed, as Bull outlines, through five key institutions: diplomacy, international law, balance of power, great power management, and war.[48] This is not the place to elaborate on these institutions. Suffice it to say that international law in this conception primarily helps states maintain their independence; it is not a law of individual world citizens. Likewise, war is an institution in the sense that it is a general practice that states revert to when other states violate the norms of sovereignty and nonintervention enshrined in article 51 of the UN Charter.

In contrast to this pluralist view is what in English school terms is often called a "solidarist" conception of international society, in which the responsibilities of states go beyond those of looking out for their citizens and preserving national identity.[49] In such a society, "saving strangers" becomes an ethical imperative.[50] In other words, the pluralism of Bull's international society is at least mitigated by humanitarian claims arising from world society. Two crucial aspects link this debate to our present discussion about Normative Power Europe: first, that the past two decades have witnessed a solidarization of international society, however contested this may be; and, second, that we can link EU claims to be a normative power to this solidarization.

There is ample evidence of solidarization in international society. The emergence of human security as the core UN security definition; the installation of the ICC; the increase in the UN Security Council's authorization of humanitarian interventions in the name of peace and security; the strengthening of the human rights regime through the introduction of the Universal Periodic Review; the increasing number of world summits covering a range of governance issues; the development of the responsibility to protect with its redefinition and conditionalization of sovereignty; the agreement on a global treaty dealing with climate change—the list could go on. None of these, of course, are uncontested. Human security remains a vague concept; not every UN member has ratified the Rome Statutes of the ICC (the United States, of course, is the most prominent holdout), and some have actively prevented their citizens from being prosecuted; humanitarian interventions have been accused of fostering Western interests; the Universal Periodic Review operates via discursive power with no proper means of enforcement; world summits may be strong on declarations and weak on actual policy; the Responsibility to Protect has been challenged in Libya and is abused by states that intervene claiming it is to protect minorities; the Paris Agreement still relies on self-defined CO_2 emission reduction targets; and so on. Yet the point is not that solidarization is uncontested or complete; the point is that in comparison to the international society of the 1970s (when Bull was writing), we have come a long way—not to a perfect solidarist society, but to an international society whose main institutions have changed, some significantly, others less so.

The contradictions and problems of this process are worthy of another paper; I cannot adequately deal with them here, although I want to insist that I make no claim whatsoever that solidarization brings us closer to the idealized world that Kagan calls paradise.[51] Partly this is because of the contestations with which such a process is fraught, and partly it is because even a solidarist world will create new normative tensions. The transformative process of solidarization is thus inherently ambiguous. Yet the important point here is that solidarization chimes not only with the internal transformation process of European integration, but also with what I have outlined as the core aims of EU foreign policy to the extent that these are linked to the idea of normative power. As such, the EU has played an active part in solidarization, from its active support of the Rome Statute (often in direct confrontation with the United States) to its promotion of regionalism beyond its own borders, from EU member state involvement in the Human Rights Council to its role in developing the global climate regime.[52]

Where, then, is the tragedy that allows us to account for the failures of normative power? In a nutshell, even as the EU has socialized international society into greater solidarization, it has had to work within the constraints set by the institutions of international society that are still significantly characterized by pluralism. These constraints have hampered and limited EU efforts as much as they have also had a socializing effect on the EU: rather than only the EU shaping conceptions of the normal on the international level, the international context has also shaped conceptions of what counts as normal within the EU and among EU member states. In other words, while international society has become solidarized, the EU has become pluralized. To see this more clearly, it is helpful to go back to two classic authors—Bull and Mitrany.

Already, in the *Anarchical Society*, Bull saw the EU as an alternative to his conceptualization of international society. He thought of the EU as a "neo-medieval" society that challenged the basic structure of the society of states by replacing state-to-state relations with a mixture of relations along territorial and functional lines and across different levels, which he compared to the medieval system of overlapping claims to authority.[53] It is ironic that the neo-medieval label has stuck in later treatments of the EU, since Bull thought it unlikely that the EU would remain in this shape and form.[54] He predicted that, given the pressure of the pluralist institutions of international society, the EU would have to develop state-like features or face disintegration. For Bull, then, the EU was a temporary aberration rather than an indicator of permanent change. In his later rejection of Duchêne's argument, Bull stated that the idea of civilian power was a contradiction in terms.[55] In an international society in which war is a core institution, no institution or alliance could sustain a-military values, goals and instruments while being a great power responsible for managing its relations with other great powers as well as order in international society more generally.

Manners's ultimate challenge for NPE is exactly the opposite: it relies on a fundamental—in English school terminology, "revolutionist"—transformation of international society. If the EU succeeded in this, state-to-state relations would have to be replaced by something close to what Bull called "neo-medievalism." Such a revolution would move the transformations within the regional international society of Europe, the main analytical focus of most of those analyzing the EU and its challenge to global governance, onto the global level.

This ultimately exceeds mere solidarization, and it is fair to say that the present EU neither validates Bull's expectations of an EU state or disintegration nor meets Manners's demands. This is mainly because the EU's agenda has been reformist rather than revolutionist—and it had no choice in this. Solidarization takes place *within* international society; thus it cannot be expected to lead to "another world," as Manners puts it. As such, solidarization needs to work with and within the pluralist institutions of international society. This makes the socialization pressures Bull outlined start to work. On the one hand, the EU has helped international society move away from pluralism, yet to do so it engages with a world still largely organized along pluralist lines—and this is its tragedy. Not ready to fully take on board the demands of world society, the EU falls back into defending the very territorial borders that, in its most radical form, normative power was supposed to overcome. Confronted with a variety of actors both in and out of the EU that play the pluralist game, and blind to its own complicity with territorial claims, the EU (or those acting in its name) fails to see the geopolitical dimensions of an association agreement with Ukraine; it reinscribes borders by creating rings of friends around itself, and it keeps migrants at bay by sending them back to supposedly safe third countries.[56]

The domestic constraints put forward by liberal-intergovernmentalist accounts, can, meanwhile, be linked to the failure to fully socialize political elites or the broader public into a new conceptualization of international society. To repeat, the reformist agenda leaves the idea of states and national identities intact. Even the Responsibility to Protect redefines sovereignty as a state's responsibility to its *own* people. And, within European integration itself, the territorial dimension of "Europe" breaks through the radical transformation claims of both functionalism and neo-medievalism. This is why David Mitrany, considered the father of functionalism, rejected the idea of regional integration. He asked:

> Could a European union, in the long run, benefit its own peoples if it tends in the least to split the world afresh into competing regional sovereignties? Is not breaking through that dour barrier of sovereignty the ultimate test? In a world of a hundred and more states sovereignty can in simple fact never be dismantled through a formula but only through function, shedding national functions and pooling authority in them; unless we are to give up all purpose of wide all-round international sharing in the works of peace.[57]

For Mitrany, regional integration only goes halfway toward the "working peace system" that he envisaged.[58] While we can understand his preferred model of functionalist organizations as one form of a political organization of world society, regional integration does not solve the problems of the territorial organization of world politics in what ultimately remains a society made up of states.

A Tragic Dilemma—and a Normative Imperative of Transcendence and Ambiguity

From the perspective outlined in this chapter, the foreign policy crisis of the EU, its failures as a normative power, are not solely a consequence of the predominance of interests over norms or domestic pressures. They result, at least in part, from the structure of the international society. On the one hand, this structure is itself in a process of transformation from pluralist to solidarist principles, even though the movement on this continuum is contested and ambiguous. The EU has played a considerable part in this process, in that sense fulfilling its normative power aims. On the other hand, the pluralist traits of international society are still strong enough to constrain the EU in its actions, to provide for an ambiguous self-understanding of its international role, and to socialize it into a considerable degree of pluralist normality.

As a consequence, the EU is in a tragic dilemma. If it continues to follow a reformist agenda, it is likely to be further socialized into a statist structure of international society, with slow and piecemeal transformations at best, and with resistance always leaving possibilities for reversal. If it follows a revolutionist agenda, it is likely to be ridiculed and marginalized (especially if populists such as Trump remain influential), and some of its member states would likely sabotage any attempt to go down that route. Neither path would lead to the fundamental transformation of international society NPE strives to achieve. They end with either the EU as a normal great power in an only slightly reformed and recognizably statist international relations structure, or consigned to irrelevance.

But this rather bleak analysis disregards the full extent of the demands of normative power. Understood less as an empirical description than as an ethical stance, normative power is an idea that cannot be guided solely by considerations of present de facto irrelevance. Transforming international society is only possible given the belief that not only another Europe, but another world, is possible. Realists and pluralists would disagree—but they too are acting out of belief, not out of any objective or correct analysis. Much of classic realist writing is founded on the idea of original sin that condemns humans to never achieving real progress in this world.[59] Similar ideas can be found in the more pluralist quarters of the English school—for instance, in Herbert Butterfield.[60] And, like Butterfield, Martin Wight read international history through the lens of his Christian beliefs.[61] Yet, in his recollection of lectures by Wight, Bull notes that while Wight seemed to agree that theological optimism was for a world beyond the human one, he also seemed to advocate a "moral passion to abolish suffering and sin."[62]

As a normative political stance, NPE only makes sense if it comes out of such moral passion. As a political theology, whether rooted in religious beliefs or appropriating religious concepts and integrating them into broader conceptions of politics as Habermas and others have done, it needs to oppose the classic Niebuhrian conception of otherworldliness. It needs to stand on a belief that we can transcend the present world that we live in to achieve a better one, albeit one that remains imperfect. As Michael Loriaux notes in his critique of the realist reading of Saint Augustine, "The Christian, animated by *caritas* and guided by the vision of the perfect peace that reigns in the heavenly city, intervenes to promote a 'better' peace, that is, to move the earthly city along the continuum toward the more perfect peace, knowing all the while that he or she will inevitably encounter setbacks and failures."[63]

This is a strong normative imperative. The mirror function of the normative power argument, in this context, is a reminder that working toward such a world is not merely a pipe dream, but a reality we can already witness in the present. The only way to deal with the tragic dilemma of NPE is to follow a more radical path of going back to integration as a substantial transformation of international society. This would necessitate a more stringent analysis of the structural constraints of the present to avoid sleepwalking into boundary-producing practices as in Ukraine. It would necessitate more creative thought about how a "better peace" can be organized—for instance, by thinking carefully about how regional international societies can be linked without falling into the trap of reproducing state territoriality, against which, as I have argued, Mitrany warned us. And it would necessitate a much greater degree of reflexivity about the EU's own actions and their conformity with the EU's own moral standards, with which the treatment of Turkey—or, for that matter, refugees—over the past decades has hardly been commensurate.

Understood in these terms, the current (and perhaps long-standing) EU foreign policy crisis can be seen as a turning point that could lead to a proper appreciation of the ethical demands of NPE. Following my argument, these demands imply that, unlike in previous debates, the tensions that stem from the inherent ambiguities of the transformations of integration cannot and ought not be suppressed. NPE as outlined in this chapter involves both a global horizon for a transformation of international society and the negotiation of this horizon in a world of cultural diversity that remains largely organized in states. In fact, the EU Global Strategy bears traces of the acceptance of this ambiguity in formulating both an alternative vision and a humbler stance toward others,[64] encapsulated in its core slogan of "principled pragmatism,"[65] which some have misread as giving up on normative claims.[66]

If this humbler yet at the same time determined stance were realized, NPE as a *mission civilisatrice* would give way to a NPE as a truly revolutionizing force. Perhaps this is not a likely scenario. Yet it is one that today's world badly needs if it hopes to avoid turning the claims of self-styled realists and populists into self-fulfilling prophecy.

Notes

Epigraph: European Council, *European Security Strategy: A Secure Europe in a Better World* (Brussels: European Council, 2003), 10.

1. Felix Berenskoetter, "Mapping the Mind Gap: A Comparison of U.S. and European Security Strategies," *Security Dialogue* 36, no. 1 (2005): 71–92.
2. European Union, *Shared Vision, Common Action: A Stronger Europe—a Global Strategy for the European Union's Foreign and Security Policy* (Brussels: European External Action Service, 2016).
3. European Union, *Shared Vision*, 8.
4. For assessments of the EU in Ukraine, see, e.g., David Cadier, "Eastern Partnership vs Eurasian Union? The EU-Russia Competition in the Shared Neighbourhood and the Ukrainian Crisis," *Global Policy* 5, supplement 1 (2014): 76–85; and Hiski Haukkala, "From Cooperative to Contested Europe? The Conflict in Ukraine as a Culmination of a Long-Term Crisis in EU-Russia Relations," *Journal of Contemporary European Studies* 23, no. 1 (2015): 36–37.

5. Ian Manners, "Normative Power Europe: A Contradiction in Terms?," *Journal of Common Market Studies* 40, no. 2 (2002): 235–58.

6. Manners, 239.

7. Ian Manners, "Normative Power Europe Reconsidered: Beyond the Crossroads," *Journal of European Public Policy* 13, no. 2 (2006): 182–99.

8. Thomas Diez and Ian Manners, "Reflecting on Normative Power Europe," in *Power in World Politics*, ed. F. Berenskoetter and M. J. Williams (London: Routledge, 2007), 179.

9. Manners, "Normative Power Europe," 253.

10. Thomas Diez, "Normative Power as Hegemony," *Cooperation and Conflict* 48, no. 2 (2013): 194–210.

11. Nathalie Tocci, *Who Is a Normative Foreign Policy Actor? The European Union and its Global Partners* (Brussels: Centre for European Policy Studies, 2008).

12. Robert Kagan, *Of Paradise and Power: America and Europe in the New World Order* (New York: Vintage, 2004).

13. Sibylle Scheipers and Daniela Sicurelli, "Normative Power Europe: A Credible Utopia?," *Journal of Common Market Studies* 45, no. 2 (2007): 435–57.

14. Bettina Ahrens and Thomas Diez, "Solidarisation and Its Limits: The EU and the Transformation of International Society," *Global Discourse* 5, no. 3 (2015): 341–55.

15. Thomas Diez and Nathalie Tocci, eds., *The EU, Promoting Regional Integration, and Conflict Resolution* (Basingstoke: Palgrave Macmillan, 2017).

16. Ali Bilgic and Michelle Pace, "The European Union and Refugees: A Struggle Over the Fate of Europe," *Global Affairs* 3, no. 1 (2017): 89–97.

17. Tobias Schumacher, "Uncertainty at the EU's Borders: Narratives of EU External Relations in the Revised European Neighbourhood Policy Towards the Southern Borderlands," *European Security* 24, no. 3 (2015): 381–401.

18. Sonja Theron, "The Great Lakes and the EU: Formal and Informal Regionalism and Conflict Transformation," in Diez and Tocci, *EU*, 131–49.

19. Robert Falkner, "The Political Economy of 'Normative Power' Europe: EU Environmental Leadership in International Biotechnology Regulation," *Journal of European Public Policy* 14, no. 4 (2007): 507–26.

20. Nicholas J. Wheeler, *Saving Strangers: Humanitarian Intervention in International Society* (Oxford: Oxford University Press, 2000).

21. John G. Ruggie, "Territoriality and Beyond: Problematizing Modernity in International Relations," *International Organization* 47, no. 1 (1993): 139–74.

22. Hedley Bull, *The Anarchical Society: A Study of Order in World Politics* (Basingstoke: Palgrave, 1977); Hedley Bull, "Civilian Power Europe: A Contradiction in Terms," *Journal of Common Market Studies* 21, no. 2 (1982): 149–70.

23. David Mitrany, "The Prospects of Integration: Federal and Functional," *Journal of Common Market Studies* 4, no. 2 (1965): 119–49.

24. David Mitrany, *A Working Peace System* (London: Quadrangle, 1966).
25. Ian Manners, "Another Europe Is Possible: Critical Perspectives on European Union Politics," in *The SAGE Handbook on European Union Politics*, ed. K. E. Jørgensen, M. Pollack, and B. Rosamond (London: SAGE, 2007), 77–95.
26. Kalypso Nicolaïdis and Robert Howse, "'This Is My EUtopia . . .': Narratives as Power," *Journal of Common Market Studies* 40, no. 4 (2002): 782.
27. François Duchêne, "Europe's Role in World Peace," in *Europe Tomorrow: Sixteen Europeans Look Ahead*, ed. R. Mayne (London: Fontana, 1972), 32–47.
28. François Duchêne, "The European Community and the Uncertainties of Interdependence," in *A Nation Writ Large*, ed. M. Kohnstamm and W. Hager (London: Palgrave, 1973), 20.
29. Manners, "Normative Power Europe."
30. Manners, 242.
31. Jennifer L. Erickson, "Market Imperative Meets Normative Power: Human Rights and European Arms Transfer Policy," *European Journal of International Relations* 19, no. 2 (2013): 209–34.
32. Adrian Hyde-Price, " 'Normative' Power Europe: A Realist Critique," *Journal of European Public Policy* 13, no. 2 (2006): 217–34.
33. Thomas Diez, "Constructing the Self and Changing Others: Reconsidering 'Normative Europe,'" *Millennium: Journal of International Studies* 33, no. 3 (2005): 613–36.
34. Ian Manners, "The Normative Ethics of the European Union," *International Affairs* 84, no. 1 (2008): 45–46.
35. Nils Feller, "Turning the Tide on EU Migration Policy" (Jacques Delors Institute Policy Paper 213, December 14, 2017), https://institutdelors.eu/en/publications/turning-the-tide-on-eu-migration-policy/; Olivia Valone, "Finding Hell in Libya: The Failure of the EU's Human Rights Regime," World Mind, March 27, 2018, https://www.theworldmind.org/home/2018/3/27/finding-hell-in-libya-the-failure-of-the-eus-human-rights-regime.
36. Thomas Diez, Ian Manners, and Richard G. Whitmann, "The Changing Nature of International Institutions in Europe: The Challenge of the European Union," *Journal of European Integration* 33, no. 2 (2011): 117–38.
37. Owen Parker and Ben Rosamond, "'Normative Power Europe' Meets Economic Liberalism: Complicating Cosmopolitanism Inside/Outside the EU," *Cooperation and Conflict* 48, no. 2 (2013): 229–46.
38. Falkner, "Political Economy."
39. Diez, "Normative Power."
40. Kagan, *Paradise and Power.*
41. Alexander Wendt, *Social Theory of International Politics* (Cambridge: Cambridge University Press, 1999).
42. Falkner, "Political Economy."

43. Maili Vilson, "The Foreign Policy of the Baltic States and the Ukrainian Crisis: A Case of Europeanization?," *New Perspectives* 23, no. 2 (2015): 49–76.

44. Nathaniel Copsey and Karolina Pomorska, "The Influence of Newer Member States in the European Union: The Case of Poland and the Eastern Partnership," *Europe-Asia Studies* 66, no. 3 (2014): 421–33.

45. Bull, *Anarchical Society*, 10–11.

46. Bull, 13.

47. Donald J. Trump, "Remarks by President Trump to the 72nd Session of the United Nations General Assembly," September 19, 2017, https://www.whitehouse.gov/the-press-office/2017/09/19/remarks-president-trump-72nd-session-united-nations-general-assembly.

48. Bull, *Anarchical Society*.

49. Barry Buzan, *From International to World Society? English School Theory and the Social Structure of Globalisation* (Cambridge: Cambridge University Press, 2004), 45–62.

50. Wheeler, *Saving Strangers*.

51. Thomas Diez, "Not Quite 'Sui Generis' Enough: Interrogating European Values," *European Societies* 14, no. 4 (2012): 522–39.

52. Ahrens and Diez, "Solidarisation."

53. Bull, *Anarchical Society*, 265–66.

54. Jan Zielonka, *Europe as Empire: The Nature of an Enlarged Europe* (Oxford: Oxford University Press, 2007); Andreas Faludi, *The Poverty of Territorialism: A Neomedieval View of Europe and European Planning* (Cheltenham: Edward Elgar, 2018).

55. Bull, "Civilian Power Europe."

56. Thomas Diez, "Transforming Identity in International Society: The Potential and Failure of European Integration," *Comparative European Politics*, March 29, 2019, https://link.springer.com/article/10.1057%2Fs41295-019-00170-9.

57. Mitrany, "Prospects of Integration," 145.

58. Mitrany, *Working Peace System*.

59. Michael Loriaux, "The Realists and Saint Augustine: Skepticism, Psychology, and Moral Action in International Relations Thought," *International Studies Quarterly* 36, no. 4 (1992): 401–20.

60. Charles A. Jones, "Christian Realism and the Foundations of the English School," *International Relations* 17, no. 3 (2003): 371–87.

61. Ian Hall, "History, Christianity, and Diplomacy: Sir Hedley Butterfield and International Relations," *Review of International Studies* 28, no. 4 (2002): 724–25.

62. Hedley Bull, "Martin Wight and the Theory of International Relations: The Second Martin Wight Memorial Lecture," *Review of International Studies* 2, no. 2 (1976): 101–16.

63. Loriaux, "Realists," 414.

64. European Union, *Shared Vision*.

65. European Union, 8; Nathalie Tocci, "From the European Security Strategy to the EU Global Strategy: Explaining the Journey," *International Politics* 54, no. 4 (2017): 487–502.

66. Sven Biscop, "The EU Global Strategy: Realpolitik with European Characteristics" (Egmont Security Policy Brief 75, June 29, 2016), http://www.egmontinstitute.be/eu-global-strategy/.

CHAPTER XI

Is There a Coherent Ideology of Illiberal Modernity, and Is It a Source of Soft Power?

JACK SNYDER

Over the past few decades, public commentary has swung wildly in anticipation of which side history is on. As recently as 1989, the "end of history" thesis declared a decisive winner in the competition among the grand ideologies: only liberal capitalist democracy governed by impersonal rule of law could sustain a stable modern society enjoying economic growth and technological progress. Illiberal forms of social organization seemed like vestiges that would be phased out in due course.[1] The concept of "soft power," the idea that America's hegemonic liberal magnetism could induce people worldwide to want what America wanted them to want, dates from that era.[2]

Liberalism's triumphalist confidence has since been shaken by a host of troubles: the unprecedented rise of modernizing but illiberal China; the resurgent role of illiberal religion and ethnicity in politics; rampant inequality in liberal as well as illiberal states; and the liberal states' struggle to deal with endemic crises of immigration, climate change, and global economic management. Doubts have arisen about whether institutions created by the leading liberal states can incorporate developing countries into a global liberal order.

In both the developed and developing worlds, the ideological initiative has shifted from liberalism toward various forms of illiberal nationalist populism.[3] Populists portray a mythologized communitarian version of the people as the repository of virtue; these people, however, suffer under a parasitical, immoral elite.[4] Populists claim to be majoritarian with respect to the those who are truly the people. The people's will is seen as unitary, not pluralistic, and often best expressed by referenda that allow for a direct relationship between the people and their leader, unmediated by laws and institutions that hinder the implementation of the popular will. Populists see a world in crisis and favor the rhetoric of bad manners as a way of defying the genteel elites and polite mainstream discourses that obfuscate the urgency for action. Populists may be nationalists, anchored in the traditionally dominant religious, ethnic, or racial groups, or they may make claims based on social class or connection to the land.

Nationalist populists are on the march.[5] Russian president Vladimir Putin markets his authoritarian kleptocracy as a traditionalist cultural reaction against the decadent West and makes common cause with the self-described champion of "illiberal democracy" inside the European Union (EU) and NATO, Hungary's prime minister Viktor Orban. Elected leaders in Turkey and India divide and rule along ethnic and religious lines in attempts—with mixed results—to heighten their powers and move closer to a tyranny of the majority. Chinese president Xi Jinping exploits internet nationalism to coerce neighbors on island claims even as he bids for leadership of the climate issue at Davos and lines up European states to participate in China-led development banks. The Philippines wins a World Court case on island sovereignty, but its populist president Rodrigo Duterte cuts a deal with China instead. Even in some old democracies, voters increasingly support nationalists, protectionists, and politicians who disdain the institutions of liberal multilateralism, cut corners on the rule of law, and are willing to cozy up to Putin. Only 30 percent of American millennials say it is important to live in a democracy.[6]

Decentering and Discrediting Liberal Soft Power?

To what extent is this shift in global political momentum due to a diffusion of soft power—the power to shape desires and attract emulation? Much of the shift comes from hard, material power, especially China's unparalleled increase in productive capacity over the last two decades and economic spurts in other rising illiberal or semiliberal powers. Also in the mix are improvements in Russian and, to some extent, Chinese military capabilities, and their increased willingness to use them coercively. Along with these developments, however, there has also been a change in ideological fortunes that cannot simply be explained by international material power calculations. Developments in the world political economy have changed the material hierarchy of states and affected the ways regimes legitimate their rule, attract support in an era of mass politics, and identify collaborators abroad.

The framing chapters of this volume by Victoria de Grazia and Burcu Baykurt offer two conceptual prisms for viewing the cultural and ideological dimensions of influence: Joseph S. Nye Jr.'s concept of soft power, based on attraction and emulation; and Antonio Gramsci's concept of social hegemony, based on the ability of a dominant social class or coalition to rule by persuading society of the naturalness, inevitability, and universal benefits of its worldview and the social order it maintains. My own analysis, in which ideology is rooted in sociological circumstances and the historical path of economic development, is closer to Gramsci's approach, though I do not adopt his terminology.

At the end of the Cold War, one of the most powerful instruments in the arsenal of liberal democratic soft power was its claim of historical inevitability. Ideas become particularly persuasive when they are taken for granted as common sense; assumptions can be insulated from critical examination when they are convincingly presented as embedded in an irresistible movement of history. The greatest of all public intellectuals, Karl Marx, used this rhetorical strategy on the grandest level. At the so-called unipolar moment when the Soviet Union fell, Francis Fukuyama made the case that liberalism rather than communism was—as was inevitable— the winner of the global teleological competition. Surprisingly, Fukuyama denied that liberalism's inevitable global victory was mainly due to its economic superiority (perhaps presciently, in light of the subsequent rise of China), stressing instead that only liberalism solves the problem of "thymos"—everyone's need for personal recognition.[7] Fukuyama disarmingly expressed some regret at the too egalitarian, insufficiently Nietzschean form of personal recognition under liberalism. This distinguished him from cruder liberal triumphalism, let him escape the trap of self-congratulatory "Whig history," and made him a palatable narrator. In a similar way, Nye's account of American hegemony rested not on its vast material resources, but on the more acceptable basis of its irresistible soft power.

Now, however, adverse trends of hard power, especially economic power, have chipped away at the narrative of liberal inevitability. Ideological and cultural challengers to liberalism have piled on these material trends, attempting to accelerate them. In the international realm, China and Russia have tried to discredit the hegemonic liberal narrative by pointing out the moral flaws underlying liberal material performance: cultural degeneracy, ethical hypocrisy, and imperial arrogance.[8] Domestic populist resistance to dominant liberal elites employs similarly impolite weapons of the weak to delegitimate hegemonic soft power, tarnishing liberal claims to historical inexorability.

In the short run, these trends favor the tide of populist nationalism in domestic politics and international relations. Populist nationalism is a response to the inherent tension between two central elements of liberal modernity: free markets and mass participation in politics.[9] The taproot of the current mismatch between markets and mass politics is economic and cultural globalization, but it takes different forms in the advanced democracies and in rising semidemocratic or illiberal states.

In the more established capitalist democracies, the globalization of trade and finance, increased mobility of labor across borders, and technologically driven shifts in the structure of work and wealth leading to greater economic inequality have spurred the self-perceived losers to demand economic and cultural protection from their nation-states. Historically, such demands have come in two forms: nativist nationalism calling for political control over markets and resources at home and abroad, or the social welfare state buffering against the pain of market adjustments. The prominence of libertarian, antiregulation, market fundamentalism in the period since the collapse of Communism has fueled global market mobility at the same time as it has hindered welfare state adaptations to some of its social costs. This has opened the door to nationalist and nativist demands within the framework of the democratic nation-states. The populist character of these movements has disrupted traditional liberal norms in established democracies, but so far has seriously undermined liberal democracy only in some of the more peripheral newcomers to that status, such as Hungary.

Among some of the larger developing states, however, the mismatch between markets and mass politics is more fraught with potential for an illiberal, mass-energized, national populist politics, since it comes at a stage when the liberal economic and political institutions that are crucially needed for further stable development are not yet in place. This trend reflects a particular phase in the economic modernization process in which rising powers are facing the institutional adjustment challenges characteristic of middle-income states along with a weakening of political regulation of the global market economy—a fraught conjuncture that echoes developments in the early twentieth century.

In these circumstances, populist nationalists have the ideological initiative in domestic and international affairs. They offer a package of policies and ideological appeals based on (1) a political economy in which patron-client relations structures market opportunities; (2) heavy state influence over markets, including international trade and investment; (3) the exclusion of cultural out-groups such as foreigners and immigrants from economic and social benefits; (4) the cultural glorification of the in-group and an obsession with perceived threats to it and its unjust humiliations; and (5) a political rhetoric that praises order, force, and direct action by executive command to do the bidding of the true people.

What accounts for the convergence of nationalist populist regimes and movements on this formula? First, this is the normal formula of rule in modernizing states that are experiencing the beginning stages of mass politics in a setting that lacks modern liberal institutions and other cultural supports of liberal democracy. In such societies, this is the default system of rule when things go wrong. Second, the convergence on this political and ideological formula is the result of common circumstances brought about by increasing social challenges rooted in global capitalism at a time when nation-states are unwilling or unable to control the social consequences of rapid market change. A third-order mechanism is the demonstration effect of nationalist populist movements that have gained traction in a number of important states, invigorating and legitimating copycats. Insofar as this demonstration effect is based on attraction and emulation, this might be fairly called illiberal soft power. Insofar as it reflects underlying flaws in the development of these nations' modern liberal institutions, common patterns in ideological struggles between their social classes, or perceptions of some inevitable tide of history, it might better be called a rising illiberal, Gramscian counterhegemony.

That said, I will argue that the internally focused nature of these diverse nationalist movements limits their ability to coalesce around a positive common formula for mutual attraction. They may be able to agree that strict national sovereignty is a better political principle than liberal cosmopolitanism, but beyond that these illiberal states and movements are too dissimilar and autonomy-focused to be attracted to a common way of life. Their relations are transactional, as befits their ideology and regime type.

Since my argument grounds ideological effects in underlying social and economic structure, I will begin by laying out its structural underpinnings in modernization theory, tracing the connection between economic development and nationalism. I will then address the consequences for illiberal soft power in international politics and the oxymoron of transnational nationalist ideology.

The Logic of Modernity

Since Ferdinand Tönnies's breakthrough work on community and society, *Gemeinschaft und Gesellschaft* (1887), modernization theorists have argued that the crucial shift that defines modernity is from personalistic social relations based on family, lineage, patron-client networks, and cultural in-group favoritism to impersonal social relations based on rules that apply to all individuals.[10] Similarly, Emile Durkheim's 1983 work *Division of Labor in Society* posited a transition between two distinct forms of social solidarity, from traditional society's group solidarity based on similarity to modern society's solidarity based on complementarity of functional roles in its complex division of labor. Durkheim went so far as to claim that the whole idea of the individual and individualism emerged from this change in social organization. Other foundational figures of social science made similar points: Karl Marx analyzed the breakdown of feudal caste privileges as ushering in capitalist relations of production based on free contracting, while Max Weber discussed the shift from organized nepotism to rational, legal, meritocratic, rule-following bureaucracies.

In this framework, culture matters, as well as institutions. The crucial cultural divide is not between civilizations bearing different cultural legacies, as in the theory of multiple modernities, but rather between the culture of tradition and that of modernity.[11] Viewed this way, the list of so-called Asian values does not reflect cultural distinctiveness at all, but instead expresses values typical of traditional societies everywhere, including the premodern West (e.g., patriarchy, duties rather than rights, priority of society over individuals) as well as policy concerns typical of developing countries (e.g., asserting state sovereignty or the priority of economic development over civil rights).

Modernization theory became unpopular in the 1960s when it became associated with hegemonic American foreign policies based on the obviously incorrect view that all developing societies would seamlessly become modern along the same path as Great Britain.[12] Nonetheless, the basic insights of more thoughtful modernization theorists remain the assumptions (often unspoken) that are central to much contemporary social science on the evolution and efficacy of the modern state. Francis Fukuyama's two-volume, 1,250-page masterwork argues that the central problem of political order and decay from prehistory to the present has been the struggle to overcome the inefficiencies embedded in lineage-based, clientelist social systems by supplanting them with modern systems of impersonal rules and accountable government.[13] Ending on a somber note, however, Fukuyama argues that remnants of the old corruption are endemic in institutional legacies in even the most advanced democracies, not to mention rising state-dominated capitalist powers such as China, with dangerous implications for inefficiency and disorder.

A crucial question for the debate over multiple modernities is how far a society must go in adopting the full package of liberal social arrangements to achieve self-sustaining economic growth. The purist view emphasizes that virtually all societies that have been highly successful over a long period have moved quite far toward the fully liberal model, both in formal arrangements and in effective rights for most segments of society. This includes due process of law, nondiscrimination, rule-based protections of property and sanctity of contracts, and widespread rights to political participation through free speech, political organizing, and fair, competitive elections of representatives who are bound by law. Setting aside oil sheikdoms and city-state entrepots protected by their liberal customers, the correlation between high per-capita income and stable, liberal democracy remains overwhelming.[14]

That said, China's unprecedented run of sustained economic growth raises the question of whether its illiberal formula, based largely on the technocratic skill of its elite, can succeed indefinitely.[15] Modernization theory might pose it this way: Is Weberian technical and administrative rationality enough to sustain modern economic performance and political stability, especially if the system's legal rationality is poorly developed and its social practices retain significant remnants of patrimonial traditionalism?

The most prominent historical scholarship on illiberal development traces the dire consequences of taking shortcuts to modernity.[16] This research—none by naïve or dogmatic liberals—highlights late-development traps leading to nationalism, including its populist version, and then to political turmoil and regime crisis. Karl Polanyi explains how free markets and mass politics clashed in the Great Depression, spurring populist fascist nationalism to assert national political control over domestic and international markets. Alexander Gerschenkron shows how late, copycat development required centralized financing and policy leadership by a strong state, which led in turn to authoritarian political coalitions and the co-optation of mass support through nationalist ideology. Barrington Moore analyzes the authoritarian nationalist alliance in late-developing states between the old aristocratic state and the rising but still weak bourgeoisie against the working class. Samuel Huntington illustrates how rapid economic development produced turbulent illiberal politics when the demand for mass political participation outstripped the development of state institutions. Ernest Gellner describes the strife that resulted when national marketization impelled ethnic stratification and forced assimilation. These dire outcomes were averted only in states that had shifted decisively to liberal institutions, ideas, and political coalitions before navigating these development traps.

Modernization theorists are not as pessimistic as Fukuyama about political decay in wealthy democracies. They note that the richest democratic country that has ever reverted to autocracy was Argentina in 1976, and it was hardly wealthy; its per-capita income was comparable to that of middle-income countries today.[17] The historical track record suggests that it is nonreforming middle- and lower-income states that revert to autocracy, not wealthy democracies with established political institutions.

The Mismatch of Markets and Governance in the Late-Development Trap

Over the past two decades, several large states in the developing and post-communist worlds have experienced significant economic growth as they introduced liberalizing reforms in their domestic markets and international economic relations. Impressive improvements in mass living standards, along with spikes in economic inequality and corruption, have often accompanied this growth. In many of these states, the emergence of an illiberal nationalism with populist overtones reflects a growing contradiction between economic development and governance institutions, sometimes called the middle-income trap.

During the Cold War, large developing states were able for a time to pursue strategies of state-led economic development and import-substituting industrialization (ISI) under "bureaucratic authoritarian" regimes.[18] This strategy depended on what Gerschenkron called the "advantages of backwardness": mobilizing underutilized labor and resource inputs, copying well-known industrial processes, and exerting state power to accumulate capital and protect infant industries from foreign competition. Politically, these states usually featured authoritarian or single-party politics in which the state aligned with a coalition of domestic manufacturers and sometimes organized labor. Subsidies and protectionism were a drag on productivity growth, however, so the system gradually stalled out.

As ISI was losing momentum, global policies of easier capital mobility and deregulation of markets, increasingly favored by advanced capitalist states and international financial institutions, offered opportunities for more dynamic, export-led growth. China, India, Brazil, Turkey, and other large developing states signed up for liberalization, and each experienced an acceleration of economic growth as a result. Russia went through its more superficial, petro-state version of market reform.

In many of these states, the initial liberalization phase was based on many of the same advantages of backwardness as ISI, only the market was now global. Cheap labor, easily extracted natural resources, copycat technology, and development-pushing state policies were now harnessed to foreign direct investment and the integration of production into internationally managed processes. Late-developing states cherry-picked the liberal institutional package of modernity, assimilating features narrowly needed for liberalized trade and finance, but approaching broader features like the rule of law, freedom of speech, and open democratic political competition warily. Clientelist economic and political arrangements more commonly associated with traditional societies and state-run economies continued. In many of these states, "neoliberal" became an epithet, meaning "crony capitalism."

There are strong signs that this phase of the globalized market development model is leading rising states into a transition trap. Growth has been based largely on adding more inputs: more labor coming off the farm, more land foreclosures, higher rates of capital investment, the exploitation of already-known technologies on a wider market scale. Knowing in advance the outcome they are aiming to achieve, the state and centralized financial institutions have used command authority to requisition and deploy resources. This model, while fully compatible with authoritarian rule and administrative control of labor, can also accommodate partial democratization. This is done with a heavy hand in China and with a lighter set of state policy tools, including steering investment through favoritism, in the other BRICS and near-BRICS.

It is the very success of this phase that leads to its demise. Wage rates rise once most of the useful labor force is employed. New land for commercial enterprises is harder to come by, and requisitioning it creates more resistance. The levers of state power ratchet the rates of savings and investment higher and higher, but force-feeding growth in this way demands more and more capital inputs to generate less and less incremental output. This syndrome constitutes exactly the impasse that China now faces.

The solution is to shift from the strategy of extensive growth, based on mobilizing additional labor and underutilized resources, to that of intensive growth, driven by increases in the combined productivity of all factors of production. This depends not on ever-increasing inputs, but on applying more efficient techniques to existing production factors and improving their allocation through improved responsiveness to market incentives. In countries in China's situation, this would require the development of its vast internal consumer market, currently stunted by the strategy of enforced savings. But what is really needed is the strengthening of liberal institutions such as the rule of law and governmental accountability to reduce the inefficiency drag of corruption, insecure rights of property and contracting, and inequality.

While slower-than-average growth can happen at every level and stage of development, a study by Brookings economist David Dollar finds that improving institutional quality is especially important for sustaining economic growth in middle-income countries because of its role in supporting the shift from extensive to intensive growth.[19] China and Vietnam were able to develop relatively good institutions for their lower level of income and stage of development, and for a time they were able to sustain a good rate of growth without developing the whole panoply of civil liberties. However, for high-income countries, Dollar finds a tight connection between good economic institutions such as well-defined property rights, the rule of law, effective government, and limits on corruption and greater liberal rights as measured by Freedom House's civil liberties index. Not counting oil states, Singapore is the only exception to this rule. In the 1990–2010 period, for countries at low levels of per-capita income, authoritarian countries grew faster than democratic ones, but among countries whose per-capita incomes were above one-fourth of U.S. per-capita income, democracies grew faster. The developmental histories of Korea and Taiwan illustrate this pattern.

Dollar reports that by 2010, China and Vietnam no longer had above-average institutional quality for their income level. China fell well below average, and Vietnam was average for its reference group. The subsequent growth slowdowns in both countries are consistent with Dollar's overall argument. As of this writing, most of the BRICS and near-BRICS are facing economic problems and growth slowdowns that fit the pattern of the late-development trap, including endemic government corruption.

By some measures, China is taking a number of positive steps to avoid getting stuck in the middle-income trap. Compared to other large developmental states, China looks more like success cases—Japan, South Korea, and Taiwan—in its efforts to prioritize education, invest in research and development, limit foreign direct investment, and avoid expansion of the informal sector of the economy. On the other hand, its economic inequality and systemic corruption must be seen as warning signs.

If Dollar is right about the need to continually liberalize institutions as a country moves up the per-capita-income food chain, why don't more countries, especially large ones, follow the example of South Korea and Taiwan? Several factors may come into play. Large size and substantial capital accumulated in the extensive growth phase give them leeway to pursue their preferred strategy. Moreover, administrative methods and patronage-based bargaining is what they know how to do, and they are good at it.[20]

A more fundamental reason is that the ruling elite, state apparatus, patronage networks, ethnic or religious majorities, and rising middle classes of these emerging powers have vested interests in maintaining the incompletely liberalized system. Many businessmen and officials make big money through favoritism, arbitrage, and self-dealing between the state and private sectors. The alternative to this partial reform equilibrium is accepting complete liberal reform and handing political and economic power to the mass of the population, which in many of these countries has been stockpiling grievances against crony capitalists for years. When the dem-onstrators in Tahrir Square learned that former Egyptian president Hosni Mubarak and his sons would get a slap on the wrist rather than a death sentence, the crime that focused their outrage was the ill-gotten vacation villas, not the suppression of human rights activists.

To keep the game going while avoiding reforms that would endanger their power and privileges, the ruling elite and their key support con-stituencies have a few options. Outright repression is one, but in a global-ized market economy that needs an educated population with enough information, initiative, and rule-following habits to do their jobs effi-ciently, some pressure for accountability is inevitable from both the regime's citizens and its international trading partners.

Trickle-down economics can also be used to justify wealth inequality. China's growing middle class, though still small compared to the mass of the population, is much better off than their parents were. Turkey's Erdo-gan is busting the national budget to disperse construction patronage throughout the backwaters of Anatolia to build poor-quality universities and shiny new airports. This cements the loyalty of his base, and, to the gullible, it looks like modernity.

When trickle-down patronage wears thin, however, nationalism is a tested tool for shifting the main axis of politics away from economic grievances to concerns about culture and identity. Nationalism allows unaccountable or semiaccountable elites to pretend to be one with the people. This is a game that can be played in rising powers to blunt or exploit the political consequences of the middle-income trap and in devel-oped democracies facing harsh market adjustments.

Populist Nationalism: Shifting the Axis of Politics from Economics to Identity

Viewed from the perspective of privileged elites, democratic or democra-tizing systems inherently bring the risk of the median voter using govern-mental power to equalize wealth. In the struggle over economic policy, populism is a game two can play. Bolshevik outsiders campaigned on the promise of land, peace, and bread. Similarly, Latin American populists like Hugo Chavez and Evo Morales promised redistribution to the poor and the excluded. However, the defenders of economic privilege also have cards to play. As mentioned, one tried-and-true method elites in democracies use to escape confiscatory taxation is moving the axis of political cleavage from economics to group identity, nationalism, and culture. In the United States, this dynamic was colorfully captured in the 2004 book *What's the Matter with Kansas?*, in which the journalist Thomas Frank argued that wealthy Republicans were duping low-income, small-town white citizens into voting against their own economic interests by hyping what he called cultural wedge issues like abortion, gay rights, racism, and threat-inflated militaristic patriotism.

Variants of this tactic are widespread across time and space, including seminal cases of late development. In the wake of Germany's rapid industrialization, the aristocratic monarchist Chancellor Otto von Bismarck responded to middle-class demands for constitutional government and limited parliamentary democracy by going them one better: universal manhood suffrage that included the working class and the peasantry. Bismarck gambled that the peasants would vote the way conservative landlords told them to, and that appeals to true German national identity could split up any hypothetical progressive coalition among labor, Catholics, and middle-class Protestant nationalists. He was right. In nine national parliamentary elections between 1870 and 1914, the conservative coalition did much better in the five that were fought on national or cultural issues defined by the Kulturkampf against the Catholics, colonial expansion, and increased military budgets to defend Germany against "hostile encirclement" by the Entente powers, which German diplomacy had largely provoked in the first place.[21] It was not until after Germany's defeat in World War I that the potential progressive coalition of organized labor and free-trade interests came to power.

The all-purpose logic of shifting the axis of electoral politics from economics to identity politics also explains urban rioting in India. Steven Wilkinson's definitive research shows that riots occur when municipal elections between an elite-dominated, identity-based party like the Hindu nationalist BJP and a lower class–based party attempting to appeal across identities such as Hindu and Muslim are expected to be close.[22] At these junctures, rumormongers polarize politics around identity and thugs foment rioting, inducing lower-class Hindus to vote their cultural ties rather than their pocketbook. The strategy only works, says Wilkinson, when the state's governing party coalition, which controls whether state police will intervene to prevent the riot, does not include the identity group targeted in the rioting. For example, when India's current Hindu nationalist prime minister, Narendra Modi, was governor of Gujarat, he declined to intervene in the 2002 Ahmedabad riots against Muslims. Following the electoral success of the BJP's populist anti-Muslim campaign in India's largest state of Uttar Pradesh in March 2017, Modi's selection of the divisive, religious rabble-rouser Yogi Adityanath as chief minister updates this pattern.

Often elites play the nationalist card in response to outsiders' earlier efforts to mobilize mass support for progressive change. Bismarck's strategy was a response to the revolutionary upheavals of 1848 and the initial successes of Germany's "national liberals." The BJP's strategy was shaped by the political landscape that the populist tactics of the Congress Party—including the foundational efforts of Mahatma Gandhi and the later populist authoritarianism of Indira Gandhi's emergency-rule period—created. Similarly, the Chinese government's flirtation with mass nationalism since the mid-1990s is a direct response to the threat from the 1989 mass protests in Tiananmen Square. Those protests and the nationalist response to them arose when traditional Communist legitimations of authority fit poorly with Deng Xiaoping's turn to market economics.

A typical danger is that nationalist gambits from above and below feed on each other in a contest of outbidding. Before 1914, for example, German middle-class mass nationalist and colonialist groups exploited the ruling elite's embrace of nationalist threat-mongering, arguing that if Germany really was encircled by the hostile Entente powers, then the army should be increased in size, the aristocracy should be taxed for it, and middle-class officers should be allowed into the aristocratic preserve of the general staff. While Bismarck cannot be called a populist by my definition, the discourses of nationalism and identity politics that he and his successors fueled played into the hands of mass nationalist groups. This ultimately set the stage for the quintessential right-wing populist group, the National Socialists, to emerge from the collapse of global markets that ended the Weimar Republic.

Outbidding dynamics are in play in China, too. After Tiananmen made liberal symbolism off limits, some of the leaders of that demonstration realized that the state-approved discourse of nationalism offered a more promising point of entrée into the public sphere. They collaborated on an anti-Western bestseller, *China Can Say No*, outbidding the regime's more controlled expressions of nationalism. Ever since, the Chinese

Communist regime has been playing a dangerous game, first allowing, stoking, and then limiting popular protest on social media and in the streets in response to nationalist grievances such as the bombing of the Chinese embassy in Belgrade, anti-Chinese pogroms in Jakarta, and Japan's bid for a permanent United Nations Security Council seat.

The nationalist discourse has become entwined with left-wing populist discourse that revives the glorification of Mao Zedong and the Cultural Revolution. These themes were combined in the egalitarian nationalist rhetoric of the fast-rising regional party boss Bo Xilai, whom the Chinese sometimes anxiously compared with Thaksin Shinawatra, Thailand's billionaire populist prime minister from 2001 to 2006. Bo's charismatic left nationalist appeal and wire-tapping of rivals was a threat to the Communist Party hierarchy, and he was brought down in a 2012 murder and corruption scandal. This cleared the way for president Xi Jinping to co-opt both the nationalist and Maoist mantles, but in a form intended to shore up party rule rather than destabilize it.

In rising powers, the updraft of outbidding is difficult to dampen. With national wealth and power on the rise, constituencies who consider themselves the core of nation, the sons of the soil, expect to be given both economic rewards and cultural hegemony. When Modi was Gujarat's governor, he abetted Hindu nationalists by allowing riots targeted largely at Muslim shopkeepers, and as prime minister he tolerates his supporters' persecution of Christians for beef-eating and trumped up charges of cow desecration.

Pride in the nation's newfound economic or political success gives the regime an automatic boost, but it can also set up popular expectations that may be hard to fulfill. The anticipation among Chinese nationalists that their century of humiliation was at an end has run into resistance from neighboring states and international courts over territorial claims and from economic nationalists in China's indispensable trading partner, the United States. In Russia, Putin has alternated economic and political prestige strategies, riding the invasion of Chechnya to power in his first landslide election, rising still higher along with oil and gas prices, and now, as his economic miracle deflates, needing to manufacture prestige with speculative gambits in Ukraine and Syria.

In short, rising powers facing late-development traps find both motives and opportunities to shift the national discourse from the reform demands and economic grievances of those left behind to manipulating the cultural agenda of their base. Brazil, the one BRIC that came late to the game of playing the nationalist card in the face of these traps, shows how risky this is. Maintaining corrupt patronage politics without the distraction of populist nationalism left the Brazilian political elites dangerously exposed. In due course, the populist Jair Bolsonaro emerged from the nationalist political fringes to win the presidency by rallying rural, evangelical, and military constituencies around the standard set of authoritarian, repressive, culturally regressive, antiminority, environmentally destructive themes. While his affinity toward international populist nationalists like Donald Trump is evident, this outcome seems better explained by the structural impasse in Brazil's political economy than by emulation stimulated by Trump's soft power. Bolsonaro had been promoting the same themes for decades, but only recently did the opportunity to cash in on them arise. Meanwhile, in other countries that have moved toward illiberal nationalism, there have been a variety of outcomes: a series of stalled modernization reforms, as in Turkey; intermittent liberal spurts and illiberal reversals, as in Argentina; or spectacular failure and liberal rebirth with the help of international efforts, as in Germany and Japan.

Populist Nationalism, Markets, and Governance in the Advanced Democracies

If populist nationalism is associated with problems of modernization, why are the already modern democracies of the West also experiencing a rising tide of nationalist, nativist, culturally conservative, illiberal populism? Even the most liberal and consolidated democratic states are struggling through a period in which globalization has weakened economic governance and put markets at odds with democratic accountability. Advanced democracies suffer from the same problem that Karl Polanyi pointed to in the interwar period: the contradiction between unregulated market forces and frustrated demand for effective mass political participation. In Europe this is exacerbated by the disconnection between democratic accountability, which resides in the national states, and economic policy, which emerges from the far less accountable realm of EU bargaining and bureaucracy. In that sense, the causes of the rise of populist nationalism in the core democratic states echo those in the modernizing late developers. Moreover, EU members most afflicted by illiberal populism in eastern and southern Europe are barely a generation beyond dictatorship—with their weak liberal institutions and cultures, they are not fully modernized.

The question of whether populist nationalism in the advanced democracies is mainly a backlash to economic or cultural disruption has attracted much debate and research. Many conclude that the answer is both—that attitudes about these two dimensions intertwine, and that the taproot in both cases is frustration at the governance system's nonresponsiveness to popular concerns. Studies vary in the extent to which they focus on the situation of individual voters and survey respondents, the challenges facing their communities as a whole, or the perceptions that shape their subjective worldviews.[23]

Successful populists craft narratives that integrate economic and cultural grievances. Economically, they emphasize themes of loss under globalization, capital mobility, the knowledge economy, and deindustrialization. Culturally, their narratives also target feelings of status loss in an era of growing cultural diversity and changing gender roles. The familiar litany has this double-barreled quality: immigrants are taking our jobs, siphoning off our welfare benefits, making our streets unsafe, contributing to terrorism, and making our towns unrecognizable. The educated, privileged elite looks down on us, sends our jobs abroad, and coddles historically stigmatized minorities, the undeserving poor, who don't work half as hard as we do. We want our respectable jobs and country back, but nobody listens to us. These narratives resonate where economic and cultural factors interact. In Britain, for example, nativist rivalry with immigrants happens especially in locations where economic scarcity combines with immigrant voting power to shift public resources away from the native population, triggering resentment.[24]

The mixture of economic and cultural themes, combined with the primacy of style over content in populist rhetoric, gives populist political entrepreneurs—like nationalists more generally—considerable latitude to be elusive, shape-shifting, or even contradictory in their policy stances. This is especially true of their attitude toward free markets. While reviling actually existing corporate capitalism, some populists idealize free markets in the abstract. From the American populist farmers of the 1890s to the small-town entrepreneurs of the Tea Party, they can be strongly pro-market, seeing it as a potential independent refuge from alien domination by big city elites. Populists just want markets to work in their favor, with marketing cooperatives for small farmers, cheap money to pay off loans, or low taxes for small business. Often these sons of the soil point to ethnic or national outgroups, in addition to the sellout elites of their own group, as the cause of rigged markets: e.g., cheap labor in China, welfare for immigrants and racial minorities, or cosmopolitan financiers whose loyalties respect no borders. Turning Polanyi on his head, some populists believe that unregulated markets would work fine if the people who manipulate them were neutralized.

Illiberal Populist Nationalism as a Source of International Soft Power

I have argued that the rise of illiberal populist nationalism as an assertive competitor to liberalism stems from an endemic and growing tension in liberalism: the mismatch between free markets and prevailing institutions for mass political participation. Broadly speaking, this leads to popular pushback against the so-called creative destruction caused by globalized markets that are insufficiently responsive to democratic political control. Among the newly rising major powers, there is a disconnection between the illiberal institutions that propelled the countries to middle-income status and the fully liberal institutions they need to modernize further. In this context, illiberal populist nationalism functions as an ideology to assert mass political control over the market in the interest of the nation's core cultural group. Populist demands may arise from below, but populist ideologies are also co-opted, articulated, harnessed, and exploited by elites.

Just as this can generate soft power—the power to persuade an audience to want what you want them to want—in domestic politics, it also creates the potential for soft power in international affairs among states or social constituencies across borders. This can happen in two ways. The first is when political ideas of actors and groups in different countries are similar. The success and vibrancy of these ideas in one country offer proof of their credibility and legitimacy in others. Early adopter countries can thus exert soft power by serving as a model, an inspiration, and a promoter of like-minded movements elsewhere. An example is the spread and consolidation of the democratic welfare state model after World War II. The second comes when different countries have similar international positions and a shared interest in advancing complementary arguments, even if their domestic political ideologies are quite different. An example is cooperation over several decades among capitalist, communist, military, civilian, democratic, and authoritarian states on the sovereign basis of live-and-let-live bargaining in the Association of Southeast Asian Nations (ASEAN).

Illiberal populist nationalist movements and demagogues seem to believe in a mutually empowering comradery of the first kind. Donald Trump explicitly recognized the Brexit vote as the success of a kindred movement that would add to his credibility and momentum. Vladimir Putin believes that it is in his interest to provide financial aid to right-wing nationalist populist movements and regimes in western and eastern Europe and to target propaganda and disinformation campaigns to aid their prospects. Surveys show that antisystem parties on the left and right in Europe agree on three things: the people are being sold out by their elites, referenda are wonderful, and Russia is not a significant threat.[25] Among the common themes that generate the potential for cross-national soft power among populist constituencies are cultural conservatism, resentment of cosmopolitanism, and defense of the interests of the nation's ethnocultural majority.

Nonetheless, these superficial commonalities do not necessarily generate soft power in the sense of a desire to cooperate intensively toward mutual emulation and the adoption of a common way of life. It may be that these sentiments are simply parallel developments generated by common causes such as exposure to market competition, influxes of culturally different migrants, and liberal multilateralism's failures of economic management and political accountability. Transactional collusion in Belt-and-Road infrastructure schemes between Chinese bribe-givers and Sri Lankan and Malaysian bribe-takers, sometimes with the help of Western management consultants and investment bankers, does not count as soft power in Nye's terms. Attempts to explain earlier waves of liberal democratization raised some of the same questions of causality as the contemporary wave of illiberal populism does: Were the liberal waves caused by soft-power diffusion of liberal ideas and examples, or triggered by similar structural causes including the collapse of liberalism's authoritarian competitors, the rise of literacy and per-capita income, and carrots and sticks offered by hegemonic liberal powers?

Moreover, attempts to exercise illiberal populist soft power may backfire. Xenophobic populists failed to live up to expectations in the 2017 Dutch and French elections. In the French case, the embarrassingly bungled Russian hacking effort on the eve of the vote certainly did not help

Marine Le Pen's already stumbling campaign. Conversely, the illiberal Polish national populist regime lost none of its cachet in domestic politics by positioning itself in defiance of both Moscow and Brussels.

The nationalism of many illiberal populists creates both opportunities and limitations for soft power. On one hand, many illiberal populist movements and the regimes that court them can make common cause in resisting liberal cosmopolitanism. They can join together in pushing back against the International Criminal Court, humanitarian interventions opposing rights-abusing dictators, pressures to liberalize markets, and shaming campaigns from gay-rights advocates. They can assert the counternorms of sovereignty, national self-determination, and non-Western civilizational values. Alexander Cooley argues that these efforts do not just reflect a coincidence of uncoordinated interests, but a concerted effort to export illiberal norms and institutionalize them in international organizations like the Shanghai Cooperation Council and illiberal election monitoring organizations.[26]

On the other hand, illiberal populist nationalism has inherent limitations as a vehicle for transnational influence. Its root appeal is to the narrow interests of its own country's dominant identity group. Its instinctive economic policy preference—or at least rhetoric—tends toward beggar-thy-neighbor nationalist economic protectionism, as in the Trump, anti-EU, and antiglobalization movements. Its rallying cry often revolves around an emotional core of resentment of past humiliations. The Chinese are still upset about the Opium War.[27] Even when illiberal populist nationalists would like to cooperate, as in the awkward bromance between Trump and Putin, their style and mindset makes it hard to deploy soft power constructively. In April 2018, the Italian nationalist populist leader Mario Salvini announced an "alliance" of nationalist populist parties in the European Parliament, but many of the presumed allies failed to endorse the effort, citing the Italian populists' demand that their countries should share more equitably the harboring of refugees stuck in Italy, the country of first landfall.[28] Indeed, the alliance of populist nationalist parties quickly fell apart, even in Italy itself.

It is true that the original philosopher of nationalism's virtues, Johann Gottfried Herder, argued that all nations should have the opportunity to fully achieve their national destiny. However, Woodrow Wilson learned that in the face of incompatible claims even liberal doctrines of national self-determination created friction. It took the creation of a much better institutionalized liberal international system, stronger democracies, and (to be painfully honest) a century of homogenizing ethnic cleansing in Europe to achieve what we now call democratic peace among liberal self-determining nation-states.[29] There is no comparable evidence of an illiberal nationalist peace. Liberalism, while nationalist in its commitment to the right of self-government by historically distinctive peoples, also relies on a common set of transnationally valid principles of human rights and rule of law for which there is no counterpart in illiberal nationalism.

It is true that illiberal states that succeed in generating economic growth, military power, and stable authoritarianism can become objects of emulation and focal points for cooperation. China is a current example, and some past illiberal powers have achieved this as well. For example, as liberal alternatives collapsed in the interwar period, East Europeans jumped on the Nazi bandwagon, emulating some of its features. But, as Albert Hirschman's famous study showed, it is easier to generate soft power when the demonstration effect of success is reinforced by dependency-promoting economic and military aid.[30] Other examples suggest that it also helps when the illiberal major power shares a religion or ethnic culture with the target of influence, though Slavophilism brought the Russians few reliable allies, and Islam has not proved to be enough to cement stable relations between would-be soft-power wielders and their clients. Communism did better by basing its soft power on illiberal but universalistic principles, but could not sustain the economic performance and political dynamism that was the real attraction. Any soft-power effects in such examples seem closely tied to underlying structural realities that shape basic material power realities and interests.

I have argued that liberalism's soft power has suffered because of a deepening tension between its two central principles of free markets and popular self-government. Illiberal populist nationalism has much deeper contradictions in its basic ideas and natural support coalitions. Populists believe in rule by the people and suspicion of elites, yet they are also suspicious of the regularized legal process and institutions that are indispensable to prevent reversion to corrupt and exploitative autocracy. Right-wing populists often favor market-based economics, but they are also attracted to strongmen who cut through red tape and implement by decree popular policies that defy market logic. The basic complaint of populists is often the power of corrupt elites, yet when populists come to power, especially in developing states with weak institutions, the most common outcome is a Fujimori-style corrupt dictatorship. These contradictions mean that the soft power of illiberal populism is often a flash in the pan, though its potential for superficial appeal is timeless.

Finally, the appearance of illiberal national populist developments in contemporary world politics does not necessarily mean that liberalism will face a cohesive competing model—or indeed any competing model. Despite certain commonalities stemming from late development and the middle-income trap, the BRICS and other large developing countries like Turkey and Indonesia are so different that it is hard to imagine them cohering around a single model. None offers an undisputable blueprint for its own future, much less a clear model of modernity for other states to emulate. And, despite the political ambivalence of their rising middle classes, many of these countries share institutional and ideological features with the established liberal states, making further liberal evolution possible. This is likely to produce a loose convergence on a rhetoric of national autonomy coupled with a policy of selective, sometimes grudging, support of liberal multilateral governance arrangements, rather than an attraction to any one state's soft power.

China's one-party technocratic model seems plausible only for Vietnam, which geopolitically is more foe than friend to Beijing. Meanwhile, the other BRICS are a hodgepodge: Russia is a continent-sized petrostate. Brazil and India are democracies burdened by a large underclass of impoverished, unskilled citizens and flawed rule of law. South Africa is a unique amalgam of white settlers, British institutions, and an impoverished African majority. Turkey, a non-BRIC, adds a religion-wielding ruling party to the mix of semidemocracy in an ethnically divided middle-income country with disadvantaged minorities. Indonesia has outperformed all expectations, given its authoritarian past, cultural diversity, and low per-capita income, but there is little talk of an Indonesian model, which appears to consist of slowly liberalizing reforms of the economy and politics with a pragmatic accommodation of the country's diverse cultural features and organized interests. Recent elections suggest that Indonesia is struggling to maintain a stable balance between more reform-minded left-populist political forces and those trying to marry a patron-based political economy to appeals to a stricter form of Islam. Another possibility is that progressive autocrats in some countries could aspire to emulate Singapore, where efficient administration defeats corruption without fully competitive party politics, but this model has not traveled smoothly to the city-states of Dubai and Qatar, let alone to rising great powers.

Notwithstanding these substantial differences, if there is any single ideology that characterizes the majority of rising powers it is nationalism. By its nature, though, nationalism is an ideology that proclaims "Let me be me," not "Let's all be the same." Still, despite the diverse characteristics of the rising powers, Xi's China, Putin's Russia, Erdogan's Turkey, and elsewhere might be seen as having common features that arise from common governance dilemmas. These include neoliberal economics at home and abroad, authoritarian or flawed democratic politics, social traditionalism among the regime's core support groups, and cultural nationalism, based on some mix of national history, ethnolinguistic distinctiveness, and/or politicized religion.

The social coalition backing such regimes often includes newly middle-class supporters who have risen from humble origins and seek a place at the table alongside more established elites, even as they look over their shoulder at impoverished masses with whom they share no common interests. Examples include China's antidemocratic east coast urban techno-structure and entrepreneurial class, the Anatolian entrepreneurs at the core of Erdogan's AKP, South Africa's new African governing class, and the middle-class Hindus who anchor Modi's BJP.[31] Many newly democratizing countries share with these rising powers the curse of corrupt officials and entrepreneurs who exploit what Joel Hellman calls the "partial reform equilibrium" that creates opportunities to extract rents through the use of state power in the market.[32]

Of course, nativist political parties and illiberal social movements also exist in the most developed, long-standing democratic states, often drawing on the same kinds of sentiments and constituencies. There may be a fine line between states where such groups are routine participants in the political system, as in many advanced democracies, and states where they *are* the system, as in some transitional "illiberal democracies."

Soft Power or Political Ideology

Arguably the most distinctive element in Joseph Nye's concept of soft power was the link between the inherent attractiveness of a nation's broad cultural attributes and its state's ability to accomplish its international objectives. But there is a lot of slippage in this purported link. A young man in Iraq might be very attracted by the idea of attending the University of Southern California, but that might not be a meaningful option for him, so he may join a ruthless sectarian militia instead. Along these lines, a survey of world attitudes toward the law of war stipulating the protection of civilians gets the same degree of support in Somalia as it does in Detroit, but Somali respondents say they don't think such laws stand any chance of shaping behavior in their locale.[33]

Moreover, a given culture's attributes may vary in their attractiveness. Japanese in the Meiji era found the industrial and military aspects of Western society very attractive, and they liked Louis Armstrong and baseball even before the American army occupied their country. But many Japanese were suspicious, uncertain, or downright terrified of other aspects of the liberal, capitalist, imperial Western package. They wanted to pick and choose, sometimes in order to fight back against the attractive outsider.

Trying to harness the attractive elements of one's culture to one's state objectives may destroy the attraction. At the very moment when cultural spontaneity is exploited to achieve specific political goals, soft influence is likely to collapse unless it is supported by the kind of power and common interest that is hard, not soft. Confucius Institutes have zero impact because they are a top-down effort to promote Chinese soft power for strategic purposes and because Confucius is not seen as especially relevant to many of the national cultures in which those institutes are deployed. Sun-Tsu's writings on the art of war, however, are avidly consumed by U.S. defense intellectuals, military veterans, and West Point undergraduates, but not in a way that helps the national interests of China.

Although there is no incompatibility between the soft power and the Gramscian ideological approaches laid out in this volume's framing chapters, and although soft power narrowly understood may be a helpful concept in some contexts, expanding soft power to encompass a topic such as the challenge of illiberal populist nationalism seems too much of a stretch. Treating illiberal populist nationalism as an ideology, whether Gramscian or otherwise, seems more productive. This approach has the advantage of highlighting both the underlying structural factors that favor these ideological developments and the causal mechanisms that describe specific ideological processes.

Notes

1. Francis Fukuyama, "The End of History?" *National Interest* 16 (Summer 1989): 3–18.
2. Joseph S. Nye Jr., *Bound to Lead: The Changing Nature of American Power* (New York: Basic Books, 1990).
3. Matt Golder, "Far Right Parties in Europe," *Annual Review of Political Science* 19 (2016): 477–98; Sheri Berman, "The Pipedream of Undemocratic Liberalism," *Journal of Democracy* 28, no. 3 (July 2017): 29–38.
4. Benjamin Moffitt, *The Global Rise of Populism: Performance, Style, and Representation* (Stanford, CA: Stanford University Press, 2016), 44–45.
5. Fareed Zakaria, "Populism on the March: Why the West Is in Trouble," *Foreign Affairs* 95, no. 6 (November–December 2016): https://www.foreignaffairs.com/articles/united-states/2016-10-17/populism-march.
6. Roberto Stefan Foa and Yascha Mounk, "The Signs of Deconsolidation," *Journal of Democracy* 28, no. 1 (January 2017): 5–16; Sheri Berman and Maria Snegovaya, "Populism and the Decline of Social Democracy," *Journal of Democracy* 30, no. 3 (July 2019): 5–19.
7. Francis Fukuyama, *The End of History and the Last Man* (New York: Avon, 1993).
8. Randall L. Schweller and Xiaoyu Pu, "After Unipolarity: China's Visions of International Order in an Era of U.S. Decline," *International Security* 36, no. 1 (Summer 2011): 41–72.
9. Karl Polanyi, *The Great Transformation* (New York: Farrar & Rinehart, 1944).
10. This and the following section draws on Jack Snyder, "The Modernization Trap," *Journal of Democracy* 28, no. 2 (April 2017): 77–91.
11. S. N. Eisenstadt, "Multiple Modernities," *Daedalus* 129 (Winter 2000): 1–29; Peter J. Katzenstein, ed., *Civilizations in World Politics: Plural and Pluralist Perspectives* (New York: Routledge, 2010).
12. Robert A. Packenham, *Liberal America and the Third World* (Princeton, NJ: Princeton University Press, 1973).
13. Francis Fukuyama, *The Origins of Political Order from Prehuman Times to the French Revolution* (New York: Farrar, Straus & Giroux, 2011); Francis Fukuyama, *Political Order and Political Decay* (New York: Farrar, Straus & Giroux, 2014).
14. Adam Przeworski, Michael Alvarez, Jose Cheibub, and Fernando Limongi, *Democracy and Development* (Cambridge: Cambridge University Press, 2000).
15. Daniel Bell, *The China Model: Political Meritocracy and the Limits of Democracy* (Princeton, NJ: Princeton University Press, 2015).
16. Barrington Moore, *Social Origins of Dictatorship and Democracy* (Boston: Beacon, 1966); Alexander Gerschenkron, *Economic Backwardness in Historical Perspective* (Cambridge, MA: Harvard University Press, 1962); Samuel P.

Huntington, *Political Order in Changing Societies* (New Haven, CT: Yale University Press, 1968); Ernest Gellner, *Nations and Nationalism* (Ithaca, NY: Cornell University Press, 1983).

17. Przeworski et al., *Democracy and Development*, 98.
18. Guillermo O'Donnell, *Bureaucratic Authoritarianism: Argentina, 1966–1973, in Comparative Perspective* (Berkeley: University of California Press, 1988).
19. David Dollar, "Institutional Quality and Growth Traps" (Pacific Trade and Development Working Paper Series, No. YF37-07, Institute of Southeast Asian Studies, Singapore, June 3–5, 2015).
20. Yuen Yuen Ang, *How China Escaped the Poverty Trap* (Ithaca, NY: Cornell University Press, 2016).
21. Brett Fairbairn, "Interpreting Wilhelmine Elections: National Issues, Fairness Issues, and Electoral Mobilization," in *Elections, Mass Politics, and Social Change in Modern Germany*, ed. Larry Eugene Jones and James Retallack (Cambridge: Cambridge University Press, 1992), 22–30.
22. Steven I. Wilkinson, *Votes and Violence: Electoral Competition and Ethnic Riots in India* (Cambridge: Cambridge University Press, 2004).
23. Matthijs Rooduijn, "What Unites the Voter Bases of Populist Parties? Comparing the Electorates of 15 Populist Parties," *European Political Science Review* 10, no. 3 (2018): 351–68; Matt Golder, "Far Right Parties in Europe," *Annual Review of Political Science* 19 (2016): 477–98.
24. Rafaela M. Dancygier, *Immigration and Conflict in Europe* (Cambridge: Cambridge University Press, 2010).
25. Susi Dennison and Dina Pardijs, "The World According to Europe's Insurgent Parties: Putin, Migration, and People Power," *European Council on Foreign Relations*, June 27, 2016, https://www.ecfr.eu/publications/summary/the_world_according_to_europes_insurgent_parties7055.
26. Alexander Cooley and John Heathershaw, *Dictators Without Borders: Power and Money in Central Asia* (New Haven, CT: Yale University Press, 2017).
27. Peter Hays Gries, *China's New Nationalism: Pride, Politics, and Diplomacy* (Berkeley: University of California Press, 2004).
28. Jason Horowitz, "Matteo Salvini Announces New European Alliance of Far-Right Populists," *New York Times*, April 8, 2019, https://www.nytimes.com/2019/04/08/world/europe/italy-salvini-far-right-alliance.html.
29. Rogers Brubaker, "Nationhood and the National Question in the Soviet Union and Post-Soviet Eurasia: An Institutionalist Account," *Theory and Society* 23, no. 1 (February 1994): 47–78.
30. Albert Hirschman, *National Power and the Structure of Foreign Trade* (Berkeley: University of California Press, 1945).
31. Kellee Tsai, *Capitalism Without Democracy: The Private Sector in Contemporary China* (Ithaca, NY: Cornell University Press, 2007).

32. Joel Hellman, "Winners Take All: The Politics of Partial Reform in Post-Communist Transitions," *World Politics* 50, no. 2 (January 1998): 203–34.

33. Greenberg Research, *The People on War Report: ICRC Worldwide Consultation on the Rules of War, Geneva: International Committee of the Red Cross*, October 1999, http://www.icrc.org/en/doc/assets/files/other/globalreport.pdf (accessed October 21, 2020).

Power, Culture, and Hegemony

A Selected Bibliography

The soft-power problematic stands at the intersection of several fields: international history, history of diplomacy, and history of concepts and ideas, international relations, political theory, communications, and cultural studies—just to start. This bibliography is conceived for anybody who is a beginner in at least one of these fields, with the premise that anybody who wants to use the term in any serious way will want to know where it came from. Otherwise, why not just use the old binary of carrot and stick? Those interested in exploring the origins of soft power, why it is such an imprecise yet unexpectedly loaded term, and whether it is too squishy to use as a key concept in scholarly work, will find that it takes us into one of the most fundamental and fascinating issues in international affairs in the early twenty-first century—namely, the asymmetric relations underlying the forces of persuasion, attraction, and consent.

Anyone putting together a bibliography on soft power must recognize that the global rise in interest in the concept coincided practically perfectly with the globalization of information brought by the internet, and that the term has been a favorite in punditry and academic and policy circles, so that the sheer amount of online papers, journal articles, master's theses, doctoral dissertations, and books—not to mention op-eds and other commentaries that use the term loosely, even casually—is incalculable. This bibliography is deliberately selective and idiosyncratic, with the goal of illuminating the theoretical debates that gave birth to the concept; conceptual terms associated with it, like "hegemony," "*mission civilisatrice*," "symbolic capital," and "cultural capital"; and the age-old question as posed by Machiavelli's *Prince* of whether it is better to be feared or loved. It wants to understand whether soft power and normative power operate differently under imperialist, neoliberal, or illiberal regimes, and how the modern modalities of its use differs from its historic use—when hegemons communicated their power through, say, coins stamped with the emperor's face, seals, the press, trade fairs, radio, and so on. In tandem with the goals of this volume, the bibliography, too, suggests the need to deprovincialize, to challenge conventional Eurocentric perspectives by looking outside the West to understand more clearly the universality of the phenomenon and the specificity of national and regional examples.

How Does Power Work in International Relations?

Is "soft power" actually a new concept? Has power changed the way it operates? Is power in the study of international order different from power in the study of social relations? This volume treats power not in the conventional IR sense, but rather in the classical sense of the Greeks, who distinguished between *hegemonia* (legitimated leadership) and *arkhe* (control), and between the two aspects of influence and persuasion: *dolos*, based on deceit and coercion, and *peitho*, which is achieved by common identities and friendship. For more on this, Stephen Lukes's *Power: A Radical View* (New York: Palgrave Macmillan, 2nd. ed., 2005) is a good place to start, together with the less classically informed article by Michael Barnett and Raymond Duvall, "Power in International Politics" (*International Organization* 59 [Winter 2005]: 39–75). The debate over the meaning of power starts from classic IR positions, notably those of Robert A. Dahl ("The Concept of Power," *Behavioral Science* 2 [1957]: 201–15), and David A. Baldwin ("Power Analysis and World Politics," *World Politics* 31, no. 2 [January 1979]: 161–94), who reaffirms that tradition in his *Power and International Relations: A Conceptual Approach* (Princeton, NJ: Princeton University Press, 2016). The constructivist turn in international relations significantly advanced the prospect of historical and comparative analysis; see Alexander Wendt, "Anarchy Is What States Make of It: The Social Construction of Power Politics," *International Organization* 46, no. 2 (1992): 391–425. This trend is felicitously developed in *Power in World Politics*, edited by Felix Berenskoetter and Michael J. Williams (Abingdon: Routledge, 2007), and especially vividly from the European continental perspective in Ulrich Beck, *Power in the Global Age* (Cambridge, MA: Polity, 2005).

Political economy combines with international relations and historical perspective in the Cambridge Studies in International Relations series, starting with *Protean Power,* edited by Peter J. Katzenstein and Lucia A. Seybert (Cambridge: Cambridge University Press, 2007), especially Katzenstein and Seybert's conclusion (267–301). John M. Hobson deprovincializes ideas of power in *The Eurocentric Conception of World Politics: Western International Theory, 1760–2010* (Cambridge: Cambridge University Press, 2012); so, too, do the British constructivists working from the perspective of the English School of international relations, starting with the master work of its progenitor, E. H. Carr. In his *Twenty Years' Crisis: 1919–1939: An Introduction to the Study of International Relations* (London: Palgrave Macmillan, 2016), Carr worried that Nazi-Fascist revisionism presented itself as making moral claims that were as valid as those made by law-abiding powers. Also relevant are Edward Keene, *Beyond the Anarchical Society: Grotius, Colonialism and Order in World Politics* (Cambridge: Cambridge University Press, 2005) and Edward Keene, "Social Status, Social Closure, and the Idea of a Normative Power Europe," *European Journal of International Relations* 19, no. 4 (2013): 939–56, which brings French sociologist Pierre Bourdieu's notion of status and cultural capital to foreign relations; see Pierre Bourdieu, "What Makes a Social Class? On the Theoretical and Practical Existence of Groups," *Berkeley Journal of Sociology* 32 (1987): 1–17. Equally vital, but from another angle altogether, the perspective of domestic struggles over the meaning of great power is offered by Robert Vitalis, *White World Order, Black Power Politics: The Birth of American International Relations* (Ithaca, NY: Cornell University Press, 2015).

The reflections of Antonio Gramsci, the Italian Communist Party leader and theorist, on how elites combine force and persuasion to legitimate their rule nationally and internationally, are often referred to. Though he actually wrote very little about international relations, he had truly original views on the pressure that rising hegemons exercise internationally as they use their domestic upheavals to present themselves to the world as leading social models. He is interesting, too, for the premise that just as what he called a "historical bloc" achieves dominance at home not only by force, but also by establishing institutions and elaborating values that are at least partially shared by class allies and subordinate classes and groups, they represent themselves to allies and client states abroad by contesting alternative models and providing such a quantity of institutions and inventions (e.g., public goods) that they can make regimes that are changing more slowly undergo a "passive revolution." The 1970s Gramscianism of Canadian constructivist R. W. Cox, in "Gramsci, Hegemony, and International Relations: An Essay in Method" (in *Gramsci, Historical Materialism, and International Relations*, ed. S. Gill, 49–66, Cambridge: Cambridge University Press, 1993), marked the opening of the Gramscian moment, though he himself did not use the category of "symbolic capital," or otherwise underscore the cultural, prestige, and status factors that matter in establishing dominant and subaltern relations in global order. By way of introduction, read Andreas Bieler and Adam David Morton, "The Critical Theory Route to Hegemony, World Order, and Historical Change: Neo-Gramscian Perspectives in International Relations," *Capital & Class* 82 (Spring 2004): 85–113; John Agnew, *Hegemony: The New Shape of Global Power* (Philadelphia: Temple University Press, 2005) is also useful, as is, if one stretches the applicability of the approach by considering the Vatican as a cultural-religious power, his "Deus Vult: "The Geopolitics of the Catholic Church," *Geopolitics* 15, no. 1 (2010): 39–61. Whether he calls himself a Gramscian or not, Alfredo G. A. Valladão, in "Democratic Hegemony and American Hegemony" (*Cambridge Review of International Affairs* 19, no. 2 [2006]: 243–60), offers keen insights into the challenge to national elites, including American, of American-led globalization.

Soft power and, especially, normative power calls for reflecting on culture, understood broadly as institutions that create meaning. Japanese American historian Akira Iriye is the pioneer here. Overlapping at Harvard University with Joseph S. Nye Jr., Iriye sees intercultural—really interinstitutional—arrangements as the bedrock of a more peaceful international order, as he describes in "Culture and Power: International Relations as Intercultural Relations," *Diplomatic History* 3, no. 12 (April 1979): 115–128 and subsequent books, including *Cultural Internationalism and World Order* (Baltimore: John Hopkins University Press, 2001) and *The Global Community: The Role of International Organizations in the Making of the Contemporary World* (Berkeley: University of California Press: 2004). For a similar line of reasoning, see Robert O. Keohane and Joseph S. Nye Jr., *Power and Interdependence: World Politics in Transition* (Boston: Little, Brown, 1977); Robert O. Keohane, *After Hegemony: Cooperation and Discord in the World*

Political Economy, (Princeton, NJ: Princeton University Press, 1984); and John G. Ruggie, "International Regimes, Transactions, and Change: Embedded Liberalism in the Postwar Economic Order," *International Organisation* 36, no. 2 (1982): 379–415.

For all of its self-evidence, there is no clear theorization about why culture has become a preeminent arena of conflict since the 1990s. Is it because culture became more and more commercialized under neoliberalism? Or because cybersystems so radically changed the modes of its diffusion across national borders? Or because economy, by undercutting society and political community, made culture the last bastion of social defense? In *Hybridity, or the Cultural Logic of Globalization* (Philadelphia: Temple University Press, 2005), Marwan M. Kraidy offers a good start to rethink the role of culture in international relations.

What Can History Tell Us?

We can better demystify soft power and how different national states and international regimes capitalize on their national and global resources to rise to preeminence if we consider the issue historically. Politicians and leaders have been worrying about their capacity to systematically use domestically generated ideological and cultural sources to distinguish their world-historical role, mollify and mobilize their subjects, and subdue foreign enemies at least since the French Revolutionary War. David Bell is good on the cold war/hot war dimensions in *The First Total War: Napoleon's Europe and the Birth of Warfare as We Know It* (New York: Houghton Mifflin, 2007), with the British playing the role that America would eventually embrace, and the French as the Bolsheviks of that era. Arno J. Mayer Jr. captured the clash of ideology between the United States and USSR coming out of World War I in *Wilson vs. Lenin: Political Origins of the New Diplomacy, 1917–1918* (New York: Meridian, 1967), as, from a different perspective, does Adam Tooze, in *The Deluge: The Great War, America, and the Remaking of the Global Order, 1916–1931* (New York: Penguin, 2015), who recognizes that the United States had the capacity to be the hegemon, but opted to hold back militarily and institutionally, to the grave destabilization of the liberal world era. For a full introduction to Wilsonianism as a progenitor of 1990s neoliberal internationalism, read John A. Thompson, "Wilsonianism: The Dynamics of a Conflicted Concept,"

International Affairs 86, no. 1 (2010: 27–42. Victoria de Grazia addresses the cultural underpinnings of the U.S. market empire in *Irresistible Empire: America's Advance Through Twentieth-Century Europe* (Cambridge, MA: Belknap Press of Harvard University Press, 2006); in *The Nazi-Fascist New Order for European Culture* (Cambridge, MA: Harvard University Press, 2016), Benjamin Martin underscores the cultural-hegemonic dimension of late 1930s European fascist states and movements. Paul W. Schroeder is good on the conflicts of legitimacy at the Congress of Vienna—which is helpful in thinking more broadly about persuasion and attraction—in his "Commentary on Nigel Gould-Davies: Rethinking the Role of Ideology in International Politics During the Cold War," *JCWS* 1, no. 1 (Winter 1999): 90–109. To exclude Russia from this discussion would be foolhardy, since, long before the establishment of the USSR and the Comintern, the Russian government was famous for its surveillance-communication-cultural networks and the indispensable role they played in keeping a multicultural and far-flung empire together. To start: see Larry Ray and William Outhwaite, "Communist Cosmopolitanism," in *European Cosmopolitanisms: Colonial Histories and Postcolonial Societies,* edited by Gurminder K. Bhambra and John Narayan, 41–56 (Abingdon Routledge, 2016; Michael David-Fox, *Showcasing the Great Experiment: Cultural Diplomacy and Western Visitors to the Soviet Union, 1921–1941* (Oxford: Oxford University Press, 2011); Tobias Rupprecht, *Soviet Internationalism After Stalin: Interaction and Exchange Between the USSR and Latin America During the Cold War* (Cambridge: Cambridge University Press, 1999); Tony Shaw and Denise J. Youngblood, *Cinematic Cold War: The American and Soviet Struggle for Hearts and Minds* (Lawrence: University Press of Kansas, 2010); and Susan E. Reid, "Who Will Beat Whom? Soviet Popular Reception of the American National Exhibition in Moscow, 1959," *Kritika* 9, no. 4 (2008): 855–904. For contemporary Russia set against the background of the "world of influence operations run amok," see Peter Pomerantsev, *This is Not Propaganda: Adventures in the War Against Reality* (London: Faber & Faber, 2019).

Soft Power, the United States, and Its Critics

At this point, Joseph S. Nye Jr.'s bibliography should be read as an important archival source, rather than as the horse's mouth, the subject of a full-blown concept history, or an intellectual biography. Key moments include

Joseph S. Nye Jr., "Soft Power," *Foreign Policy*, 80 (1990): 153–71; with William A. Owens, "America's Information Edge," *Foreign Affairs* 75 (1996): 20–36; and Nye, "The Decline of America's Soft Power: Why Washington Should Worry," *Foreign Affairs* 83 (2004): 16–20. Also useful is Nye, "Public Diplomacy and Soft Power," *Annals of the American Academy of Political and Social Science* 616 (March 2008): 94–109; Richard L. Armitage and Joseph S. Nye Jr., "Implementing Smart Power: Setting an Agenda for National Security Reform," statement before the Senate Foreign Relations Committee, April 24, 2008, https://www.foreign.senate.gov/imo/media /doc/042408_Transcript_Implementing%20Smart%20Power.pdf ; Nye Jr., "Get Smart: Combining Hard and Soft Power," *Foreign Affairs* 88, no. 4 (2009): 160–63; "Transcript of Witness Testimony to the House of Lords Select Committee on Soft Power and UK Influence," October 15, 2013, https://www.parliament.uk/documents/lords-committees/soft-power-uk -influence/uc151013Ev10.pdf; and, finally, "China's Soft and Sharp Power," *Project Syndicate*, January 4, 2018, https://www.project-syndicate.org/com mentary/china-soft-and-sharp-power-by-joseph-s--nye-2018-01.

Critiques are innumerable: Janice Bially Mattern, "The Concept of Power and the (Un) Discipline of International Relations," in *Oxford Handbooks Online*, edited by Christian Reus-Smit and Duncan Snidal, 691–98, https://www.oxfordhandbooks.com/view/10.1093/oxfordhb /9780199219322.001.0001/oxfordhb-9780199219322-e-40 (accessed October 8, 2020); Laura Roselle, Alister Miskimmon, Ben O'Loughlin, "Strategic Narrative: A New Means to Understand Soft Power," *Media, War & Conflict* 7, no. 1 (March 2014): 70–84; and Todd Hall, "An Unclear Attraction: A Critical Examination of Soft Power as an Analytical Category in Chinese Thought," *Chinese Journal of International Politics* 3, no. 2 (2010): 189–211, count among the most persuasive. Nye has responded good-naturedly to Western critics in "Responding to My Critics and Concluding Thoughts," in *Soft Power and U.S. Foreign Policy: Theoretical, Historical, and Contemporary Perspectives*, edited by Inderjeet Parmar and Michael Cox, 215–27 (Abingdon: Routledge, 2010). He has reiterated and expanded his views on how the United States must adapt "power resources" to remain at the pinnacle in *The Future of Power* (New York: Public Affairs, 2011).

To glimpse the cyberindustry devoted to soft-power metrics, see "The Soft Power 30: A Global Ranking of Soft Power 2018," available at http://www.aalep.eu/global-ranking-soft-power-2018 (accessed October 21, 2020).

Normative Power, Europe, and Its Critics

For a good introduction to the concept, see *Normative Power Europe: Introductory Observations on a Controversial Notion,* edited by André Gerrits (The Hague: Netherlands Institute of International Relations, 2009). For a critical retrospective, see Thomas Diez and Ian Manners, "Reflecting on Normative Power Europe," in *Power in World Politics,* edited by Felix Berenskoetter and M. J. William, 173–88 (Abingdon: Routledge, 2007).

For the historical precedents, see François Duchêne, "Europe's Role in World Peace," in *Europe Tomorrow: Sixteen Europeans Look Ahead,* edited by R. Mayne, 32–47 (New York: Fontana/Collins, 1972); and Hedley Bull, "Civilian Power Europe: A Contradiction in Terms?," *Journal of Common Market Studies* 21, no. 2 (December 1982): 149–70.

For an especially wide-ranging approach—really, a supersession of the concept that brings in the military dimension—see the brilliant Zaki Laïdi, *Norms Over Force: The Enigma of European Power* (New York: Palgrave Macmillan, 2007), and, especially, his recent intervention "Is Europe Ready for Power Politics?" (Robert Schuman Centre for Advanced Studies Research Paper No. RSCAS, June 2019, 2019), https://papers.ssrn.com/sol3/papers.cfm?abstract_id=3405237 (accessed October 2, 2020), 42.

With a focus on Europe's problem with immigration and diversity, see Lisbeth Aggestam, "Introduction: Ethical Power Europe?," *International Affairs* 84, no. 1 (2008): 1–11; and Lisbeth Aggestam and Christopher Hill, "The Challenge of Multiculturalism in European Foreign Policy," *International Affairs* 84, no. 1 (2008): 97–114. Adding in Russia, see Andrey Makarychev, "Hard Questions About Soft Power: A Normative Outlook at Russia's Foreign Policy," *DGAPanalyse Kompakt* 10 (October 2011), https://www.academia.edu/7667026/DGAPanalyse_kompakt_Hard_Questions_About_Soft_Power_A_Normative_Outlook_at_Russias_Foreign_Policy (accessed October 2, 2020). Also useful is *The Return of Geopolitics in Europe? Social Mechanisms and Foreign Policy Identity Crises,* edited by Stefano Guzzini (Cambridge: Cambridge University Press, 2012).

The concept of "normative power," like the policies identified with it, is much debated. An essay by Raja Noureddine who won the twenty-second annual essay competition by the Contemporary European Studies Association of Australia (CESAA), provides an excellent review and bibliography criticisms in "Critically Assess and Analyse the Notion That the EU Is a Normative Power," November 24, 2016, https://eeas.europa .eu/delegations/venezuela/15688/22nd-annual-cesaa-essay-competition -winners-awarded-dr-bruno-scholl_nb. For a clear-eyed, realist position, there is Adrian Hyde-Price, "'Normative' Power Europe: A Realist Critique," *Journal of European Public Policy* 13, no. 2 (2006): 217–34; and Jan Zielonka, "Europe as a Global Actor: Empire by Example?," *International Affairs* 84, no. 3 (2008): 471–84. Zielonka's more recent "Europe's New Civilizing Missions: The EU's Normative Power Discourse," *Journal of Political Ideologies* 18, no. 1 (2013): 35–55 is also important.

Is Twenty-First-Century Soft Power Comprehensible Without Cybercommunications?

Assuming that rising hegemons have always mobilized communication resources and that hegemonic powers always use them to sustain themselves and challenge others, is there a specific dimension to their employment under soft-power internationalism? For a grand, problematic, historical-conceptual overview, read two books by the indispensable Harold Adams Innis: *Empire and Communications* (Toronto: Dundurn, 2007), and *The Bias of Communication* (Toronto: University of Toronto Press, [1951] 2008). Assuming every power rests on a particular technological basis that shapes the relationship between humans and things, for the United States see Norbert Wiener, *The Human Use of Human Beings: Cybernetics and Society* (New York: Hachette, 1988). Also useful is Lucy A. Suchman, *Plans and Situated Actions: The Problem of Human-Machine Communication* (Cambridge: Cambridge University Press, 1987). From its inception, cybernetics in the United States has been linked to the government and the military: see Paul N. Edwards, *The Closed World: Computers and the Politics of Discourse in Cold War America* (Cambridge, MA: MIT Press, 1997). For the effort to distinguish propaganda from other kinds of persuasion, mostly self-serving, see J. Michael Sproule, *Propaganda and Democracy: The American Experience of Media and Mass Persuasion* (Cambridge: Cambridge University Press, 1997).

The peculiarities of U.S. development become clearer if read against the European experience, a fact now amply recognized in Andreas Fickers and Pascal Griset's *Communicating Europe* (London: Palgrave Macmillan, 2019);

and *The Handbook of European Communication History*, edited by Klaus Arnold, Paschal Preston, and Suzanne Kinnebrock (New York: Wiley & Sons, 2019). For Russia and the USSR, see the important work of Benjamin Peters, *How Not to Network a Nation: The Uneasy History of the Soviet Internet* (Cambridge, MA: MIT Press, 2016). On China, see Shen Hong, "China and Global Internet Governance: Toward an Alternative Analytical Framework," *Chinese Journal of Communication* 9, no. 3 (2016): 304–24. To recall the illusory view that the internet would promote an egalitarian liberal internationalism, read Manuel Castells, *The Rise of the Network Society* (New York: John Wiley & Sons, 2011); and Rebecca MacKinnon, *Consent of the Networked: The Worldwide Struggle for Internet Freedom* (New York: Basic Books, 2012). To understand the new modes of citizenship and exclusion enabled by new media technologies, see *Global Communications: Toward a Transcultural Political Economy*, edited by Paula Chakravartty and Yuezhi Zhao (Lanham, MD: Rowman & Littlefield, 2008). Also useful is Miriyam Aouragh and Paula Chakravartty, "Infrastructures of Empire: Towards a Critical Geopolitics of Media and Information Studies," *Media, Culture & Society* 38, no. 4. (April, 2016): 559–75. Also worth a look are Shawn M. Powers and Michael Jablonski. *The Real Cyber War: The Political Economy of Internet Freedom* (Champaign: University of Illinois Press, 2015); Jack Goldsmith and Tim Wu, *Who Controls the Internet? Illusions of a Borderless World* (Oxford: Oxford University Press, 2006); and Laura DeNardis, *The Global War for Internet Governance* (New Haven, CT: Yale University Press. 2014). On the recent securitization and militarization of cybercommunications, start with Tanner Mirrlees, *Hearts and Mines: The U.S. Empire's Culture Industry* (Vancouver: University of British Columbia Press, 2016); Christian Marazzi, *Capital and Language: From the New Economy to the War Economy* (Los Angeles: Semiotext(e) Foreign Agents Series, 2011); and Lisa Parks and Caren Kaplan, *Life in the Age of Drone Warfare* (Durham, NC: Duke University Press, 2017).

How Are Soft and Normative Power Operationalized?
From New Diplomacy to Public Diplomacy

To start, there is Harold Nicolson, *Diplomacy* (Oxford: Oxford University Press, [1939] 1963); and *The Evolution of the Diplomatic Method* (Westport,

CT: Greenwood, 1954). Nicholson targets Woodrow Wilson and the United States when he argues that diplomacy degenerated into a public fray the moment demagogic rulers began to solicit mass opinion. Nicholas J. Cull explores the big changes in the Transatlantic world with the onset of the Cold War in "Public Diplomacy before Gullion: The Evolution of a Phrase," in *Routledge Handbook of Public Diplomacy*, edited by Nancy Snow and Philip M. Taylor, 19–24 (Abingdon: Routledge, 2006). And Akira Iriye, "Culture and Power: International Relations as Intercultural Relations," *Diplomatic History* 3, no. 2 (April 1979): 115–28, underscores the need for cultural diplomacy once multilateral institutions became so prominent in international affairs.

For a history of American public diplomacy, a good starting place is Jason Hart, *Empire of Ideas: The Origins of Public Diplomacy and the Transformation of U.S. Foreign Policy* (Oxford: Oxford University Press, 2013). For a thoughtful set of introductory essays and bibliography on current transatlantic practice, see *Soft Power and U.S. Foreign Policy: Theoretical, Historical, and Contemporary Perspectives*, edited by Inderjeet Parmar and Michael Cox (Abingdon: Routledge, 2011).

Three Rising Hegemons: Turkey, Brazil, China

Our three cases compellingly underscore the number of theoretically and empirically rich studies being generated both from the regions themselves and from neighboring regions. We have listed these alphabetically; the large numbers of salient works are another signal that the concept of "soft power" has great political and intellectual vibrancy outside of its origin point, the United States, where policy interest in the problematic has waned.

Republic of Turkey

Angey-Sentuc, Gabrielle. "Challenging the Soft Power Analysis." *European Journal of Turkish Studies* 21 (2015): 1–21.
Atalay, Zeynep. "Civil Society as Soft Power: Islamic NGOs and Turkish Foreign Policy." In *Turkey Between Nationalism and Globalization*, edited by Riva Kastaryano, 165–86. Abingdon: Routledge, 2013.

Balcı, Bayram. "The Gülen Movement and Turkish Soft Power in the South Caucasus and the Middle East." In *The Great Game in West Asia*, edited by Mehran Kamrava, 183–201. London: Hurst, 2017.

Barlas, Dilek. "Turkish Diplomacy in the Balkans and the Mediterranean: Opportunities and Limits for Middle-Power Activism in the 1930s." *Journal of Contemporary History* 40, no. 3 (2005): 441–64.

Benhaïm, Yohanan, and Kerem Öktem. "The Rise and Fall of Turkey's Soft Power Discourse." *European Journal of Turkish Studies* 21 (2015): 1–24.

Davutoğlu, Ahmet. "Turkey's Humanitarian Diplomacy: Objectives, Challenges, and Prospects." *Nationalities Papers: The Journal of Nationalism and Ethnicity* 41, no. 6 (2013): 865–870.

Fisher Onar, Nora. "Neo-Ottomanism, Historical Legacies, and Turkish Foreign Policy." Center for Economics and Policy Studies, German Marshall Fund, EDAM Discussion Paper Series, October 2009. Accessed October 2, 2020. http://www.gmfus.org/publications/neo-ottomanism-historical-legacies-and -turkish-foreign-policy.

Fuller, Graham, Ian O. Lesser, Paul B. Henze, and James F. Brown. *Turkey's New Geopolitics: From the Balkans to Western China*. New York: Westview/Routledge, 1993.

Huijgh, Elen, and Jordan Warlick. *The Public Diplomacy of Emerging Powers, Part 1: The Case of Turkey*. Los Angeles: Figueroa, 2016.

İpek, Pınar. "Ideas and Change in Foreign Policy Instruments: Soft Power and the Case of the Turkish International Cooperation and Development Agency." *Foreign Policy Analysis* 11, no. 2 (2015): 173–93.

Kalın, İbrahim. "Soft Power and Public Diplomacy." *Perceptions* 16, no. 3 (2011): 5–23.

Kirişçi, Kemal. *Turkey and the West: Fault Lines in a Troubled Alliance*. Washington, DC: Brookings Institution, 2017.

Mabley, Bruce. "Is the World Humanitarian Summit Part of Turkey's Soft Power Strategy." Open Canada, May 13, 2016. https://www.opencanada.org/features /world-humanitarian-summit-part-turkeys-soft-power-strategy/.

Öktem, Kerem. "Projecting Power: Non-Conventional Policy Actors in Turkey's International Relations." In *Another Empire: A Decade of Turkey's Foreign Policy Under the Justice and Development Party*, edited by Kerem Öktem, Ayşe Kadioğlu, and Mehmet Karli, 77–108. Istanbul: Istanbul University Press, 2012.

Öner, Selcen. "Soft Power in Turkish Foreign Policy: New Instruments and Challenges." *Euxeinos* 10 (2013): 1–37.

Parlar Dal, Emel, and Emre Erşen. "Reassessing the 'Turkish Model' in the Post-Cold-War Era: A Role Theory Perspective." *Turkish Studies* 15, no. 2 (2014): 258–82.

Rapis, Alexander. "Turkish Pillars of Soft Power in Southeastern Europe." Master's thesis, University of Macedonia, 2012.

Yanık, Lerna K. "Bringing the Empire Back In: The Gradual Discovery of the Ottoman Empire in Turkish Foreign Policy." *Die Welt des Islams* 56, nos. 3–4, (2016): 466–88.

Yavuz, M. Hakan, "Social and Intellectual Origins of Neo-Ottomanism: Searching for a Post-National Vision." *Die Welt des Islams*, 56, nos. 3–4 (2016): 438–65.

Republic of Brazil

Amorim, Celso. *Acting Globally: Memoirs of Brazil's Assertive Foreign Policy: Rethinking Global Democracy in Brazil*. Lanham, MD: Hamilton, 2017.

Anderson, Perry. "Bolsonaro's Brazil." *London Review of Books* 41, no. 3 (2019): 11–22.

Bethell, Leslie. "Brazil: Regional Power, Global Power." Open Democracy, June 8, 2010. https://www.opendemocracy.net/leslie-bethell/brazil-regional-power -global-power.

Dauvergne, Peter, and Déborah B. L. Farias. "The Rise of Brazil as a Global Development Power." *Third World Quarterly* 33, no. 5 (2012): 903–17.

de Freitas Barbosa, Alexandre, Thais Narciso, and Marina Biancalana. "Brazil in Africa: Another Emerging Power in the Continent?" *Politikon: South African Journal of Political Studies* 36, no. 1 (2009): 59–86.

Dumont, Juliette, and Anaïs Fléchet. "Pelo que é nosso! a diplomacia cultural brasileira no século XX." *Revista Brasileira de História* 34, no. 67 (January–June 2014): 203–21.

Flynn, Matthew. "Pharmaceutical Diplomacy in the Americas and Beyond—Social Democratic Principles Versus Soft Power Interests." *International Journal of Health Services* 43, no. 1 (2013): 67–89.

Fraundourfer, Markus. *Rethinking Global Democracy in Brazil*. London: Rowman & Littlefield, 2018.

Furtado, Celso. *Global Capitalism*. Translated by Jorge Navarrete. Mexico City: Fondo de Cultura Economica, 1999.

Furtado, Celso. *Obstacles to Development in Latin America*. New York: Anchor/Doubleday, 1970.

Herz, Mônica. "A dimensão cultural das relações internacionais: proposta teórico-metodológica." *Contexto Internacional* 6 (July 1987): 61–76.

Milani, Carlos R. S. "Educational Cooperation as Soft Power: The Case of Brazil's Foreign Policy." Paper presented at ISA/Global South Caucus, Singapore, January 8–10, 2015.

Passarinho, Nathalia. "Dilma diz na ONU que espionagem fere soberania e direito internacional." G1, September 24, 2013. http://g1.globo.com/mundo/noticia /2013/09/dilma-diz-onu-que-espionagem-e-direito-internacional.html.

Ribeiro, E. T. *Diplomacia Cultural: seu papel na política externa brasileira*. Brasília: Fundação Alexandre Gusmão, 1989.

Rolland, Denis, Saraiva, José Flavio Sombra, and Amado Luiz Cervo. *Le Brésil et le Monde: Pour une histoire des relations internationales des puissances émergentes*. Paris: L'Harmattan, 1998.

Rolland, Denis, Katia de Queirós Mattoso, and Idelette Muzart Fonseca Santos. *Matériaux pour une histoire culturelle du Brésil: Objets, Voix et Mémoires*. Paris: L'Harmattan. 1999.

Stuenkel, Oliver. "Brazil as a New Global Agenda Setter?" In *Shifting Power and Human Rights Diplomacy*, edited by Thijs van Lindert and Lars van Troost, 25–33. Netherlands: Amnesty International, 2014.

Suppo, Hugo, and Mônica Leite Lessa. *A quarta dimensão das relações internacionais: a dimensão cultural*. Rio de Janeiro: Contra Capa, 2012.

Visentini, Paulo Fagundes. *A projeção internacional do Brasil, 1930–2012*. Rio de Janeiro: Elsevier, 2013.

Visentini, Paulo Fagundes. "South-South Cooperation, Prestige Diplomacy or 'Soft Imperialism?' Lula's Government Brazil-Africa relations." *Século XXI* 1, no. 1 (January–December 2010): 65–84.

People's Republic of China

For a synopsis of the thought of leading Chinese commentators on questions of soft power, see the Wilson Center Website: https://www.wilsoncenter.org/scholars-and-media-chinas-cultural-soft-power (accessed October 2, 2020). For a range of primary documents that helps situate the debates, the Center for Strategic and International Studies is useful. A good place to start is Bonnie S. Glaser and Melissa E. Murphy, "Soft Power with Chinese Characteristics," https://csis-website-prod.s3.amazonaws.com/s3fs-public/legacy_files/files/media/csis/pubs/090310_chinesesoftpower_chap2.pdf (accessed October 20, 2020). Also rich is Ming-jiang Li, "China Debates Soft Power," Chinese Journal of International Politics 2, no. 2 (Winter 2008): 287–308. More generally:

Alden, Chris, and Ana Cristina Alves. "China's Regional Forum Diplomacy in the Developing World: Socialisation and the 'Sinosphere.'" *Journal of Contemporary China* 26, no. 103 (January 2, 2017): 151–65.

Amako, Satoshi. "China's Diplomatic Philosophy and View of the International Order in the 21st Century." *Journal of Contemporary East Asia Studies* 3, no. 2 (January 2014): 3–33.

Breslin, Shaun. "The 'China Model' and the Global Crisis: From Friedrich List to a Chinese Mode of Governance?" *International Affairs* 87, no. 6 (November 1, 2011): 1323–43.

Di, Dongsheng. "Continuity and Changes: A Comparative Study on China's New Grand Strategy." *Historia Actual Online* 12 (2007): 7–18.

Dirlik, Arif. *Complicities: The People's Republic of China in Global Capitalism.* Chicago: University of Chicago Press, 2017.

Kurlantzick, Joshua. *Charm Offensive: How China's Soft Power Is Transforming the World.* New Haven, CT: Yale University Press, 2007.

Macaes, Bruno. *Belt and Road: A Chinese World Order.* London: C. Hurst, 2018.

Sum, Ngai-Ling. "The Intertwined Geopolitics and Geoeconomics of Hopes/ Fears: China's Triple Economic Bubbles and the 'One Belt One Road' Imaginary." *Territory, Politics, Governance,* October 5, 2018, 1–25.

Wang, Gungwu. "China and the International Order: Some Historical Perspectives." In *China and the New International Order,* edited by Gungwu Wang and Yongnian Zheng, 21–31. Abingdon: Routledge, 2008.

Wang, Jian., ed. *Soft Power in China: Public Diplomacy Through Communication.* Palgrave Macmillan Series in Global Public Diplomacy. New York: Palgrave Macmillan, 2011.

Womack, Brantly. "International Crises and China's Rise: Comparing the 2008 Global Financial Crisis and the 2017 Global Political Crisis." *Chinese Journal of International Politics* 10, no. 4 (December 1, 2017): 383–401.

Xiang, Lanxin. "China and the International Liberal (Western) Order." In *Liberal Order in a Post-Western World,* edited by Trine Flockhart, Charles A. Kupchan, Christina Lin, Bartlomiej E. Nowak, Patrick W. Quirk, and Lanxin Xiang, 107–20. German Marshall Fund, EDAM Discussion Paper Series, May 5, 2004. http://www.gmfus.org/profiles/lanxin-xiang.

Zhang, Denghua. "The Concept of 'Community of Common Destiny' in China's Diplomacy: Meaning, Motives, and Implications." *Asia & the Pacific Policy Studies* 5, no. 2 (May 1, 2018): 196–207.

Zhou, Weifeng, and Mario Esteban. "Beyond Balancing: China's approach towards the Belt and Road Initiative." *Journal of Contemporary China* 27, no. 112 (July 2018): 487–501.

China in Africa, China in the Developing World

Alden, Chris, and Ana Cristina Alves. "China's Regional Forum Diplomacy in the Developing World: Socialisation and the 'Sinosphere.'" *Journal of Contemporary China* 26, no. 103 (January 2, 2017): 151–65.

———. "History and Identity in the Construction of China's Africa Policy." *Review of African Political Economy* 35, no. 115 (2008): 43–58.

Alden, Chris, and Daniel Large. "On Becoming a Norms Maker: Chinese Foreign Policy, Norms Evolution, and the Challenges of Security in Africa." *China Quarterly*, no. 221 (March 2015): 123–42.

Ang, Yuen, Yuen. "How China's Development Story Can Be an Alternative to the Western Model." *South China Morning Post*, February 3, 2017, https://www.scmp.com/comment/insight-opinion/article/2067512/how-chinas-development-story-can-be-alternative-western.

Bräutigam, Deborah. *The Dragon's Gift: The Real Story of China in Africa*. Oxford: Oxford University Press, 2009.

Benabdallah, Lina. "Towards a Post-Western Global Governance? How Africa-China Relations In(Form) China's Practices." *Rising Powers Quarterly* 1, no. 1 (2016): 135–45.

Chau, Donovan. "The French Algerian War, 1954–1962: Communist China's Support for Algerian Independence." In *Military Advising and Assistance: From Mercenaries to Privatization, 1815–2007*, edited by D. Stoker, 111–26. New York: Routledge, 2007.

Easterly, William. *White Man's Burden: Why the West's Efforts to Aid the Rest Have Done So Much Ill and So Little Good*. Oxford: Oxford University Press, 2007.

Jackson, Steven F. "China's Third World Foreign Policy: The Case of Angola and Mozambique, 1961–93." *China Quarterly* 142 (June 1995): 388–422.

Larkin, Bruce D. *China and Africa, 1949–1970: The Foreign Policy of the People's Republic of China*. Berkeley: University of California Press, 1971.

Snow, Philip. *The Star Raft: China's Encounter with Africa*. London: Weidenfeld & Nicolson, 2008.

Xi, Jinping. "Open a New Era of China-Africa Win-Win Cooperation and Common Development." Discourse at the opening ceremony of the Johannesburg Summit of the Forum on China-Africa Cooperation, December 4, 2015. http://www.fmprc.gov.cn/mfa_eng/zxxx_662805/t1321614.shtml

Comparing EU and Chinese Approaches

Ferenczy, Zsuzsa Anna. *Europe, China, and the Limits of Normative Power*. London: Edward Elgar, 2019.

Jakimów, Małgorzata. "Desecuritisation as a Soft Power Strategy: The Belt and Road Initiative, European Fragmentation, and China's Normative Influence in Central-Eastern Europe." *Asia Europe Journal* 17, no. 4 (December 2019): 369–85.

Jakóbowski, Jakub. "Chinese-Led Regional Multilateralism in Central and Eastern Europe, Africa and Latin America: 16 + 1, FOCAC, and CCF." *Journal of Contemporary China* 27, no. 113 (September 3, 2018): 659–73.

Kavalski, Emilian. "The Struggle for Recognition of Normative Powers: Normative Power Europe and Normative Power China in Context." *Cooperation and Conflict* 48, no. 2 (2013): 247–67.

Kowalski, Bartosz. "Central and Eastern Europe as a Part of China's Global South Narrative." Asia Dialogue, August 27, 2018. http://theasiadialogue.com/2018/08/27/central-and-eastern-europe-as-a-part-of-chinas-global-south-narrative/.

Vangeli, Anastas. "Diffusion of Ideas in the Era of the Belt and Road: Insights from China–CEE Think Tank Cooperation." *Asia Europe Journal* 17, no. 4 (2019): 421–36.

——. "On Sino-Balkan Infrastructure Development Cooperation." In *Experiences with Chinese Investment in the Western Balkans and the Post-Soviet Space: Lessons for CEE?*, edited by Łukasz A. Janulewicz. Budapest: Center for European Neighborhood Studies, Central Europe University, 2018.

Contributors

DILEK BARLAS is a professor of history at Koç University, Istanbul.

MARTINA BASSAN is an associate doctor at the Center for International Studies (CERI) at Sciences Po Paris and a former lecturer in China's foreign policy at the Paris School of International Affairs.

BURCU BAYKURT is an assistant professor of urban futures and communication at the University of Massachusetts Amherst.

THOMAS DIEZ is a professor of political science and international relations at the University of Tübingen.

VICTORIA DE GRAZIA is Moore Collegiate Professor of History at Columbia University and a founding editor of *Radical History Review*.

MUSTAFA KUTLAY is a lecturer in the Department of International Politics at City, University of London.

FERNANDO SANTOMAURO is the learning officer at United Cities and Local Governments (UCLG) in Barcelona. Formerly he was a postdoctoral researcher at the University of Brasília.

JACK SNYDER is the Robert and Renée Belfer Professor of International Relations in the Department of Political Science and the Saltzman Institute of War and Peace Studies at Columbia University.

OLIVER STUENKEL is an associate professor of international relations at the Getulio Vargas Foundation (FGV) in São Paulo.

JEAN TIBLE is a professor in the Department of Political Science at the University of São Paulo.

ANASTAS VANGELI is a Research Fellow at the EU*Asia Institute, ESSCA School of Management, and a Senior Non-Resident Fellow at the ChinaMed Project, Turin World Affairs Institute (T.wai).

LERNA K. YANIK is a professor in the Department of Political Science and Public Administration at Kadir Has University, Istanbul.

ZHONGYING PANG is a distinguished professor of International Relations at the Institute of Marine Development, Ocean University of China in Qingdao

Index

Adalet ve Kalkınma Partisi. *See* Justice and Development Party

Africa: Bandung Conference influencing, 182, 185, 200*n*23; Brazilian foreign policy and, 158–60; Brazil prioritizing, 139–40; CADF, 189; CATTF and, 187; China-Africa Cooperative Partnership for Peace and Security, 193, 205*n*69; Chinese ideology and, 184–85; Chinese noninterference and, 194, 206*n*75; Chinese soft power applied in, 186–88; Chinese soft-power roots in, 182–84; conclusions, 197–98; as contested terrain, 183; Djibouti, 193, 205*n*71; donor-recipient model and, 189–90; Du Bois and, *184*, 185; infrastructure building and, 190, 203*n*46; joint projects implemented in, 187; Lula da Silva and, 139; media influencing, 187, 200*n*29; multilateralist approach used in, 197–98, 207*nn*88–89; peace-building and, 193–94, *195*; policy shift in, 189, 202*n*39; programs launched in, 183; Rousseff and, 138, 139; security and, 193–94; topics addressed, 181–82. *See also* Development aid, Chinese; Forum on China-Africa Cooperation; Middle East and North Africa; *specific countries*

Africa-China Poverty Reduction and Development Conference, 187–88

Afro-Asian solidarity, *184*, 185

AIIB. *See* Asian Infrastructure Investment Bank

Alliance of Civilizations Conference, 91

Alliance of Civilizations Initiative, 91

"America's Information Edge" (Nye and Owens), 31–32, 63

Amorim, C., 161, 162

Anarchical Society (Bull), 261–62, 265–66

"Anarchy Is What States Make of It" (Wendt), 302

Angola, 176*n*46, 176*n*48, 189, 202*n*44

Anticorruption operation. *See* Lava Jato

Arab Spring, 67
Arab uprisings, 67, 113–14
Argentina, 157, 281
Armitage, R. L., 46–47
Asian Infrastructure Investment Bank
    (AIIB), 192, 204n61, 217

Baldwin, D. A., 302
Balkans, 42–44, 89. *See also* Serbia
Bandung Conference (1955), 182, 185,
    200n23
Barber, B., 30
Barchard, D., 85–86
Barnett, M., 302
Barroso, J. M., 50
Batista, E., 165
Beers, C., 45
Beijing Consensus, 189, 202n43, 213
Belo Monte dam project, 165, 175n40
Belt and Road Initiative (BRI): actors
    own contexts influencing, 226,
    230–32; actors participating in, 224,
    242n1; asymmetric roles in, 230;
    CCD and, 234–35; as China-
    centered, 229–30; Chinese actors
    work reshaped by, 231–32;
    classification struggles and, 237–39;
    competition of Chinese actors in,
    231; development aid and, 192,
    204n63; developmentalist vision of,
    235; economies linked via, 12; EU
    criticisms of, 241; five areas
    emphasized in, 207n84; FOCAC and,
    196; forums advancing, 227–28,
    244n15; frame realignment in,
    239–40; future-oriented discourse
    and, 234–35; geoeconomic
    imagination and, 233–37; GFC and,
    234; global governance and, 216–17;
    global internet and, 71, 72; Marshall
    Plan contrasted with, 216; microlevel

complexity and, 225–26; motivations
    related to, 231; non-Chinese
    coperformers in, 229–30, 232;
    non-Chinese demands in, 229–30;
    people-to-people interactions in,
    236; purpose and vision of, 233, 235;
    relations between actors in, 226,
    227–30; routinization of symbolic
    practices and, 228–29; scripts
    followed in, 229; self-conception and
    worldview related to, 237, 247n43;
    Silk Road Spirit and, 234;
    socialization under framework of,
    226; storytelling and, 233; symbolic
    power in action, 2011–2015, 237–40;
    symbolic power limits, post-2015,
    241–42; symbolic power of
    infrastructure and, 235–37, 246n38,
    246n41; triangular temporal rhetoric
    and, 234–35; U.S. and, 241–42
Bibliography: on Brazil, 313–14; on
    China, 314–17; on culture, 304–5; on
    cybercommunications, 309–10; on
    diplomacy, 310–11; on Europe and its
    critics, 308–9; on Gramsci, 303–4; on
    history, 305–6; on normative power,
    308–9; of political economy, 303; of
    power in international relations,
    302–5; purpose and goal of, 301–2;
    on Turkey, 311–13; on U.S. and its
    critics, 306–7
Bismarck, O. von, 286, 287
Bolivia, 157
Bolsa Familia (Family Stipend policy),
    145, 152n31, 157
Bolsonaro, J., 289
Bolsonaro government, 129, 134, 138,
    149
Bound to Lead (Nye), 28
Bowling Alone (Putnam), 33
Bo Xilai, 288

Braman, S., 76n20

Bräutigam, D., 189–90

Brazil: Africa as priority for, 139–40; bibliography on, 313–14; B. Clinton and, 130–31; Cold War collapse and, 129–30; conclusions about, 147–49; cyber war and, 70–71; DAC and, 140; democracy and, 131, 132; developing world and, 144–45; diplomacy of, 137–38, 155; domestic issues, 141; domestic policies legitimized in, 145, 152n31; donor agreements and, 140–41; economic interests of, 146; as emerging power, 155–60; *500 Years of Periphery* and, 153; foreign policy principles held by, 138, 151n14; global order resisted by, 142–43; Haiti and, 131–32, 139, 143–44; hard-power investments of, 137–38; Honduras and, 133; humanitarian aid motives of, 143–47; humanitarian cooperation versus assistance and, 142; as humanitarian donor, 139–43; illiberal populist nationalism in, 289; image projected by, 135–36; international system reform and, 140; Lampreia and, 155–56; liberalism and, 132–33; megaprojects in, 165, 175n40, 176n42; moral vision and, 146; More Doctors health program in, 165–66; neoliberalism and, 6; 1990s wariness of, 130–31; on periphery, 153–54; petrochemical sector, 169; prestige, loss of, by, 172, 178n64; racism in, 137, 140, 151n20; random, unpredictable aid from, 146–47; rebalance of power and, 3–4; regional influence of, 145; reputation of, 161, 175n28; rules and norms-based global governance and, 138; RwP concept

and, 138, 139, 151n16; security and, 143–44; soft-power narratives of, 135–39; topics addressed about, 11, 129; unique contributions to global affairs, 136; UNSC and, 136, 161–62; U.S., distrust of, by, 133–34; violence and, 173n9; wait-and-see approach of, 130–31; WikiLeaks scandal and, 168–69, 176n49. *See also* Foreign policy, Brazilian

Brazil, Russia, India, China, and South Africa (BRICS), 144, 196, 283, 284, 295. *See also specific members of*

BRI. *See* Belt and Road Initiative

BRICS. *See* Brazil, Russia, India, China, and South Africa

Bull, H.: *Anarchical Society* and, 261–62; civilian power and, 34, 35; EU as neo-medieval society and, 265; human rights claims and, 262; international system and, 261–62; pluralist international society and, 254, 263; sovereignty/ nonintervention and, 263

Bush, G. W., 7–8; DFI and, 66; journalists embedded by, 44; Lula and, 132–33

CADF. *See* China-Africa Development Fund

Capitalism: Brazilian foreign policy and, 163–64; China's rise via, 233, 243n8, 244n25; U.S. versus European, 35–36

Cardoso, F. H.: B. Clinton and, 131; democracy development and, 131; Haiti and, 131–32

Carnes, L., 46

CATTF. *See* China-Africa Think Tanks Forum

CCD. *See* Community of common destiny

CCP. *See* Chinese Communist Party

CELAC. *See* Community of Latin American and Caribbean States

Cem, İ., 91

Censorship, of internet, 69, 71, 77n36

Center for Strategic and International Studies (CSIS), 46

Central, East, and Southeast Europe (CESEE): anticommunist attitudes in, 238–39, 240; anticommunist foreign policy and, 237; "Beijing's Mistaken Offer" and, 247n50; classification struggles and, 237–39; conclusions about, 242; economic geography of, 238; EU criticisms of, 241; as former socialist states, 238; frame realignment of, 239–40; Global South and, 238; history reimagined, 238–39; hysteresis and, 239; members of, 238, 243n13, 247n44; paradoxical realizations of, 238–40; South-South cooperation and, 239–40, 247n50; symbolic power in action and, 237–40; symbolic power limits, post-2015, 241–42; topics addressed about, 12, 227; U.S. and, 241–42; USSR and, 238–39

Central Intelligence Agency (CIA), 65–66

CESEE. *See* Central, East, and Southeast Europe

China: Afro-Asian solidarity and, *184*, 185; AIIB and, 192, 204n61, 217; bibliography on, 314–17; capitalism uplifting, 233, 243n8, 244n25; CATTF and, 187; censorship of internet by, 69; conclusions, 197–98, 219; cultural diplomacy of, 182–83, 185–88, 199n8; cultural revival in, 185–88, 200n27, 216; Cultural Revolution, 185, 186, 200n25;

development model, 188–92, *191*, *192*; Djibouti and, 193, 205n71; economic system of, 185–98, 213–14; Egypt and, 183, 199n12; Five Principles of Peaceful Coexistence and, 182; global internet shaped by, 71–72; Go Out policy of, 188, 201n37; harmonious world theory and, 186; ideology and Africa, 184–85; illiberal peace-building and, 194; learning/importing stage, 209–14; Maoist Era, 182–85; Memorandum of Understanding on U.S.-China Development Cooperation, 207n88; modernization of politics and, 208, 219n2; moral realism and, 148; multilateralist approach of, 197–98, 207n88; Namibia and, 193, 204n66; nationalism and, 200n27; neoliberalism and, 6; noninterference and, 194, 206n75, 211, 215; origins of soft power in, 181; outbidding dynamics in, 287; peace-building and, 193–94, *195*; peaceful rise and, 214–15; poor countries and, 144; post-Western approach and, 185–98; programs launched in Africa by, 183; projection stage, 216–17; rebalance of power and, 3–4; responsible stakeholder trope and, 216–17; rise and fall, 208–9; rise of, Western discourses of, 225, 243n8; scholarship on soft power from, 210; sharp power and, 218–19; since economic reform period, 185–98; socialist cultural soft power of, 214; soft power applied in Africa, 186–88; soft-power challenges of, 217–18; soft-power rise in, 186–87; soft-power roots, in Africa, 182–84; soft-power theme of, 134–35; Somalia and, 193, 204n67;

Foreign policy: conservative groups and, 171, 177n63; outside Euro-Atlantic context, 9

Foreign Policy (magazine), 28–29

Foreign policy, Brazilian: Africa and, 158–60; Amorim and, 161; anticorruption and, 167–68; assertive, 155–60; background related to, 153–55; capitalism and, 163–64; Constitution of 1988 and, 155; defeat of assertive, 165–67; defense issues facing, 170; "Ecumenical and Responsible Pragmatism," 156; goals of, 159; hard power pressures and, 167–71; hard power themes of, 163; humanitarian aid and, 159–60; illiberal liberals and, 171–72; inhibition of assertive, 160–64; internal limitations to, 163–64; internet regulation and, 162; Iran sanctions and, 163; Mozambique and, 160; multilateral forums pursued by, 158; overview, 154–55; principles of, 137–38, 151n14; PT and, 164; Rousseff impeachment and, 166–67; RwP and, 161–62; South American regional integration via, 157–58; Tehran Declaration and, 161; UN and, 161–62

Foreign policy, Chinese: Africa as testing ground for, 182; conclusions, 197–98, 219; evolution of, 224–25; FOCAC as platform for, 196–97; ideology, nonexport of, and, 212; international order and, 211; multilateralist approach used in, 197–98, 207n88; no, not, non policies of, 211–12, 217; nonalliance principle of, 211–12; as nonhegemonic, 211; no strings policy of, 212; as not challenging, 211; peace and security, 193; symbolic power and, 224–25

Foreign policy, EU: international transformation via, 255–56; liberal-intergovernmentalist account of, 260–61; Mars/Venus metaphor related to, 259–60; military power and, 259–60; multilateralism of, 251; narrative of, 37; norm transfer paths and, 256; political theology and, 254; principled pragmatism and, 251; topics addressed, 254–55; tragedy of, 251–55; transformative power limitations of, 251–52; Turkey and, 252; Ukraine and, 252; unilateral tendencies of, 252

Foreign policy, Turkish: neo-Ottomanism and, 85; periods of JDP, 108; regional integration strategy of, 110–12; regional power and, 108–9; stateness problems and, 113–14, 117; Syria and, 112

Foreign policy, U.S.: Asia focus of, 259–60; overhauling of, 47; smart power and, 47–48; soft power and, 1–2

Forum on China-Africa Cooperation (FOCAC): background, 195–96; BRI and, 196; Chinese focus on, 195–97; as foreign policy platform, 196–97; global governance and, 196; organization of, 215; side events of, 187, 201n33

Four Olds, 200n25

Frank, T., 286

Free Trade Area of the Americas (FTAA), 130, 157

Freitas, J. de, 170

Friedman, T., 30

FTAA. *See* Free Trade Area of the Americas

Fukuyama, F.: liberalism and, 276; modernity and, 280; stateness components and, 113

Fuller, G. E., 86–87

Gaddafi, M. al-, 50

Garcia, A., 172

GDPR. *See* General Data Protection Regulation

Gellner, E., 281

Gemeinschaft und Gesellschaft (Tönnies), 279

General Data Protection Regulation (GDPR), 71

Geoeconomic imagination: symbolic power of, 233–37; triangular temporal rhetoric and, 234–35

Germany: electoral and identity politics in, 286, 287; normative thinking of, 36–37; outbidding dynamics in, 287; post-Soviet, 36; Yugoslavia and, 36–37

Gerschenkron, A., 281

GFC. *See* Global financial crisis

Ghana, 183

GII. *See* Global Information Infrastructure Initiative

Glassman, J. K., 45

Global financial crisis (GFC), 234

Global Information Infrastructure Initiative (GII), 64–65

Global internet: adoption of, 64; "America's Information Edge" and, 63; Brazilian foreign policy related to, 162; censorship, 69, 71, 77n36; China shaping, 71–72; H. Clinton and, 68–69, 70; conclusions, 72–74; design, 62; DFI and, 66; economic globalization and, 64–65; empire building and, 61; fragmented, 61; Gore and, 64–65; hegemons,

regional, and, 67–68; ICANN and, 65, 71; infrastructure, 64–66; In-Q-Tel and, 65–66; issues addressed, 10; multilateral liberal internationalism and, 60; narrative broadcasting and, 61; nationalism and, 275; networked public sphere and, 66–67; Rousseff and, 70–71; scope of, 60–61; Silicon Valley companies and, 66–67; soft-power beginnings, 1990–2000, and, 63–66; surveillance and, 66, 68, 76n20; topics addressed, 61–63; U.S. and, 63–74; U.S.-dominated tech decline, 2010–2015, 68–72; U.S. freedom agenda of, 68–69, 70; U.S. liberal mission, 2000–2010, 66–68; WikiLeaks and, 69–70

Global South, 175n36; CESEE and, 238; megaevents supported by, 163

Google Citation Index, 49, 49–50

Go Out policy, 188, 201n37

Gore, A., 64–65

Gramsci, A., 276, 303–4

Guangkai Xiong, 210

Guimarães, S. P., 153, 156, 173n1

Gül, A.: soft-power terminology used by, 94–95; "Turkish model" and, 94; virtuous power and, 97

Gülen community, 97, 100, 101

Habermas, J., 257

Haiti, 131–32, 139, 143–44

Hamilton, D., 51

Hard power: Brazilian foreign policy of, 163, 167–71; Brazil investments in, 137–38; soft power compared with, 20. *See also* War

Harmonious world theory, 186

Hegemony: global internet and, 67–68; normative power as, 253; social, 276

Herder, J. G., 293

High-speed rail, 236, 246*n*42

Honduras, 133

Hong Kong, 212

Hongying Wang, 210

Hughes, K., 45

Hu Jintao, 49, 186

Humanitarian aid, Brazilian: Africa as priority of, 139–40; conclusions about, 147–49; cooperation versus assistance and, 142; domestic policies and, 141, 145, 152*n*31; economic interests and, 146; exports and, 159–60; international aid structures and, 140–41; moral vision and, 146; motives for, 143–47; random and unpredictable, 146–47; security and, 143–44; volatility in, 139

Humanitarian power, 96

Human rights, 262

Hungary, 240

Huntington, S. P., 30, 281

ICANN. *See* Internet Corporation for Assigned Names and Numbers

Illiberal populist nationalism: in advanced democracies, 289–91; in Brazil, 289; capitalist democracies and, 277; China peace-building and, 194; competing models and, 295–96; conclusions about, 296–97; contradictions, 294–95; developing states and, 277–78; from economics to identity shift and, 285–89; economy and, 285–89, 290; emulation of, 294; EU and, 289–90; European international society contesting, 262–63; free markets and, 290–91; Germany and, 286, 287; ideological formula of, 278; India and, 286–87, 288; internally focused nature of, 278–79; as international soft-power source, 291–96; late-development trap and, 281–85; liberals and, 171–72; liberal soft-power discrediting and, 275–79; markets and mass politics related to, 277–78; modernity logic applied to, 279–81; modernity shortcuts and, 281; mutually empowering comradery and, 291–92; narratives of economic and cultural grievances, 290; outbidding dynamics in, 287–88; policies of, 278; representatives of, 275; shift toward, 274–75; soft-power backfiring for, 292–93; soft-power opportunities and limitations, 293; soft power or ideology and, 296–97; topics addressed about, 13–14; will of people and, 275

India, 286–87, 288. *See also* Brazil, Russia, India, China, and South Africa

Indonesia, 295

Information technologies: "America's Information Edge" and, 63; H. Clinton embracing, 48–49. *See also* Communication technologies

Infrastructure: Africa and, 190, 203*n*46; AIIB, 192, 204*n*61, 217; benefits of, 236; as complex policy issue, 246*n*41; drawbacks related to, 246*n*38; embodied experience of, 236, 246*n*42; symbolic power of, 235–37, 246*n*38, 246*n*41; tech, 64–65

In-Q-Tel, 65–66

"Integrated Strategy for Expanding Russia's Humanitarian Influence in the World" (Russian soft power doctrine), 135

International society: belief and, 267–68; conclusions, 267–69; ethical claims and, 267–69; EU as neo-medieval society, 265; functionalism and, 266–67; human rights and, 262; illiberal state contesting, 262–63; international system contrasted with, 261–62; Manners and, 265–66; normative power and, 261–67; pluralist, 254, 263; solidarist conception of, 263; solidarization in, 263–66; world society and, 262

Internet. *See* Global internet

Internet Corporation for Assigned Names and Numbers (ICANN), 65, 71

Iran: Tehran Declaration and, 161; UNSC sanctions against, 163

Iraq: *Soft Power* and, 44–45; Turkish trade with, 114, 117; U.S. invasion of, 22–23, 44–45

Islam, S. El-, 50

Italy, 169, 293

Jakóbowski, J., 247n50

Japan, 205n71, 297

JBS Group, 168, 176n45

JDP. *See* Justice and Development Party

"Jihad vs. McWorld" (Barber), 30

Journal of Common Market Studies, 25, 34

Justice and Development Party (JDP): Alliance of Civilizations Conference and, 91; conclusions about, 99–102; Davutoğlu and, 92–93, 94; financial aid and, 97–98; foreign policy periods of, 108; Gülen community and, 97; neo-Ottomanism and, 93; organizations established by, 98; regional integration strategy of, 110–12; "Soft Power 30" and, 101–2; soft-power terminology used by,

94–96; transformative power terminology used by, 92; Turkey's transformative power and, 84–85, 92–102; "Turkish model" and, 93–94; virtuous power and, 99

Kaczmarski, M., 247n50

Kagan, R., 23, 259–60

Kalın, I., 98–99

Kennedy, P., 28

Kenya, 204n63

Keohane, R., 27

Kirişçi, K., 109–10

Kohl, H., 42

Kosovar Albanians, 43

Kurlantzick, J., 189

Kutlay, M., 110

Laïdi, Z., 51–52

Lampreia, L. F., 155–56

Lantos, T., 45

Late-development trap, 281–85

Lava Jato (anticorruption operation): Freitas on, 170; ideological vision of, 169; impeachment and, 166–67; JBS Group and, 168

Lesser, I.O., 86–87

Liberal-intergovernmentalism, 260–61

Liberalism: Brazil and, 6, 132, 133; challenges to, 277; competing models and, 295–96; end of history thesis and, 274; Fukuyama and, 276; grassroots movements and, 67; inevitability of, 276–77; internet design and, 62; markets and political participation influencing, 291; techno-utopianism and, 63–64; U.S. mission of, 2000–2010, 66–68. *See also* Multilateralism; Neoliberalism

Libya, 117, 162, 175n34, 193

Lin, J. Y., 192, 240

Nye, J. S., Jr. (*Continued*)
  diplomacy and, 83–85; Serbia and, 43;
  Soft Power by, 44–45; soft power
  coined by, 1–2; "Think Again: Soft
  Power" by, 83

Obama, B., 163
Obama administration, 68
OBOR. *See* Belt and Road Initiative
Odebrecht (engineering company), 168,
  169, 176n46, 176n48
OECD. *See* Organization for Economic
  Co-operation and Development
Office of Public Diplomacy, 98–99
Of Paradise and Power (Kagan), 23
One Belt, One Road initiative. *See* Belt
  and Road Initiative
Open Door policy, 185–86
Operation Allied Force, 43–44
Orban, V., 240
Organization for Economic Co-
  operation and Development
  (OECD), 140, 141, 189–90
Owens, W. A., 31–32, 57n49, 63

Pakistan, 174n23
Paraguay, 157–58
Paranhos, J. *See* Rio Branco, Baron of
Patriota, A., 145
Peace-building, 193–94, *195*, 205n72
Petrobras, 169–70
Poland, 240
Polanyi, K., 281
Politics of persuasion, 5
Power: bibliography, selected, on,
  302–5; blurred lines of, 8–9; defined,
  20; Deng on, 187; Greeks and, 302;
  international relations and, 302–5.
  See also specific forms of
Power (Lukes), 302
Power, T. J., 175n28

"Power Analysis and World Politics"
  (Baldwin), 302
Power and Interdependence (Nye and
  Keohane), 27
"Power in International Politics"
  (Barnett and Duvall), 302
Pozen, D., 74
Prodi, R.: normative power and, 39;
  "other" and, 40
PT. *See* Workers Party
Putin, V., 135, 275, 288, 292
Putnam, R., 33

Racism, Brazil and, 137, 140, 151n20
Reagan, R., 35, 42
Renda, K. K., 110
Ren Lei Ming Yun Gong Tong Ti
  (Shared future), 217
Responsibility while Protecting (RwP):
  Brazil and, 138, 139, 151n16, 161–62;
  Brazilian foreign policy and, 161–62;
  failure of, 163
Revolution in Military Affairs (RMA),
  31
Rio Branco, Baron of: background
  about, 154–55; legacy, 137
Rise and Fall of Great Powers, The
  (Kennedy), 28
Rise of the Trading State, The
  (Rosecrance), 35
RMA. *See* Revolution in Military
  Affairs
Rosecrance, R., 35, 109
Rousseff, D.: Africa and, 138, 139; global
  internet and, 70–71; Haiti and, 131;
  impeachment of, 166–67;
  megaprojects and, 165, 175n40,
  176n42; More Doctors health
  program of, 165–66; NSA scandal
  and, 162; smaller politics of, 165;
  WikiLeaks scandal and, 168, 176n49

Russia: economic and political prestige
strategies in, 288; phases of smart
power in, 8; sharp power and, 8–9;
soft-power doctrine of, 135; Ukraine
and, 252. *See also* Brazil, Russia,
India, China, and South Africa
RwP. *See* Responsibility while
Protecting

Salvini, M., 293
Schmidt, E., 72–73
Schmidt, W., 1
Schwarzenegger, A., 246n42
Serbia, 43
Seven Sisters (oil companies), 169
Seventeenth CCP National Congress,
210
Shared future. *See* Ren Lei Ming Yun
Gong Tong Ti
Sharp power: China and, 218–19; Russia
and, 8–9; U.S. and, 218
Sheehan, J., 24, 41
Sikkink, K., 26
Silicon Valley companies, 66–67
Silk Road Spirit, 234
Silva, L. P. da, 170
Silveira, A. da, 156
Singapore, 295
Smart power, 8, 47–48, 68
Snowden, E., 70
Soft power: defined, 2, 83–85; self-
conception and worldview related to,
237, 247n43. *See also specific topics*
Soft Power (Nye), 44–45
"Soft Power 30" (global ranking of soft
power), 101–2, 178n64
"Soft Power and Public Diplomacy in
Turkey" (Kalın), 98–99
Soft Power Index, 50
Soft-power internationalism: Cold War
aftermath and, 1–4; demise of, 4;

features, 5–8; illusion and promise of,
9; overview, 1–5, 9–14. *See also specific
topics*
Solidarist society, 254
Solidarization, 263–65
Somalia, 193, 204n67
South Africa. *See* Brazil, Russia, India,
China, and South Africa
South America, 157–58. *See also specific
countries*
South-South cooperation, 239–40, 247n50
Spektor, M., 142
Stateness: Arab uprisings and, 113–14;
components of, 113; problems of,
113–14, 117
Strategic Depth (Davutoğlu), 92–93
Sudan, 204n67
Symbolic power: in action, 2011–2015,
237–40; actors own contexts related
to, 226, 230–32; asymmetric roles
normalized with, 230; CCD and,
234–35, 245n32; change dynamics of,
226–27; classification struggles and,
237–39; defined, 224; foreign policy,
Chinese, and, 224–25; forums
utilizing, 227–28, 244n15; frame
realignment via, 239–40; future-
oriented discourse of, 234–35; of
geoeconomic imagination, 233–37;
GFC and, 234; of infrastructure,
235–37, 246n38, 246n41; limits of,
post-2015, 241–42; macro versus
micro view and, 227; overview
about, 224–27; relations between
actors, 226, 227–30; rise of China
and, 225, 243n8; routinization of,
228–29; Silk Road Spirit and, 234;
storytelling and, 233; topics addressed
on, 227; triangular temporal rhetoric
and, 234–35; as world-making, 226
Syria, 112, 114

Tahir, M., 7

Taiwan, 183, 184–85

Tanzania, 204n63

Tao Guang Yang Hui (Deng teaching doctrine): no, not, non policies and, 211–12; revision of, 215; two schools of, 210

Technology: countries blocking, 69; internet freedom and, 68–69; NSA revelations and, 69–71; U.S. decline in, 2010–2015, 68–72. *See also* Global internet

Tehran Declaration, 161

Temer, M, 131, 166, 169

"Think Again: Soft Power" (Nye), 83

TIKA. *See* Turkish Cooperation and Coordination Agency

Tocci, N., 253

Tönnies, F., 279

Trade: FTAA and, 130; politics of persuasion and, 5; *The Rise of the Trading State*, 35; WTO, 212–13

Trading state, Turkish: conclusions about, 120–21; domestic political economy capacity problems, 117–20; Egypt relations with, 117; EU and, 117; foreign trade breakdown, *115–16*; foreign trade deficit and, 119; Iraq and, 114, 117; Kirişçi and, 109–10; middle-income trap and, 118–20; R&D needed in, 119–20; regional integration strategy of, 110–12; stateness problems and, 113–14, 117; structural problems of, 119; Syria and, 112; territorial state versus, 109–10; transformative states and, 118; Turkish lira and, 119, 125n52

Transformative power, of EU, 251–52

Transformative power, of Turkey: Balkans and, 89; civilization and, 91; conclusions, 91–92, 99–102;

education and, 89–90; financial aid and, 97–98; JDP rule and, 84–85, 92–102; in 1990s, 90–91; "Soft Power 30" and, 101–2; terminology surrounding, 92, 99–100, 102n5; topics surrounding, 84; "Turkish model" and, 88–90

Transformative states, 118, 124n42

Triangular temporal rhetoric, 234–35

Trump, D.: mutually empowering comradery and, 292; nation-state centrism of, 262

Trump administration, Brazil distrusting, 134

Turkey: Alliance of Civilizations Initiative and, 91; bibliography on, 311–13; censorship of internet by, 69, 71, 77n36; collective identity and, 121; Cyprus and, 252; education and, 89–90; EU foreign policy and, 252; EU soft power influencing, 84; Iran sanctions and, 163; liberal-intergovernmentalism related to, 261; neoliberalism and, 6; 1990s, 90–91; rebalance of power and, 3–4; regional economic integration strategy, 110–12; shared history used by, 86, 102n11; "Soft Power and Public Diplomacy in Turkey," 98–99; Tehran Declaration and, 161; topics addressed about, 10–11, 84–85; "Turkish model" and, 84–85, 88–90, 93–94; as virtuous power, 85, 92, 94, 97. *See also* Neo-Ottomanism; Trading state, Turkish; Transformative power, of Turkey

Turkey and the West (Barchard), 85–86

"Turkey's Humanitarian Diplomacy" (Davutoğlu), 96

"Turkey's New Eastern Orientation" (Fuller), 86–87